COUNSELLING SKILLS AND KNOWLEDGE FOR SCoPEd B

COUNSELLING SKILLS AND KNOWLEDGE FOR SCoPEd B

FOR SCoPEd B

DIVERSITY, SELF-AWARENESS, ASSESSMENT AND RESEARCH

Edited by

Felicitas Rost, Naomi Moller, Tanya Frances, Claudine McFaul, Gina Di Malta and Hayley Ness

Published by

SAGE Publications Ltd, 1 Oliver's Yard, 55 City Road, London EC1Y 1SP

SAGE Publications Inc, 2455 Teller Road, Thousand Oaks, California 91320

SAGE Publications India, Unit No 323–333, Third Floor, F-Block International Trade Tower, Nehru Place New Delhi 110 019

SAGE Publications Asia-Pacific Pte Ltd, 8 Marina View Suite 43-053, Asia Square Tower 1, Singapore 018960

The Open University, Walton Hall, Milton Keynes MK7 6AA

First published 2025

 ® The Open University has had Woodland Carbon Code Pending Issuance Units assigned from Doddington North forest creation project (IHS ID103/26819) that will, as the trees grow, compensate for the greenhouse gas emissions from the manufacture of the paper in D230 *Book 1*. More information can be found at https://www.woodlandcarboncode.org.uk/

This publication forms part of the Open University module D230 *Advancing your counselling practice*. Details of this and other Open University modules can be obtained from Student Recruitment, The Open University, PO Box 197, Milton Keynes MK7 6BJ, United Kingdom (tel. +44 (0)300 303 5303; email general-enquiries@open.ac.uk).

Alternatively, you may visit the Open University website at www.open.ac.uk where you can learn more about the wide range of modules and packs offered at all levels by The Open University.

Edited and designed by The Open University.

Typeset by The Open University.

Printed in the United Kingdom by Halstan Printing Group, Amersham.

Paperback ISBN 978 1 0362 1241 4   Hardback ISBN 978 1 0362 1242 1   eBook ISBN 978 1 0362 1244 5

1.1

Contents

Introduction

Contents

Introduction

Welcome to *Counselling Skills and Knowledge for SCoPEd B: Diversity, Self-awareness, Assessment and Research*. This book is intended to support counsellors and psychotherapists in developing their professional competence. Mapping on to the SCoPEd framework, it helps counsellors whose current competence aligns with 'Column A' requirements work towards meeting 'Column B' requirements.

What is the SCoPEd framework?

The framework was developed by a coalition of UK counselling and psychotherapy professional bodies to provide shared standards of education and professional practice for adult counselling and psychotherapy. The framework provides a cross-professional agreement about what counsellors and psychotherapists should be able to do at different levels of qualification and practice. It sets out training, practice and competence requirements across three columns: Column A (average 2 years' core training with a minimum of 100 client hours), Column B (minimum 3 years' training with a minimum of 450 client hours) and Column C (minimum 4 years' training, equivalent to an MSc or MA, with a minimum of 450 client hours).

The competencies (SCoPEd Framework, 2022) cover five areas:

- *Theme 1: Professional framework* covers 'professional and ethical boundaries, and working within an ethical, legal and professional framework to create a safe therapeutic space for the counselling or psychotherapy to take place' (p. 16).
- *Theme 2: Assessment* focuses on 'assessing the needs of diverse clients or patients within a clear framework for understanding psychological distress, which takes account of risk and the need to work within personal limits' (p. 18).
- *Theme 3: Therapeutic relationship* focuses on 'establishing and developing an authentic and enabling therapeutic relationship which concentrates on the particular needs of diverse clients or patients, from the first stages of establishing rapport through to a safe ending' (p. 21).
- *Theme 4: Knowledge and skills* emphasises the 'ability to relate theory to practice, which shows understanding of the individual, their difficulties and the process of change within a clear framework of skills and knowledge' (p. 26).
- *Theme 5: Self-awareness and reflection* covers 'the ability to use self-awareness, self-knowledge, self-challenge, reflexivity and supervision to ensure the best interests of diverse clients and patients are at the forefront of the work' (p. 30).

This book focuses on Column B competencies while also providing you with an opportunity to revisit and refine the core skills covered in Column A. Of the 25 Column B competencies, this volume includes 14, primarily those focused on assessment, self-awareness, and knowledge and skills. Table 1 lists which chapters cover which SCoPEd competencies.

Table 1 SCoPEd competencies by chapter

Chapter	SCoPEd competency
Chapter 1	**2.5.B** Ability to conceptualise, evaluate and take account of a range of mental health problems, symptoms of psychological distress, functioning and coping styles (with due understanding of cultural norms), during assessment and throughout therapy
Chapter 2	**4.11.B** Ability to recognise and explore with the client or patient the assumptions that underpin understanding of identity, culture, values and worldview
Chapter 3	**5.4.B** Ability to critically challenge own identity, culture, values and worldview
Chapter 4	**4.2.B** Ability to critically appraise a range of theories underpinning the practice of counselling and psychotherapy **4.7.B** Ability to demonstrate the capacity, knowledge and understanding of how to select and adapt interventions and (or) approaches to respond to the needs of the client or patient
Chapter 5	**5.4.B** Ability to critically challenge own identity, culture, values and worldview
Chapter 6	**5.1.Bii** Ability to work with 'unconscious' and 'out of awareness' processes
Chapter 7	**5.1.Bi** Ability to be emotionally prepared for intense and complex work, which requires sustained reflexivity
Chapter 8	**5.6.B** Ability to review and evaluate supervision arrangements and take responsibility for adapting supervision to the evolving and changing requirements of ongoing practice
Chapter 9	**2.1.B** Ability to use an initial and ongoing clinical assessment strategy that is informed by a consistent, coherent and in-depth theoretical approach
Chapter 10	**2.8.B** Ability to devise and use a comprehensive risk assessment strategy
Chapter 11	**2.5.B** Ability to conceptualise, evaluate and take account of a range of mental health problems, symptoms of psychological distress, functioning and coping styles (with due understanding of cultural norms), during assessment and throughout therapy
Chapter 12	**4.15.B** Ability to utilise audit and evaluation tools to monitor and maintain standards within practice settings
Chapter 13	**4.16.B** Ability to draw upon and evaluate published research on counselling and psychotherapy, and integrate relevant research findings to enhance practice

Chapter 14	**4.16.B** Ability to draw upon and evaluate published research on counselling and psychotherapy, and integrate relevant research findings to enhance practice
Chapter 15	**4.16.B** Ability to draw upon and evaluate published research on counselling and psychotherapy, and integrate relevant research findings to enhance practice
Chapter 16	**4.16.B** Ability to draw upon and evaluate published research on counselling and psychotherapy, and integrate relevant research findings to enhance practice
Chapter 17	**2.11.B** Ability to identify and respond to the impact of the technologically mediated environment on issues of identity and presence, including fantasies and assumptions about the therapist and client or patient
Chapter 18	**4.9.B** Ability to reflect upon the complex and sometimes contradictory information gained from clients or patients and to coherently describe their present difficulties and the potential origins using a clear theoretical model or approach
Chapter 19	**4.2.B** Ability to critically appraise a range of theories underpinning the practice of counselling and psychotherapy
Chapter 20	**4.7.B** Ability to demonstrate the capacity, knowledge and understanding of how to select and adapt interventions and (or) approaches to respond to the needs of the client or patient

(Adapted from SCoPEd Framework, 2022)

Looking beyond SCoPEd

This book goes beyond the SCoPEd framework to provide a focused theoretical, empirical and reflexive foundation in two ways. First, the book contextualises the framework by emphasising the need to consider any differences between client and counsellor – in particular, differences that have socio-cultural meaning (e.g. those associated with stigma or discrimination) – because the broader social context inevitably shapes how both clients and counsellors approach each other and the process. Part 1 of this book offers ideas for diversity-informed and culturally sensitive ways of working.

Second, given that the core training in counselling varies substantially in how much time it dedicates to understanding research, Part 4 of this book orientates and introduces the reader to research methods. These chapters emphasise an understanding of research as a key resource for theoretical and practical development. In doing so, it fosters the applied value of research on counselling and counsellors' critical thinking in relation to concepts, theories and practices. This emphasis also reflects the fact that many of this book's authors are researchers and therefore believe it is important to test counselling theories and techniques, rather than accept that they 'work' on faith. It also reflects a broader goal for counsellors: to be able to critically evaluate counselling theories and approaches, and in turn one's own practice.

Book structure

This book focuses on competencies in key areas including assessment, self-awareness, knowledge and skills. Specifically, the book is structured into the following parts:

- Part 1: Diversity (Chapters 1–4)
- Part 2: Reflexivity (Chapters 5–8)
- Part 3: Assessment (Chapters 9–12)
- Part 4: Research (Chapters 13–16)
- Part 5: Developing as a practitioner (Chapters 17–20).

These five parts all relate to and build on each other. Each chapter includes examples of client material, discussion of relevant research, encouragement to pause and reflect on the content, and suggestions for further reading.

How to use this book

You can read the chapters in the order they appear, or you can be guided by the topic or competency. As with all Open University learning materials, this book has been written in a way that encourages you to actively engage with the content. To help you process and assimilate your learning, you may also find it helpful to do some of the following:

- Look at the competence (or competencies) for the chapter before you read it and consider how confident you feel about your ability to meet it. Consider whether there are some aspects you feel more confident about and some less – and why.
- After reading a chapter, journal about how it resonated with you. For example, you could reflect on whether your own understandings were validated or challenged, and if so, why and how. You could also reflect on whether reading the chapter led to an emotional response.
- Summarise the key learning points from each chapter in a way that emphasises the areas most useful for you. In other words, rather than take notes about things you already know or feel confident about, focus on any new understandings you have developed.
- Note down any topics for further investigation. Each chapter provides further reading suggestions at the end, but the final references section will also provide you with potential topics or issues that you could investigate further.

Book authors and varied perspectives

This book has been written by a diverse group of practitioners (counsellors, psychotherapists, and clinical and counselling psychologists) at The Open University, and by invited experts in the field. Our diverse experiences in counselling practice – as supervisors, as trainees and trainers, as researchers, as clients, as well as in our personal lives – have inevitably shaped the content of this book. We do not all see the world – or counselling – the same way; you can therefore expect to encounter a range of different perspectives in this book, some of which might align with yours, while others may not. The intent of showcasing a range of understandings is to support you in honing your own, and to reflect the diversity of the broader counselling and psychotherapy profession. The views expressed in each chapter belong to the author(s) alone and do not represent the views of the editors or all contributors to this book, nor of any organisation they are affiliated with.

Emotional impact

While you might disagree with some of the opinions expressed by the authors, some content can also bring up unwelcome emotions, thoughts and memories, or even trigger unpleasant psychological and physical reactions. The work of counselling centres around difficult experiences, severe states of mind and distressing behaviours, and is thus inevitably emotive. However, knowing that this can happen and paying attention to it matters because it can interfere with your learning. Given that this book is aimed at qualified (SCoPEd Column A) counsellors, we assume that your core training will have prepared you for such eventualities and that you know how best to look after yourself while studying. Recognising both your professional experience and expertise, and wishing to avoid any potential negative impacts on your learning, we have occasionally included content warnings for material giving details of potentially difficult experiences or content. In keeping with this book's focus on fostering self-awareness, we encourage you to monitor your responses to the chapters and engage in appropriate self-care if necessary.

Terminology

The use of words can be both relative and context-dependent, and different counselling approaches often use different terminology. This can be confusing, especially when you are trying to grasp complex phenomena and relate them to your practice. Authors have therefore explained their use of terminology wherever possible, and included margin definitions of concepts that might not be familiar to everyone. We are also mindful that words can have a strong impact, which can negatively affect your curiosity or sense of safety.

While we have not imposed a specific style or language on authors, we have worked with a commitment to avoid discriminatory, stigmatising or oppressive language. To that effect, we have also asked critical readers to review each chapter, and their helpful and invaluable comments have not only increased the clarity of the content, but also assisted us in our commitment towards ethical and inclusive education and practice.

Book images and case examples

Many of the images in this book have been contributed by Open University counselling and psychology students and staff. We thank everyone who submitted an image to us and hope that you enjoy seeing them in this book. Other images were created by chapter authors, and a few have come from commercial sources. The case examples used in the book are either fictional, composites of clients or anonymised examples with important details changed to protect clients.

We very much hope that you'll find the approaches offered in this book informative, creative, supportive and beneficial.

The Editorial Team

References

SCoPEd Framework (2022), collaboratively developed by Association of Christian Counsellors (ACC), British Association for Counselling and Psychotherapy (BACP), British Psychoanalytic Council (BPC), Human Givens Institute (HGI), National Counselling and Psychotherapy Society (NCPS) and United Kingdom Council for Psychotherapy (UKCP). Available at: https://www.bacp.co.uk/about-us/advancing-the-profession/scoped/scoped-framework (Accessed: 12 June 2024).

Part 1

Diversity

Chapter 1

Developing culturally sensitive understandings of psychological distress

Tanya Frances

Contents

Introduction

Moss on stone by Tanya Frances. The colours, textures and patterns represent the diversity of life and the potential for exploring many perspectives. There are many unique and often overlooked qualities of moss: it plays an essential role in developing ecosystems and is able to survive in extreme conditions.

Take a moment to consider factors that impact your emotional, physical and psychological well-being. It is likely that social, global and political concerns do not just relate to the 'external' world, but are present in your own life and in the therapy room. For example, these issues could include the climate crisis, Brexit, reproductive rights, the Black Lives Matter and #MeToo movements, societal Islamophobia and antisemitism, war and conflict, and trans rights. This suggests that our individual and collective emotional and psychological well-being are interconnected with broader socio-cultural systems and the natural environment. This chapter offers ways of understanding human diversity and the interconnectedness of individuals and socio-cultural environments.

The first four chapters in this book offer ideas for diversity-informed ways of working. This chapter provides a foundation for thinking about the theoretical and philosophical underpinnings of counselling, which inform how counsellors conceptualise and work with psychological distress. The chapter focuses on cultural diversity because effective practice relies on a meaningful consideration of cultural norms. The chapter highlights how counselling that is practised in the UK is largely based on white, Western systems of knowledge and that, just as these systems will not be appropriate and effective for all clients, they do not reflect the cultural identities of all counsellors either. Hopefully, this chapter offers ways to consider your cultural identity, what diversity means for you, your interpersonal and therapeutic relationships, and your counselling practice.

While reading, try to stay with any discomfort that you notice. Sara Ahmed (2017) has suggested that knowledge is generated in moments of difficulty or discomfort. Rather than avoiding it, 'the task is to stay with the difficulty', as Ahmed puts it (p. 13), which can help us to learn truths about ourselves, the systems we operate within, and how we relate to others and the world. You are therefore encouraged to embrace a spirit of curiosity and openness throughout this chapter.

This chapter contributes towards achieving the **SCoPEd competency 2.5.B**:

Ability to conceptualise, evaluate and take account of a range of mental health problems, symptoms of psychological distress, functioning and coping styles (with due understanding of cultural norms), during assessment and throughout therapy.

(SCoPEd Framework, 2022, p. 19)

This chapter aims to:

- outline the rationale for taking a culturally sensitive approach to conceptualising mental health problems and symptoms of psychological distress

- explore what diversity means, and encourage critical thought about how it is conceptualised in the counselling and psychotherapy profession

- highlight the importance of cultural humility and cultural equity, both theoretically and in practice

- consider ways of working that can support a culturally sensitive approach to practice.

1 Why diversity matters for clients

Understanding diversity and working effectively within diverse therapeutic relationships matters for clients because it helps reduce harm (as covered below; Sue, 2015) and reduce the risk of drop-out (Owen *et al.*, 2012). You might note the phrasing 'within diverse therapeutic relationships', above. This draws on Myira Khan's (2023) invitation for therapists to consider diversity as located 'within' relationships and social contexts; thus, diversity is not an individual issue defined by the client's individual differences or identity characteristics, but instead is produced relationally and contextually.

Working with diversity links with social justice because it requires recognising both privileged and minoritised identities along with any resulting power differentials and barriers to inclusive and ethical practice. 'Social justice' and 'diversity' are, therefore, terms used by well-intentioned institutions and individuals, but they risk becoming little more than buzzwords (Winter, 2019), addressed more as a 'tick-box exercise' than meaningfully in practice (Ahmed, 2017). Further, engaging with diversity can feel confusing to 'do' or 'get right'. Research evidence also suggests that trying to bring 'politics' into therapy can lead to therapists feeling lonely or like they are going against their training, especially if they have been trained to leave politics 'at the door' (Winter, 2021, p. 308) and remain neutral. Before thinking more about this, it might be helpful to consider what 'diversity' means.

1.1 Defining diversity

Human diversity refers to aspects that make us different from one another, including individual, social or cultural differences (Jones, Dovidio and Vietze, 2014). General understandings are based on demographic differences, such as those related to religion, disability, sexuality, age, race, ethnicity and gender. However, diversity is also about other aspects of who we are, such as personality, preferences, culture and heritage, socio-economic background, politics, health and our physical bodies. Diversity is also about similarities: how we perceive and experience ourselves to be similar, and how we might share social categories with one another.

The individual and social, therefore, are clearly interdependent. Social difference can be thought of as something that is *constructed by*, but also has an *influence on*, individuals (Blaine and McClure Brenchley, 2020):

- *Social difference as socially constructed and maintained by individuals.* How we act affects how social categories are reproduced and maintained. For example, what it means to be a 'man' or 'woman' can be understood as socially constructed, and is also maintained by those who identify with those **cisnormative** gender categories.

cisnormative

Refers to the belief that cisgender people (those whose gender identity matches the body they were born with) are 'normal' and 'right', and therefore those who transgress this norm are 'abnormal' and 'wrong'.

- *Social difference as exerting influence on individuals.* Various intersecting social forces influence our behaviour. Identity (how we see ourselves) is partly shaped by the beliefs and views that others (individuals, society and culture) hold about us and the social groups we belong to (or are seen as belonging to). This then shapes behaviour. For example, the categories of 'woman' and 'man' are categories of social difference which (a) determine what constitutes 'womanhood' or 'manhood', and (b) influence how a person sees themselves according to these gender norms.

Scott Page (2007) proposed four categories of diversity:

heuristics
General rules that guide our decision making in situations where we have limited information but need to make a decision quickly.

- *Cognitive diversity* refers to differences in patterns of thinking, perspectives or points of view, **heuristics**, interpretations (how we categorise and make sense of the world, others and the self, based on events and experiences) and how we make predictions or inferences (how we make meaning out of information and experience).

- *Identity diversity* refers to how an individual identifies or affiliates themselves with categories such as gender, sexual orientation, ethnicity, religion and age.

- *Demographic diversity* refers to social categories such as the ones above, but without explicit regard for how the person identifies. This might relate to the difference between how someone identifies and how they are perceived socially. For example, a person who is autistic might identify as being disabled, as they experience the disabling effect of neurotypical-centric contexts. However, they may not be perceived by others as disabled because their difference is largely 'invisible'.

- *Preference diversity* refers to difference in likes, dislikes and values. This includes fundamental preferences (the outcomes we prefer) and instrumental preferences (the preferred means by which we achieve outcomes).

1.2 Similarity and difference in practice: the relevance of cultural history

In this chapter you are invited to consider diversity in relation to the fictional case of Huang, the client, and Claudia, the therapist. This case is introduced below.

Case example: Huang and Claudia – background context

Huang is a 24-year-old Chinese woman who lives in London. She is in her fifth year of studying medicine at university. Huang grew up in Beijing and moved to London five years ago for her studies. Huang is experiencing depression symptoms and suicidal ideation but has no plans to end her life. She feels low and isolated, struggles to motivate herself to study and lacks hope for the future. She feels she cannot talk to her parents in Beijing, as the cultural and societal stigma about mental illness in China could bring shame to her family. She also does not feel she can talk to her partner, Sara, who is concerned and encouraged Huang to seek therapy. Through her university's counselling service, Huang has begun working with Claudia.

Claudia is a white, British, integrative therapist from a middle-class background, who grew up in a rural part of Devon, England. She lived there until her early twenties, when she moved to Brighton to study psychology and became interested in further training in counselling. Her interest in counselling came about as a result of her own experience of therapy following her father's death. In her mid-twenties – after staying in Brighton for a few years and learning more about her queer identity – she moved to London with her partner and trained as a humanistic counsellor. Claudia identifies as a middle-class, lesbian woman, and is currently studying for her PhD alongside her work as a counsellor. Now in her early forties, she is content with her professional life. She is infertile and is trying to come to terms with her grief for the children she wished for but does not have.

Pause for thought 1.1

From your first impressions, which aspects of diversity would you want Claudia to be mindful of? What aspects might impact Huang's experience of therapy?

There are differences between Huang and Claudia regarding cultural background, ethnicity and age. Of course, many demographic and identity categories are not visible and may or may not become significant in therapy (e.g. Claudia and Huang may share some similarities, such as sexual orientation, political views or class).

The following case illustration focuses on the first therapy session.

Case example: Huang and Claudia begin therapy

Claudia: It sounds like your girlfriend is quite worried. You say you are unsure about whether counselling will help you. Can you tell me more?

Huang: She has been worried for a while, but I don't think she understands how I feel. I'm worried I'll fail this year, but that isn't enough to motivate me to study any more. Thinking about going into practice next year fills me with dread. I'm not sure how counselling can help.

Claudia: It sounds like you're worried about next year. Can you say a bit more about dread?

Huang: It's not that I don't like medicine – I do. But at uni, I feel like I'm looked at differently. People on my course say things about me behind my back, and sometimes it makes me feel like I don't belong – like they don't like me being here.

Claudia: I hear you sometimes feel isolated and like you don't belong. Is this a familiar experience for you?

Huang: I'm an only child, like most people my age in my country, so being alone is a familiar experience. In a way, I'm used to it, but I had a volatile relationship with my mum when it was only her and I at home. She'd get angry with me, and I didn't understand it then. I think she put all her hopes and expectations on me. I think she was grieving children she never had or couldn't keep. I think she took it all out on me. Yeah, I did feel alone with that as a kid.

Claudia: You must have felt quite alone with that – and it sounds like some of your experiences now might bring back those feelings of aloneness.

Huang: Partly. But this feels different. Sometimes, my classmates don't even have to say anything, they just look at me with disgust. There have been times when, you know, I was reading articles about how it was for people working in healthcare through the Covid-19 pandemic, especially Chinese people. They were getting lots of hate, getting attacked. People don't need to say anything, but I know they don't want me there. I don't see the point in thinking about the future any more.

Huang's dread about the future and experiences of social isolation are – in part – due to her observations of racism towards her, and towards Chinese people in general, increasing in the UK. You may also consider that Huang's cultural history is important here and provides cultural, familial and political context for understanding Huang's experience of isolation or feelings of being alone. Huang mentions that she is an only child, like most people her age in China. She brings her cultural history, albeit not explicitly, into the dialogue: between 1979 and 2016, China had a 'one-child policy', restricting urban couples to one child, except for those in a minority ethnic group and couples with a disabled child (Cameron *et al.*, 2013). Huang suggests that her mother was grieving children she did not have or perhaps could not keep. Her theory is that her mother directed her unprocessed grief and anger towards her, and this amplified feelings of loneliness. Viewed in this way, current social isolation might activate fear, threat and trauma for Huang. Awareness of Huang's cultural history may be central to understanding her current psychological distress.

Pause for thought 1.2

If Huang were your client, how comfortable would you feel identifying racism as a relevant factor? Does your identity, background and culture shape how comfortable you feel naming racism, exploring cultural history and asking more?

Your experiences, identity, background and culture likely shape how you might recognise yourself as similar to and/or different from Huang. These similarities and differences may affect how comfortable you would feel naming racism and exploring Huang's cultural history and its psychological significance.

1.3 The relational dimensions of sameness and difference

What happens within therapeutic relationships matters, as it is widely recognised that the therapeutic relationship is a central component of positive therapy outcomes (Wampold *et al.*, 2017). In the context of diversity in the therapeutic relationship, as mentioned earlier, you might consider yourself working *within* diversity rather than working with the diverse 'other' (Khan, 2023; Winter and Charura, 2023). This **relational** approach is a way of understanding 'otherness' – or the process of **othering** – as produced between the therapist and the client *and* within the structures in which they meet.

Attending to the relational production of 'otherness' has implications for counselling, as therapists can consciously or unconsciously project their biases and assumptions, which may cause harm or oppression (Turner, 2021). In later chapters, you will explore these concepts, including why understanding positionality is key (Chapter 3) and how to use reflexivity (Part 2 of this book). Framing diversity relationally helps to show the interdependence of individuals and social context; that social difference is constructed and maintained *by* individuals; and that social difference exerts influence *on* individuals.

relational

Refers to the philosophy that knowledge is produced within relationships (with other people and non-human animals) and contexts (including environmental, historical, socio-cultural and political), and therefore shifts and changes over time and place.

othering

A process whereby an individual or a group is labelled as being different to oneself or one's group. Assumptions made about that individual or group may be prejudicial.

2 Cultural sensitivity

You have probably encountered concepts such as cultural competence, cultural sensitivity and cultural adaptations. These terminologies can get confusing. Pilar Hernández-Wolfe (2011) proposes a **decolonial approach** to mental health to define cultural sensitivity. She suggests that cultural sensitivity integrates cultural equity and cultural humility:

decolonial approach

The process of moving away from white, Western-centric, Global North systems of knowledge production towards those that embrace understandings and practices of the Global South.

- *Cultural equity* refers to seeing how dimensions of structural privilege and marginalisation shape how we relate to the self and others, and how this can vary depending on context. It encourages us to examine our privileges and marginalisations in relation to others (e.g. clients), rather than inherently centring our own norms and values as the status quo.

- *Cultural humility* refers to the flexibility and humbleness required to engage in ongoing learning, by letting go of theories, stereotypes or assumptions we might hold tightly. It is the ability to say 'I do not know' when we truly don't know. This is not a devaluing of training or experience, but a recognition that sometimes, especially when working with cultures different to our own, there might be elements that we are unaware of, or 'truths' presented by clients that are different to our own norms.

Integrating cultural equity and humility is one way of working with cultural differences in therapy. This promotes a willingness to share power with clients, learn from and with them, and practise self-reflexivity, especially when working with clients from cultures different from one's own.

2.1 Working with cultural differences

In the previous case example, Huang described feelings of not belonging. The following case example provides dialogue from later on in the session.

Case example: Huang and Claudia explore cultural differences

Claudia: You told me about classmates saying upsetting things and your sense that you do not belong. Can you tell me more about the upsetting things your classmates say or what you think they think about you?

Huang: They look at me and immediately think, 'Oh, that's just another Chinese student. Another international student', you know? Someone who shouldn't be here.

Claudia: I'm not sure I fully understand that feeling, as I have not experienced what it is like to be an international or Chinese student. Can you tell me a little more? How do you feel when you see others making judgements about you?

Huang: I don't know. I might as well give up. Part of me is angry because all they see is my face, and they make assumptions. I am not this quiet, Covid-spreading girl that they think I am. But a part of me also feels like, what's the point? Is it worth trying any more? I look at the news and I feel like, you know, immigrants are just not welcome. And I think my mother needs me to be there back home.

Claudia: Thank you for letting me understand. It feels to me like racism is a big factor here. It seems that you are tuned into how, perhaps, racist attitudes and behaviours are directed towards you in both explicit ways and more nuanced ways? I wonder how it feels for you to come to therapy with me, a white therapist, who cannot understand this fully?

Claudia shows cultural humility by acknowledging that she is unlikely to understand what being a female, Chinese international student in the UK is like. The relational impacts of this are important, and they are situated in a time of anti-immigration politics, post-Brexit atmosphere, terrorist attacks, the rise of xenophobic hate crimes and discrimination in the UK, and what some have described as the political legitimisation of such attitudes and crimes (Piatkowska and Lantz, 2021).

Pause for thought 1.3

In practice, do you acknowledge and reflect on your similarities and differences with clients, either in a session or during supervision? What makes this easier or more challenging to do?

Let's look at how the session could have gone if Claudia had responded differently to the experiences and feelings being expressed by Huang.

Case example: Huang and Claudia explore cultural differences (alternative)

Huang: They look at me and immediately think, 'Oh, that's just another Chinese student. Another international student', you know? Someone who shouldn't be here.

Claudia: That must be hard. You know, my experience is that you are intelligent and eloquent. Your commitment to your work and studies is commendable, and you being here despite feeling unwelcome shows your resilience. I am sure your family are proud of you, even if your peers don't value your intelligence as much.

Huang: I don't know. I guess I feel that they don't want me here. It sounds silly. Like, it's small things. When I use our shared kitchen to cook, everyone leaves. Or if I'm at the shop wearing a mask because I have a cold, people stare at me. Some people in my classes also say, 'Oh, your English is so good, patients will never know you have only been here for a few years'. Sometimes, though, random people yell things at me. Someone last year threw a pack of face masks at me and told me to go back home.

Claudia: That sounds awful. I'm sorry this is your experience. I'm sure you're bright. I know of a couple of Asian professors in your department, and they are very well respected. I wonder how you see those professors.

Huang: I don't know. Do you mean Professor Akio and Professor Lee, the Japanese and South Korean professors?

Claudia: Ah, I'm sorry; they seem similar to you in many ways. Where I am coming from, though, is that perhaps it might help to know it is possible to find your path despite the challenges you face.

Pause for thought 1.4

In the spirit of tuning into gut feelings, tensions or hesitancies, is there anything about the last case example that stands out to you as potentially dismissive or invalidating?

Claudia's humanistic orientation means that she offers core conditions such as empathy and congruence, and she values Huang as an expert on herself, taking on board Huang's meaning making about her childhood and attempting to offer Huang a way of seeing herself where positive growth is possible. However, the alternative session example also demonstrates a lack of cultural humility and cultural equity. Claudia may not be aware of it, but instead of acting with humility about what she does not know, her assumptions inform what she says. There are some racial and ethnic microaggressions; for example, Claudia ascribes intelligence to Huang based on her assumption that Chinese people are intelligent and have a strong work ethic. She also demonstrates invalidation of interethnic differences by assuming that Huang is the same as the other Asian people she knows, even though they are South Korean and Japanese, and do not share the same cultural heritage as Huang. These are two types of microaggressions that can commonly occur in therapy (Kuo, Imel and Tao, 2021).

Claudia's interventions may have missed aspects of Huang's cultural history. Further, they may be experienced as dismissive or invalidating, because there's an assumption that the problem is Huang's lack of individual resilience rather than related to the systemic context. Multicultural psychologists have described this as monocultural bias (Betancourt and López, 1993; Gone, 2009), whereby they suggest 'the procedural norms of the discipline as a source of cultural insensitivity' (Rogler, 1999, cited in Gone, 2009, p. 751) – the norm in this case is the tendency towards individualism.

2.2 The importance of cultural equity and cultural humility

The following case example shows how the session between Huang and Claudia could progress.

Case example: Huang and Claudia conclude their session

Claudia: I understand your uncertainty about counselling. Are you willing to give it a go?

Huang: I can try. Things can't go on like this. I can't talk to my parents because they don't understand, but I'm not sure they want to hear. My mother always left me alone to get on with it, or I'd be receiving all her unprocessed emotions. I feel pressure as she's getting older and may need me to look after her in a few years.

Claudia: It sounds like multiple aspects of the future bring a sense of pressure or dread. Pressure to take care of your mother as she ages, and dread about your future here. It feels to me like you are describing racist comments and behaviours from strangers and from your peers, too. I wonder if this is how you see these experiences of hostility and feeling unwelcome?

Huang: Yeah, I do think about that. I do see it in that way.

Claudia: I wonder what it is like to have assumptions made about you based on how you are 'read' by others?

Claudia attempts to show cultural equity by noticing how structural privilege and marginalisation might shape Huang's experience. She also indicates cultural humility by demonstrating a willingness to learn from Huang, instead of imposing stereotypes and biases about Chinese culture. As you will explore in later chapters, this emphasises the importance of training, reflexivity, supervision and personal therapy. Working with Huang could activate Claudia's conscious and unconscious biases or aspects of her trauma history; for instance, the isolation she might have felt losing her father at a young age or her own grief around infertility.

> ### Pause for thought 1.5
>
> In what instances might it be helpful to educate yourself when taking on a client from a cultural background different from your own? What are the benefits and limitations of educating yourself?

Being attuned to and interested in your client is always necessary, but for some clients there might be a requirement to educate yourself around specific issues. However, there are limitations to such training in terms of assuming homogeneity – that is, that all members of a specific culture or social group are similar or the same (Lekas, Pahl and Fuller Lewis, 2020). For example, Reeves *et al.* (2024) interviewed transgender and non-binary people about seeking general healthcare. Participants valued the cultural humility shown by clinicians who were willing to take their lead about the use of pronouns and the correct names and language to describe their anatomy. However, participants experienced having to educate their providers about their needs and identities as burdensome, uncomfortable and detrimental; it got in the way of building relationships with their healthcare providers. Further, correcting mistakes (such as misgendering) increased feelings of alienation. This suggests that intentions to practise with cultural humility do not always suffice, and it may not always be appropriate to expect clients to educate their providers.

3 Understanding psychological distress

Intertwined by Tanya Frances. The trunk and different-sized twines of this tree have grown together and are almost interconnected, reflecting how the self, others and our social, cultural and political environments are interconnected.

Critical psychologists (who emphasise the need to consider power differences between social groups) and community psychologists (who focus on addressing related issues in society) have a long-standing history of drawing attention to the limitations of traditional or mainstream counselling and psychotherapy theories and methods (e.g. Smail, 2001; 2015). One critique is that dominant psychological narratives provide particular 'truths', ones that understand psychological distress as an individual pathology rather than resulting from the interconnections with social, cultural, historical and relational factors (Samuel and Ortiz, 2021).

Factors beyond the individual could be societal, such as the racism that Huang experiences, and/or trauma-based, such as experiencing sexual or domestic violence, or war and conflict. Theories around how mental health difficulties arise, including biomedical understandings and the impact of trauma, are explored further in Chapter 11.

3.1 How we know what we know in counselling

This section briefly examines the 'epistemic' underpinnings of counselling (how we justify claims of 'truth', and how we come to know what we know). Evidence-based practice, informed by values of **empiricism**, has grown in popularity and discourse, and this is not all a bad thing – it is useful to critically examine what works and for whom. However, one might argue that not all evidence is created equally (Hunsley and Mash, 2007), and an evidence hierarchy determines the theories and practices we use and what is held as 'true' (Ghaemi, 2010).

In contrast, cultural humility and cultural equity require the counsellor to examine not only personal values and experiences, but also the values and experiences of the cultures within which counselling theories were produced. Some criticisms draw attention to the limits of Western world-views and values, such as empiricism, objectivity and individualism. The argument is that Western, white, North American and Western European ways of understanding human distress are grounded in colonial ideologies and, as such, fail to appreciate and embrace Indigenous and non-Western approaches to healing (Singh, Appling and Trepal, 2020; Oulanova, Hui and Moodley, 2023). Colonisation refers to the practice of a nation seizing the territory of another people and subjugating the original inhabitants. The process of colonisation today can more often be seen as:

> visible and invisible attempts to socialize and resocialize those 'at the margins' to fit into dominant cultural values and experiences. Thus, the dominant White, Eurocentric society maintains its sense of order, power, structural privilege, and supposed 'normalcy' to which those from other cultures are supposed to accommodate, value, and acclimate.

> *(Singh, Appling and Trepal, 2020, p. 262)*

Implications of **coloniality** are vast and have been described as a 'soul wound' (Duran, 2006), impacting on the loss of identity, culture, spirituality and language, and leading to ongoing intergenerational trauma. Mignolo (2005) suggests that there are two interconnected aspects of coloniality: (a) the systemic oppression of local knowledges – knowledge grounded in Indigenous cultures; and (b) the emergence of alternative knowledges as a result of the oppression of local knowledges. As such, anti-colonial thinking and culturally sensitive practice seeks to deconstruct, challenge and resist systems that centre dominant truths about normality/abnormality, healthy/unhealthy and what we see as 'common sense' (Wada and Kassan, 2021). It has been argued that even if counsellors are practising in a culturally competent way, the dominant theories used do not typically or explicitly seek to dismantle and critically question systems of power, privilege and oppression, and as such, they may well uphold the status quo through their assumed superiority and generalisability (Singh, Appling and Trepal, 2020).

All theories are situated within a particular context, which is not in and of itself problematic. The fact that white, Western Eurocentric theories and clinicians make assumptions about white, Western European clients is, in part, helpful in understanding what works and for whom among this specific

empiricism

The idea that true ('objective') knowledge comes from experience – from that which can be measured, controlled and separated from emotion – as opposed to ('subjective') knowledge based on one's feelings.

coloniality

The system of power relations that outlives colonial administration. It is the living legacy of colonialism in contemporary societies.

population. However, assuming that these theories are generalisable to all diverse clients, and that they are superior and universal, is a problem and puts the profession in a position of power (Sue, 2015).

While this chapter focuses on cultural diversity, many of us in counselling occupy various marginalised identities. It is important to note that while the emphasis here is on the UK context, and thus there is an assumed element of shared 'British' culture, there are cultural diversities within this context across the four nations related to differences such as class, religion and familial migration.

Pause for thought 1.6

Can you think of a time when you have been treated in a particular way based on a marginalised part of your identity (such as gender, age or disability)? What was that like? Have you experienced this in a healthcare or therapy setting?

3.2 (Re)examining assumptions and going beyond what we do and say with clients

Examining assumptions requires going beyond particular interventions, such as what you do (for example, collaborative formulation) and what you say (for example, offering empathy). Returning to Huang, in the 'alternative' case example in Section 2.1, Claudia demonstrated microaggressions towards her. Claudia must examine the assumptions and values that inform her work with Huang, which could be both conscious and unconscious. Failure to do so could cause harm to her client (Sue, 2015). One argument is that to avoid microaggressions, you need to go beyond simply avoiding specific behaviours or statements which may invalidate clients:

> microaggressions are reflections of a worldview of inclusion–exclusion, superiority–inferiority, desirability–undesirability, and normality– abnormality. Racial microaggressions are deeply embedded implicit racial biases, and it is this element that is harmful to clients of color, not just the specific behaviors. What is dangerous here is that implicit biases are outside the level of conscious awareness and cannot be separated from their behavioral expressions. Thus, avoiding harm does not occur through simply eliminating behavioral or non-verbal manifestations of microaggressions but requires major personal change and self-reckoning by clinicians.

(Sue, 2015, p. 363)

You'll read more on how you can work with unconscious processes in Chapters 2 and 6. For now, consider that going beyond what you do or say with a client might look like creating space for divergences and differences in world-views, and holding both/all as credible 'truths' (Hernández-Wolfe, 2011; Sue, 2015; Yahalom and Hamilton, 2024). Sue (2015, p. 368) has also explored building interventions from the 'ground up' rather than 'top-down'. This speaks to cultural equity by valuing the legitimacy of modes of healing that are different to one's own culture. This 'self-reckoning' that is carried out by examining assumptions must be ongoing and not a one-off at the beginning of therapy.

Pause for thought 1.7

What, if any, responses do you notice as you reach the end of this chapter? Do you notice any gut feelings, tensions or hesitancies? Are there curiosities or areas of comfort or discomfort? What might you learn from reflecting on how working with diversity makes you feel?

Conclusion

Understanding and working effectively with diversity matters for clients, and can also be generative for therapists in increasing awareness of personal and professional identity. This chapter focused on cultural diversity and examined the 'truths' from which Western, white, Eurocentric counselling and psychotherapy theory and practice operate. It is not necessarily a problem that in a Western context, Western modes of working and understanding psychological distress are practised with clients who are from the same culture. However, an assumption (conscious or otherwise) that (a) any given theory or approach is generalisable to all diverse cultures and (b) it is superior and universal needs to be critically examined. This chapter invites you to continue thinking critically and reflexively.

Further reading

- The following book offers ideas about anti-oppressive practice:

  Khan, M. (2023) *Working within diversity: a reflective guide to anti-oppressive practice in counselling and therapy.* London: Jessica Kingsley Publishers.

- The following book recounts lived experiences of racism in counselling and psychotherapy:

  Zahid, N. and Cooke, R. (eds) (2023) *Therapists challenging racism and oppression: the unheard voices.* Monmouth: PCCS Books.

- For more information about colonial histories, microaggressions, race and dynamics of power, you can explore the following resource:

  Charura, D. and Lago, C. (eds) (2021) *Black identities and white therapies: race, respect and diversity.* Monmouth: PCCS Books.

References

Ahmed, S. (2017) *Living a feminist life*. London: Duke University Press.

Betancourt, H. and López, S.R. (1993) 'The study of culture, ethnicity, and race in American psychology', *American Psychologist*, 48(6), pp. 629–637. Available at: https://doi.org/10.1037/0003-066x.48.6.629

Blaine, B.E. and McClure Brenchley, K.J. (2020) *Understanding the psychology of diversity*. 4th edn. London: SAGE Publications.

Cameron, L., Erkal, N., Gangadharan, L. and Meng, X. (2013) 'Little emperors: behavioral impacts of China's One-Child Policy', *Science*, 339(6122), pp. 953–957. Available at: https://doi.org/10.1126/science.1230221

Duran, E. (2006) *Healing the soul wound: counseling with American Indians and other native peoples*. New York: Teachers College Press.

Ghaemi, S.N. (2010) 'Levels of evidence', *Psychiatric Times*, 27(1), pp. 24–26.

Gone, J.P. (2009) 'A community-based treatment for Native American historical trauma: prospects for evidence-based practice', *Journal of Consulting and Clinical Psychology*, 77(4), pp. 751–762. Available at: https://doi.org/10.1037/a0015390

Hernández-Wolfe, P. (2011) 'Decolonization and "mental" health: a mestiza's journey in the borderlands', *Women and Therapy*, 34(3), pp. 293–306. Available at: https://doi.org/10.1080/02703149.2011.580687

Hunsley, J. and Mash, E.J. (2007) 'Evidence-based assessment', *Annual Review of Clinical Psychology*, 3, pp. 29–51. Available at: https://doi.org/10.1146/annurev.clinpsy.3.022806.091419

Jones, J.M., Dovidio, J.F. and Vietze, D.L. (2014) *The psychology of diversity: beyond prejudice and racism*. Hoboken,NJ: Wiley-Blackwell.

Khan, M. (2023) *Working within diversity: a reflective guide to anti-oppressive practice in counselling and therapy*. London: Jessica Kingsley Publishers.

Kuo, P.B., Imel, Z.E. and Tao, K.W. (2021) 'An experimental analogue evaluation of Asian and Asian Americans' immediate reactions to therapist microaggressions', *Counseling Psychologist*, 49(5), pp. 754–780. Available at: https://doi.org/10.1177/00110000211001368

Lekas, H.-M., Pahl, K. and Fuller Lewis, C. (2020) 'Rethinking cultural competence: shifting to cultural humility', *Health Services Insights*, 13, pp. 1–4. Available at: https://doi.org/10.1177/1178632920970580

Mignolo, W.D. (2005) *The idea of Latin America*. Malden, MA: Blackwell Publishing.

Oulanova, O., Hui, J. and Moodley, R. (2023) 'Engaging with minoritised and racialised communities "inside the sentence"', in L.A. Winter and D. Charura (eds) *Handbook of social justice in psychological therapies: power, politics, change*. London: SAGE Publications, pp. 10–21.

Owen, J., Imel, Z., Adelson, J. and Rodolfa, E. (2012) '"No-show": therapist racial/ ethnic disparities in client unilateral termination', *Journal of Counseling Psychology*, 59(2), pp. 314–320. Available at: https://doi.org/10.1037/a0027091

Page, S.E. (2007) 'Making the difference: applying a logic of diversity', *Academy of Management Perspectives*, 21(4), pp. 6–20. Available at: https://doi.org/10.5465/amp.2007.27895335

Piatkowska, S.J. and Lantz, B. (2021) 'Temporal clustering of hate crimes in the aftermath of the Brexit vote and terrorist attacks: a comparison of Scotland and England and Wales', *The British Journal of Criminology*, 61(3), pp. 648–669. Available at: https://doi.org/10.1093/bjc/azaa090

Reeves, K., Job, S., Blackwell, C., Sanchez, K., Carter, S. and Taliaferro, L. (2024) 'Provider cultural competence and humility in healthcare interactions with transgender and nonbinary young adults', *Journal of Nursing Scholarship*, 56(1), pp. 18–30. Available at: https://doi.org/10.1111/jnu.12903

Samuel, C.A. and Ortiz, D.L. (2021) '"Method and meaning": storytelling as decolonial praxis in the psychology of racialized peoples', *New Ideas in Psychology*, 62, article number 100868. Available at: https://doi.org/10.1016/j.newideapsych.2021.100868

SCoPEd Framework (2022), collaboratively developed by Association of Christian Counsellors (ACC), British Association for Counselling and Psychotherapy (BACP), British Psychoanalytic Council (BPC), Human Givens Institute (HGI), National Counselling and Psychotherapy Society (NCPS) and United Kingdom Council for Psychotherapy (UKCP). Available at: https://www.bacp.co.uk/about-us/advancing-the-profession/scoped/scoped-framework (Accessed: 12 June 2024).

Singh, A.A., Appling, B. and Trepal, H. (2020) 'Using the multicultural and social justice counseling competencies to decolonize counseling practice: the important roles of theory, power, and action', *Journal of Counseling & Development*, 98(3), pp. 261–271. Available at: https:/doi.org/10.1002/jcad.12321

Smail, D. (2001) 'De-psychologizing community psychology', *Journal of Community & Applied Social Psychology*, 11(2), pp. 159–165. Available at: https://doi.org/10.1002/casp.621

Smail, D. (2015) *Origins of unhappiness: a new understanding of personal distress.* London: Routledge.

Sue, D.W. (2015) 'Therapeutic harm and cultural oppression', *The Counseling Psychologist*, 43(3), pp. 359–369. Available at: https://doi.org/10.1177/0011000014565713

Turner, D. (2021) *Intersections of privilege and otherness in counselling and psychotherapy.* London: Routledge.

Wada, K. and Kassan, A. (2021) 'The internalization of counseling, psychology, and psychotherapy: decolonizing diversity and social justice training', in A. Kassan and R. Moodley (eds) *Diversity and social justice in counseling, psychology, and psychotherapy: a case study approach.* Solana Beach, CA: Cognella, pp. 355–368.

Wampold, B.E., Flückiger, C., Del Re, A.C., Yulish, N.E., Frost, N.D., Pace, B.T., Goldberg, S.B., Miller, S.D., Baardseth, T.P., Laska, K.M. and Hilsenroth, M.J. (2017) 'In pursuit of truth: a critical examination of meta-analyses of cognitive behavior therapy', *Psychotherapy Research*, 27(1), pp. 14–32. Available at: https://doi.org/10.1080/10503307.2016.1249433

Winter, L.A. (2019) 'Social justice and remembering "the personal is political" in counselling and psychotherapy: so, what can therapists do?', *Counselling and Psychotherapy Research*, 19(3), pp. 179–181. Available: https://doi.org/10.1002/capr.12215

Winter, L.A. (2021) 'Swimming against the tide: therapists' accounts of the relationship between p/Politics and therapy', *Counselling and Psychotherapy Research*, 21(2), pp. 303–312. Available at: https://doi.org/10.1002/capr.12401

Winter, L.A. and Charura, D. (eds) (2023) *The handbook of social justice in psychological therapies: power, politics, change.* London: SAGE Publications.

Yahalom, J. and Hamilton, A.B. (2024) 'Cultural pragmatism: in search of alternative thinking about cultural competence in mental health', *Journal of Theoretical and Philosophical Psychology*, 44(1), pp. 59–73. Available at: https://doi.org/10.1037/teo0000230

Chapter 2

Identity, culture and engagement in the therapeutic relationship

Sharon Frazer-Carroll

Contents

Introduction

Underneath the Surface by Maria Kenyon. This image represents the complex connections that exist beneath apparent calm and the convoluted pathways that lead to the root of the matter.

Chapter 1 shone light on ways of understanding human diversity and what this might mean for the way therapists think about difference. It positioned difference as borne out of the relationship between individuals, rather than as a label belonging to specific groups of individuals. This chapter builds on that approach, shifting attention to think more closely about the therapist's contribution to the range of diverse relationships they will develop in the therapeutic space. Today's counsellors and psychotherapists must consider the intersecting impacts of race, culture, gender, sexual orientation, socio-economic status, disability and other influences in both the therapy room and in their clients' lives.

The content in this chapter is based on the premise that openness and a willingness to learn about yourself, as well as your client, is essential to working effectively as a therapist (Chin, Hughes and Miller, 2022).

Largely focusing on racial difference, I draw on my experience as a Black British, cisgender woman and psychodynamic therapist to illustrate many of the ideas discussed. Given limitations in space, most of the examples relate to working with racial difference; however, the principles explored apply to working with all categories of difference. Furthermore, as practising therapists, the efforts we make to enhance awareness of ourselves, our identities and our position in the world has importance for our work across the board, irrespective of the client we are working with. Judy Ryde (2009), co-founder of Psychotherapists and Counsellors for Social Responsibility and who works with refugees and asylum seekers, expresses this as the need to understand who we are within a diverse world as we touch the lives of those we seek to help.

Please note that the chapter covers personal experiences of racism. These are included to help you understand the concepts explored and to encourage you to reflect on both your own cultural assumptions and aspects of identity.

This chapter contributes towards achieving the **SCoPEd competency 4.11.B**:

Ability to recognise and explore with the client or patient the assumptions that underpin understanding of identity, culture, values and worldview.

(SCoPEd Framework, 2022, p. 28)

This chapter aims to:

- consider cultural assumptions and their relationship with world-view, identity, values and client work

- encourage you to reflect on aspects of your own identity and position in society, and consider the influence of these when you engage with clients

- explore methods for increasing relational depth when working with the diverse range of clients you may encounter.

1 The influence of world-view, position and perspective on practice

As outlined by Sigmund Freud in 1915, our position in society contributes to the shaping of our identities, affecting the way we feel, think and interact with others (Freud, 1984). This also has an impact on our relationship with our clients, for example in how we make sense of their communication or the level of curiosity we show when we help them to explore the content they bring to a session. Even the level of receptivity you have to the ideas shared in this chapter will be influenced by your position in the world and your experiences in relation to that.

On entering the profession I was taken aback by what I perceived as limited attention to difference and diversity. I later learned that, traditionally, socially constructed categories like race (used in this chapter to refer to colour, nationality and ethnicity), gender, disability and class had been considered as having little significance to personality development (Bhui and Morgan, 2007; Tummala-Narra, 2013). Consequently, there has been comparatively little consideration of the ways in which social factors impact mental health and well-being, both in diagnosis and treatment.

Since the murder of George Floyd in 2020, and the subsequent protests against racism and police brutality, there has been accelerated interest in anti-oppressive practice and an influx of initiatives aimed at promoting equality, diversity and inclusion in counselling and psychotherapy. Speculation might suggest that the inclusion of difference and diversity in the SCoPEd competency framework, and even in this chapter, is a part of that retrospective attempt to begin filling this longstanding void, which was previously unseen or overlooked by those with the power to influence.

> ## Pause for thought 2.1
>
> Consider your own experience. How much of your core training was given to looking at difference and diversity? Which aspects of diversity were included, and which were not?
>
> What are your feelings about the relatively recent mainstream emphasis on equality, diversity and inclusion, and anti-oppressive practice? Is it useful, genuine and proportionate? Or perhaps it is irrelevant, excessive, insufficient or performative? Consider the influences on your feelings and whether they constitute barriers to, or motivators for, the way you think about the information in this chapter.

Chapters 1, 3 and 4 help answer the question of why we are discussing difference and diversity by thinking about counselling theories and their underpinning assumptions, in addition to working reflexively and practising in culturally sensitive and decolonial ways. Factors such as client safety, the avoidance of harm, and offering a fair and equitable service are important here, both legally and ethically. This chapter emphasises a further dimension by reminding us that we are considering difference and diversity because the psychotherapy profession has, for most of its time, been dominated by white, European, middle-class men whose perspectives led to a focus on factors that were deemed important by them and to them. In this way, the architects of modern-day psychotherapy could be described as having a common **world-view** steeped in the affairs of previous centuries, where deeply ingrained European standards of knowledge production, mental health and treatment were seen as truths and the 'correct' way of being, thinking and doing (Thomas, 2013).

In the Western world, **social hierarchies** typically place white, cisgender, heterosexual, non-disabled, middle-class men at the top, due to historical and systemic advantages. This positioning grants them greater access to resources, opportunities, and social and economic influence. As a result, we are now living with the consequences of past decisions which have left factors like race, class and disability poorly considered in counselling and psychotherapy. The sector still has significant progress to make; for instance, in the context of race:

world-view

A set of shared beliefs, values, attitudes and behaviours that stem from a largely unconscious understanding of the world, forming a lens through which interactions and events are interpreted.

social hierarchies

A system that ranks individuals or groups in a society based on factors like power, status, wealth or other social attributes.

- There is little racial diversity in the UK counselling and psychotherapy profession, with most practitioners identifying as white and not from any minority ethnic group (Bansal *et al.*, 2022).
- Theories remain Eurocentric, are assumed by the sector to be universal and are criticised for their failure to take account of Indigenous approaches (Bhui and Morgan, 2007).
- Research too frequently assumes universality, despite being based on predominantly white participants and having poor representation of racial demographics (Comas-Díaz, 2016; Smart and Harrison, 2017).
- Few training courses pay meaningful attention to race, culture or ethnicity (Ragaven, 2018; Daloye, 2022; Grewal *et al.*, 2024) and professional bodies have yet to specify consideration of racial factors as a requirement for reaccreditation.
- Racial discrimination and implicit bias negatively affect experiences and contribute to inequalities for service users from Black and minority ethnic communities (Naz, Gregory and Bahu, 2019).

Research suggests that the more likely a person is to believe in their own objectivity, the greater chance there is of bias unknowingly influencing their decision making (Pronin, 2007). Consequently, appreciating that you make assumptions because of the position you have in society is a foundational step in reducing bias, prejudice and errors of judgment that may affect your therapeutic relationships.

2 Unmasking assumptions: navigating identity, culture and values

Your world-view is based on cultural assumptions that you will have developed simply as a matter of growing up in the environment you did, while occupying the position in society that you have. Cultural assumptions exist as part of implicit memory (which is acquired and used unconsciously), which means you may not be aware of when you acquired them or when you display them (Jost *et al.*, 2009). Acquisition usually happens at critical times in life, including early childhood, or through repetition over long periods of time. Such assumptions form a central part of your identity and have significant influence on the way you view and interact with the world (Beagan, 2018). Cultural assumptions allow you to make generalisations and predictions, and therefore navigate the situations you meet with relative ease. The automated nature of assumptions means they also create blind spots, which can lead to bias and discrimination.

2.1 Counsellor and psychotherapist assumptions

In a clinical setting, a therapist's cultural assumptions can threaten therapeutic goals (Drustrup, 2020; Alleyne, 2023). They can, for example, lead to misunderstanding and upset, or questioning of the client's reality.

Consider the following case example. The therapist's comments are based on the assumption that she and her client share a similar experience of the police force and law enforcement. The client is a Black woman of Antiguan descent in her forties and the therapist is a white British woman aged 60.

Case example: Cultural assumptions between counsellor and client

Client: I was quite freaked out by the treatment of that Black man they arrested recently. It was all over the news and social media.

Therapist: That sounds difficult. Do you want to tell me more about how you felt?

Client: I kept thinking of his family – his parents, his partner, his children. [Gasps]

Therapist: Hmm, it seems to have really affected you and led you to think about how those close to him may have been impacted as well.

Client: Yes, I ended up reinforcing the messages that I'm always telling my boys. If the police stop you, don't try to assert yourself. Try to clear yourself, but don't interrupt. Do as they say and remain polite. Demonstrate that you respect their authority even if they are younger than you. Don't ask questions. I'm so sick and tired of having to do this. It makes me really angry, but what can I do?

Therapist: It sounds as though this horrible incident left you understandably upset and full of anxiety.

Client: Yes, it did. I had disturbed sleep and felt sick and agitated.

Therapist: It sounds as if it may have been so distressing that it spilled over a little and left you passing the worry to your sons, as if they were in danger too?

Client: They are in danger; every Black and Brown boy needs to know that they can't hide their skin, and they can be treated differently in these situations. And I need to teach them to keep themselves safe.

Therapist: I wonder if it might be helpful to look at ways of managing your anxiety, and maybe to explore that feeling that your sons might be treated differently to everybody else bound by the law?

Client: I don't think you quite understand. I don't have anxiety; well, I do, but not about my sons. Um, my anxiety is needed – I'm not over-anxious or paranoid.

Global Majority

A collective description for Black, Indigenous, Brown and Latinx people, who constitute approximately 85 per cent of the world's population. Used as an alternative to Black, Asian and minority ethnic (BAME), it reflects proportion and disrupts traditional definitions of identity in relation to whiteness.

In this situation, the therapist is unaware that her experiences have left her oblivious to some of the concerns of the **Global Majority** surrounding this sense of duty in keeping their children safe (Harris and Amutah-Onukagha, 2019). Historic inequality, including disproportionate use of force and unexplained deaths in custody, continue to fuel feelings of fear and mistrust in these communities (Beagan, 2018). A range of strategies are used to prepare children for the very real law enforcement threats experienced over decades. Black males in particular are stereotypically portrayed as violent, intimidating and aggressive. Without this understanding, therapists are left making sense of client information by applying assumptions based on their own experience. This can feel invalidating to clients and, in replicating cross-racial interactions in wider society, clients may also feel that misreadings of this kind signify difference, distance and a lack of understanding, thereby hindering the working alliance.

Recent research suggests that the therapeutic alliance tends to be poorer for Global Majority clients, leading to poorer outcomes particularly for Asian, Pacific Islander and Black clients (Li *et al.*, 2024).

Identifying your own cultural assumptions is an important step in building a therapeutic alliance with the client, one which is robust enough to tolerate exploration of *their* assumptions.

2.2 Client assumptions

Social hierarchies establish power dynamics that affect how individuals perceive both themselves and others. These hierarchies often play a crucial role in the process of **racialisation**, which Omi and Winant (2015, p. 13) describe as 'the extension of racial meaning to a previously racially unclassified relationship, social practice, or group'. The example in Box 2.1 highlights the experiences I had which contributed to my own racialisation. These events contributed to my own understanding of how I was perceived by those around me and how I was expected to behave. I see these events as helping to shape my understanding of who I was in the world. In this respect, they helped to shape my identity as a racialised being.

racialisation

The process of ascribing a racial character to something such as a relationship, social practice or group.

Box 2.1 Racialisation in primary years: a personal experience

Our world-view shapes how we interpret our own identities as well as those of others, which often reinforce existing social hierarchies. This illustration is from my own experience.

Growing up in the 1960s and 70s as a first-generation Black British girl, I remember the relief I experienced when friends, teachers or assistants defended me from onslaughts of racist abuse in the playground. They would say things like 'leave her alone, we're all the same underneath' or 'we are all made of blood, skin and bone, you know'.

Although I absorbed this message, as time passed many instances indicated that I was not the same as my white friends in terms of the way I was treated. For example, in primary school, when we knocked on doors for each other to walk to school in the morning, some of my white friends' parents asked the Black children to stand behind the gate. In the playground I learned the song: 'If you're white, you're alright; if you're yellow, you're mellow; if you're brown, stick around; if you're black, get back.' In junior year textbooks, the only people that looked like me were in chains. And in secondary school, when we were allowed out at lunchtime, security guards more frequently followed me around in stores, which was particularly unnerving.

This was an early start to realising the difference that was associated with the place I had been assigned in the world by the nature of my skin colour.

The term 'racialised' is usually applied to individuals from marginalised communities; however, in actuality, we are all racialised. We all acquire a set of privileges and disadvantages that are based on characteristics associated with race, and which give us a place in a socially constructed hierarchy that has become a societal reality. A variety of factors can contribute to individuals ascribing these racial categories to themselves; for example, noticing power differentials and becoming fearful of being rejected or excluded by the majority and thereby losing social status.

internalised oppression

Refers to the process where the marginalised group adopts the negative attitudes, beliefs and stereotypes perpetuated by the dominant society.

Multiple studies demonstrate the phenomenon of internalised racism – which is just one form of **internalised oppression** – whereby people of colour adopt the negative attitudes, beliefs and stereotypes perpetuated by the dominant (white) society (Davids, 2011; David and Derthick, 2013; Seet, 2020). This occurs through both conscious and unconscious processes, and can lead to a weak sense of self. Research suggests that in some instances, this internalisation can have a moderating effect on mental health by reducing psychic conflict (Thomas, 2007; Garcia, David and Mapaye, 2019), although other research has shown a negative health effect over time (James, 2021).

The Clark test (Clark and Clark, 1939), which explored bias in the 1940s, showed children as young as 3 years old demonstrating preference for white dolls over Black ones. Black dolls were predominantly identified as 'bad' and white dolls as 'good' by children of various racial origins. Disturbingly, even Black children labelled the Black doll as 'bad', despite identifying it as looking most like them. The study has since been recreated many times in a variety of countries, and today produces similar but much less pronounced results in many instances (Byrd *et al.*, 2017).

Racial attitudes and the assumptions associated with them persist over time and are reinforced intergenerationally through families and social relationships, systemically through institutions and structurally through the collective influence of social, political and economic operations (Alleyne, 2007; Frosh, 2013).

It may be your responsibility as a therapist to support your client in reframing experiences and working through trauma associated with their oppression; however, to do that effectively, you will need to have worked on the unconscious assumptions you hold as well.

2.3 Raising awareness of your own cultural assumptions

The concept of identity encompasses who you are, the traits that make up 'you', the way others feel about you and how you feel about yourself. Individuals hold multiple and intersecting identities (explained further in Chapter 3), which include both privileged and marginalised aspects (Goodman, 2015).

Our social identities – which include our race, gender, class, sexuality, age and religious beliefs – intersect to create unique combinations of privilege and marginalisation. In British (and wider Western) society, a person who is female, has a disability and is Muslim is likely to face a greater number of societal challenges than a person who is female, not disabled and Christian, for example. Government statistics show that Muslims were targets for 44 per cent of religious hate crimes in 2023 across England and Wales (Home Office, 2023), and that people with physical disabilities face stereotyping, stigma and physical, communication and economic barriers on an everyday basis (Barbareschi *et al.*, 2021). Privileges are explored more fully in Chapter 3; however, here we can think of them simply as advantages available to an individual that are inaccessible to others, and which are derived because of personal characteristics rather than personal control. Privileged aspects of one's identity encounter less challenge in society and indicate areas where one's cultural assumptions are likely to be greater.

An increasing number of scholars have begun to discuss methods which can support you in understanding and challenging your cultural assumptions (Comas-Díaz, 2016; Drustrup, 2020). Some key areas for consideration are listed below.

- *Personal therapy*: Self-exploration with a therapist who has spent time reflecting on their own identity can be an effective way to think about your own values and beliefs. Consider developing questions to identify a therapist who can support your specific goals. If you want a therapist to help you explore your racial identity, for example, you might ask them for their thoughts on the relevance of racial identity to personal therapy.

- *Professional development activities*: You can familiarise yourself with the institutionalised and systemic oppression which affects the lives of marginalised clients. Researching these topics can improve your understanding of your own identity and positioning in society, and will help you focus on your clients' concerns while avoiding placing a burden on them to educate you on these topics. Workshops, conferences, journals, books, the internet and supervision can all help. Choose providers that have expertise in the specific areas that are important for you. If you intend to work on racial identity, for example, you might attend events by the Black, African and Asian Therapy Network, the Muslim Counsellor and Psychotherapist Network or the Community Trauma Conference. Pink Therapy also puts on specialist events around gender inclusive therapy. Additionally, to stay in touch with wider political action, you could join Psychologists for Social Change.

- *Reflective activities*: Exploration of your assumptions is more effective when you have other people who can help you interrogate your feelings. However, reflective activities can encourage increased awareness of your identity, the privileges associated with your position, the bias you hold and the assumptions you may be prone to. It can be helpful to think about the messages and understandings that you acquired in childhood.

There are common experiences of racial marginalisation, racial discrimination and social exclusion, which together provide a common experience of oppression; however, since subcultures exist within marginalised communities, there may be significant differences between subgroups. It therefore remains important to treat each client as an individual.

Many clients of colour will have different early experiences to the ones I describe, for example. Individuals brought up in Africa or the Caribbean report being less likely than their Black British or African American counterparts to have considered race and racism until moving to predominantly white countries (Jackson and Cothran, 2003). Significant divisions were also created between Africans who remained in the continent and those who were forcibly taken into enslavement. Familiarisation with the culture and type of oppression which marginalised groups face is not synonymous with understanding individual client experience, but it does aid at least a partial understanding of the world they live in.

Pause for thought 2.2

Consider your own racial identity. What were your early memories related to race (including physical characteristics like skin colour, hair texture and facial features)? What do you recall adults around you saying? What events come to mind, and what might they tell you about the way you feel about your own racial identity, the way you see others and the way others see you?

Racial identity theories that suggest how the racial component of our identities is formed can help you to reflect on aspects of your personality that you may not automatically spend time thinking about. Identity theories can also contribute to thinking about the client's world and ways of working with trauma, discrimination, internalised oppression and minority stress (Frost and Meyer, 2023). Models of Black racial identity development, for example, can support work with clients of colour, enhancing their sense of self by working through negative self-images which have been internalised through the process of racialisation (Helms, 1993). In addition, identity theories can help provide a framework for practitioners and psychologically prepare them for working with the anger and guilt which marginalised clients may unconsciously carry, which stems from suppressing their authentic selves during the process of socialisation, racialisation and being forced to accept the inequalities associated with their place in the societal hierarchy.

Janet Helms (1993) and other theorists have also proposed white racial identity models, which include being aware of racial identities, understanding the privileges associated with white identity, reducing the intensity of emotional responses like guilt and shame, and being committed to dismantling racism. In traditional counselling training, Erik Erikson's psychosocial development model is commonly taught, but there are many other models available which may assist your work with clients who have marginalised identity characteristics. You may find it helpful to consult some of these in exploring your own identities as well as thinking about the client groups you work with.

3 Working with difference

Reflection by Simon Whitmore. This image conveys a flickering insight and a sense of clouded reflection.

A deeper understanding of who you are and how your position in society informs your perspective will strengthen your ability to work with clients. Similarly, deeper knowledge of the realities associated with the world your client lives in can help foster a more meaningful connection, avoid inadvertently reinforcing wounds you might hope to heal, prevent unnecessary ruptures in the relationship and avoid premature abandonment of treatment by the client.

3.1 Exploring cultural assumptions in practice

Bringing identity into the room early in the therapeutic relationship can help to establish a foundation for open discussion on which later exploration of assumptions can build. It can signal to the client that this will be a relationship where conversation on difference is welcomed. During assessment sessions you might, for example, ask clients why they chose you. This gives you the opportunity to explore the way the client sees you, in the moment as well as later on.

The methods you use to establish a foundation where difference can be explored will depend on you: who you are, the modality you are trained in, how you work and the setting you work in. You might work in an organisation with greater constraints on flexibility compared to working in private practice, or if you work with couples or children you may need to factor in additional dimensions or specific concerns.

Pause for thought 2.3

How can you begin to establish a foundation for discussing difference in your practice? Consider where you work, how you work and the type of clients you work with. Think back to specific clients you have had – consider any phrasing and approaches to practice that may have helped with any difficulties that arose.

It can be helpful to continue reflecting on your approach from time to time as you work with different clients, move between settings or as you continue to evolve your practice.

3.2 Spotlighting difference

Recent decades have seen increasing diversity in both client and therapist populations, so there is a greater need to think about the therapeutic dyad and the way differences in social and cultural position might influence treatment outcomes (Bhui and Morgan, 2007).

Considering 'who you are' in relation to societal hierarchies can add insight which supports the client in their own exploration in the therapy room. Consider this next case example where the therapist, a 50-year-old Black British woman, explores relational context to support a 45-year-old Black British woman in thinking about racial assumptions.

Case example: Drawing on identity in therapy

Client: I am so pleased to find a Black therapist willing to have in-person sessions with me. My previous therapist was an old white woman with white hair, and I found it difficult to share issues related to my race.

Therapist: What kind of things did you find difficult to share?

Client: I didn't think she would understand why the racist events I experienced at school had affected me so badly. White people can have difficulty understanding the things that hurt people of colour. Also, I struggled to talk to her about the things that having a white husband and biracial children brought up for me – I felt guilty, it felt like I was criticising her.

Therapist: And what about me – are there things you find difficult to share with a Black woman?

Client: [Short silence] I suppose it feels difficult talking to you about my mental health.

Therapist: That could be tricky given that one of the goals you shared at the beginning of therapy was to improve your mental health. Do you have a sense of why that might be?

Client: [Laughs] Yes, it's confusing. I think the things I want to talk about would seem trivial to many Black women, and you always seem so together. I can't come in complaining that I don't have the energy to cook and clean – there would be too much judgement and you'd be thinking I'm nasty [laughs again] – it's just everything is piling up at work, at home … It was easier to talk to my white therapist about the need to rest.

Bringing the therapist's own identity into the exchange revealed significant information about the client's previous experiences, her perception of the situation and what was happening between the therapist and client. It also opened avenues for further exploring assumptions associated with the client's world.

3.3 Working with fear, avoidance and difficult emotions

The discomfort associated with discussing aspects of identity can be intense and has the potential to interfere with, or even deter, meaningful thought processes and discussion in therapeutic interactions. Topics that evoke emotions such as shame or guilt are difficult to discuss and can hinder honest exchange through conscious and unconscious processes, irrespective of the therapist's background (Alleyne, 2023). Talking about things to do with race, for example, can trigger deep emotions (Sue, 2015). A white therapist who feels blame and shame, or fear of association when discussing racial oppression, may retreat from fully engaging with their Black clients (Knight, 2013). On the other hand, a Black therapist who suspects their white client may feel blame or anger at ongoing oppression may also fear upset and hesitate to discuss the topic. In both instances there is an unconscious propensity to avoid discomfort (Morgan, 2014; Smith, Proctor and Akondo, 2021).

In offering a model for addressing racism in the therapy room, Drustrup (2021) describes racial literacy as a lifelong process. As such, it can help to accept yourself as a 'work in progress'. Engage in conversations about race outside of the therapy room and recognise that you will make mistakes. If you intentionally create space in therapy in which it is safe to discuss race, this will make it easier to apply skills throughout the therapeutic process that you would otherwise use to repair ruptures in the relationship.

Conclusion

This chapter has looked at the ways in which cultural assumptions can impact the therapeutic space, alongside how and why it is essential for practitioners to explore their own implicit assumptions. As a counsellor, you will be aware of the attention, caution and care that is needed when approaching sensitive topics in therapeutic encounters, as well as the range of states and emotions that can arise in clients. However, there is an added challenge when working with marginalised and stigmatised groups who may have a lifetime's worth of oppressive experience, where key aspects of their identities have been hidden and denied. Associated feelings may be worsened when the appearance of their therapist gives them little reason to believe discussion in therapy will be different to their encounters in the wider world. You may also approach sessions with an awareness of the distance you still have to travel in working on your own bias, with an understanding that deep culture is transferred through implicit memory and assumptions. Bias and prejudice in this respect are inescapable. On this basis, you may find a platform for creating relationships based on openness and trust, where difficulties can be worked through, and the respectful care and containment you offer can give rise to the required healing in your client as well as incidental growth in yourself.

Further reading

- The following chapter explores world-view and the implications for counselling marginalised communities:

  Ibrahim, F.A. and Heuer, J.R. (2016) 'Worldview: implications for culturally responsive and ethical practice', in *Cultural and social justice counseling: client-specific interventions*. Cham, Switzerland: Springer, pp. 51–75.

- The following book considers culturally sensitive reflexive practice in counselling and psychotherapy:

  Lago, C. and Smith, B. (eds) (2010) *Anti-discriminatory practice in counselling and psychotherapy*. 2nd edn. London: SAGE Publications.

- The following book introduces and prompts reflection on work with trauma and adversity across a variety of client groups:

  Treisman, K. (2024) *Trauma-informed health care: a reflective guide for improving care and services*. London: Jessica Kingsley Publishers.

References

Alleyne, A. (2007) 'The internal oppressor: the veiled companion of racial oppression', *The Black, African and Asian Therapy Network*. Available at: https://www.baatn.org.uk/bwl-knowledge-base/the-internal-oppressor-the-veiled-companion-of-external-racial-oppression-3/ (Accessed: 11 December 2024).

Alleyne, A. (2023) *The burden of heritage: hauntings of generational trauma on Black lives.* London: Karnac Books.

Bansal, N., Karlsen, S., Sashidharan, S.P., Cohen, R., Chew-Graham, C.A. and Malpass, A. (2022) 'Understanding ethnic inequalities in mental healthcare in the UK: a meta-ethnography', *PLoS Medicine*, 19(12), article number e1004139. Available at: https://doi.org/10.1371/journal.pmed.1004139

Barbareschi, G., Carew, M.T., Johnson, E.A., Kopi, N. and Holloway, C. (2021) '"When they see a wheelchair, they've not even seen me" – factors shaping the experience of disability stigma and discrimination in Kenya' *International Journal of Environmental Research and Public Health*, 18(8), article number 4272. Available at: https://doi.org/10.3390/ijerph18084272

Beagan, B.L. (2018) 'A critique of cultural competence: assumptions, limitations, and alternatives', in C.L. Frisby and W.T. O'Donohue (eds) *Cultural competence in applied psychology: an evaluation of current status and future directions.* Cham, Switzerland: Springer International Publishing, pp. 123–138.

Bhui, K. and Morgan, N. (2007) 'Effective psychotherapy in a racially and culturally diverse society', *Advances in Psychiatric Treatment*, 13(3), pp. 187–193. Available at: https://doi.org/10.1192/apt.bp.106.002295

Byrd, D., Ceacal, Y.R., Felton, J., Nicholson, C., Rhaney, D.M.L., McCray, N. and Young, Y. (2017) 'A modern doll study: self concept', *Race, Gender and Class*, 24 (1–2), pp. 186–202. Available at: https://www.jstor.org/stable/26529244 (Accessed: 11 December 2024).

Chin, J., Hughes, G. and Miller, A. (2022) 'Examining our own relationships to racism as the foundation of decolonising systemic practices. "No time like the present"', *Journal of Family Therapy*, 44(1), pp. 76–90. Available at: https://doi.org/10.1111/1467-6427.12384

Clark, K.B. and Clark, M.P. (1939) 'The development of consciousness of self and the emergence of racial identification in Negro preschool children', *Journal of Social Psychology*, 10(4), pp. 591–599.

Comas-Díaz, L. (2016) 'Racial trauma recovery: a race-informed therapeutic approach to racial wounds', in A.N. Alvarez, C.T.H. Liang and H.A. Neville (eds) *The cost of racism for people of color: contextualizing experiences of discrimination.* Washington, DC: American Psychological Association, pp. 249–272.

Daloye, D. (2022) 'The experiences of Black and Minority Ethnic trainee counselling psychologists: an interpretative phenomenological analysis', *Counselling Psychology Review*, 37(1), pp. 31–40. Available at: https://doi.org/10.53841/bpscpr.2022.37.1.31

David, E.J.R. and Derthick, A.O. (2013) 'What is internalized oppression, and so what?', in E.J.R. David (ed.) *Internalized oppression: the psychology of marginalized groups.* New York, NY: Springer Publishing Company, pp. 1–30.

Davids, M.F. (2011) *Internal racism: a psychoanalytic approach to race and difference.* London: Palgrave Macmillan.

Drustrup, D. (2020) 'White therapists addressing racism in psychotherapy: an ethical and clinical model for practice', *Ethics & Behavior*, 30(3), pp. 181–196. Available at: https://doi.org/10.1080/10508422.2019.1588732

Drustrup, D. (2021) 'Talking with white clients about race', *Journal of Health Service Psychology*, 47, pp. 63–72. Available at: https://doi.org/10.1007/s42843-021-00037-2

Freud, S. (1984) 'The discovery of the unconscious', in A. Richards (ed.) *On metapsychology: the theory of psychoanalysis, Vol. 11*. Translated from the German by J. Strachey. London: Penguin, pp. 159–222.

Frosh, S. (2013) 'Psychoanalysis, colonialism, racism', *Journal of Theoretical and Philosophical Psychology*, 33(3), pp. 141–154. Available at: https://doi.org/10.1037/a0033398

Frost, D.M. and Meyer, I.H. (2023) 'Minority stress theory: application, critique, and continued relevance', *Current Opinion in Psychology*, 51, article number 101579. Available at: https://doi.org/10.1016/j.copsyc.2023.101579

Garcia, G.M., David, E.J.R. and Mapaye, J.C. (2019) 'Internalized racial oppression as a moderator of the relationship between experiences of racial discrimination and mental distress among Asians and Pacific Islanders', *Asian American Journal of Psychology*, 10(2), pp. 103–112. Available at: https://doi.org/10.1037/aap0000124

Goodman, D.J. (2015) 'Oppression and privilege: two sides of the same coin', *Journal of Intercultural Communication*, 18, pp. 1–14. Available at: https://dianegoodman.com/wp-content/uploads/2020/05/PrivilegeandOppression.pdf (Accessed: 11 December 2024).

Grewal, C.S., Khan, M.B., Panesar, J.K.K., Asher, S. and Mehan, N. (2024) 'Exploring BAME student experiences in healthcare courses in the United Kingdom: a systematic review', *Journal of Advances in Medical Education & Professionalism*, 12(1), pp. 8–17. Available at: https://doi.org/10.30476/jamp.2023.98882.1825

Harris, A. and Amutah-Onukagha, N. (2019) 'Under the radar: strategies used by Black mothers to prepare their sons for potential police interactions', *Journal of Black Psychology*, 45(6–7), pp. 439–453. Available at: https://doi.org/10.1177/0095798419887069

Helms, J.E. (1993) *Black and white identity development: theory, research and practice*. Santa Barbara, CA: Greenwood Press.

Home Office (2023) *Hate crime, England and Wales, 2022 to 2023*. Available at: https://www.gov.uk/government/statistics/hate-crime-england-and-wales-2022-to-2023/hate-crime-england-and-wales-2022-to-2023 (Accessed: 16 August 2024).

Jackson, J.V. and Cothran, M.E. (2003) 'Black versus Black: the relationships among African, African American, and African Caribbean persons', *Journal of Black Studies*, 33(5), pp. 576–604. Available at: https://doi.org/10.1177/0021934703033005003

James, D. (2021) 'The seemingly "protective" effect of internalised racism on overall health among 780 Black/African Americans: the serial mediation of stigma consciousness and locus of control', *Psychology & Health*, 36(4), pp. 427–443. Available at: https://doi.org/10.1080/08870446.2020.1797028

Jost, J.T., Rudman, L.A., Blair, I.V., Carney, D.R., Dasgupta, N., Glaser, J. and Hardin, C.D. (2009) 'The existence of implicit bias is beyond reasonable doubt: a refutation of ideological and methodological objections and executive summary of ten studies that no manager should ignore', *Research in Organizational Behavior*, 29, pp. 39–69. Available at: https://doi.org/10.1016/j.riob.2009.10.001

Knight, Z.G. (2013) 'Black client, white therapist: working with race in psychoanalytic psychotherapy in South Africa', *The International Journal of Psychoanalysis*, 94(1), pp. 17–31. Available at: https://doi.org/10.1111/1745-8315.12034

Li, Y., Whiston, S., Wong, Y.J. and Gilman, L. (2024) 'Clients' race/ethnicity as a moderator of the relationship between the therapeutic alliance and treatment outcome', *International Journal for the Advancement of Counselling*, 46(2), pp. 219–241. Available at: https://doi.org/10.1007/s10447-024-09546-3

Morgan, H. (2014) 'Between fear and blindness: the white therapist and the Black patient', in F. Lowe (ed.) *Thinking space: promoting thinking about race, culture and diversity in psychotherapy and beyond*. London: Routledge, pp. 56–74.

Naz, S., Gregory, R. and Bahu, M. (2019) 'Addressing issues of race, ethnicity and culture in CBT to support therapists and service managers to deliver culturally competent therapy and reduce inequalities in mental health provision for BAME service users', *The Cognitive Behaviour Therapist*, 12, article number e22. Available at: https://doi.org/10.1017/s1754470x19000060

Omi, M. and Winant, H. (2015) *Racial formation in the United States*. 3rd edn. New York, NY: Routledge.

Pronin, E. (2007) 'Perception and misperception of bias in human judgment', *Trends in Cognitive Sciences*, 11(1), pp. 37–43. Available at: https://doi.org/10.1016/j.tics.2006.11.001

Ragaven, R.N. (2018) *Experiences of Black, Asian and Minority Ethnic clinical psychology doctorate applicants within the UK*. PhD thesis. University of Hertfordshire. Available at: https://uhra.herts.ac.uk/handle/2299/21590 (Accessed: 11 December 2024).

Ryde, J. (2009) *Being white in the helping professions: developing effective intercultural awareness*. London: Jessica Kingsley Publishers.

SCoPEd Framework (2022), collaboratively developed by Association of Christian Counsellors (ACC), British Association for Counselling and Psychotherapy (BACP), British Psychoanalytic Council (BPC), Human Givens Institute (HGI), National Counselling and Psychotherapy Society (NCPS) and United Kingdom Council for Psychotherapy (UKCP). Available at: https://www.bacp.co.uk/about-us/advancing-the-profession/scoped/scoped-framework (Accessed: 12 June 2024).

Seet, A.Z. (2020) 'Surviving the survival narrative part 1: internalised racism and the limits of resistance', *Cosmopolitan Civil Societies: An Interdisciplinary Journal*, 12 (2–3), pp. 36–50. Available at: https://doi.org/10.5130/ccs.v12.i2-3.7154

Smart, A. and Harrison, E. (2017) 'The under-representation of minority ethnic groups in UK medical research', *Ethnicity & Health*, 22(1), pp. 65–82. Available at: https://doi.org/10.1080/13557858.2016.1182126

Smith, L., Proctor, G. and Akondo, D. (2021) 'Confronting racism in counselling and therapy training – three experiences of a seminar on racism and whiteness', *Psychotherapy and Politics International*, 19(2), article number 1579. Available at: https://doi.org/10.1002/ppi.1579

Sue, D.W. (2015) *Race talk and the conspiracy of silence: understanding and facilitating difficult dialogues on race*. Hoboken, NJ: John Wiley & Sons.

Thomas, L.K. (2007) 'Discussion of "The internal oppressor: the veiled companion of racial oppression"', *Attachment: New Directions in Relational Psychoanalysis and Psychotherapy*, 1(3), pp. 275–279.

Thomas, L.K. (2013) 'Empires of mind: colonial history and its implications for counselling and psychotherapy', *Psychodynamic Practice*, 19(2), pp. 117–128. Available at: https://doi.org/10.1080/14753634.2013.778484

Tummala-Narra, P. (2013) 'Psychoanalytic applications in a diverse society', *Psychoanalytic Psychology*, 30(3), pp. 471–487. Available at: https://doi.org/10.1037/a0031375

Chapter 3

Developing self-awareness in working with diversity

Zoë Boden-Stuart

Contents

Introduction

Coastal Erosion of Sandstone by Stuart Timms. This photograph speaks to the way we are all shaped by our histories and environments.

Imagine you are about to start working with a new client. From the little you know about them, you will already be forming judgements: some conscious and some not. As emphasised in Chapter 2, these judgements will be shaped by your own experiences and prevailing social norms. We quickly build up an initial picture of a person by drawing on our own frames of reference, even when we think we are being non-judgemental (see Cook, 2021). This means that who we are – our identities, values and world-views – shape our interactions with our clients from the very first moment.

It is also worth remembering that your client will do the same with you. They may have chosen you because they believe you share some significant aspect of their identity (e.g. being a Black woman or identifying as part of the LGBTQ+ community). Or perhaps they see you as different from them in a way that they believe will help them to confide in you. Or they may have been allocated to work with you and be wondering whether you will be 'right' for them. Things that may not hold much importance for you could be pivotal in how your client sees you; for example, where you practise, how you advertise your services, your accent or a previous career. Even 'small' decisions we make as practitioners (like what we choose to wear) can lead clients to make assumptions about who we are, our values and our world-views. Aspects of our identity that we foreground may become reasons for clients to want – or not want – to work with us. Therefore, it is important to gain an understanding of ourselves in order to understand the impact of these aspects on our clients.

This chapter will outline why and how critical self-awareness is important in building strong therapeutic relationships with your clients. It will focus particularly on core aspects of our identities – including age, race, class, gender, sexual identity and disability – and on understanding how these intersect. The chapter will touch on culture, values and world-view, all concepts that will be further explored in Chapter 5. Ongoing personal development is a key aspect of therapeutic practice, and learning more about how we see ourselves, what matters to us and our frame of reference is fundamental to becoming a more robust, ethical and effective counsellor.

The chapter contributes towards achieving the **SCoPEd competency 5.4.B**:

> Ability to critically challenge own identity, culture, values and worldview.
>
> *(SCoPEd Framework, 2022, p. 30)*

This chapter aims to:

- develop your understanding of why 'knowing yourself' is fundamental for working ethically and effectively, as well as for building strong therapeutic relationships

- outline frameworks for critically auditing your own identities, culture, values and world-view, with particular consideration of how you are positioned socially

- critically reflect on some of the ways in which our identities shape our counselling practice.

1 Who are you?

As counsellors, we spend much of our time thinking about our clients, but to work competently and ethically we must also spend time cultivating a deep understanding of how we feel about *ourselves*. Counsellors know that a strong therapeutic alliance is key to good counselling outcomes (Norcross and Lambert, 2018), and it follows that we need to think deeply about both the client *and* the therapist in that relationship. You are encouraged to approach this chapter with a commitment to self-care as you explore your identity (self-care will be explored further in Chapter 7). Pay attention to your bodily responses, any memories that surface, and your feelings as you reflect on who you are and what that means to you. Take your time, consider what you need and try to adopt a compassionate stance towards yourself and others.

Pause for thought 3.1

Briefly try to answer the question 'who am I?'

Notice what ideas of yourself first came to mind, what followed and anything you excluded. You might have considered your gender, race, ethnicity, disability status, sexuality, age, nationality and religion, along with your relationship identities (e.g. 'father', 'wife', 'son', 'aunt') or migration status. You might have included things that you care about or values that you hold dear.

Are some aspects of yourself more important than others? Why might this be?

Working with a client who is different to you can summon up a range of feelings – anxiety, embarrassment, shame, curiosity, anger, envy, guilt – and thoughts such as: 'Will I know what to say?'; 'Will I use the right language?'; 'Will the client want to work with me?'; and 'Will they make assumptions about me?' Working with a client who you perceive as similar to you will also bring up feelings and thoughts, perhaps including feelings of identification, comfort or familiarity, assumptions about shared perspectives or an expectation of connection. Exactly which thoughts and feelings emerge with each client will, at least partially, depend on how we feel about certain aspects of ourselves, as illustrated through the following fictional case example.

Case example: Kristi reacts to a shared characteristic

Kristi is a bisexual counsellor in her sixties. She has started working with a client in their twenties who has listed their sexuality as 'bi' on their assessment forms. So far in their sessions, the client hasn't mentioned this. Kristi assumes that the client is hesitating because they have trouble trusting others to accept their sexuality. Kristi is basing this on her own ambivalence: she feels both proud and ashamed of her bisexuality. She struggles with internalised biphobia and fears being rejected by both straight and gay communities. Kristi also feels teacherly at the prospect of helping her younger client accept their sexuality, though this was not something that the client had said they wanted to work on. Kristi has assumed that the client will have 'issues' to bring to therapy around their sexuality.

Sharing a minoritised sexual identity with her client sensitises Kristi to a range of potential issues that affect bisexual people. However, Kristi is allowing her own experiences and feelings about her sexuality to shape how she understands her client's issues. It may be that the client *does* want to talk about difficult feelings surrounding their sexuality during sessions; however, it could also be that they accept and enjoy their sexual identity. Indeed, as the counsellor and client differ significantly in age, the context and culture in which they experience their sexuality could be radically different. In this case, both difference in age and similarity in sexual identity are shaping how the counsellor thinks about and works with her client. This counsellor would benefit from reflecting more deeply on what her age and sexuality mean to her, how these dimensions of her identity shape her position in relation to others, and how this has influenced her values and world-view.

1.1 The changing nature of identity

Reflecting deeply on our own identities as counsellors is important for several reasons. Counsellors may **project** unacknowledged feelings about their own identities (e.g. shame, worthlessness, fear, hatred) on to their client, thus positioning themselves as superior and avoiding anxiety-inducing feelings. In Jungian terms (Jung, 1969, para. 131), those feelings remain in **the shadow**. Dwight Turner (2021), who authors Chapter 4, speaks about how this happens on a collective level too through a process of 'othering' (defined in Chapter 1, Section 1.3), whereby one social group projects their fears, hatred and shame on to another group. Counsellors and clients are individuals, but they are also part of these social groups that are othered or are involved in the othering process.

Relatedly, however, identities are multiple and mutable: we all have many different aspects to who we are, and over time these can change. Migration, for example, may take you from being in the majority social group to being viewed as 'other' – an outsider. Disabilities may be with us for our entire lifetime or may be something that we acquire or only become aware of later in life. Age is an identity characteristic that is always changing: at some points we might experience our age as something that brings us power or authority, and at others (perhaps when we are very young or very old), it might signify fewer opportunities or privileges. Age is also approached differently across cultures; for example, in Britain, older people are viewed and cared for differently from how they are in China, where there is a

project

Projection is the unconscious process of directing unacceptable or unbearable thoughts or feelings outwards, attributing them to other people. Projection is a defence mechanism that helps the individual avoid aspects of themselves that elicit difficult emotions.

the shadow

Refers to the unconscious aspects of a person that do not fit with their good opinion of themselves, and that the person would deny or find hard to own or acknowledge.

stronger expectation that younger generations will look after and respect their elders (e.g. Laidlaw *et al.*, 2010). How we describe and react to our identities therefore depends, at least in part, on our context, culture and world-view.

1.2 Understanding intersectionality and privilege

It may seem like counselling theory and practice have only recently started thinking about identity, difference and social inequalities, but these ideas are not new. Intersectionality and privilege, two key concepts for understanding how identities matter, were developed by third-wave feminist scholars and activists working in the 1980s and 1990s. At that time, academics recognised that focusing on gender inequalities in isolation was hampering efforts towards social justice for *all* women. Black women and other women of colour occupied particularly precarious social positions, as they were marginalised and oppressed both because of their gender *and* their race. Legal scholar Kimberlé Crenshaw (1989) used the term **intersectionality** to describe how social structures impact certain social groups in unequal ways, and cause double – or multiple – disadvantages. This term has become significant across a wide range of disciplines, and now frequently refers to intersections between all social categories, including disability, sexual identity, age and religion, for example. More recently, intersectionality theory has been taken up within the social sciences as a framework for thinking through individual lived experiences. For counsellors, an intersectional perspective brings the opportunity to 'see' others – and oneself – more fully. As Turner explains, intersectionality allows us:

> to bring to the surface, like a free diver, that which has increasingly been left in the depths of the unconscious … [A]s Crenshaw herself recognised, without these increasing efforts too many minority groups will continue to fall between the gaps of our knowledge and understanding, and will remain invisible.

(Turner, 2021, p. 21)

The 1980s was also an important time for questioning what it meant to have *privileged identities*, especially in terms of race, gender and sexual identity. Privilege in this context refers to the opportunities to feel at home in the world, to avoid penalty or danger, to escape anxiety or insult, to avoid having to hide or disguise oneself, or to avoid feeling angry or aggrieved (McIntosh, 2001). It is often possible to use words like 'power' or 'dominance' instead of 'privilege'. However, Turner (2021) describes how privilege used as supremacy is about having power over others, with traumatic outcomes, whereas privilege that is accepted with humility, and from a relational stance, is a gift. Turner's message, therefore, is that privilege is not 'bad', but rather it is how we use our social privileges that is important.

Belonging to a socially privileged group may not equate to feeling privileged or enjoying a life without hardships. Privileged social identities tend to be those shared with the majority (e.g. in the UK, this means being white, non-disabled and heterosexual), but they can also represent historical injustices

intersectionality

A concept that describes how social and political systems of power intersect in multiple and coexisting ways to produce different experiences of identity-based privilege and marginalisation in the same individual.

and systems of control (e.g. the patriarchy and colonialism). Privileged identities also tend to avoid scrutiny. Research or personal reflection on male, white or heterosexual privilege, for example, is a way of turning the spotlight back on to those groups (e.g. Connor *et al.*, 2021). Recognising privilege is therefore an opportunity for us all to reflexively consider the meanings and experiences associated with holding positions of power. Most, if not all, people will have at least one domain of their identity that has a relatively privileged position in society.

Pause for thought 3.2

Which socially privileged identities do you hold? Which aspects of your identity are less socially privileged?

The following case example explores the complexity of one individual's identity.

Case example: Farah's context and identity

Farah is a British-Persian woman in her late forties, who describes herself as Brown. She is Muslim. Her mother and father were first-generation immigrants to the UK. She attended a private school and then a highly regarded university, graduating with both a bachelor's and a master's degree. Farah grew up in an affluent family; her mother was a doctor and her father, a lawyer. She trained as a counsellor while raising her three children and caring for her ageing parents. She is heterosexual and cisgender, and she has no disabilities. She is married to a man with whom she has a stable and supportive relationship. They live in good economic circumstances and in good health.

Some aspects of Farah's identity are privileged, bringing with them certain powers and opportunities, and some aspects are more oppressed or marginalised in British society. Farah's race, religion, skin colour, gender and status as a second-generation immigrant, as well as potentially her age and caring role, position her in social groups that hold less power within British society. For example, Farah has frequently been told to 'go back home', despite living in the city in which she was born. However, her affluence, class, educational background, heterosexuality, cisgender and non-disabled status also mean that she holds some privilege. For example, Farah does not have to worry about being able to access her counselling practice which is up several flights of stairs. Together, these make up just some of the complexities inherent in Farah's identity. The wheel of power/privilege (Figure 3.1), which was created by Canadian teacher Sylvia Duckworth, can help you to think through this example.

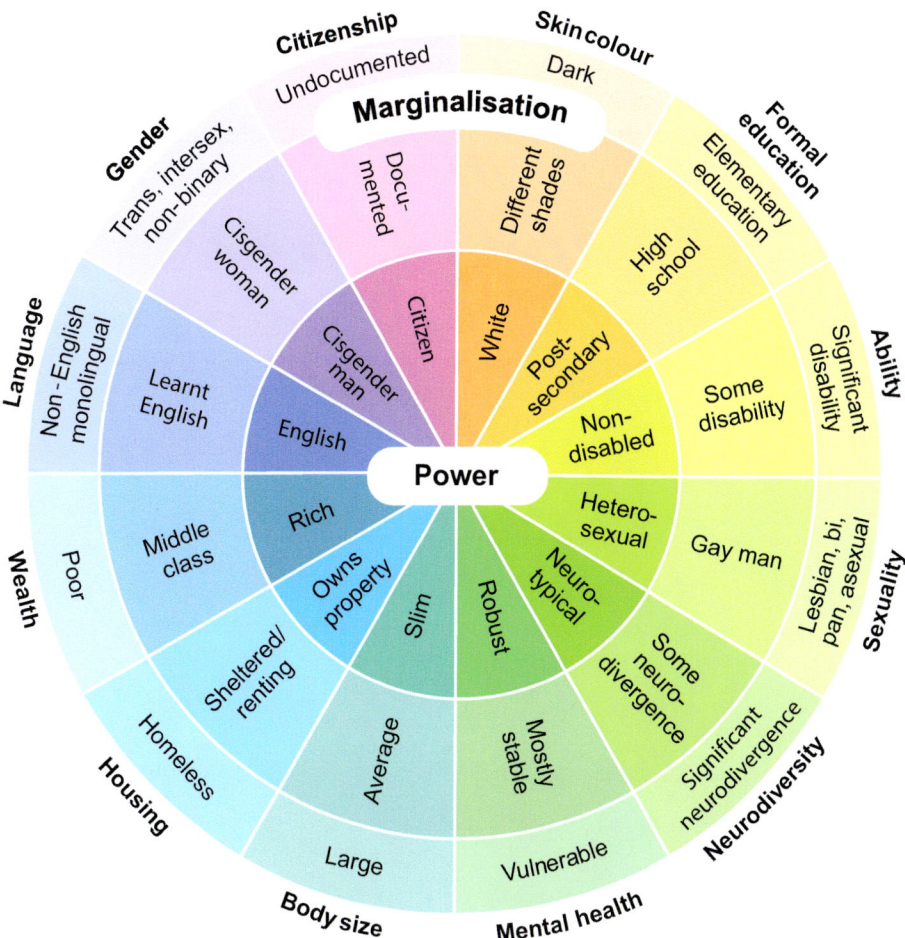

Figure 3.1 The wheel of power/privilege, based on Global North culture and values. A characteristic's position on the wheel indicates whether it is more marginalised or more privileged/powerful. (Adapted from Duckworth, 2020)

Pause for thought 3.3

Is there anything about the wheel of power/privilege that you think is missing or that you would change?

All counsellors will hold multiple identities, each contributing to different amounts of social privilege. These identities also intersect. In Farah's example, as a Muslim woman she will experience different levels and types of Islamophobic harassment than her Muslim husband (Alimahomed-Wilson, 2020). For example, how she chooses to dress may be more closely scrutinised. Thinking about your own identity through the lenses of intersectional theory and power/privilege can help you to reflect on the complex ways in which you are positioned in relation to others, including your clients.

This reflective work can be challenging, and you may be questioning whether it is necessary to do it. The next section will consider why counsellors need to develop critical self-awareness around identity, values and world-view, and how it can affect our ethical integrity, competence and efficacy.

2 Why is it important to understand who you are?

The work of confronting ourselves can be emotionally demanding. So, why is it necessary? Self-awareness is a key part of all therapy training for good reason, and it is a key aspect of working ethically and competently (Knapp, Gottlieb and Handelsman, 2017). Self-awareness can refer to both moment-to-moment awareness and broader self-insight (both of which are covered in Part 2 of this book), but it is the latter that is the focus of this chapter. This section suggests three reasons why this self-interrogative work matters: for supporting ethical integrity, therapeutic effectiveness and therapeutic self-disclosure.

2.1 Supporting ethical integrity

The British Association for Counselling and Psychotherapy's *Ethical Framework* (BACP, 2018) provides some helpful reminders of why reflecting on our identities is fundamental to ethical counselling. One of the BACP's ethical principles is self-respect, which includes self-knowledge, self-care and integrity. Developing self-knowledge involves engaging with *all* aspects of your identity; not only those aspects viewed as 'different', but also those you share with the majority social group. It also includes looking at aspects that may be painful, perhaps because they have been persecuted or because they elicit feelings of shame, distress, guilt or complicity. Self-care can only be achieved if you are able to fully recognise your vulnerabilities and how you habitually cope with or defend against them, as well as your strengths and resources. (Chapter 6 will explore more about how aspects of ourselves remain out of awareness, or unconscious.) Having integrity in this domain means being able to act with self-awareness and in line with your own values and needs – to do this, you need a good understanding of yourself and how you relate to others, plus the courage to act on this understanding.

The BACP (2018, p. 11) also lists identity as one of the personal moral qualities that counsellors should aspire towards developing, defining it as a 'sense of self in relationship to others that forms the basis of responsibility, resilience and motivation'. Having a sense of self requires a thorough consideration of your identities and how they have shaped your values and world-view.

2.2 Supporting therapeutic effectiveness

All modalities acknowledge that self-awareness supports the counsellor to be appropriately responsive to their client (McLeod, 2013). It is also a key element of building a strong therapeutic alliance with your client:

> In our view it is always therapeutic for the therapist to be aware of her [their, his] own feelings and reactions as this awareness orients her, and helps her be interpersonally clear and trustworthy. This inner awareness and contact naturally flows from the experience of therapeutic presence.
>
> *(Greenberg and Geller, 2001, p. 151)*

Being more aware of who we are, and how that positions us socially, better enables us to offer a robust presence for the client, to empathise without losing our sense of ourselves and to 'meet' the client where they are. From a person-centred perspective, 'congruence' – a concept first associated with Carl Rogers (1957) – involves both awareness and acceptance of the counsellor's self-experience at inner, interpersonal and ecological (relating to the living world) levels of integration (Cornelius-White, 2007). To be congruent, there needs to be a 'lining-up' of bodily experience, feelings and thoughts, and an acceptance of all of those aspects (Mountford, 2011). From a psychodynamic perspective, self-awareness supports counsellors to make sense of, and manage, countertransferential feelings towards the client (this is further covered in Chapter 6). A counsellor who reacts to a client unconsciously risks harming the client and contributing to poor outcomes. When the counsellor has unresolved conflicts, these need to be brought into conscious awareness and worked through, for example in personal therapy and supervision (Hayes, Gelso and Hummel, 2011).

2.3 Supporting therapeutic self-disclosure

Different modalities follow different beliefs about counsellor self-disclosure and the extent to which transparency is valued. However, evidence suggests that counsellor self-disclosure can be beneficial for the therapeutic relationship (Henretty *et al.*, 2014) when used sparingly and to emphasise similarity (Hill, Knox and Pinto-Coelho, 2018). Disclosure of identity can happen intentionally or unintentionally, and some aspects are more visible than others. You may decide to be transparent about less visible aspects of your identity to build an authentic therapeutic relationship with your client, or you may choose to keep these private as part of your therapeutic frame. Knowing how you feel about your identity, and how this positions you in relation to others, can help determine what you are willing to share with clients, and in what circumstances.

The aim, then, is to develop the awareness necessary so that *should* you choose to disclose something, there would be no barrier to you doing so. This means having the capacity for self-awareness and for accepting self-knowledge without barriers such as defence, deflection and anxiety (Mountford, 2011). Clients can surprise us with direct or indirect questions about who we are. You may also have experience of being 'read' in a certain way that might not reflect your own identity. A whole range of identities may be assumed on the basis of appearance (e.g. skin colour, facial features, body shape and size, hair type or cut, clothing choices, style or quality), speech, mannerisms, names, or the use of mobility or sensory aids. Whether or not we choose to self-disclose aspects of our identities within the therapeutic relationship will depend on many factors.

Hearn and West-Olatunji (2015), for example, detail the complex nature of counsellors disclosing an LGBTQ+ identity. They note that while any disclosure should always be done in service of the client, the counsellor should also consider how they feel about their LGBTQ+ identity and how this may be influenced by internalised prejudices and anxieties, the sexual or gender identity of the client, and the prevailing culture and norms. For those of us with minoritised identities, choosing whether to be transparent about who we are is not necessarily straightforward, and may have consequences for the counsellor's safety or reputation. Thinking through these issues in advance means that a counsellor is less likely to be caught off-guard.

Pause for thought 3.4

Can you think of a time when your identity became relevant in your work with a client? Reflect on whether or not you voiced this aspect of your identity, and how you feel about that choice now.

So far, you have considered some theoretical lenses through which to reflect on who you are, and some practical rationales for why this work matters. The next section suggests some tools for reflecting more deeply on your identity, values and world-view.

3 Taking stock of who you are: conducting an identity audit

This section provides two frameworks relevant to exploring your own identity: the Social GGRRAAACCEEESSS, and the dimensions of visible–invisible and voiced–unvoiced. Section 4 will then encourage you to think through how you respond affectively to your identities.

In the early 1990s systemic family psychotherapist John Burnham and his colleague Alison Roper-Hall developed a mnemonic to help trainees explore issues of identity to enhance their practice. As of writing in 2025, the mnemonic is 'Social GGRRAAACCEEESSS' – the acronym stands for gender, geography, race, religion, age, ability, appearance, class, culture, ethnicity, education, employment, sexuality, sexual identity and spirituality (this framework will be referred to as the 'Social Graces' from this point onwards). Burnham (2012) emphasises the fluid nature of the mnemonic: it has changed a lot since its inception, and he recognises it is not all-inclusive. For example, it does not include migration status, mental health diagnosis or adoption status. He also recognises that people's identities are complex and cannot simply be summed up in such a list. In addition, Burnham (2012, p. 146) draws attention to intersectionality, describing the mnemonic as a 'collide-scope', in that different aspects of identity intersect and can be contextualised and understood in different ways, with varying impacts.

Burnham (2012) also notes that although they originally thought of these identity aspects as social in nature, they are also personal. Our social positions and the relative social power that we wield as a group (e.g. of women, of Black people, of people with disabilities) does not account for the in-group differences that comprise people's personal experiences and meanings. As counsellors, we need to carefully interrogate what our present identities mean to us, how we feel about them and how they shape our experiences with others. The Social Graces can therefore be thought of as a scaffolding for thinking about ourselves (Nolte, 2017) – and for defining different aspects of our identities (rather than for considering our social position in terms of relative privilege, as you saw with the wheel of power/ privilege shown in Figure 3.1).

How we feel about aspects of our identities shapes how we think, talk about and act on them. Burnham (2012) describes how each of the Social Graces sits on *visible–invisible* and *voiced–unvoiced* continuums (see Figure 3.2). A 'visible' identity, as race or gender sometimes are, will be seen by others, which can be both helpful and unhelpful in different circumstances. If your visible identity is similar to that of the client with whom you are working (i.e. you both look similar), this may bring feelings of congruence, comfort and familiarity, or build trust or openness within the relationship. However, it may also lead to assumptions or over-identification (such that it becomes difficult to take an appropriately detached therapeutic perspective). Being visibly different may bring feelings such as anxiety, curiosity, surprise, relief or shame. Visible difference can be desired, for example where a female client chooses a male therapist to explore issues related to an absent father. Invisibility comes with its own complexities too: less obvious aspects of identity (such as a person's spirituality) may generate connection, but this is only possible if they are made visible (i.e. disclosed).

A voiced aspect of identity is one that you choose to talk about, regardless of whether or not it is visible. In your counselling work, you may believe it is important to share, for example, your religion, cultural background or sexuality, perhaps on your website or in your biography. Unvoiced aspects are those you do not speak about, intentionally or unintentionally. They may have been silenced within your family of origin, or are so taken for granted you never considered needing to name them. Alternatively, you may be hyper-aware of the consequences of voicing a hidden aspect of yourself.

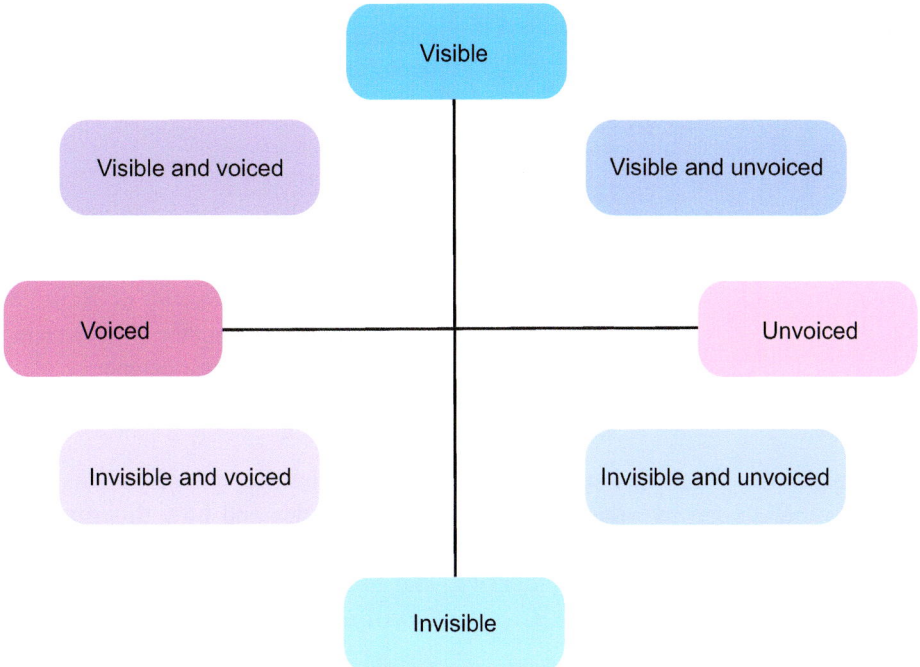

Figure 3.2 Dimensions for reflecting on the extent to which aspects of identity are visible/invisible and voiced/unvoiced (Adapted from Burnham, 2012, p. 146)

Understanding our identities and how we feel about them is key for understanding their role in our therapeutic relationships. Table 3.1 draws on the case of Farah (introduced in Section 1.2) to provide an example of how a counsellor might deepen their understanding of their own identities. In this example, Farah considers her female gender identity.

Table 3.1 Farah's visible–invisible and voiced–unvoiced dimensions of gender

Visible–invisible	Voiced–unvoiced	Thoughts and feelings	Possible impact on clients
Believes she is easily viewed as a woman because of the way she dresses, her hair styles and her makeup. Feels her voice also indicates that she is a woman.	Rarely voices her gender. Assumes she doesn't need to but will do so to identify herself as part of the 'sisterhood' when talking to other women about male privilege. States her pronouns to introduce herself in support of others with minority gender identities.	Can be anxious around men in certain contexts, which she attributes to an abusive relationship with a man in her teens. Feels comfortable and accepting of her gender. Some shame and internalised/self-directed misogyny and hatred. Feels pride in being a woman, which gives her a sense of belonging. She supports women's causes.	Risks projecting her feelings of vulnerability as a woman on to her female clients. May judge female clients who do not conform to the same norms of femininity as she does. May overlook her cisgender privilege when working with trans and/or non-binary clients. Risks treating male clients as if they are threatening, or may try to assert authority over them as a defence against her anxiety.

In this example, Farah has started to think about what her gender means to her, how she is seen by others in respect to her gender and how this might affect her therapeutic relationships. You can use this table as a framework to interrogate aspects of your own identity. The following section illustrates how you can strengthen this process; Chapter 5 will also support you in this work.

4 Reflecting on the impact of identity on practice

This final section provides an approach to thinking more deeply about an aspect of your identity: in this case, your gender. You may find it helpful to journal your reflections; alternatively, just take your time to think about the prompts as you work through the section. For some people, gender is a contentious term. It is used here to bring to mind how you live in the world and the sense you have of yourself as, for example, non-binary, intersex, trans, female or male. This may or may not be the same as the sex you were assigned at birth.

Gender is a powerful force in shaping how we experience the world. Below is a set of reflective steps for thinking about how and, importantly, *why* an aspect of your identity has impacted your counselling journey. Asking 'why?' is a method for thinking critically about your responses; that is, questioning and challenging yourself. There may not be one simple answer to 'why?', but it may help you to deepen your understanding of how you came to have certain thoughts, feelings or experiences. As with everything in this book, approach this task with self-compassion and an awareness of your needs and well-being.

Step 1: Reflections on early life

Start by thinking about your early life. Do you remember receiving any particular messages, and developing particular **scripts** or **introjects** – either voiced or implicit? How easy is it to reflect on this aspect of childhood? You may or may not have already spent considerable time thinking about this.

- Notice whether you feel any resistance, and explore that.
- Consider where those messages came from and who provided you with alternatives (e.g. parents, friends, educators, the media).
- Reflect on how your gender was more or less socially privileged and if/when you became aware of that.
- Reflect on how your perception of your gender changed as you developed; perhaps around puberty, when you started dating or when you left home.
- Consider whether your gender ever made you feel vulnerable, whether it created or prevented opportunities for you in education or work, or whether you felt constrained or empowered by the expectations that came with your gender. Has any of this changed since you were a child, either for you personally or societally?

scripts

Describes the beliefs, expectations and behaviours that we inherit from our families and societies. These can be replicated, challenged or changed.

introjects

Refers to the ideas, values and beliefs that we inherit from significant authority figures in our lives (e.g. parents/carers).

Step 2: Reflections on counselling training

Now think about gender within the context of the counselling profession, starting with your training.

- How many people shared your gender? What was it like to be part of that majority or minority?
- What gender-related topics were or were not discussed and why might that be? You might consider topics such as gender norms, misogyny or misandry, intimate partner violence/domestic violence, sexual violence, trans rights, menstruation and menopause, toxic masculinity, parenting, diet or body shape, gendered health issues (like prostate or ovarian cancer), and social movements (e.g. #MeToo).
- Reflect on how well represented your gender is in the history of your modality. For example, how many authors of your gender were included on your reading list? How many classic case studies covered people sharing your gender? Were your tutors or assessors the same gender as you? What about the person leading your course or training institute?
- Reflect on the wider distribution of gendered power within the profession, historically and today, and what this means for you personally. For example, did having a tutor of the same/a different gender affect how you contributed to your personal development groups?

Step 3: Reflections on counselling practice

The third area to consider is your practice. This may help you become aware of any thoughts or beliefs you hold about particular genders. You may have experience working in a gendered service or specialise in a gendered area.

- How do you feel about working with clients of the same/a different gender? Do you have a preference? Why might this be? You might consider factors such as emotional comfort, familiarity, safety or attraction.
- Reflect on which presenting issues you most associate with which genders: anger, violence, panic, parenting issues, relationship breakdown, suicidality or substance use, for example. Gender is one of the most basic **schemas** that people develop to organise information (see Starr and Zurbriggen, 2017), and this can lead to us hold rigid gender beliefs.
- You could also look at how you present your gender in your marketing materials or biography. Perhaps gender is implied through your name and/or a photograph, or perhaps you explicitly name your gender or include your pronouns. Reflect on what you have done intentionally and what may have happened outside of your awareness.
- Finally, consider how the context of gender appears within your supervisory relationship. Is it a topic that you are comfortable discussing? Was it a consideration in your choice of supervisor?

schemas

A cognitive or socio-cognitive concept or framework that helps people organise and make sense of complex information.

Step 4: Reflections on intersectionality

So far, this section has focused solely on gender. Now, revisit the questions above, but this time take an intersectional approach and see whether doing so produces more nuanced responses. For example, disclosing to your personal development group that you are a survivor of sexual abuse as a Black man or as a white woman is likely to be experienced differently, as there are dominant (and sometimes sexist and racist) cultural beliefs about who can be victimised and in what contexts. It is likely that if you are a white woman, you will be part of the majority in your personal development group, and because violence and abuse against women and girls is increasingly spoken about in society, other women may also share similar experiences. However, if you are a Black man, you may well find yourself in the minority in your training, both because of your gender and your race. Additionally, as sexual abuse against boys remains relatively hidden in society (e.g. Sivagurunathan *et al.*, 2019), you may find that people struggle to connect with your experiences. Thinking about the intersectional identities within your training group or supervisory relationship might be a good place to start when reflecting on how gender shapes your relationships with others.

This section has hopefully given you the opportunity to reflect more deeply on one aspect of your identity. You can use this exercise as a model to explore other aspects like age, disability, race or sexual identity, for example.

Conclusion

The aim of this chapter was to help you think about how your identities matter for your counselling practice. You have considered why engaging in a thorough and ongoing audit of your identity, and understanding how this shapes your values and world-views, is fundamental to being an ethical and effective counsellor. None of us is only one thing – we hold multiple identities that become more or less significant as we journey through life, and different aspects of our identities intersect to provide us with more or less social power. Identities change over time and are contingent on our own context; however, knowing who we are in relation to our clients is essential for developing strong therapeutic relationships. Hopefully, the theoretical and practical grounding this chapter has provided can help you further explore who you are and why that matters for your clients.

Further reading

- The following book provides background and context to the many ways in which gender intersects with counselling:

  Miville, M.L., Vera, T. and Bensmiller, N. (2024) *Counseling and gender: intersectional approaches for practice, research, and advocacy.* Cham, Switzerland: Springer Nature.

- The following chapter focuses on understanding the Social Graces framework:

  Burnham, J. (2012) 'Developments in Social GGRRAAACCEEESSS: visible–invisible and voiced–unvoiced', in I.-B. Krause (ed.) *Culture and reflexivity in systemic psychotherapy: mutual perspectives.* London: Karnac Books, pp. 139–160.

- This book provides useful exercises for further intersectional self-reflection:

  Khan, M. (2023) *Working within diversity: a reflective guide to anti-oppressive practice in counselling and therapy.* London: Jessica Kingsley Publishers.

References

Alimahomed-Wilson, S. (2020) 'The matrix of gendered Islamophobia: Muslim women's repression and resistance', *Gender & Society*, 34(4), pp. 648–678. Available at: https://doi.org/10.1177/0891243220932156

BACP (2018) *Ethical framework for the counselling professions*. Available at: https://www.bacp.co.uk/events-and-resources/ethics-and-standards/ethical-framework-for-the-counselling-professions/ (Accessed: 22 February 2024).

Burnham, J. (2012) 'Developments in Social GGRRAAACCEEESSS: visible–invisible and voiced–unvoiced', in I.-B. Krause (ed.) *Culture and reflexivity in systemic psychotherapy: mutual perspectives*. London: Karnac Books, pp. 139–160.

Connor, S., Edvardsson, K., Fisher, C. and Spelten, E. (2021) 'Perceptions and interpretation of contemporary masculinities in Western culture: a systematic review', *American Journal of Men's Health*, 15(6), article number 15579883211061009. Available at: https://doi.org/10.1177/15579883211061009

Cook, M. (2021) *Perceiving others: the psychology of interpersonal perception*. London: Routledge.

Cornelius-White, J. (2007) 'Congruence', in M. Cooper, M. O'Hara, P.F. Schmid and G. Wyatt (eds) *The handbook of person-centred psychotherapy and counselling*. Basingstoke: Palgrave Macmillan/Springer Nature, pp. 168–181.

Crenshaw, K. (1989) 'Demarginalizing the intersection of race and sex: a Black feminist critique of antidiscrimination doctrine, feminist theory and antiracist politics', *University of Chicago Legal Forum*, 139, pp. 139–167.

Duckworth, S. (2020) *Wheel of power/privilege*. Available at: https://www.flickr.com/photos/sylviaduckworth/50500299716/ (Accessed: 27 January 2022).

Greenberg, L.S. and Geller, S. (2001) 'Congruence and therapeutic presence', in G. Wyatt (ed.) *Rogers' therapeutic conditions: evolution, theory and practice. Volume 1: congruence*. Monmouth: PCCS Books, pp. 131–149.

Hayes, J.A., Gelso, C.J. and Hummel, A.M. (2011) 'Managing countertransference', *Psychotherapy*, 48(1), pp. 88–97. Available at: https://doi.org/10.1037/a0022182

Hearn, B.G. and West-Olatunji, C. (2015) 'Deciding to disclose: the LGBTQ counselor's unique challenge', *Vistas Online*, 74, pp. 1–8.

Henretty, J.R., Currier, J.M., Berman, J.S. and Levitt, H.M. (2014) 'The impact of counselor self-disclosure on clients: a meta-analytic review of experimental and quasi-experimental research', *Journal of Counseling Psychology*, 61(2), pp. 191–207. Available at: https://doi.org/10.1037/a0036189

Hill, C.E., Knox, S. and Pinto-Coelho, K.G. (2018) 'Therapist self-disclosure and immediacy: a qualitative meta-analysis', *Psychotherapy*, 55(4), pp. 445–460. Available at: https://doi.org/10.1037/pst0000182

Jung, C.G. (1969) *The collected works of C.G. Jung. Volume 11: psychology and religion: West and East*. 2nd edn. Edited and translated from the German by G. Adler and R.F.C. Hull. Princeton, NJ: Princeton University Press. Bollingen Series.

Knapp, S., Gottlieb, M.C. and Handelsman, M.M. (2017) 'Self-awareness questions for effective psychotherapists: helping good psychotherapists become even better', *Practice Innovations*, 2(4), pp. 163–172. Available at: https://doi.org/10.1037/pri0000051

Laidlaw, K., Wang, D., Coelho, C. and Power, M. (2010) 'Attitudes to ageing and expectations for filial piety across Chinese and British cultures: a pilot exploratory evaluation', *Aging & Mental Health*, 14(3), pp. 283–292. Available at: https://doi.org/10.1080/13607860903483060

McIntosh, P. (2001) 'White privilege and male privilege: a personal account of coming to see correspondences through work in women's studies', in M.L. Anderson and P.H. Collins (eds) *Race, class, and gender: an anthology*. 4th edn. Belmont, CA: Wadsworth, pp. 95–105.

McLeod, J. (2013) *An introduction to counselling*. 5th edn. Maidenhead: McGraw-Hill Education.

Mountford, C.P. (2011) 'Unpacking the congruence box', *Self & Society*, 38(4), pp. 5–17.

Nolte, L. (2017) '(Dis)gracefully navigating the challenges of diversity learning and teaching – reflections on the Social Graces as a diversity training tool', *Context*, 151, pp. 4–6.

Norcross, J.C. and Lambert, M.J. (2018) 'Psychotherapy relationships that work III', *Psychotherapy*, 55(4), pp. 303–315. Available at: https://doi.org/10.1037/pst0000193

Rogers, C.R. (1957) 'The necessary and sufficient conditions of therapeutic personality change', *Journal of Consulting Psychology*, 21(2), pp. 95–103. Available at: https://doi.org/10.1037/h0045357

SCoPEd Framework (2022), collaboratively developed by Association of Christian Counsellors (ACC), British Association for Counselling and Psychotherapy (BACP), British Psychoanalytic Council (BPC), Human Givens Institute (HGI), National Counselling and Psychotherapy Society (NCPS) and United Kingdom Council for Psychotherapy (UKCP). Available at: https://www.bacp.co.uk/about-us/advancing-the-profession/scoped/scoped-framework (Accessed: 12 June 2024).

Sivagurunathan, M., Orchard, T., MacDermid, J.C. and Evans, M. (2019) 'Barriers and facilitators affecting self-disclosure among male survivors of child sexual abuse: the service providers' perspective', *Child Abuse & Neglect*, 88, pp. 455–465. Available at: https://doi.org/10.1016/j.chiabu.2018.08.015

Starr, C.R. and Zurbriggen, E.L. (2017) 'Sandra Bem's gender schema theory after 34 years: a review of its reach and impact', *Sex Roles*, 76, pp. 566–578. Available at: https://doi.org/10.1007/s11199-016-0591-4

Turner, D. (2021) *Intersections of privilege and otherness in counselling and psychotherapy: mockingbird*. London: Routledge.

Chapter 4

Recognising and working with the decolonised self

Dwight Turner

Contents

SCoPEd Framework (2022), collaboratively developed by Association of Christian Counsellors (ACC), British Association for Counselling and Psychotherapy (BACP), British Psychoanalytic Council (BPC), Human Givens Institute (HGI), National Counselling and Psychotherapy Society (NCPS) and United Kingdom Council for Psychotherapy (UKCP). Available at: https://www.bacp.co.uk/about-us/advancing-the-profession/scoped/scoped-framework (Accessed: 12 June 2024).

Thomas, L.K. (2000) 'Attachment issues between a Caribbean mother and daughter', *Separation & Reunion Forum and Goldsmiths College joint conference*, London (UK), 23 June.

Turner, D. (2021) *Intersections of privilege and otherness in counselling and psychotherapy: mockingbird*. London: Routledge.

Williams, W. (2020) *Windrush lessons learned review*. Independent report, HC 93. Available at: https://www.gov.uk/government/publications/windrush-lessons-learned-review
(Accessed: 18 December 2024).

Young, N.J. (2018) 'Gay "conversion therapy" in "Cameron Post," "Boy Erased" is far from a thing of the past', *Huffington Post*, 25 August. Available at: https://www.huffingtonpost.com/entry/opinion-conversion-therapy-movies_us_5b7f1e64e4b0348585fee692 (Accessed: 18 December 2024).

Introduction

A girl walking in nature. This image represents the passage through self-exploration to discovering who one truly is.

This chapter builds on the ideas introduced in the three previous chapters. It uses a critical and decolonial lens to examine how the theories and epistemic underpinnings used in counselling and psychotherapy can reinforce systems of privilege, oppression and marginalisation. The aim of this chapter is to help you think critically about 'decolonising' the self and developing a decolonial approach to your work (a concept introduced in Chapter 1).

The chapter considers the importance of addressing one's own colonised identities – moulded by systems such as colonialism and patriarchy to the point where the individual is 'accepted' within these systems – to enhance awareness of and address how we as individuals might reinforce and continue systems of marginalisation and oppression.

Note that this chapter includes descriptions of colonisation and enslavement. These are included to help you critically reflect on the colonisation of counselling and psychotherapy, and to apply a decolonial lens to client work. As a therapist, you are probably used to monitoring your own reactions and responses to material that might be troubling, evocative or difficult to hear. This chapter is about addressing our own colonised identities and working with those of clients. This is a very particular kind of work; it is not neutral, and it might present challenges to you. The chapter uses terms such as 'white supremacy', 'racism' and 'colonisation'. These are not neutral terms, and they may well evoke responses. You are invited now to consider the concept of 'white fragility', which can occur when white people:

> consider a challenge to our racial worldviews as a challenge to our very identities as good, moral people. Thus, we perceive any attempt to connect us to the system of racism as an unsettling and unfair moral offense. The smallest amount of racial stress is intolerable – the mere suggestion that being white has meaning often triggers a range of defensive responses … These responses work to reinstate white equilibrium as they repel the challenge, return our racial comfort, and maintain our dominance within the racial hierarchy.

> *(DiAngelo, 2018, p. 2)*

As you read this chapter, you might notice personal reactions to particular words or ideas. You are invited to be curious about how your own colonised self and the colonised spaces you occupy might shape these responses.

This chapter contributes towards achieving the **SCoPEd competencies 4.2.B and 4.7.B**:

> Ability to critically appraise a range of theories underpinning the practice of counselling and psychotherapy.
>
> Ability to demonstrate the capacity, knowledge and understanding of how to select and adapt interventions and (or) approaches to respond to the needs of the client or patient.
>
> *(SCoPEd Framework, 2022, pp. 26–27)*

This chapter aims to:

- outline the nature of coloniality and its impact on the client
- think critically about how theories and epistemologies underpin counselling and psychotherapy practice
- suggest ways to recognise signs of colonisation in clients and yourself, and to support clients in working through these.

1 Critical appraisal of theoretical approaches to counselling practice

Historically, education in the **Global North** was afforded to those who were identified as white, European men, and were of a higher class and power (Schaverien, 2004). This meant that most women, working-class people and those under colonial rule received, at best, only the most rudimentary education or, at worst, were castigated for knowing anything of worth (Akbar, 1996). The UK educational system has been set up to maintain these structures of supremacy. US author, academic and activist bell hooks, whose work addresses feminism, race, intersectionality and capitalism, put forward the idea that education systems are framed out of the **patriarchy**, **white supremacy** and empire/colonialism (hooks, 2016; Golash-Boza, Duenas and Xiong, 2019).

Pause for thought 4.1

Think about your own counselling training, continued professional development or supervision. Have you been encouraged to think critically about the theories or teaching material you use? How has your critical thinking been received by trainers or supervisors?

In the UK, counselling and psychotherapy education has been critiqued for its cultural monotony and erasure of important conversations around difference, diversity and colonial thinking (Lago and Charura, 2021). Such critiques are both central and generative in terms of developing training and practice to engage with the history of coloniality in the profession and, as such, to better equip therapists to address their own internalised colonised ideas as well as those of clients. Most practitioners are not taught to consider the range and diversities of clients' intersectional identities, or the ways in which socially located experiences of privilege and oppression may have been a factor in their current psychological distress. It is therefore important to go beyond your current experiences and understandings when thinking about diversity.

1.1 Colonised narratives in counselling and psychotherapy

This section examines the wider cultural, socio-economic and colonial world within which we reside. It looks at colonised psychotherapeutic narratives and how difficult it can be to think beyond this frame of understanding. To do this, the section draws on ideas from psychodynamic theory, although the same challenges can occur within other modalities, too.

Global North

A term used to denote the nations of the world with a high level of economic and industrial development and political freedoms. It contrasts with the Global South, a term used to denote comparatively less development and freedoms.

patriarchy

A societal system in which a male figure sits at its head and holds dominance and privilege (such as the father, the male elder or a male political leader).

white supremacy

The belief that white people constitute a superior race and should therefore dominate societally.

This chapter draws on the case example of Michael (introduced below) which covers our work together; this case is an amalgamation of several client cases I have encountered.

Case example: Michael – background context

Michael is a 65-year-old man of African-Caribbean descent. Michael's parents were part of the Windrush generation who travelled to the United Kingdom in the later 1950s to find work during the time of the British Empire. At this time, Michael was left in Jamaica, in the Caribbean, where he was raised for some of his early years by his grandparents. He remembers very little of his life before this time, except that he was happy with his parents and older brother. When his parents left, Michael said that he felt very little emotion about the separation; he simply enjoyed spending time with his older brother at the beach or playing in the yard in and around the coconut trees.

His grandmother became ill, so although he got to spend a lot of time with his grandparents, there were occasions when his grandfather was preoccupied with looking after his grandmother, thereby leaving both Michael and his brother to their own devices. After several years, when Michael was 11 years old, his parents sent for Michael and his brother; they travelled to the United Kingdom, where they were reunited with their parents in Luton, England. By this stage, his parents had two further children, siblings that Michael knew nothing about and with whom he initially struggled to form bonds. Michael's older brother, who by this time was of secondary school age, struggled not just with the change of environment, but with being parachuted into a school where he was very different to the other children in his classes.

Michael's mother died suddenly of a serious stroke when Michael was an adult. Michael found himself feeling emotions that he had not experienced before, and his friends encouraged him to seek therapy. Michael was initially reluctant to do this, based on his feeling that counselling was a 'white undertaking' and that he would find it difficult to find a therapist of colour who might understand him. By the time he approached me for therapy, it had been a year since his mother had passed, and his emotional struggles had failed to dissipate.

Pause for thought 4.2

What are your initial reactions to reading about Michael? What do you make of his feeling that counselling is a 'white undertaking'? How might your own racial identity shape your response to this?

You might find that aspects of your own internalisations of colonisation – your colonised self – shape your initial reading of and reactions to Michael and, as such, how you might make sense of and work with Michael's psychological distress.

Now read the following account of the early stages of my counselling work with Michael.

Case example: Michael and I begin therapy

During the early stages of our work, Michael would consistently arrive about 10–20 minutes late. While my supervisor, who was a white man, encouraged me to challenge Michael around these instances of lateness, what struck me during the early weeks of our work was that this was a symptom of the disconnect that he had endured when he was a child.

Upon exploring this further, this disconnect played out in various ways, some of which often led to Michael being seen as a 'problem' or as 'different' in some way; my supervisor felt that Michael's lateness was a problem, for example. If I were to negatively pathologise Michael's lateness and make assumptions about it, I might have missed out on exploring the pain that Michael still held, which related to the separation from his parents. Additionally, on reflection, I might have been rather blasé about Michael's tardiness. It could be that not taking it seriously was a way of playing into the historical cultural bias against Black men: seeing Black men as 'less than', often meaning they are not held in mind or taken seriously.

From a decolonial lens, client presentations such as Michael's – which are seen as contrary to the norm, or the 'ideal' of whiteness, patriarchy, class superiority and heteronormativity – risk becoming marked out as 'wrong', 'other' and as a form of illness or pathology. The pain of this pathologisation, of having been marked out as other, is not only specific to Michael or to being marked out as racially different. This is the case for many marginalised and oppressed groups. For example, in the LGBTQ+ community there is painful confusion and consternation around the inclusion of 'gender dysphoria' in diagnostic systems, and around the failures of varying medical and governing bodies to ban conversion therapies in the UK and the US (Nichols, 2016; Young, 2018; *Memorandum of understanding*, 2024).

1.2 Critical considerations of theoretical context from a decolonial lens

As already emphasised, theory and epistemology underpin counselling and psychotherapy practice. This means that the wider context within which truths are born is an important factor in understanding those truths. The reductionist frameworks instituted in many training courses have failed to account for this. Together with the drive for acceptance by the medical establishment that marked the counselling profession's inception, this makes clear that all forms of counselling and psychotherapy have been embedded within structures of oppression (Kizito, 2017; Lev Kenaan, 2021). This can be seen from the earliest stories of Carl Jung and his travails through Africa, where he met people whom he viewed as less than him in his research into the collective unconscious (Burleson, 2005), or in the well-known recording of Carl Rogers inviting a Black client to express difficult feelings of anger and resentment towards him as a white male psychotherapist (Moodley, Lago and Talahite, 2004). While these stories often aimed to gain information, or explore the core conditions of person-centred therapy, what they also did was to ignore, and therefore reinforce, the oppressive power dynamics which Black people often have to endure.

More contemporary examples arise out of the works of Eugene Ellis (2021) and Jane Czyzselska (2022), who explore the experiences of Black and LGBTQ+ therapists and clients, utilising their stories to explore the structural marginalisations still embedded within our profession.

Psychotherapy, in its desire to establish truth, has often adopted the same colonised, supremacist narratives as any other form of knowledge production. Sigmund Freud, for example, a man who is much maligned for some of his views around difference and diversity, was himself a Jewish immigrant who fled from Vienna in Austria before the First World War (Freud, 1964). One might wonder whether Freud, driven by a desire to have his ideas accepted within the medicalised establishment, chose to push aside some of his arguably more interesting and less extreme viewpoints around the influence of culture upon mental health.

Pause for thought 4.3

What external factors influence your own understanding of yourself? What about information from family members, society, culture or elsewhere? Think back to Chapter 3 and its idea of forming intersectional identities: how do these external factors inform these identities?

---

2 Decolonising practice

A modern-day Black family engaged in raising their children away from the colonised, stereotypical gender roles and structures which would have affected the older generation of such a family.

In Chapter 1 you briefly explored how we come to know what we know in counselling; that is, you explored the epistemic underpinnings of the profession. You were encouraged to think critically about **epistemology**, examining how we justify claims to 'truth' and what kind of knowledges are given credence or attention.

epistemology

Theory of knowledge (i.e. the nature of learning and generating knowledge about the world).

This section will explore how theory and epistemology underpin counselling and psychotherapy practice. It will start by applying a particular theoretical approach to Michael's case, using a decolonial lens. It will then focus on establishing safety and reconnection through therapy, specifically by looking at the client's intergenerational history.

2.1 A decolonial perspective on attachment and intergenerational wounds

As explored in the chapter so far, colonised ideas and forms of knowledge production, along with the limited training available to address such issues, can result in a loss of theoretical nuance and critical thinking. This can in turn negatively affect the counsellor's attunement with the client. By drawing on the case example of Michael, this section will critically apply attachment theory using a decolonial lens. Attachment theory (Bowlby, 1988) broadly refers to a framework or model of our early life relationships with caregivers and our community, and their influence on our view of self in relation to others. In the theory's original iteration there were assumed to be three attachment styles: secure, avoidant and ambivalent (sometimes referred to as anxious). Later, a fourth style – disorganised attachment – was added by Ainsworth *et al.* (2015).

According to attachment theory:

- a child develops a *secure attachment* when their needs have largely been met, with the caregiver providing a consistent sense of safety and security for exploration and learning about the world

- a child develops an *avoidant* or *ambivalent/anxious attachment* (where they avoid or respond inconsistently to their caregiver, respectively) as a way of adapting to a lack of safety from the caregiver, which affects the child's understanding of the world and themselves

- a child develops *disorganised attachment* when experiencing ongoing fear, inconsistency or abuse; for example, when raised in chaotic or unpredictable circumstances or those that lead to trauma.

All four attachment styles will affect relationships in adulthood, whether romantic or otherwise. This section focuses on ideas from attachment theory to exemplify how the colonisation of ideas occurs and how this can be addressed.

Case example: Michael – background context (continued)

Through the therapy sessions with Michael, I began to understand that he felt very marginalised in his family as a child, to the extent that he would often spend a lot of time kicking a ball in the yard on his own while his brother was doing his own thing, and his younger siblings were playing with their parents. When Michael was 14, his older brother departed back to the Caribbean to live with his grandparents once more, having found life in England too difficult and the racism too much to contend with. Michael remained in the United Kingdom, and while he found himself able to secure work in factories in Luton, he found it incredibly difficult to form close relationships.

None of his romantic relationships lasted particularly long, and it was not until he was in his early twenties that he found himself in a relationship with somebody with whom he felt comfortable and safe. They lived together for a while and had two children. However, his girlfriend moved away with the children to London when their relationship fell apart. Michael found it difficult to reconnect with his children, given that the travel was difficult. The stress of this meant that Michael slowly withdrew from his children's lives, choosing instead to live life as a bachelor until he entered therapy with me.

When working from a decolonial perspective, I first explore how the client has developed ways of inhabiting **colonised spaces**. I might then explore the potential impacts of these strategies, which might include exploring the parts of the self that can be harmed or distressed by being marginalised and hidden in order to inhabit colonised spaces with a greater degree of safety. With Michael, to avoid misattunement, my work involved understanding the colonised aspects of himself and his family. We looked at the historical narratives that sat alongside some of his parents' decisions.

In doing this, I learnt that Michael now knew that his parents had been educated in ways which would have been seen as English, taught to speak the Queen's English, and also taught to reject anything which might have made them seem as if they were less civilised – such as speaking patois (speech that is considered non-standard by people in a particular area or country) and dressing in more traditional clothing – or anything which suggested they were 'unworthy' to travel to the United Kingdom. I wanted to encourage Michael to consider the impact of this intergenerational history. I understood that Michael had spent most of his life in a kind of disconnect from both his racialised identity and the intergenerational history that led him to now be in the United Kingdom. In therapy, and over time, Michael began to remember that in the care of his grandparents, after his parents left, he was not permitted to cry. He linked this to his current disconnect from his own emotional experience, whereby he often could not connect with, name or express his emotions. However, he had a sense that when grieving his mother's death, while he could not cry and felt quite numb, 'something' wasn't OK.

I brought into the sessions the idea in society that the Windrush generation should be celebrated, for example through Windrush Day, a commemoration held annually on 22 June. I noted that, while in many ways admirable, this centring of celebration does not always recognise important facts (Williams, 2020). The first of these is that Windrush is a part of colonisation, and many of those who were invited to the United Kingdom from the Caribbean were often required to leave behind their own families in order to gain passage (Thomas, 2000). This internalisation of the colonising of whiteness is a core facet, which had a huge impact on Michael's early life. What this means is that for his parents, as for many during this time, the 'internalised coloniser', and the drive to be seen as acceptable by this internalised figure, would have played a part in their move to the motherland, thereby echoing ideas posited by Frantz Fanon in his book *Black Skin, White Masks* (2021). Practically, this internalisation would have meant that as his parents were leaving, his grandparents would have encouraged him not to cry. While logical in many ways – because not crying was seen as the best thing for the family – this response does not fully acknowledge the emotional impact of losing a parent at such an early age.

The Supporting Relationships and Families organisation (formerly known as the Separation and Reunion Forum) discusses some of this in papers that explore the experiences of children left behind with relatives in the Caribbean while their parents came to the United Kingdom (e.g. Aymer, 2000; Thomas, 2000). The initial disconnect between parent and child was often

colonised spaces

Geographical spaces that have been taken over and controlled by European colonisers, who have established political, social and economic power over the Indigenous peoples and land.

repeated when the child was sent for and parachuted into a family where they did not know their newer, younger, British-born siblings. This meant that some children not only lost their parents once, but also had to leave loving uncles, aunts and grandparents to attempt to reform attachments with parents who had moved on with their lives. Without acknowledging and understanding the psychological impact of this separation, Michael and many children like him found themselves unable to make sense of themselves and relate to others in an environment which othered them.

Pause for thought 4.4

What, for you, are the limitations of attachment theory as explored here? What do you feel are the possibilities, opportunities and/or challenges of decolonising your own work as a counsellor or psychotherapist? Given your own intersectional identities, how might you work with a client like Michael from a decolonised perspective?

As discussed in Chapter 1, remaining with difficulty and critically examining the 'truths' you hold, or have been taught, can be a helpful way to address your own internalised biases. You might find that reflecting on the opportunities and challenges of decolonising your practice highlights some of these areas of work. Returning to a decolonial way of working with Michael, it was important to recognise that Eurocentric understandings of attachment do not match the experiences of children from other cultures. Attending to the intergenerational and racial history here helped to examine the role of safety, connection and early child–caregiver–community relationships in context.

2.2 Critical reflection on safety and reconnection

While reading this chapter, you might have found yourself reflecting on the close relationships in Michael's early life and how they could have shaped how Michael formed close relationships in adulthood. Secure attachment within a community context can be understood as something provided by all of the caregivers around the child. What I understood about Michael's experience is that while Michael and his brother did experience some level of community caregiving, I also needed to consider the intergenerational wounding that makes separation and reunion such a relatively 'easy' experience to recreate and re-constellate. 'Intergenerational wounding' is used here to reflect the ongoing impact of the days of slavery, when children were forcibly removed from their parents by enslavers, thereby disrupting and distorting the more secure attachment patterns which other children may have experienced. So, when thinking about safety and reconnection in Michael's close relationships, it was important to remember Michael's intergenerational history and integrate an examination of this history in the therapy work. The following case example describes how this worked, and the impact of this context on the possibility of reconnection with himself and those important to Michael.

Case example: Michael and I progress therapy

It became clear that Michael needed to explore his relational patterns. We explored not just Michael's relationship with his mother, but also his relationships with romantic partners and his children. We discussed his experience of having two children within an intermittent relationship spanning several years, in which he chose not to live with his partner but conversely needed to keep her close, both physically and emotionally. These explorations helped Michael understand the intergenerational and cross-cultural internalisations that shaped his relational patterns. This led him to begin to view his life so far as painful and unsatisfactory.

Our work took Michael to a place where he could safely mourn the loss of his mother and reconnect with aspects of himself and his history. This reconnection enabled him to begin to make amends for the distance he had created between himself and his own children.

To understand Michael's relational patterns, we also needed to bring his intergenerational racialised history into dialogue. We discussed how, historically, when we factor in the experiences of slavery, the idea of 'family' did not really exist for many people of colour (Akbar, 1996). For example, Black people were forced to bear children in order for the enslaver to maintain their status. As such, the idea of attachment between a Black slave woman and her child, never mind the formation of family, was something which was feared and was often destroyed. Enslaved people were 'sold', families were broken up and parent–child attachment relationships were not permitted.

While Michael had not directly experienced enslavement, connecting to his intergenerational and racialised history meant that we could identify the intergenerational impact of this and better understand Michael's fear-based responses in the context of colonialism. For Michael, this was centred around the trauma of separation, and this had a particularly traumatising impact given what separation has meant historically for Black people. As such, for Michael to connect with the emotional impact of separation, he needed to also connect with his colonised and decolonised self.

Pause for thought 4.5

Do you relate to the idea of having been colonised into a white, patriarchal world? Do you feel this has hampered or held you back? On the other hand, do you feel that these experiences have been positive for you?

3 Challenging the colonisation of counselling and psychotherapy

A prevalent concept within counselling and psychotherapy is that practitioners should 'meet' their clients 'where they are'. This ultimately suggests that we are not there to lead our clients; we are there to be led by them and to acknowledge and accept their unique perspectives, experiences and challenges. However, this idea fails to recognise that a more culturally competent way of working involves not just meeting clients where they are, but also acknowledging and responding to changes that the therapist or counsellor go through to achieve this cultural meeting.

theoretical performativity

The performance of a student within their modality so that they present themselves as a safe student. Within this performance comes an added psychological inauthenticity.

Counselling and training courses generally encourage us to be more authentic, and we might take part in personal therapy and therapy groups to work towards better self-awareness. The changes brought about by such experiential self-explorations might motivate us to understand ourselves and our histories, but this might come with a caveat: **theoretical performativity**, whereby a counselling student from a minoritised group performs to meet the particular standards and principles of their modality – not just to demonstrate that they are capable, but also to feel *culturally safe* within colonised environments.

> ## Pause for thought 4.6
>
> In what ways do you feel you might 'perform' your therapist identity? How have you learnt this? Have colonised spaces informed how you perform this role comfortably and 'well'?

Meeting with various clients may involve the counsellor encountering their own intersectional identities, which they may have put to one side in order to perform as a good therapist. Furthermore, trying to shoehorn clients' intersectional identities and experiences into the narrow confines of colonised ways of working and counselling assessments will mean that we miss diversities and ways of being which could enhance both our own knowledge and the understanding of the profession as a whole (Turner, 2021; Czyzselska, 2022). Yet, for those counsellors and psychotherapists who are willing to stretch beyond those colonised confines of the training courses, the modalities and the ways of being, there is a wealth of experiences that they might encounter, endure and be moulded by. These will not only help them to become their more authentic selves, but also better or more truly engage with the range of different clients and psychotherapists that they will inevitably encounter.

3.1 Reflecting on how clients may change the counsellor

Throughout this chapter you have likely had many responses to the case of Michael, and to the invitations to think about a decolonial way of working with this client. You are encouraged here to stay with your reflections and to consider how aspects of your own colonised self and your intergenerational history might inform how you have read and responded to this case. I want to share some of my reflections on how you (and I) may be changed by meeting clients.

> ### Case example: Personal reflections on working with Michael
>
> In working with Michael, one of the most important things for me to recognise was that the experience of meeting this client would inevitably change me. Understanding and researching the colonised nature of his parents' experiences allowed me to understand how that experience had informed that of my own parents, who were themselves from the Windrush generation. Although different in many respects, our parents shared enough similarities that I learnt important things about my own colonised self. I was challenged to explore – in supervision and in therapy – what it was like to work with a client with a similar cultural background and experiences. I was also challenged to critically reflect on how the modalities and theories I had learnt about were not useful for understanding Michael's experience.

The personal reflections and self-exploration that can come about through working with a client such as Michael can be profound and long-lasting; these are, in my experience, an important part of examining and understanding the colonised self. Alongside exploring the cultural similarities between myself and Michael, I also physically connected to the emotional pain that Michael had endured in his cultural movement from one world to another. To me, this was a pain built out of the varying layers of rejection and abandonment. However, it was also about how this African-Caribbean cultural norm – which I knew well enough about, but also had started to recognise as flawed – would have impacted upon the internalised intergenerational messages which I myself would have internalised as a child.

Counselling and psychotherapy within these sorts of lenses involves a form of cultural alchemy, where one endures the 'disassemblement' of one's cultural self and the deeper re-exploration in a type of cultural underworld of what it means to be, for example, a person of colour, gay, trans, a woman, a feminist, non-disabled or of a specific age. This leads to us stripping away those social constructs that have informed such identities before rebuilding them through a deeper understanding of who we want to be. In the same way that Michael explored who he was beyond these cultural frameworks, the counsellor or psychotherapist can do the same.

This means that the more diverse the range of clients we dare ourselves to work with and the more curious we are – not just about the client groups that we encounter, but also about how that meeting of cultures may change us – the more a constant ebb and flow of growth and renewal will be possible. Only through a willingness to constantly challenge our intersectional identities can the cultural growth of our profession become established.

Conclusion

This chapter has argued that thinking critically about the theories we adopt as counsellors and where our knowledge comes from will create more productive and generative grounds for counsellors, clients and the counselling profession in general. Specifically, it will help counsellors think creatively and beyond the boundaries of knowledge structures that shape ideas which are taught as 'truths', but which are both limited and limiting. The chapter has described how critical decolonial thinking can help counsellors and psychotherapists connect to and examine the internalised narratives of the colonial systems we have all imbibed.

Hopefully, this chapter has prompted some critical thinking of your own about the nature of knowledge and its origins. This chapter has drawn on attachment theory and psychoanalytical thinking to exemplify how you might approach these theories from a decolonial lens. The case of Michael was used to give some insight into how this might look in practice, and how you might further develop your own critical thinking and capacity to consider what a decolonial lens might do for your practice and self-understanding. A decolonial lens can help counsellors understand their colonised selves and the colonised spaces they occupy, and thus can free up space to 'meet' clients and work with aspects of their colonised identities. Working in the spirit of curiosity and with an awareness of colonised selves and histories can support you in assisting clients towards connection, integration and 'wholeness', especially where there is a colonised–coloniser split or where aspects of the self are marginalised.

Further reading

- The following book explores the nature of white fragility and the psychological reasons why people who identify as white may find issues of race and racism difficult to stay connected with:

  DiAngelo, R. (2018) *White fragility*. London: Penguin Books.

- The following book closely considers how race appears in the therapy room from a theoretical perspective:

  McKenzie-Mavinga, I., Black, K., Carberry, K. and Ellis, E. (2023) *Therapy in colour*. London: Jessica Kingsley Publishers.

- The following book offers a psychodynamic and existential exploration of the role of privilege and otherness in the therapy space:

  Turner, D. (2021) *Intersections of privilege and otherness in counselling and psychotherapy: mockingbird*. London: Routledge.

References

Ainsworth, M.D.S., Blehar, M.C., Waters, E. and Wall, S.N. (2015) *Patterns of attachment: a psychological study of the strange situation*. Classic edn. London: Routledge.

Akbar, N. (1996) *Breaking the chains of psychological slavery*. Tallahassee, FL: Mind Productions & Associates.

Aymer, C. (2000) 'A good enough migration experience', *Separation & Reunion Forum and Goldsmiths College joint conference*, London (UK), 23 June. Available at: https://www.serefo.org.uk/assets/a_good_enough_migration_experience~cathy_aymer.pdf (Accessed: 29 January 2025)

Bowlby, J. (1988) *A secure base: parent–child attachment and healthy human development*. New York: Basic Books.

Burleson, B. (2005) *Jung in Africa*. London: Continuum.

Czyzselska, J.C. (ed.) (2022) *Queering psychotherapy*. London: Karnac Books.

DiAngelo, R. (2018) *White fragility*. London: Penguin Books

Ellis, E. (2021) *The race conversation: an essential guide to creating life-changing dialogue*. London: Confer Books.

Fanon, F. (2021) *Black skin, white masks*. Translated from the French by R. Philcox. London: Penguin Classics.

Freud, S. (1964) 'The disillusionment of the war', in *Thoughts for the times on war and death*. Translated from the German by E.C. Mayne. Surrey: Hogarth Press.

Golash-Boza, T., Duenas, M.D. and Xiong, C. (2019) 'White supremacy, patriarchy, and global capitalism in migration studies', *American Behavioural Scientist*, 63(13), pp. 1741–1759. Available at: https://doi.org/10.1177/0002764219842624

hooks, b. (2016) 'Feminism is for everybody', in R. Dagger and D.I. O'Neill (eds) *Ideals and ideologies: a reader*. 10th edn. New York: Routledge, pp. 23–24.

Kizito, K. (2017) 'Bequeathed legacies: colonialism and state-led homophobia in Uganda', *Surveillance and Society*, 15(3–4), pp. 567–572. Available at: https://doi.org/10.24908/ss.v15i3/4.6617

Lago, C. and Charura, D. (eds) (2021) *Black identities and white therapies: race, respect and diversity*. Monmouth: PCCS Books.

Lev Kenaan, V. (2021) 'Digging with Freud: from hysteria to the birth of a new philology', *American Imago*, 78(2), pp. 341–366. Available at: https://doi.org/10.1353/aim.2021.0015

Memorandum of understanding on conversion therapy in the UK (2024). Version 2, revision A. Available at: https://www.bacp.co.uk/events-and-resources/ethics-and-standards/mou/ (Accessed: 24 January 2025).

Moodley, R., Lago, C. and Talahite, A. (eds) (2004) *Carl Rogers counsels a Black client: race and culture in person-centred counselling*. Monmouth: PCCS Books.

Nichols, J.M. (2016) 'A survivor of gay conversion therapy shares his chilling story', *Huffington Post*, 18 November. Available at: https://www.huffingtonpost.co.uk/entry/realities-of-conversion-therapy_us_582b6cf2e4b01d8a014aea66 (Accessed: 18 December 2024).

Schaverien, J. (2004) 'Boarding school: the trauma of the "privileged" child', *Journal of Analytical Psychology*, 49(5), pp. 683–705. Available at: https://doi.org/10.1111/j.0021-8774.2004.00495.x

Part 2

Reflexivity

Chapter 5

Using reflexivity in counselling

Jennie Kirk

Contents

Introduction

Sea Fret at Hauxley by John Tuff

Have you ever experienced a strong reaction to a situation that has challenged your whole sense of self?

I am from the north-east of England, from a town which is predominantly white and working class. My beliefs are very liberal; I have always been keen to challenge people who express views that are sexist, racist or homophobic. In 1998 I went to university in Liverpool. During the first term I caught the bus home, alone, and sat on the empty top deck. A few stops later a group of Black teenage boys boarded the bus; I could hear them laughing as they made their way upstairs. I can still remember how terrified I felt. As they walked past me, I froze, keeping my gaze focused on the window to avoid making eye contact. The rest of the ten-minute journey was uneventful, but I can recall the huge sense of relief I felt as I stepped off the bus. Afterwards I tried to rationalise my experience: 'I felt like that because they were teenagers being loud'; 'it's because it was a group of boys'; 'it's because it was dark, and I was alone in a new city'. I didn't dare consider that it was because they were Black (and specifically young, Black boys) and I am white. That thought was too shameful.

We all experience a range of emotional reactions towards others, and these reactions are influenced by our own identity, culture, values and world-view. These aspects of the self make up our 'lens' through which we perceive the world around us. When our feelings or behaviour do not match our sense of self, the temptation is to deny or distort these emotions (Rogers, 1951), as I did in the example above. It is more difficult to acknowledge these emotions to ourselves, accept them and take a curious stance about where they come from.

In Chapter 2 you were introduced to the SCoPEd competency which focuses on core aspects of your identity. This chapter will continue with that theme, focusing on appearance and social class – the former aspect of self is immediately visible, while the latter is less so. The choice to focus on appearance and class is in part because they are covered less in counselling literature, but also partly personal; I have judged and felt judged by others in relation to both aspects. In this chapter you will be encouraged to consider your own lens and reflect on how aspects of sameness and difference between counsellor and client can both help and hinder the therapeutic process. The chapter will also encourage you to think critically about the methods of reflexivity you currently use and will introduce deliberate practice as another method for reflexivity.

This chapter contributes towards achieving the **SCoPEd competency 5.4.B**:

> Ability to critically challenge own identity, culture, values and worldview.
>
> *(SCoPEd Framework, 2022, p. 30)*

This chapter aims to:

- encourage critical reflection on your own identity, culture, values and world-view in relation to those of your past, current or potential clients

- outline the research literature on sameness and difference in identity and the impact this can have on client work

- critically discuss methods which use reflexivity as a tool to enhance the therapeutic relationship and improve client outcomes.

1 Considering your own lens: why does this matter?

In this chapter, the word 'lens' is being used as a metaphor for the way in which we view the world around us. Our lens is made up of our identity, culture, values and world-view, but as counsellors our lens is also shaped by counselling theory and the modality in which we practise. In our everyday encounters, our perceptions and reactions – both conscious and unconscious – impact our relationships. In the counselling room, they impact the therapeutic relationship and subsequent outcome of therapy.

Activity 5.1 Reviewing a reflection: Betty and Yalom

Allow about 10 minutes

A key theme in this book is compassion towards yourself and others. You are encouraged to demonstrate this here while engaging with material which is potentially distressing. **The following extract contains material which is fatphobic and misogynistic**. This activity is included to help you practise the professional counselling skills for reflection on biased and difficult thoughts around clients.

Read the following extract from Yalom's (1989) *Love's Executioner*. In this book, Yalom reflects on his experience of delivering therapy with ten different patients. This extract describes Yalom's reflections on his initial encounter with his client 'Betty'. As you read, notice your reactions to his words.

> The day Betty entered my office, the instant I saw her steering her ponderous two-hundred-fifty-pound, five-foot-two-inch frame toward my trim, high-tech office chair, I knew that a great trial of countertransference was in store for me.
>
> I have always been repelled by fat women. I find them disgusting: their absurd sidewise waddle, their absence of body contour – breasts, laps, buttocks, shoulders, jawlines, cheekbones, everything, everything I like to see in a woman, obscured in an avalanche of flesh. And I hate their clothes – the shapeless, baggy dresses or, worse, the stiff elephantine blue jeans with the barrel thighs. How dare they impose that body on the rest of us?

(Yalom, 1989, pp. 94–95)

Discussion

Yalom's words seem particularly stark, given that they are presented out of context. Nevertheless, a quick glance at the book reviews on Amazon capture the reactions to his book, which range from admiration for his candour, to anger for his misogyny and fat-shaming. Perhaps you felt some of these emotions too? How you reacted is likely shaped by your own views and experiences.

I first encountered these words during my first year of counselling training. I remember being impressed by how honest Yalom was about his feelings towards his client and wondered whether I could be as authentic as he was. As a teacher for many years, I was used to putting on a mask, hiding my emotions and my reactions towards my students. I was struggling with the personal development aspects of my training and intensely disliked the focus on self-reflection. I felt comforted that Yalom appeared human and flawed, and that it was perhaps okay for me to be too. I didn't once think about Betty and how she may feel. But then again, why would I? I am the same height, but I am of average weight. Like Yalom, I had internalised the messages I had received about body size and had positioned Betty as 'other', through a process of othering (Murray, 2007), creating distance between her and myself. My struggles at that time were focused on my inability to see myself as a counsellor. The aspects of self that troubled me meant my empathy and attention were directed towards Yalom, as the therapist.

I did not give Betty a second thought, not until I came back to Yalom as a therapist in private practice, feeling a little stuck and wanting to regain some inspiration from those books that had ignited my initial passion for the powers of therapy. This time, I felt a niggling, uncomfortable feeling that I had not noticed previously. I felt conflicted. I still felt that he was brave for admitting feelings that others may privately hold but would not say, but I also felt disgust that Betty was being objectified in this way (and shame that I had not noticed this earlier).

The wider work from which this extract is taken makes clear that Yalom's decision to work with Betty is based on his belief that it will help him develop as a therapist. Is Yalom's decision ethical? Yalom was not governed by the same ethical codes we have today. Can therapy still be effective where there is such a strong reaction to difference? The extent to which Yalom believed that therapy with Betty had a successful outcome remains unclear. What does become clear is that as Betty loses weight, Yalom becomes more positive in his depiction of her. Fuller (2018) notes that Yalom's disgust towards Betty's appearance underpins the whole therapeutic encounter.

In Yalom's case, his countertransferential reactions were evident from the moment he met Betty, but with some clients, these reactions may not arise until later. This is why it's essential that, as counsellors, we have a critical understanding of our own identity, culture, values and world-view before we begin to explore the world of another, and that we maintain this awareness during that exploration as part of an ongoing reflexive process.

1.1 Reflexivity as an essential part of the counsellor role

Self-reflection refers to those moments when you reflect on your own thoughts, feelings and experiences. In contrast, reflexivity is a more ongoing process in which you focus your awareness on your reactions to others and the world around you. In the counselling context, self-awareness is used when you relate to clients as a means of enhancing the therapeutic relationship (Etherington, 2017). Our own lens not only impacts the way we relate to clients in the room, but also influences our attitude towards charging clients, how we feel about a client missing a session, and even our own attitude towards self-care (these aspects will be picked up in Chapter 7). Willig (2019) argues that our beliefs about the nature of being human (our ontology) is likely to have influenced the type of therapy we practise (also known as our epistemology; this concept will be unpacked in Chapter 13). Therefore, reflexivity on your chosen counselling model and whether it aligns with the assumptions and goals of your client are important for establishing a solid therapeutic alliance.

How much emphasis you place on the need for ongoing reflexivity and, indeed, which areas you choose to reflect on may depend in part on your core counselling modality, as summarised in Table 5.1.

Table 5.1 Counselling modalities and associated focus on reflexivity

Modality	**Emphasis on reflexivity**
Psychodynamic	Emphasises the influence of the unconscious. Therapy involves helping to bring the client's unconscious into awareness (Freud, 1922), for example through analysis of transference and countertransferential reactions. It is important for therapists to understand how their own identity shapes their reaction to the client and how the client may be reacting to them. This may uncover ways in which the client is relating to others. The need to fully understand the self explains the weight placed on personal therapy by proponents of this modality.
Humanistic	The counsellor considers their relationship with their client, how they are experiencing therapy and how their own identity, culture, values and world-view may be impacting their ability to offer the core conditions of empathy, unconditional positive regard and congruence (Rogers, 1957). For example, a counsellor may notice moments where they feel more, or less, empathic, and reflect on why (Stedmon and Dallos, 2009). They may also make use of immediacy, disclosing how they are feeling in response to the client during the session (Wheeler and D'Andrea, 2004).

CBT	Focuses on techniques, but also acknowledges the importance of the therapeutic alliance (Boswell and Constantino, 2021). Reflexivity is important in determining why certain techniques may or may not be working; students are encouraged to try out the techniques on themselves and reflect on their experience (Bennett-Levy *et al.*, 2009). Reflexivity is also useful for identifying where client disclosures are triggering the therapist's own 'faulty' cognitions (Liu, 2011).
Pluralistic	Creating a strong therapeutic alliance is seen as the essence of pluralistic therapy, and reflexivity is at the heart of this (Cooper and Dryden, 2016). Training courses emphasise personal development through a variety of methods to develop counsellor self-awareness. Training also outlines theories from other modalities so that students develop a 'theoretical identity' which aligns with their personal identity. Understanding the client's identity is crucial, as therapy is tailored to the client through consideration of both group differences and individual differences.

1.2 The impact of identity on client work

As our own identity is always in a state of flux, self-reflection is not something which should end once we are qualified. The activity below encourages reflection on social class, an aspect of identity which receives less attention in counsellor training programmes (Kaiser and Prieto, 2018).

Activity 5.2 Reflection on your social class

Allow about 10 minutes

Consider your own experiences and assumptions in relation to both your social class and that of your clients. While doing so, you may find the following questions useful.

1   How do you define social class? What messages have you received from family, friends or society around class?

2   How would you define your own class, and has this changed? How does class intersect with other aspects of your identity?

3   How do you think your clients perceive your social class?

4   How did it feel to work with a client who was similar or different to you in terms of social class? Did it impact your work with them?

Discussion

What sort of things came up for you? Did you notice yourself thinking, 'I treat all clients equally' or 'class is irrelevant in today's society'? Perhaps you felt irritated by the exercise and disliked having to focus on an aspect of identity which you feel is less relevant to you. You may have thought about the balance of power between counsellor and client or, with respect to similarity, how you avoid overidentification with the client. What feelings or thoughts came up when you considered whether your work with clients may be impacted by your own values, attitudes and beliefs?

Despite the commonly held notion that we live in a classless society (Balmforth, 2009), socio-economic status still has a huge bearing on our lives, including our mental health. Statistics demonstrate that, in the UK, those with a low income are more likely to display symptoms of ill mental health, such as anxiety (Joseph Rowntree Foundation, 2024). Despite this link, we tend to frame psychological distress as located within the individual and separate from the structural inequalities they face (McEvoy, Clarke and Thomas, 2021). In the therapy world, class could be called 'an absent presence' (Ryan, 2019, p. 52); its bearing is felt, yet its weight is not discussed.

Clients also make judgements about their counsellors based on their identity. Classism can be seen in an account from Ryan (2019), who described a case where a client assumed their therapist would not be effective because of their 'working-class' accent. Some counsellors who work from home and have made efforts to make their space 'neutral' are surprised when clients comment on their 'middle-class' style choices (McEvoy, Clarke and Thomas, 2021). These findings stress the importance of being aware of stereotypes which may leak into the therapy room. This will be explored further in the next section, in the context of sameness and difference between counsellor and client.

2 Research findings on sameness and difference: a help and a hindrance?

This section examines how sameness and difference can affect the therapeutic relationship, both positively and negatively. Empathy is a key concept related to this.

Pause for thought 5.1

Think about the provision of empathy and how this may be impacted by perceived sameness. Do you feel more able to empathise when you believe that a client is similar to you?

2.1 Sameness between client and counsellor

When we meet someone whom we regard as similar, a connection can be formed very quickly. Similarities in experience can lead to a shared understanding where we use 'shorthand and culturally relevant terms' with ease (Sanderson-Shortt, 2022, p. 17). For example, research into client experience of class in the counselling room revealed that perceived similarity in social class led to greater equality within the relationship and allowed the client to be more genuine (Trott and Reeves, 2018).

Sameness should not mean that counsellors proceed with therapy without paying close attention to the ways in which they are relating to the client. Misunderstandings can occur when we assume that those who appear similar share our beliefs, values and experiences. This is highlighted in a research study by Georgiadou (2016), who interviewed international trainee counsellors about their experiences of counselling in the UK, in a culture different to their own. Georgiadou is Greek, and 'Claire', one of the participants she interviewed, is Asian. In her interview, Georgiadou emphasised the sameness in their identity, focusing on their shared experience of counselling in a second language. However, Claire prioritised their difference, highlighting their visible difference in ethnicity by stating 'You look like them!' (Georgiadou 2016, p. 364). Claire assumed that the researcher had more in common with people from the UK than she did, and therefore would find it easier to work with clients from the UK. This suggests that the assumptions a therapist makes should be examined and brought into awareness, as best one can, including consideration of the potential impact on therapy.

Some clients see perceived sameness as a barrier to effective therapy, whereby the therapist is seen as 'colluding' with the client or making assumptions about them based on their own frame of reference (Trott and Reeves, 2018). Lee and Prior (2013, p. 98) describe a counsellor with shared personal experience to a client who had difficulty in identifying where the sadness 'in the room' was coming from; as his client talked, he noticed that he kept thinking about his own situation. As discussed in Chapter 3, we may have the same wounds as our clients, but these wounds can heal differently.

2.2 Difference between client and counsellor

Ultimately, difference between a client and counsellor is not what matters; it is the awareness of difference and diversity, and the willingness to be able to explore that difference, that is important. In their research, Trott and Reeves (2018) demonstrated that class differences could be facilitative where an effort was made by the therapist to understand the client's experience in the context of their social class. It is necessary to recognise difference because of the potential for miscommunication, misunderstanding or failure to recognise the significance of an issue for the client (Winter *et al.*, 2016). Difference may lead to barriers in communication due to implicit assumptions that the client and counsellor have about each other. For example, Erb (2020) described a client who dismissed the notion that Erb could help, as her young, blonde, attractive appearance represented to the client a privileged identity, and therefore one that had not experienced pain. Difference between client and counsellor can create power imbalances; however, reflecting on difference can help to avoid unwittingly behaving in ways which oppress the client (Proctor, 2021).

One unintended consequence of difference may be the expression of **microaggressions**. Common client experiences of microaggressions in therapy include the therapist responding in ways which reflect cultural stereotypes, and the therapist avoiding or minimising the client's experience (Owen, Tao and Drinane, 2018). These microaggressions may be verbal, non-verbal or environmental (Sue *et al.*, 2007). Such microaggressions can be seen in Yalom's description of therapy with Betty. Yalom's (1989, p. 94) 'trim … office chair' is an aspect of the physical environment designed for an average-sized person. His lack of eye contact is representative of a non-verbal aggression. These micro-aggressions can be subtle and happen on an unconscious level: Yalom is surprised that Betty had noticed his difficulty in making eye contact when Betty discloses this to him during their last session.

microaggressions
Utterances or behaviours which may occur as part of our everyday interactions with individuals who are different from ourselves. This communication is experienced as hostile or hurtful to those who receive them.

Pause for thought 5.2

Yalom accepted Betty as a client in order to overcome his countertransferential reactions in relation to body size. What could Yalom have done to minimise the impact of his countertransferential reactions on the client?

The next section will discuss some methods which Yalom could have used to encourage reflexivity while working with Betty.

3 Being reflexive about your identity, culture, values and world-view

So far, this chapter has discussed why reflexivity and a critical understanding of your own identity, culture, values and world-view is necessary for providing ethical and effective therapy. The following section will critically discuss different ways of being reflective, both 'in action' and 'on action' (Schön, 1991) (Chapter 7 will also use this framework when discussing strategies for self-care). Lastly, this chapter will also introduce deliberate practice as a tool for reflexivity.

3.1 Reflection in action

Reflection in action is focused on the present – on the counsellor's immediate work with a client. Counselling is hard work. You need to pay attention to what the client says, how they say it, how they appear when they say it, whether this relates to things that they have said before and how you are experiencing the client's words. This information will then guide what you do next. Most of the time our interventions will encourage further exploration on the part of the client; sometimes they will lead to a real moment of insight; and at other times they may demonstrate a lack of understanding that can lead to an impasse or **therapeutic rupture**.

therapeutic rupture

A breakdown in the therapeutic relationship, wherein the client may challenge the therapist or become withdrawn during sessions.

Where awareness of a rupture occurs in session, it can be useful to explore this with the client (Winter *et al.*, 2016). This exploration can be easier when a positive therapeutic alliance, characterised by an open recognition of difference (and similarity) in identity, is established from the start. Ruptures in relationship do not necessarily mean that therapy is failing with that client; in fact, some modalities (such as psychodynamic) view these events as helpful sources of information that reveal aspects of the client's unconscious.

The fictional case example below illustrates an example of reflection in action.

Case example: Kayden and Grace start working together

Kayden is 18 years old, from a working-class background, and has been referred to a counselling service by his GP. The service is a charity that offers six free sessions to clients and is staffed by volunteer counsellors in training placements. Kayden is allocated a person-centred counsellor, Grace, who is in her fifties and is from a middle-class background.

Grace suggests that their first session went well. She conducted some initial assessments and explained what is involved in person-centred counselling. The rest of the session involved Kayden explaining why he had been referred for therapy.

At the start of their second session, Kayden arrives a few minutes late. As he sits down, he looks uncomfortable. Grace begins the session in her usual way by asking him where he would like to start. Kayden remains silent, and Grace starts to feel tension rising in her chest. She recalls feedback from her course leaders, who asserted that 'holding silence' was an area Grace found challenging. However, Grace has also been reading some research which suggested that clients with a working-class background may find the therapeutic experience 'alien' (Holman, 2014, p. 544). Grace decides to break the silence and suggests that perhaps Kayden does not know where to start, that she sensed some tension and that she wonders whether something is worrying him. Kayden comments that he has said everything he needs to say in the last session. He was worried because Grace had told him that counselling involves discussing your emotions, and he thought that she would tell him what was wrong and how to get better. He didn't know how he felt, and he wasn't used to talking about feelings. Grace asks Kayden if there were situations where he felt that he did connect with emotion; Kayden mentions that this happens when he listens to music. He feels his favourite artists are able to express what he is feeling, and he wonders whether he could bring some of those lyrics to his sessions.

In listening to Kayden, it appears that his ideas of therapy and those of his counsellor do not match. He sees the counsellor as an expert, someone who will tell him what is wrong. Grace has used immediacy here to guide her response to Kayden. She experiences tension but wonders how much of this is due to her own insecurities (avoidance of silence) and how much of this is coming from the client's worries about where to start. She decides to name the tension that she is experiencing, and this leads to Kayden revealing his fears and subsequently to a method in which he feels comfortable in accessing emotional material.

3.2 Reflection on action

Reflection on action is more focused on past and future events. It can occur in a number of practical contexts, some of which are discussed in turn below.

Supervision can be used as a safe space to reflect on the process of therapy, where counsellors can explore their feelings in relation to sameness and difference with their clients (Lago, 2011). Discussion of issues pertaining to identity, values, culture and world-view between supervisor and supervisee can be an opportunity to practise open communication in areas which may lead to discomfort for the supervisee. For example, supervision would have been a useful place for Yalom to reflect on his reactions towards Betty and the impact of these on the therapeutic process.

Personal therapy is also useful. Many training courses contain a requirement for personal therapy as a tool to increase self-awareness. The positive impact of personal counselling on matters related to the self is acknowledged by trainees (Murphy *et al.*, 2018), who see therapy as a way of gaining more insight on themselves, as well as distinguishing between personal issues and those belonging to their clients. Despite this, therapists who are counselling trainee or qualified counsellors may be reluctant for them to discuss topics related to client work in their own therapy sessions. This blurring between the role of supervision and personal counselling can lead to uncertainty about where to take issues pertaining to the self in relation to others. Returning to personal counselling as a practising counsellor can be useful for a variety of reasons, such as navigating changes in identity like becoming a parent or entering midlife. Yalom's issues, which had been stirred up by his work with Betty, could have been explored in therapy.

Continuing professional development (CPD) can encompass an array of activities, such as reading, attending conferences, online learning and watching TV programmes. Research suggests that although counsellors believe CPD is helpful, there is a lack of evidence that it leads to better client outcomes (Taylor and Neimeyer, 2017, cited in Mahon, 2023, p.). CPD may be a useful way of engaging in further training on issues which come up during reflexive processes. This could include attending workshops on any barriers to empathy that may be revealed through client work, such as around body image, class, race, disability, sexuality and gender. The case study example of Kayden, discussed in the previous section, highlighted one way in which CPD (in this case, reading research) has the potential to enhance practice.

People generally associate *mindfulness* and counselling with a client being taught techniques to identify thoughts and emotions in the present moment rather than simply avoiding them because they are difficult (Barker, 2013). However, mindfulness, in the form of attending to experience in a non-judgemental manner, is useful for being reflexive about our identity, culture, values and world-view. This is especially useful for those areas which cause us discomfort, as it allows for a means of exploration through a lens of compassion.

Client work can involve working with people whose experience is different to our own. This can help to increase knowledge and understanding of other groups. It is recommended that when embarking on work with clients from a different background, supervision is sought from someone who is competent in that area (Liu, 2011). Although client work can be a useful tool for increasing awareness, it is important that we do not expect our clients to 'teach' us, as this places additional emotional labour on them (Sanderson-Shortt, 2022). The case of Yalom and Betty highlights the problematic nature of using client work alone as a tool for self-development.

Pause for thought 5.3

Which of the above methods do you favour for increasing self-awareness? Is there anything that has been missed?

3.3 Deliberate practice

Another method that can be used to increase self-awareness is deliberate practice. This offers a systematic approach to improving client work, with exercises aimed at rehearsing skills and activities that are designed for use with recordings of one's client work (Rousmaniere, 2017). Deliberate practice is based on evidence that effective learners pay attention to errors and spend time on activities designed to improve their skills under the guidance of someone with greater expertise (Miller, Hubble and Chow, 2020).

Applying this to the case of Kayden and Grace (where there was difference in identity between client and counsellor), Grace could use deliberate practice as a method to assess her emotional attunement towards Kayden. This would require seeking Kayden's consent to record sessions in order to conduct focused activities using the recordings, which would then be discussed in supervision. One of the concerns Grace had was whether the emotions she was sensing were those of the client or arising from her own insecurities. Rousmaniere (2017) describes an activity which involves listening to a client recording, paying attention to bodily sensations, thoughts and feelings stirred up while listening, pausing the recording when a strong reaction is experienced and then noting whether or not this was clearly connected to the client's material.

A thorough consideration of deliberate practice is beyond the scope of this chapter. However, several modality-specific books have been written about deliberate practice, which focus on skills pertinent to particular methods, including cognitive behavioural therapy (Boswell and Constantino, 2021) and psychodynamic psychotherapy (Levenson, Gay and Binder, 2023). Although the use of deliberate practice in counselling is still in its infancy, research suggests that it has the potential to improve relational factors such as empathy and therapeutic alliance (Mahon, 2023). However, some practitioners (Rousmaniere, 2017) have noted that focusing on areas of weakness can lead to feelings of shame and distress, and the activities themselves can be very time-consuming.

What about Yalom? If he had used some of the methods outlined above, he may have noticed his desire to look away from Betty, and that his feelings of disgust in relation to her body size were a barrier to his empathy. Instead of feeling concern for his office chair when he saw her walk towards it, he may have felt concern for Betty and the way that she may feel having to squeeze uncomfortably into it. Perhaps he would have discarded that high-tech office chair?

Conclusion

This chapter has highlighted that sameness and difference can impact the therapeutic relationship. Critically challenging one's own identity, culture, values and world-view is therefore important in counselling. There are several methods which can be used to encourage reflexivity, both at the point of client work and also around it. What matters less is the method or methods that are chosen; it is the very act of ongoing reflexivity that is crucial for counsellor development and for delivering ethical and effective therapy.

Further reading

- If you wish to explore deliberate practice further, the following book is useful for all counselling modalities:

  Rousmaniere, T. (2017) *Deliberate practice for psychotherapists: a guide to improving clinical effectiveness*. Abingdon: Routledge.

- For further in-depth discussion on the impact of attitudes towards body size in a clinical setting, you can read the following book chapter, which is published online in *The Psychologist*:

  Fuller, C. (2016) 'When a body meets a body: fat enters the consulting room', *The Psychologist*, 15 December. Available at: https://www.bps.org.uk/psychologist/when-body-meets-body-fat-enters-consulting-room.

References

Balmforth, J. (2009) '"The weight of class": clients' experiences of how perceived differences in social class between counsellor and client affect the therapeutic relationship', *British Journal of Guidance & Counselling*, 37(3), pp. 375–386. Available at: https://doi.org/10.1080/03069880902956942

Barker, M. (2013) *Mindful counselling and psychotherapy: practising mindfully across approaches and issues*. London: SAGE Publications Limited. Available at: https://doi.org/10.4135/9781473915084

Bennett-Levy, J., Thwaites, R., Chaddock, A. and Davis, M. (2009) 'Reflective practice in cognitive behavioural therapy: the engine of lifelong learning', in J. Stedmon and R. Dallos (eds) *Reflective practice in psychotherapy and counselling*. Maidenhead: McGraw-Hill Education, pp. 115–135.

Boswell, J.F. and Constantino, M.J. (2021) *Deliberate practice in cognitive behavioral therapy*. Washington, D.C.: American Psychological Association.

Cooper M. and Dryden, W. (2016) (eds) *Handbook of pluralistic counselling and psychotherapy*. London: SAGE Publications Ltd.

Erb, J. (2020) 'Politics of appearance: bodily transference and its implications for the counselling relationship', *Psychotherapy and Politics International*, 18(2), article number e1538. Available at: https://doi.org/10.1002/ppi.1538

Etherington, K. (2017) 'Personal experience and critical reflexivity in counselling and psychotherapy research', *Counselling and Psychotherapy Research*, 17(2), pp. 85–94. Available at: https://doi.org/10.1002/capr.12080

Freud, S. (1922) *Introductory lectures on psychoanalysis*. London: Allen & Unwin.

Fuller, C. (2018) *The fat lady sings: a psychological exploration of the cultural fat complex and its effects*. Abingdon: Routledge.

Georgiadou, L. (2016) '"You look like them": drawing on counselling theory and practice to reflexively negotiate cultural difference in research relationships', *International Journal for the Advancement of Counselling*, 38(4), pp. 358–368. Available at: https://doi.org/10.1007/s10447-016-9277-4

Holman, D. (2014) '"What help can you get talking to somebody?" Explaining class differences in the use of talking treatments', *Sociology of Health & Illness*, 36(4), pp. 531–548. Available at: https://doi.org/10.1111/1467-9566.12082

Joseph Rowntree Foundation (2024) *UK Poverty 2024: the essential guide to understanding poverty in the UK*. Available at: https://www.jrf.org.uk/uk-poverty-2024-the-essential-guide-to-understanding-poverty-in-the-uk (Accessed: 31 May 2024).

Kaiser, D.J. and Prieto, L.R. (2018) 'Trainee estimates of working alliance with upper- and working-class clients', *Counselling and Psychotherapy Research*, 18(2), pp. 154–165. Available at: https://doi.org/10.1002/capr.12170

Lago, C. (ed.) (2011) *The handbook of transcultural counselling and psychotherapy*. Maidenhead: Open University Press.

Lee, B. and Prior, S. (2013) 'Developing therapeutic listening', *British Journal of Guidance & Counselling*, 41(2), pp. 91–104. Available at: https://doi.org/10.1080/03069885.2012.705816

Levenson, H., Gay, V. and Binder, J.L. (2023) *Deliberate practice in psychodynamic psychotherapy*. Washington, D.C.: American Psychological Association.

Liu, W.M. (2011) *Social class and classism in the helping professions: research, theory, and practice.* London: SAGE Publications Ltd.

McEvoy, C., Clarke, V. and Thomas, Z. (2021) '"Rarely discussed but always present": exploring therapists' accounts of the relationship between social class, mental health and therapy', *Counselling and Psychotherapy Research*, 21(2), pp. 324–334. Available at: https://doi.org/10.1002/capr.12382

Mahon, D. (2023) 'A scoping review of deliberate practice in the acquisition of therapeutic skills and practices', *Counselling and Psychotherapy Research*, 23(4), pp. 965–981. Available at: https://doi.org/10.1002/capr.12601

Miller, S.D., Hubble, M.A. and Chow, D. (2020) *Better results: using deliberate practice to improve therapeutic effectiveness.* Washington, D.C.: American Psychological Association. Available at: https://doi.org/10.1037/0000191-000

Murphy, D., Irfan, N., Barnett, H., Castledine, E. and Enescu, L. (2018) 'A systematic review and meta-synthesis of qualitative research into mandatory personal psychotherapy during training', *Counselling and Psychotherapy Research*, 18(2), pp. 199–214. Available at: https://doi.org/10.1002/capr.12162

Murray, S. (2007) 'Corporeal knowledges and deviant bodies: perceiving the fat body', *Social Semiotics*, 17(3), pp. 361–373. Available at: http://doi.org/10.1080/10350330701448694

Owen, J., Tao, K.W. and Drinane, J.M. (2018) 'Microaggressions: clinical impact and psychological harm', in G.C. Torino, D.P. Rivera, C.M. Capodilupo, K.L. Nadal, D. W. Sue (eds) *Microaggression theory: influence and implications.* Hoboken: John Wiley & Sons, Inc, pp. 65–85. Available at: https://doi.org/10.1002/9781119466642.ch5

Proctor, G. (2021) *The dynamics of power in counselling and psychotherapy: ethics, politics, and practice.* 2nd edn. Monmouth: PCCS Books.

Rogers, C. (1951) *Client-centered therapy.* London: Constable & Company Ltd.

Rogers, C.R. (1957) 'The necessary and sufficient conditions of therapeutic personality change', *Journal of Consulting Psychology*, 21(2), pp. 95–103. Available at: https://doi.org/10.1037/h0045357

Rousmaniere, T. (2017) *Deliberate practice for psychotherapists: a guide to improving clinical effectiveness.* Abingdon: Routledge.

Ryan, J. (2019) 'Class in psychodynamic theory, research and practice', *Psychodynamic Practice*, 25(1), pp. 44–59. Available at: https://doi.org/10.1080/14753634.2018.1556725

Sanderson-Shortt, A. (2022) 'Relationships', *Private Practice*, March, p. 17. Available at: https://www.bacp.co.uk/media/14771/private-practice-march-2022.pdf (Accessed: 25 June 2024).

Schön, D.A. (1991) *The reflective practitioner: how professionals think in action.* Aldershot: Ashgate Publishing Ltd.

SCoPEd Framework (2022), collaboratively developed by Association of Christian Counsellors (ACC), British Association for Counselling and Psychotherapy (BACP), British Psychoanalytic Council (BPC), Human Givens Institute (HGI), National Counselling and Psychotherapy Society (NCPS) and United Kingdom Council for Psychotherapy (UKCP). Available at: https://www.bacp.co.uk/about-us/advancing-the-profession/scoped/scoped-framework (Accessed: 12 June 2024).

Stedmon, J. and Dallos, R. (2009) 'Reflective frameworks', in J. Stedmon and R. Dallos (eds) *Reflective practice in psychotherapy and counselling.* Maidenhead: McGraw-Hill Education, pp. 43–65.

Sue, D.W., Capodilupo, C.M., Torino, G.C., Bucceri, J.M., Holder, A.M.B., Nadal, K. L. and Esquilin, M. (2007) 'Racial microaggressions in everyday life: implications for clinical practice', *American Psychologist*, 62(4), pp. 271–286. Available at: https://doi.org/10.1037/0003-066X.62.4.271

Trott, A. and Reeves, A. (2018) 'Social class and the therapeutic relationship: the perspective of therapists as clients. A qualitative study using a questionnaire survey', *Counselling and Psychotherapy Research*, 18(2), pp. 166–177. Available at: https://doi.org/10.1002/capr.12163

Wheeler, C.D. and D'Andrea, L.M. (2004) 'Teaching counseling students to understand and use immediacy', *The Journal of Humanistic Counseling, Education and Development*, 43(2), pp. 117–128. Available at: https://doi.org/10.1002/j.2164-490X.2004.tb00012.x

Willig, C. (2019) 'Ontological and epistemological reflexivity: a core skill for therapists', *Counselling and Psychotherapy Research*, 19(3), pp. 186–194. Available at: https://doi.org/10.1002/capr.12204

Winter, L.A., Guo, F., Wilk, K. and Hanley, T. (2016) 'Difference and diversity in pluralistic counselling and psychotherapy', in M. Cooper and W. Dryden (eds) *Handbook of pluralistic counselling and psychotherapy*. London: SAGE Publications Ltd, pp. 275–287.

Yalom, I.D. (1989) *Love's executioner: and other tales of psychotherapy*. New York: Basic Books.

Chapter 6

Working with unconscious and out-of-awareness processes

Felicitas Rost and Naomi Moller

Contents

Introduction

Antarctic Iceberg by Michael Rost

The image of the iceberg has often been used to depict Western psychological theories of the mind. Freud used it as a metaphor when he developed a model that distinguished between conscious and unconscious aspects, arguing that – just as most of an iceberg's mass is under the surface – the vast majority of our mental processes happen out of the light of our awareness. He was not the first, however, to consider unconscious processes. Several philosophers, religious/spiritual thinkers and scientists (e.g. Paracelsus and Darwin) had written about this before him. Given the prominence of the concept, it is rather surprising that mental activity was seen as entirely conscious until the nineteenth century. It is even more surprising that there are still some who cannot be convinced: *Open Minded: Searching for Truth about the Unconscious Mind*, a book published in 2023, strongly disputes the masses of research evidencing the importance of unconscious processes, for example (Newell and Shanks, 2023).

Different theories have been put forward both to conceptualise the unconscious and to suggest how it functions; some of these will be briefly summarised in the first part of this chapter. While there is not yet consensus on which theories most convincingly explain what is held and transmitted unconsciously, evidence suggests that the unconscious is more than simply the storage of forgotten memories. Rather, it involves psychological processes that influence our emotions, thoughts and behaviours – and hence our relationships to ourselves and others.

Within the therapeutic setting, we can offer our clients a unique opportunity to pay attention to their unconscious inner world, unhelpful habits and relationship dynamics. Yet, it is equally crucial that we, as counsellors, do not lose track of our own unconscious processes, as these can get in the way of the therapeutic work. In Chapter 5 you read about Yalom's countertransference to Betty. As this chapter will cover, countertransference responses in particular might not always be immediately apparent to us, but they can have a damaging impact on our relationship with our clients. Working with out-of-awareness processes is a sophisticated skill that requires practice and patience. Moreover, we need to create the right conditions – and psychic space – to allow for reflexivity to take place.

This chapter contributes towards achieving the **SCoPEd competency 5.1.Bii**:

Ability to work with 'unconscious' and 'out of awareness' processes.

(SCoPEd Framework, 2022, p. 30)

This chapter aims to:

- explore different theoretical models of unconscious and out-of-awareness processes
- consider how these processes affect the views of ourselves and our relationships
- help you to develop different reflective skills to work with unconscious processes.

1 Theories of unconscious processes

Case example: Making sense of the unconscious in supervision

Counsellor: I don't know, I just feel like this client is complaining all the time. I mean, I know she has this history with an overly anxious mother and an alcoholic father, but in lots of other ways it feels like the difficulties in her life are small compared with some of my other clients.

Supervisor: Hmm, I guess I can understand that perspective. And yet, I can't help but notice that the empathy that you typically offer your clients seems to be kind of missing for this client. Have you noticed that?

Counsellor: Empathy? Yes, I know I should be feeling something warm and sympathetic towards her – but actually, I find this client kind of irritating, and I am having this strange feeling of disgust.

Supervisor: That sounds important. Perhaps this is something to be curious about?

To a varying degree, counsellors and psychotherapists are trained to think about what is going on under the surface – in other words, underneath what a client says or behind their visible behaviours. Similarly, counsellors and psychotherapists are taught to consider their own unconscious processes. Sometimes, as in the case example above, a clue can be found in uncharacteristic reactions to a client, and a supervisor can help us to notice something we have perhaps been ignoring. However, becoming aware of the signals from our unconscious is not straightforward, and neither is noticing how our own and our clients' unconscious is impacting the therapeutic encounter – this takes a lot of practice and patience. One place to start is by looking at existing understandings of unconscious processes that are drawn not only from psychotherapy and counselling, but also from broader psychological theory and research.

1.1 The psychoanalytic model

In a paper originally published in 1915, Sigmund Freud not only described mental processes that are outside our field of consciousness, but also proposed the idea of a *dynamic unconscious*. (Freud, 1957). He proposed that most of our behaviours are driven by the content held in the (inaccessible) unconscious and developed a distinct theory of the content, function and symptoms of unconscious processes. Broadly, these include:

repression

A mechanism by which unpleasant or unwanted thoughts, feelings or impulses are blocked from consciousness.

defence mechanisms

Unconscious mental processes that protect oneself from anxiety-provoking thoughts and feelings.

- *Content*: The unconscious is comprised of genetic or pre-programmed information, such as cultural norms, language, past experiences and adaptations that served our survival. It also includes aspects of **repression** – specifically repressed fantasies and memories – to help us manage conflicts between our desires/instincts and social expectations, or to cope with anxieties and mental pain that result from experiencing trauma.

- *Functioning*: Our unconscious processes serve our survival by: (a) providing cultural norms and past experiences to guide us automatically; and (b) repressing traumatic and painful experiences which would otherwise stifle our development. The assumption of an inherent conflict between two contradictory forces is important: the crux of this conflict is that the unconscious tries to keep its material hidden (it can make use of a variety of **defence mechanisms** to achieve this), but the repressed information wants to emerge. The existence of such contradictory forces makes it a *dynamic* unconscious.

- *Symptoms*: One possible response or 'solution' to the inherent conflict between the urge to repress and reveal unconscious content is symptom formation. Symptoms might be psychological (e.g. low mood) or physical (e.g. repeated headaches).

It is worth noting that this is a very simplified sketch of Freudian theory of the unconscious. Freud himself revised his theory more than once, and subsequent psychoanalysts developed their own elaborations and divergences – for example, concerning the nature and influence of unconscious fantasies and the function of repression. A further debate concerns the existence of a collective unconscious, as proposed by Jung (1969), for example.

1.2 Social cognitive theories

Another tradition of theory and research on the unconscious comes from cognitive psychology and focuses on social cognition (e.g. Bargh, 2017; Reber and Allen, 2022). Social cognitive theory is a largely research-based tradition and demonstrates the interplay between conscious and unconscious processes in studies on perception, attention, learning, memory and, more recently, on emotions. Social psychologists extended this tradition through the study of unconscious processes in attitudes, persuasion and social judgment. This social cognitive research tradition uses different terminology, referring to implicit/automatic (rather than 'unconscious') and explicit (rather than 'conscious') processes, and they have developed various ways of conceptualising unconscious processes, including:

- *Being unaware*: The person is unaware that they have been exposed to a stimulus which exerts an impact.

- *Not noticing impact*: The person is aware of being exposed to a stimulus, but is unaware that they have been influenced by it.

- *Not paying attention*: The person is not paying attention to something (e.g. background noise) but is still unconsciously monitoring it.

Extensive research suggests that unconscious processes are at work in learning and judgement, as well as in the following areas:

- *Perception*: Humans have a split perceptual system (LeDoux, 1995). Slower, rational processes involve conscious awareness to regulate thoughts, actions and behaviours, and mediate our concentration, planning, decision making, and so on. In contrast, faster processes happen unconsciously, bypassing a fine-tuned appraisal of what we perceive. Many day-to-day situations rely on the latter system, including the regulation of our breathing and making complex decisions quickly.

- *Motor skills*: **Implicit learning** is also part of smooth engagement in complex motor skills, like riding a bike or driving a car.

- *Memory*: Many laboratory studies (e.g. Bargh, 2017; Han *et al.*, 2022) have shown that the memory of a past event can influence a person's subsequent behaviour, even if they don't consciously remember that event. This type of memory is called 'implicit memory'; Box 6.1 provides a brief overview of the memory system.

- *Emotions*: There is sound evidence that emotion processing can happen unconsciously. Braunstein, Gross and Ochsner (2017) argue that alongside explicit (conscious) attempts to control one's emotions, there is both automatic implicit emotion regulation and what they term implicit 'controlled' emotion regulation.

implicit learning

The process of acquiring knowledge without conscious awareness that learning is taking place. It involves learning skills automatically and rapidly through interactions with the environment.

Box 6.1 Different types of memory

Camina and Güell (2017) outline a model that proposes different memory systems.

Explicit memory consists of facts and day-to-day experiences that can be consciously and deliberately retrieved. They are typically divided into semantic memory for general and personal facts (including our physical, mental and demographic identity) and episodic memory for specific events.

Implicit memory includes information that relates to behaviours that we rely on without consciously remembering the details (like driving a car). It also includes memory for words, sounds or shapes, which facilitate skills, habits, routines and adaptive responses. This type of memory is said to include two strands:

- *Associative memory*: This is where a person unconsciously associates things based on how events co-occur. For example, a child whose father is unpredictable and violent due to alcohol use might begin to associate the sound of the keys in the lock with danger and react with fear (classical conditioning), or they might respond by being very quiet to make themselves feel safer (operant conditioning). This has also been referred to as emotional memory, since it is a conditioned emotional response (Lemma, 2016).

- *Non-associative memory*: This involves learning new emotional responses when someone is repeatedly exposed to an event or stimuli. To return to the example of the child with the violent father, this might mean becoming habituated to angry screaming between their parents when their father is *not* drunk (and not violent), so they no longer react in fear and hide under the bed at other times due to this habituation. Alternatively, it might mean reacting more strongly, so that over time even the smell of alcohol (even when not around the father) is enough to evoke a fear response, due to sensitisation.

While psychoanalytic models focus more on the resulting conflict between two systems of awareness in trying to explain and treat mental suffering, cognitive psychology emphasises the interplay between the two. Repetition, for example, can lead to conscious processes becoming automatic. Similarly, repeated conscious avoidance of a particular feeling or thought can lead to repression as well as automated behaviour, as Box 6.1 highlighted. As such, research has emphasised that complex cognitive information processing also happens without our awareness.

1.3 Evolutionary theory

There is now sound evidence that humans inherit 'ready-made' systems of habit. In other words, we have several independent and unconscious behavioural guidance systems that we access automatically during early childhood (Bargh and Morsella, 2008). One of these includes a cultural guide to how we should behave and communicate, what we can expect and value, and what is safe and what is dangerous. These guidance systems can be seen as shortcuts: knowledge that has served previous generations (in their adaptations) is transferred to us (Campbell, 1974). Thus, when we follow our intuition or gut reactions, this is often driven by past knowledge that we hold in our unconscious. These are then said to be fine-tuned by the current local social, political and cultural system, and the behaviours and values adopted by those closest to us (Bargh and Morsella, 2008). This 'download' can include stereotypes and prejudices about certain groups of people, as well as entrenched ideologies about race, sexuality, class, and so on. Thinking specifically about the context of psychotherapy practice, the potential implications of this are:

- counsellors will have their own prejudices and assumptions, including about what the purpose of counselling is
- therapeutic ruptures may occur because clients from particular social groups may wrongly assume that counsellors share their unconscious social and relational understandings.

Thus, as stressed in Chapter 2, when working as counsellors, we need to reflect and become aware of our own unconscious social assumptions and prejudices to avoid their unhelpful impact on our relationships and work with clients. The next section suggests further strategies for working with the unconscious, with a specific focus on relationships.

2 Unconscious processes and our sense of self and others

One similarity between the Freudian understanding of unconscious processes and the account provided by cognitive and social psychologists is the idea that our past experience influences us, even if we don't remember it. This understanding aligns with the masses of research on the impact of attachment bonds in early childhood, a period said to involve 'childhood amnesia' because of how few memories most people have of their early childhood (Bauer, 2015). Thus, our early experiences and relationships play a crucial role in influencing our thoughts, emotions and behaviours. This section focuses on the impact of unconscious processes on our sense of self (identity) and our relationships, and how to become aware of some of these in ourselves and our clients.

Pause for thought 6.1

Try to imagine a scenario with a current or previous client in which you are confident and fully present; you are listening and being there for them. What emotions come up when you imagine this?

Now have another go, but this time imagine your supervisor is the person being there for you. They are being thoughtful and caring, helping you to understand something in your work with a client. Again, what do you feel?

This exercise emphasises two important points: the first is that we can will ourselves to consciously conjure up mental representations of ourselves and others; the second is that we have these stored somewhere within ourselves so we can retrieve them and use them in our reflections.

2.1 Mental representations

The psychological process behind our ability to store information about ourselves and others is called **internalisation**. Cognitive behavioural approaches conceptualise these internal representations as core beliefs, which form the self through implicit and explicit learning processes. Other counselling approaches refer to these as *schemas*, which include emotional and physiological elements in addition to cognitive aspects. Person-centred theory refers to them as forming *internal conditions of worth*. Attachment theory adds that we can internalise whole structures or templates of relating patterns, including the array of associated emotions, thoughts and fantasies we hold about the people or events involved. These structures are referred to as *internal working models*; they are said to determine our expectations, perceptions, emotions and reactions to the behaviours of others, as well as

internalisation

The unconscious process by which we integrate or assimilate beliefs, attitudes, characteristics, emotions, and so on, of other people or groups into the self and adopt these as our own.

form the basis of our attachment styles that guide all subsequent relationships unconsciously (e.g. Roisman *et al.*, 2005).

Thus, when you conjure up the idea of your supervisor, it comes with associated emotions and thoughts that can trigger specific behaviours. It might allow you not only to remember helpful advice they have given, but also to experience, consciously or unconsciously, a feeling of warmth or a sense of care that in turn might strengthen your presence with your client in that moment. That said, the way that you experience – and subsequently internalise – your supervisor could also be influenced by your early experiences of interactions with your caregivers. A possible example might be that if you experienced a relationship with a parent that was reliable and caring, you might believe that a supervisor will be interested in you and your client work. In turn, you are more likely to unconsciously perceive them as trustworthy and the interaction between you as fruitful. By contrast, if you experienced unreliable attention to your needs from your caregivers, you might not always feel deserving and have an unconscious expectation of your supervisor's reaction as being critical towards your attempts to ask for help, for example. This might therefore mean that you don't seek help easily, or you unconsciously defend against this thought (e.g. by being overly critical towards your own approach when talking to them). Conversely, you may display overt confidence and block opportunities for feedback.

Pause for thought 6.2

Thinking about your relationship with your supervisor, can you notice any habitual, repetitive thought patterns or behaviours in relation to them? Are these specific to working with your supervisor, or have you experienced them with other people too?

transference

A term used to describe the redirection of the client's feelings about someone else on to the counsellor.

countertransference

A term used to describe the redirection of the counsellor's feelings towards the client.

It requires reflexivity to understand your own internal working models and the impact these have on you and those around you. This chapter primarily focuses on the example of your relationship with your supervisor, but just as the internal working models of your clients will impact how they perceive you and how they engage with the therapeutic process, so will yours impact the relationship with them. Other terms describing these processes, especially within the therapy context, are **transference** and **countertransference**. If you are having doubts about your supervisor, you don't feel adequately 'held' by them, or you even feel rejected or misunderstood, reflecting on your possible transference to them may be particularly helpful as an additional barometer for judging their competence or how they 'fit' with you. It is also possible for your perception of them and your experiences with them to change over time. Our internalised models can be especially triggered when we feel stressed or anxious (e.g. Collins *et al.*, 2004).

2.2 Coping and defence mechanisms

Many clients reportedly seek counselling because they feel unable to cope any longer. Coping mechanisms are strategies that people use to handle difficult situations by reducing unpleasant emotions. Defence mechanisms can be used in a similar way. Although multiple different perspectives exist on how the two constructs relate to each other, coping mechanisms are commonly understood as involving conscious processes and are stressor related, while defence mechanisms are mainly unconscious processes (Silverman and Aafjes-van Doorn, 2023).

According to psychoanalytic theory, people automatically adopt defence mechanisms to help build resilience during development. These can serve in an adaptive manner during adulthood when confronted with stress or adversity, but they can also be used too rigidly or too exclusively at the cost of healthy functioning or developing mutually satisfying relationships.

> **Pause for thought 6.3**
>
> Can you think of a client who you believed used defences too inflexibly? How did that present itself or affect them in their life? Did it also somehow affect your relationship with them?

It was Anna Freud who, in 1936, developed a comprehensive theory of psychological defence mechanisms (Freud, 1992). Current research has identified about 30 different types (Di Giuseppe and Perry, 2021); Table 6.1 lists some of these. The classification of defences as levels, ranging from mature to immature, has been a helpful one (e.g. Vaillant, 1977; Perry, 1990). Research has shown that the more mature the defence mechanism, the more adaptive the person's coping ability (Silverman and Aafjes-van Doorn, 2023).

The more reliant a client is on immature defences, the more vulnerable they are. Consequently, they are less able to sustain an awareness of the cognitive and emotional aspects of their experience, and the internal and external stresses they face. Thus, recognising the level of adaptability that your client is operating at is important, whether your aim is to help your client to become aware and slowly adopt more mature defence strategies, or because you want to gauge what kind of intervention or exercise might be most appropriate at a particular moment.

Table 6.1 Defence mechanisms

Level of adaptivity	Defence mechanism	Example
Immature	Splitting, projection, rationalisation, schizoid fantasy, manic defences, passive aggression, acting out	Projection: Your client might feel hate towards someone but struggles with this, believing that it is wrong to feel this way. This conflict is resolved by the client believing that the person hates them instead.
Intermediate	Isolation of affect, intellectualisation, repression, dissociation, reaction formation, displacement, devaluation, idealisation, omnipotence	Displacement: Your client might substitute one person/thing for another. They might come to a session after a very frustrating meeting with their manager and start criticising you for being inflexible, too expensive, etc.
Mature	Altruism, humour, self-assertion, self-observation, sublimation, suppression	Sublimation: Your client might redirect a socially unacceptable desire into a more acceptable one (e.g. sexual or aggressive/violent impulses into competitive, physically aggressive sports).

2.3 Resistance

Paying attention to resistance is another important aspect of therapeutic work. This includes reflecting on your own possible resistances and those from your clients, as both can stifle progress and lead to client drop out. For example, you could consider whether there are things you don't want to pay attention to or hear from your clients. While resistance can be conscious, it is mostly unconscious and manifests to varying degrees, often through a range of defences. For example, when your client suddenly misses sessions and explains that they 'simply forgot again', this might be a sign that there is resistance at play.

Another example is when you don't pay attention to something that appears obvious, such as aspects of diversity between you and your client, which might suggest you are avoiding or denying something. Goedert (2020) stresses the importance of paying attention to racialised resistances in particular, arguing that although they are also present in clients, it is primarily the counsellor's unexplored racialised fantasies that create impediments to understanding, and often manifests in a denial of racist dynamics. Thus, working through these resistances is crucial. Practically, this might involve exploring and tolerating uncomfortable thoughts and fantasies that you might intellectually and emotionally disagree with.

Finally, signs of resistance should not necessarily be regarded as indicating that the client or counsellor wants to impede or oppose the therapeutic work. Rather, it might be a helpful sign of intense anxiety because a client is not ready for some intervention or approach, or because they need something else from you. Lemma (2016) makes a helpful distinction between resistance as a result of internal conflict or anxiety, and resistance that comes from a place of need. For instance, a client might have needed to develop a strong defensive structure to protect themselves and survive trauma or abuse. In these cases, we need to respect clients' resistance and moderate our work accordingly.

3 Working with unconscious processes

A photo of a lagoon by Ana Santos

Drawing on theory and research from psychoanalysis and social cognition, this chapter has explored how unconscious processes may influence us. But what does this research suggest about how to reduce the impact of the unconscious on clients and on ourselves as counsellors? The ability to work with the unconscious is very important for counsellors, as highlighted in the case example at the start of Section 1.

Focusing on unconscious processes is a sophisticated skill that requires us to be attuned to multiple levels of communication simultaneously. Moreover, unconscious memories or learning that shape initial perception is hard to change because you may not be aware of how you or your clients have been impacted. Conversely, it is easier to moderate the carryover impacts of previous experiences once you become aware of what is happening. Lemma (2016) talks of 'layered listening': counsellors need to pay attention to what is specifically present (manifest content) and what might be hidden underneath it (latent content). As the image above suggests so poignantly, one's experience can be layered: the image shows a calm, beautiful lagoon on the one hand (here, a metaphor for conscious communication) and the sea getting ready for a storm on the other (a metaphor for unconscious communication). Relatedly, unconscious influences are more likely to operate when a person is in a passive/experiential state versus an active/goal orientated state (Bargh, 2022). In other words, consciously paying attention to one's own moment-to-moment experiences during a counselling session is a good strategy for moderating the potential impacts of our unconscious material and for gaining insights into that of our clients. The next section unpacks some additional strategies.

3.1 Routes to your client's unconscious

Paying attention to speech

You are likely familiar with the use of mirroring and reflecting your clients' feelings back to them. These strategies can be used to provide feedback and validation, for example by remarking, 'By what you are saying, I can clearly hear how angry this person made you feel in that situation'. But these can also be used to help your clients relocate their attention to feelings or thought patterns that they may not be aware of. For example, you could say, 'I notice that while you speak about this person, your voice becomes very subdued. Have you noticed that too?' or 'Every time you mention that person, I notice that you are crossing your arms. What do you make of that?'

Questions like these enable clients to say spontaneously whatever comes to their mind; this is a useful technique to allow unconscious thoughts, feelings or associations to emerge. However, as emphasised, unconscious thoughts and feelings might not be expressed in *what* a client says, but in the *way* they say it. Therefore, you could pay attention to the kind of tone they use: is it harsh, soft, fading or inconsistent? You could also listen to the syntax of their sentences. Do they not complete their sentences or is the narrative incoherent, for example?

How people speak is determined by many factors, including culture. Consequently, verbal expressions, speed dysfluency (e.g. stammering or stuttering) and speed of talking that appears out of the ordinary for a particular client are often particularly relevant clues. These might hint at a possibility that something unconscious is being expressed, which you could bring to the fore by verbalising it to the client, as in the following example:

'I have noticed over the past few sessions that when you speak about your partner and [a particular incident], you start speaking a lot faster and the words at the end of your sentences get lost or dropped off, as it were. This leaves me needing to guess what you might mean.'

Paying attention to how your client speaks and what reaction this creates in you is an example of paying attention to 'latent' content, as introduced at the start of Section 3.

Paying attention to bodies

> ### Pause for thought 6.4
>
> Pause and pay attention to your body posture in this very moment. How are you holding or composing your body? What have your hands been doing while you read? Have you tensed up? Have you noticed any sensations or particular emotions arising while reading this chapter?

Another path for unconscious communication can be through the body. Just now you were asked to pay attention to your bodily sensations; similarly, you can also pay attention to your client's non-verbal expressions. Keeping in mind that there are cultural influences on non-verbal behaviour (Matsumoto and Hwang, 2016), can you notice anything particular about your client's body posture, for instance? Returning to defensive strategies as an example, could your client's body be expressing the opposite of what they are verbally saying? This might be seen in the case of a client who talks very favourably about their brother while their hands are in constant movement, kneading each other and making fists.

Within both humanistic and experiential counselling approaches, a range of techniques have been developed to allow clients to experience an awareness of what is held unconsciously within their bodies. These include, for example, the evocative unfolding of problematic reactions, chair exercises and focusing, to just name a few (for an overview, see Elliot, 2012). To allow your clients to gain access to their felt sense you could, for instance, ask 'What does it feel like inside right now?' or 'Where is the [sadness/anger] in your body?' You could take this a step further and ask your client to 'become' a specific non-verbal expression, such as their crossed arms or clutched fists, by asking, 'What about becoming your fist that you are clutching right now? Can you express what it might be feeling?'

Making general enquiry and leaving space

When a client tells you a story, a memory or a dream, you could ask them a follow-up question, such as 'How does that leave you feeling?', 'Are there any bodily sensations that you can notice right now?', 'What other thoughts does it bring up now you've told me?' or 'What else comes to mind?' If you keep the questions general enough, these might trigger further thoughts or feelings that are hovering just outside their consciousness. Sometimes leaving space by being silent, yet not withdrawing attention, can also be helpful to trigger further thoughts and allow space for emotions that have surfaced during the telling to come up. In these moments, you might also be able to get a glimpse of some defence mechanisms as in, for example, a client who immediately deflects from what they have said and, without a break, starts talking about something else to avoid the emotion.

Likewise, even if a client can't think of anything else to say after you ask a question or offer an inquisitive silence, their reaction might reveal something important. Do they, for example, react with irritation or indifference? Silences can also convey different meanings: sometimes they can show reflection, but at other times they can be a sign of a defence.

3.2 Working with countertransference

The last section of this chapter focuses on two psychological processes that are primarily used in psychoanalytic approaches, but that we authors believe to be important in *any* kind of psychological work. These are *projection* and *projective identification*.

The underlying mechanism is, in a way, opposite to internalisation, which was explained in Section 2.1. Projections and projective identifications direct unacceptable or unbearable thoughts or feelings outwards by attributing them to other people. A relatable example might be a colleague or friend saying to you, 'Gosh, you look a bit annoyed!' when in fact they are the one who is annoyed in that moment.

Pets are often used as objects of our projections; you might say, 'Oh, doesn't my cat look a bit irritated this morning?' Pets can indeed be helpful for us in managing our unconscious feelings, such as irritation that might have surfaced during sleep. However, if used in excess, projections can become part of an individual's problems rather than a helpful solution. Likewise, if counsellors are not aware that these unconscious processes can affect them, they can be pulled into reacting to these without being aware of it.

Pause for thought 6.5

Can you think of a client who has made you feel a particular way? For example, perhaps you felt extremely drowsy, confused and unable to think clearly while being with them, or you might have felt unusually helpless or as though you simply cannot get anything right with them.

The case example at the start of Section 1 featured a counsellor who, when exploring their reactions in supervision, discovered a feeling of irritation and disgust instead of empathy towards their client. Read the concluding part of this case to find out what happened next in this supervision session.

Case example: Making sense of the unconscious in supervision (continued)

Supervisor: You don't have to go into detail here with me, but generally, can you attribute the feeling of irritation or disgust to anything that is going on in your personal life at the moment?

Counsellor: Let me think for a moment ... Well, I can't really think of anything that makes me feel that way. Things in my private life are pretty good at present.

Supervisor: Okay, then perhaps we can assume that your feelings, which we both think are rather unusual for you, could be an indication that projective identification is happening. In other words, they could be feelings that your client, for whatever reason, can't bear to feel and thus needed to project – unconsciously – into you for you to hold and feel.

Counsellor: Okay, yes, that makes sense, since I really struggle to somehow own these feelings. I wonder if this is something about how my client feels about herself? I have found myself wondering whether she is feeling shame that she can't acknowledge. It's a strong reaction, though!

The dialogue between the counsellor and supervisor here highlights an example projection (from the client) and projective identification (by the counsellor). Therefore, when this process occurs between client and therapist (as opposed to within other relationships more generally), it is a type of countertransference, which was defined in Section 2.1.

Lemma (2016) provides some useful guidance for working with countertransference:

- Get accustomed to noting your own emotional responses to [your client's] verbal and non-verbal behaviours.
- Don't dismiss seemingly unconnected associations that may come to mind as you listen to [your client] (e.g. a song or a character from a book).
- Are the feelings you experience (or that you think you should be experiencing but are not) accountable for in terms of issues in your own life at the time? [...] Be careful to monitor what belongs to you [and what belongs to your client].
- Refrain from intervening, especially if you experience an urge to do so.
- Try to stay with the feeling(s) evoked in you. Note what it makes you feel like doing or what it makes you feel about yourself (e.g. incompetent, powerful, attractive). If you feel under pressure to say something, this may be a further indication that projective identification is operative.
- Typically, the process of internal reflection eases the psychological strain as you gain important emotional distance and hence perspective.

(Lemma, 2016, p. 256)

If you don't pay attention to projective identification when it happens, a possible danger is that you might get pulled into reacting – or colluding with something – without being aware of it. Staying with the above case example, if the counsellor hadn't explored their emotions towards the client, they might have started to react dismissively when the client talked about her difficulties. Such reactions are also called enactments. These can be subtle, such as in instances where you find yourself agreeing to change a session time and wondering afterwards why you did that despite inconveniencing yourself. However, they can also be more severe, for example if the counsellor reacts angrily to or even laughs at a client, or by crossing professional and ethical boundaries.

Conclusion

This chapter introduced you to some theories of unconscious processes and discussed how you can become more aware of these within yourself, your clients, and in the therapeutic and supervisory relationship. Working with out-of-awareness processes in counselling is a process in itself. This chapter has highlighted the importance of attending to the unconscious in counselling, which includes understanding and working with defence mechanisms and resistance. It has also provided some techniques that you can use to foster your ability to work with this hidden material, including paying attention to verbal and non-verbal aspects of behaviour (in both your client and yourself), and working with countertransference.

Further reading

- The following source is a great introduction to the psychoanalytic way of working with unconscious processes and offers many clinical examples:

  Lemma, A. (2016) *Introduction to the practice of psychoanalytic psychotherapy.* 2nd edn. Chichester: John Wiley & Sons.

- The following book about unconscious processes is an excellent resource and was written for a general audience:

  Bargh, J.A. (2017) *Before you know it: the unconscious reasons we do what we do.* London: Touchstone.

References

Bargh, J.A. (2017) *Before you know it: the unconscious reasons we do what we do.* London: Touchstone.

Bargh, J.A. (2022) 'The cognitive unconscious in everyday life', in A.S. Reber and R. Allen (eds) *The cognitive unconscious: the first half century.* Oxford: Oxford University Press, pp. 89–112

Bargh, J.A. and Morsella, E. (2008) 'The unconscious mind', *Perspectives on Psychological Science*, 3(1), pp. 73–79. Available at: https://doi.org/10.1111/j.1745-6916.2008.00064.x

Bauer, P.J. (2015) 'A complementary processes account of the development of childhood amnesia and a personal past', *Psychological Review*, 122(2), pp. 204–231. Available at: https://doi.org/10.1037/a0038939

Braunstein, L.M., Gross, J.J. and Ochsner, K.N. (2017) 'Explicit and implicit emotion regulation: a multi-level framework', *Social Cognitive and Affective Neuroscience*, 12 (10), pp. 1545–1557. Available at: https://doi.org/10.1093/scan/nsx096

Camina, E. and Güell, F. (2017) 'The neuroanatomical, neurophysiological and psychological basis of memory: current models and their origins', *Frontiers in Pharmacology*, 8, article number 438. Available at: https://doi.org/10.3389/fphar.2017.00438

Campbell, D.T. (1974) 'Evolutionary epistemology', in P.A. Schilpp (ed.) *The philosophy of Karl Popper.* La Salle, IL: Open Court Publishing, pp. 413–463.

Collins, N.L., Guichard, A.C., Ford, M.B. and Feeney, B.C. (2004) 'Working models of attachment: new developments and emerging themes', in W.S. Rholes and J.A. Simpson (eds) *Adult attachment: theory, research, and clinical implications.* New York: Guilford, pp. 196–239.

Di Giuseppe, M. and Perry, J.C. (2021) 'The hierarchy of defense mechanisms: assessing defensive functioning with the Defense Mechanisms Rating Scales Q-Sort', *Frontiers in Psychology*, 12, article number 718440. Available at: https://doi.org/10.3389/fpsyg.2021.718440

Elliott, R. (2012) 'Emotion-focused therapy', in P. Sanders (ed.) *The tribes of the person-centred nation: an introduction to the schools of therapy related to the person-centred approach.* 2nd revised edn. Ross-on-Wye: PCCS Books, pp. 103–130.

Freud, A. (1992) *The ego and the mechanisms of defence.* Translated from the German by C. Baines. London: Karnac Books.

Freud, S. (1957) 'The unconscious', in J. Strachy (ed.) *The standard edition of the complete works of Sigmund Freud. Vol. 14: on the history of the psycho-analytic movement, papers on metapsychology and other works (1914 –1916).* Translated from the German by J. Strachy. London: Hogarth Press, pp. 159–215.

Goedert, M. (2020) 'Racism in the countertransference', *The Psychoanalytic Quarterly*, 89(4), pp. 715–740. Available at: https://doi.org/10.1080/00332828.2020.1805270

Han, Y.C., Schmidt, K.D., Grandoit, E., Shu, P., McRobert, C.P. and Reber, P.J. (2022) 'Cognitive neuroscience of implicit learning: implications for complex learning and expertise', in A.S. Reber and R. Allen (eds) *The cognitive unconscious: the first half century.* Oxford: Oxford University Press, pp. 37–61.

Jung, C.G. (1969) *The collected works of C.G. Jung. Volume 9, part 1: the archetypes and the collective unconscious.* 2nd edn. Translated from the German by R.F.C. Hull. Edited by H. Read, M. Fordham and G. Adler. Princeton, NJ: Princeton University Press. Bollingen Series XX.

LeDoux, J.E. (1995) 'Emotion: clues from the brain', *Annual Review of Psychology*, 46, pp. 209–235. Available at: https://doi.org/10.1146/annurev.ps.46.020195.001233

Lemma, A. (2016) *Introduction to the practice of psychoanalytic psychotherapy.* 2nd edn. Chichester: John Wiley & Sons.

Matsumoto, D. and Hwang, H.C. (2016) 'The cultural bases of nonverbal communication', in D. Matsumoto, H.C. Hwang and M.G. Frank (eds) *APA handbook of nonverbal communication.* Washington, DC: American Psychological Association, pp. 77–101.

Newell, B.R. and Shanks, D.R. (2023) *Open minded: searching for truth about the unconscious mind.* Cambridge, MA: The MIT Press.

Perry, J.C. (1990) *Defense Mechanism Rating Scales (DMRS).* 5th edn. Cambridge, MA: J.C. Perry.

Reber, A.S. and Allen, R. (2022) *The cognitive unconscious: the first half century.* Oxford: Oxford University Press.

Roisman, G.I., Collins, W.A., Sroufe, L.A. and Egeland, B. (2005) 'Predictors of young adults' representations of and behavior in their current romantic relationship: prospective tests of the prototype hypothesis', *Attachment & Human Development*, 7 (2), pp. 105–121. Available at: https://doi.org/10.1080/14616730500134928

SCoPEd Framework (2022), collaboratively developed by Association of Christian Counsellors (ACC), British Association for Counselling and Psychotherapy (BACP), British Psychoanalytic Council (BPC), Human Givens Institute (HGI), National Counselling and Psychotherapy Society (NCPS) and United Kingdom Council for Psychotherapy (UKCP). Available at: https://www.bacp.co.uk/about-us/advancing-the-profession/scoped/scoped-framework (Accessed: 12 June 2024)

Silverman, J. and Aafjes-van Doorn, K. (2023) 'Coping and defense mechanisms: a scoping review', *Clinical Psychology: Science and Practice*, 30(4), pp. 381–392. Available at: https://doi.org/10.1037/cps0000139

Vaillant, G. (1977) *Adaptation to life.* Boston, MA: Little & Brown.

Chapter 7

Using reflexivity to develop and maintain emotional fitness

Claudine McFaul

Contents

Introduction

At the Water's Edge by Claudine McFaul

Experienced counsellors often reflect on their work as being hugely rewarding, but recognise that the rewards come at the cost of a significant and sustained level of emotional commitment. Guiding clients through the pain and joy of their lived experience is emotionally demanding, intense and complex work. So, if you sometimes find yourself waking in the small hours of the night, with your mind whirring as it processes the progress you are making in accompanying your client towards a desired outcome, you will be relieved to know that you're not alone.

In my experience as a practising counsellor, I have sometimes found myself awake at odd hours, ruminating and reflecting on my work with a particular client. These experiences have taught me that developing a capacity for sustained reflexivity is key to our emotional fitness in our role as counsellors, which in turn ensures that we can give our best to our clients while still maintaining our emotional and personal poise.

This chapter explores how the emotional complexity of counselling impacts the counsellor and how we can recognise the signs of emotional fatigue. It also considers ways to maintain and develop the emotional fitness and motivation required to carry out meaningful and rewarding work.

This chapter contributes towards achieving the **SCoPEd competency 5.1.Bi**:

Ability to be emotionally prepared for intense and complex work, which requires sustained reflexivity.

(SCoPEd Framework, 2022, p. 30)

This chapter aims to:

- explore the impact of working with 'complexity' and why it matters for your practice

- consider how to assess and monitor your own risk of vicarious trauma, burnout and compassion fatigue by noticing and learning from your emotional responses

- explore how self-care can be used as a preventive measure to avoid some of these risks

- consider how to develop your emotional fitness and maintain the motivation to carry out meaningful work.

1 The importance of being self-aware

Reflective practice can play a crucial role in your professional development as a counsellor as it involves evaluating what went well and what didn't, which enables you to refine your approach in future situations. While helpful, this process can also be considered somewhat passive, as it tends to occur after a counselling session has ended. In contrast, *reflexive* practice is often more transformative as it tends to be conducted in real-time, leading to a deeper understanding about what is happening for both the counsellor and the client. Reflexive counsellors aim to develop their self-awareness so they can actively reflect on their own feelings, thoughts and behaviours during the counselling process to ensure that they are working in the best interests of both themselves and their clients.

As the focus of this chapter is about learning to feel comfortable while working with complexity in the counselling room, developing a reflexive practice can be considered an important way to build your emotional fitness so that you feel aware and present with your clients. This will enable you to become more mindful of your internal responses so that you can critically reflect on these and make immediate adjustments if necessary.

Reflexivity isn't easy. Perhaps, as in my own experience, there have been times when you have regretted your choice of words when working with a client, or when you have listened to a recording of yourself with a client and realised that you weren't being as empathetic as you thought you were.

Although you will be used to encouraging your clients to pause for a moment to access their feelings and help them become more self-aware, it is important that you also feel comfortable doing the same. The following section starts by offering you the opportunity to put this into practice right now by exploring your feelings around what led you to choose this career.

1.1 Motivations for becoming a counsellor

Only the wounded healer can truly heal.

(Jung, 1963, p. 125)

Pause for thought 7.1

It is possible that you have already come across Jung's 'wounded healer' expression, perhaps during your counselling training. What do you think about his statement above?

Do you feel that you can be a more empathetic counsellor if you have had similar experiences to your client? Are people with unresolved emotional issues attracted to counselling as a profession? Is it harmful to work as a counsellor if you are working through your own trauma?

Notice your immediate reactions (your thoughts, feelings, body sensations) when considering these questions and keep them in mind while you read through the rest of this section.

When considering Jung's words, you may have thought about poignant experiences from your past that led you to decide to train in this field. Perhaps you experienced a loved one attending counselling and appreciated the healing value of a close and empathetic relationship? During your training you may have met fellow trainees from a variety of backgrounds, some who may have experienced significant traumas or poor mental health, and felt drawn to help others in similar predicaments. During your personal development training you may have questioned whether you, or your fellow trainees, were the right candidates for this type of work due to unresolved past experiences.

McBeath (2019) carried out a survey to understand therapists' motivations for practice. He received 540 responses and found that a large majority believed that their career choice was influenced by unconscious motivations, along with a desire to understand themselves more fully and to feel more understood by others. As counsellors frequently work with vulnerable and distressed clients, examining your own motivations for your decision to work as a counsellor is fundamental to working ethically with your clients; not doing so may risk unintentionally using clients to compensate for your own wounds or emotional vulnerabilities.

Barnett (2007) suggests that it is helpful to explore the unconscious motivations of choosing to train as a counsellor, especially around relating and experiencing intimacy at a 'safe' distance, particularly if deprived of this at a young age. Some children who experience a challenging early life may take on a kind of caretaker role in the family, and so develop a 'special' sensitivity to the emotional needs of others. This awareness of shifts in the emotional atmosphere is central to the role of a counsellor, so it could feel like a natural career choice. Others may simply feel the urge to help people due to their past experiences and consider themselves to be ideally placed to listen with empathy to others. This may be particularly relevant for those counsellors who have personal experiences related to equality, diversity and inclusion. Although there is a natural tendency to focus on the more positive aspects of why you may have chosen to do this work, Barnett hints that it is essential for both the counsellor and the client to explore the counsellor's position in order to avoid causing harm to either party.

According to the workforce mapping survey collected by the BACP (2023), the majority of UK counsellors are aged between 45–64, which might suggest that many come to this role as a second career. There could be a number of reasons for this, but Erikson (1968) puts forward an interesting theory about generativity, which is where individuals want to leave something meaningful behind for the next generation and may feel disillusioned or regress emotionally at a certain point in their life if they don't feel that they have reached their full potential. During midlife, a second career as a counsellor – a role which can promise meaning and purpose – may offer some individuals an opportunity to make peace with this existential unrest. Additionally, their 'woundedness' may offer an opportunity to work in a field that promotes personal growth for both themselves and their clients.

1.2 The myth of the counsellor as a rescuer

There can be many attractive aspects to working as a counsellor, such as seeing clients become empowered and sharing many moments of connection that can feel joyful and transcendent at times. From the very first interaction with your client, there can be an expectation that you convey a level of competence and confidence in your field, so clients feel safe to continue their counselling journey with you. When the sessions are progressing well and positive changes are taking place, inevitably clients may be impressed by your professionalism and hold your counselling skills in very high regard. Counsellors may feel tempted to simply go along with this narrative, which positions them as a 'rescuer' from life's difficulties and traumas – after all the training and hard work, who wouldn't want to hear that they are good at their job?

Yet, unquestioned positive affirmations can be hazardous both to the therapeutic relationship and to your development as a counsellor, as of course counsellors have their own flaws, imperfections and personal struggles, and may feel burdened by these unrealistic expectations. A power dynamic could potentially develop, where a counsellor's theoretical knowledge is privileged over the client's knowledge of themselves. This may create a disconnect, or even feelings of shame, which can lead the counsellor to feel that they need to hide their vulnerabilities rather than seek help when needed. Counsellors new to the profession may be reluctant to seek support from their supervisor or employer in case it compromises their self-image as a competent professional. This may be particularly relevant for trainee counsellors who have changed careers and may find it challenging to return to the position of being a novice as they start out on a new professional path. Peer support and supervision can help to address this challenge.

Activity 7.1 Reflecting on your beliefs

Allow about 15 minutes

To further explore your motivations, you may find it interesting to consider the beliefs that you hold around your practice. In 1983, Albert Ellis presented five main irrational beliefs he felt therapists should openly explore when they are struggling to work effectively. Consider whether these, or similar, beliefs resonate with your experience as a counsellor.

1   I have to be successful with all of my clients practically all of the time.
2   I must be an outstanding therapist, clearly better than other therapists I know or hear about.
3   I have to be greatly respected and loved by all my clients.
4   Since I am doing my best and working so hard as a therapist, my clients should be equally hard working and responsible, should listen to me carefully, and should always push themselves to change.
5   I must be able to enjoy myself during therapy sessions and to use these sessions to solve my personal problems as much as to help clients with their difficulties.

(Adapted from Ellis, 2003, pp. 206–207)

Discussion

You may find it helpful to consider the extent to which these issues resonate with your own feelings and reflections on your practice as a counsellor. For example, do they prompt you to consider any difficulties you have encountered or are currently encountering? Interestingly, these beliefs may be the same as those a counsellor is trying to help their clients to overcome, so you may find it helpful to be aware of these and how they may help shape communication and understandings between you and your clients.

therapeutic authenticity

The matching of a therapist's inner thoughts, feelings and core beliefs with their outer presentation and behaviour, and a consideration of how the client perceives this.

As research has found that effective therapy is more about the therapeutic relationship rather than the type of therapy itself (Wampold and Imel, 2015), it would appear that counsellors have to strike a difficult balance between having **therapeutic authenticity** and being competent. On the one hand they need to be authentic and sincere with their clients in order for the therapeutic relationship to develop, while on the other hand they need to focus specifically on the client's needs and exude a certain level of professional capability to ensure that their clients trust and want to work with them.

This section has explored how counselling is an active, dynamic process that is shaped by the personal histories and motivations of both the client and the counsellor. As such, from an ethical standpoint, it is crucial that counsellors adopt a reflexive approach in order to avoid causing unintentional harm to either themselves or their clients. The key to this is understanding your motivations for becoming a counsellor and the need to strike an appropriate balance between authenticity and competence. The following section will consider how to navigate the intense and complex work of a counsellor in more detail.

2 Defining and navigating 'intense and complex' work

Losing Yourself by Kerry Watt

Although there are clear ethical reasons for counsellors to remain vigilant in their practice and to foster self-awareness, it is important to consider how this can work in the counselling room. You may already be confident in incorporating this into your practice or, alternatively, you may perceive this as adding an extra burden on an already demanding workload. Covey (1989) uses a good analogy here of the woodcutter who is too busy chopping wood to pause to sharpen his axe and get the job done more effectively. Particularly when carrying out emotionally challenging work with conflict, loss and trauma, it may feel overwhelming to take time to explore your feelings. It can help to take a moment to contemplate what type of work you would consider to be 'intense and complex' so that you can be aware in advance of areas where you may need to stay particularly attuned.

Pause for thought 7.2

Briefly consider whether you find it draining working with particular clients or client groups, perhaps due to your own past experiences. Do you feel preoccupied by thoughts of them outside of the session? Do you experience any physical signs of stress (e.g. headaches, stomach problems, exhaustion) when working with particular clients?

Do you feel that you have professional and personal support in place? Would you feel confident referring those clients on to another practitioner?

2.1 Risks involved in emotionally challenging work

The stress that may be experienced by some professionals working in the mental health field has been an emergent issue for decades, with many studies showing that this can lead to emotional exhaustion and loneliness (Luther *et al.*, 2017; Posluns and Gall, 2020). Human suffering is universal, and common events such as financial stress, parenthood, illness, relationship breakdown, and loss can add an extra strain on counsellors, who may have been conditioned to put their feelings to one side in the therapy room.

Counsellors may be faced with ethical dilemmas about continuing to see a client at the expense of their own feelings. As an example, the experience of parenthood could influence the therapeutic relationship in a multitude of ways, according to Bienen (1990). This could develop from the counsellor or client experiencing a pregnancy or loss of pregnancy, and any resulting transference and/or countertransference. Counsellors may also feel physically and emotionally torn between the demands of pregnancy or their newborn baby and the needs of their clients, and family members could feel resentful of the energy that the therapist is giving to their clients; all of which can result in barriers to a successful therapeutic relationship.

The risks of working with complexity are not just limited to the emotional lives of counsellors. Research has shown that counsellors may be at increased risk of emotional exhaustion by systemic factors (such as ageism, racism or sexism, etc.) and organisational factors including high caseloads, challenging client issues, lack of support or supervision, a stressful work environment or a lack of resources (Green *et al.*, 2014; Thompson, Amatea and Thompson, 2014). In addition, emotional isolation and loneliness could be considered an occupational hazard, particularly by those working in private practice (Rokach and Sha'ked, 2013).

The potential risks for counsellors are typically described using four key terms: burnout, compassion fatigue, vicarious trauma and secondary traumatic stress (Maslach and Jackson, 1981; Rothschild, 2023) (see Table 7.1). These terms are commonly used interchangeably in the literature and can coexist in practice.

In 2023, a US-based study involving 550 mental health therapists found that 52% had experienced burnout (Canady, 2023). Factors that contributed to this burnout were: administrative burdens (55%), compassion fatigue (54%), low pay (44%), severity and complexity of their clients' needs (33%), high caseload (25%) and poor work–life balance (60%). The study found that around 29% of therapists were considering leaving the field due to these demands.

Table 7.1 Negative effects of stress on the counsellor

Stress impact	Description	Symptoms
Burnout	A state of emotional, mental and physical exhaustion, resulting from prolonged and intense stress associated with the demands of counselling.	Emotional exhaustion: feeling drained and emotionally depleted due to the intense emotional experiences of clients.
		Depersonalisation: feelings of cynicism, detachment or a sense of distance from clients. May start to view clients more as problems or cases than as individuals with unique needs.
		Physical symptoms: headaches, fatigue, sleep disturbances and other stress-related health issues.
		Reduced personal accomplishment and job satisfaction: decreased sense of achievement and efficacy.
Compassion fatigue	Emotional exhaustion or numbness that can result from constant exposure to the suffering and trauma of others.	Feelings of burnout, emotional numbness and a reduced ability to empathise. May experience a sense of hopelessness, guilt and/or inadequacy. Difficulty maintaining a healthy work–life balance.
Vicarious trauma Secondary traumatic stress	Negative emotional and psychological reactions that can occur following exposure to the trauma experiences of others.	Vicarious trauma: may over-empathise with their client's experiences, as if happening to them directly or someone close to them. Leads to intrusive thoughts, emotional numbing or a sense of powerlessness.
		Secondary traumatic stress: may experience actual symptoms of traumatic stress, including nightmares and flashbacks.

Counsellors may also encounter challenges in dealing with client behaviour, which can have an impact on their well-being. Clients may not feel at ease when entering therapy, and emotions may run high during the sessions. When working with clients who are guarded or angry, it is understandable that counsellors might feel vulnerable and unsafe, but this may lead them to question their competence in the role and their ability to work with risk.

There may be other aspects of a client's behaviour that at first seem benign, but end up being problematic for the therapist. Rokach and Boulazreg (2022) suggest that clients' ambivalent behaviours – like arriving late, talking about the weather rather than themselves and making false assurances that they are well – can be problematic as they are difficult to deal with directly. Counsellors may be concerned that a client will drop out or, worse, make a complaint against them. Interestingly, experiencing therapist burnout is itself considered a risk factor for ethical misconduct (Norcross and VandenBos, 2018).

According to Kottler (2022), some risk factors for burnout might include:

- a perceived lack of control over job responsibilities
- time pressures; feeling unappreciated and underpaid
- experiencing discrimination, microaggressions and marginalisation
- feeling inadequately supported by your supervisor/organisation
- a personal history of mental health difficulties/trauma
- current challenges in your personal life
- feeling physically unwell
- an imbalance between work and personal life
- maladaptive coping strategies such as an over-reliance on food, substance abuse, or behaviours that could lead to negative physical or mental health outcomes
- perfectionist tendencies and unrealistic expectations about the role.

Pause for thought 7.3

Do you feel any of these risk factors might apply to you? Do they make you more vulnerable to experiencing burnout?

You may have recognised some of these risk factors, or perhaps you have experienced burnout at some point during your career; it is worth noting, however, that not all counsellors will find that these factors make them more susceptible to burnout. In fact, as discussed earlier, some counsellors could argue that these factors increase their skills in empathy. Nevertheless, due to the multifaceted nature of client work and the reality of how life satisfaction in counsellors tends to ebb and flow, it would appear prudent to develop an early warning system to recognise initial symptoms of emotional exhaustion or secondary trauma as they emerge. The next section will explore how you can maintain your emotional fitness while working as a counsellor.

3 Maintaining emotional fitness

self-care

The practice of taking an active role in protecting and maintaining one's own well-being, particularly during periods of stress.

Having considered some of the risk factors that can lead to burnout, in this section you will explore how to maintain equilibrium when working with complexity. Practicing **self-care** is an essential and ethical part of the role, and this is reflected in the codes of practice used by professional bodies in the field. In its *Ethical Framework*, the British Association for Counselling and Psychotherapy (BACP), one of the prominent professional bodies for counselling in the UK, defines self-care in Article 91 as:

(a) taking precautions to protect our own physical safety

(b) monitoring and maintaining our own psychological and physical health, particularly that we are sufficiently resilient and resourceful to undertake our work in ways that satisfy professional standards

(c) seeking professional support and services as the need arises

(d) keeping a healthy balance between our work and other aspects of life.

(BACP, 2018)

Although research has found that practising self-care can heighten the therapist's insight into their client's problems and lead to more efficacious therapy (Malinowski, 2014), and also that neglect of self-care in therapists can cause occupational stress, there may be a stigma around prioritising self-care in the profession (Norcross and VandenBos, 2018). Kottler (2022) expresses frustrations around a superficial idea of self-care, influenced by the growing self-help movement. He suggests the following reasons for why therapists might struggle to commit to meaningful and regular self-care habits:

- They expect instant relief.
- They have unrealistic expectations and impossible goals.
- Self-care requires honest and thorough acknowledgement of difficulties.
- Self-care implies something is broken.
- There may be deeper issues to address.
- Ambivalence (there can be some gains in remaining stuck).
- There may be systemic and contextual issues limiting time and opportunity.
- There can be limits to the effectiveness of self-help and further support may be required.

Pause for thought 7.4

What is your relationship with self-care? To what degree do you feel your self-care needs are met?

Understanding your own emotions involves developing self-awareness, recognising and interpreting your feelings, and being able to manage them effectively. This process involves developing a keen sense of self, which will be influenced by your skills and experience, and may therefore be more challenging in the early years of your counselling practice. Dorociak, Rupert and Zahniser (2017) found that more experienced therapists tend to engage in more self-care behaviours and report less stress than those who are early in their career. They also reported that more experienced therapists noted greater career satisfaction and were less likely to feel overwhelmed with managing their work demands.

Norcross and VandenBos (2018) found that, during their working day, therapists tended to apply principles of self-care to their clients, whereas at home they did not apply these theories to themselves. Some research also found that self-care can work in a preventative way to manage stress and avoid negative outcomes, and can also promote good outcomes by supporting flourishing and life satisfaction in therapists (Rupert and Dorociak, 2019).

The next section will look at particularly useful self-care strategies. The need to use such strategies is expressed by Satir (2000, p. 25), through her delightful analogy comparing therapists to musical instruments: 'how it is made, how it is cared for, its fine tuning, and the ability, experience, sensitivity, and creativity of the player will determine how the music will sound'. If you would expect musicians to care for their instruments in order to create beautiful music, logically you should also see it as a priority to nurture and care for yourself in order to maintain the most harmonious interactions with clients. To explore this further, using both reflective and reflexive practice, it is helpful to consider Schön's (1983) distinction between the different ways that therapists might implement self-care: reflection on action (retrospectively reviewing your emotions and behaviour) and reflection in action (attending to your physical and emotional responses in the moment) – these concepts were first introduced in Chapter 5, Section 3.

3.1 Reflection on action

Research has revealed a number of strategies that can be employed outside of the counselling session to build a more self-compassionate approach to counselling work (many of the issues discussed so far in this chapter would fall into this category). These are handled below, in turn.

Personal therapy and supervision are highly important. A report by Ziede and Norcross (2024) found that over 90% of therapists agree that having another person hold you accountable and challenge your thinking is an excellent way to strengthen and reinvigorate your work. Bennett-Levy (2019) argues that personal therapy influences therapist characteristics, claiming that there is a correspondence between the characteristics of effective therapists and what therapists report from personal therapy; however, any causal link is disputed by Moe and Thimm (2021) in their systematic review of the literature. Interestingly, Norcross *et al.* (2008) reported that cognitive behavioural therapists and academics were less likely to seek personal therapy, and also that they were more likely to be sceptical about how effective personal therapy can be. This would suggest that it may also be important to question whether you experience any conflict between your personal philosophy on life and your theoretical stance as a practitioner. (The benefits of taking a reflexive approach in supervision will be discussed further in Chapter 8.)

It is also important to have *realistic expectations*. Recognise the inevitability of failure and disappointment in the role. Working with complexity may lead to situations where you feel helpless. Kottler (2022, p. 133) suggests that failures are 'critical to our continued development – if, that is, we are willing to acknowledge them'. Accept that peaks and troughs in the role are normal and will ultimately help you to develop greater flexibility, resilience and humility. Being compassionate towards yourself during challenging moments and remembering how your personal values and beliefs, in addition to cultural and societal factors, may be influencing your emotional responses can help to build resilience in the role.

There is also value in recognising the intricate link between *physical health* and emotional well-being (Hernandez *et al.*, 2018), and adopting measures to nurture both of these aspects of yourself. Consider your own relationship with your body, and how you understand and connect with what it needs. This might include needs in relation to movement, sleep, nutrition or rest.

As previously noted, the nature of counselling work often evokes a sense of isolation. Seeking *social support* from trusted individuals – including friends, family or colleagues – regarding your emotional experiences can offer much solace during difficult periods. Additionally, mentors and professional networks can play a valuable role in this context.

Setting boundaries is an essential skill which evolves with experience and may differ between individuals and counselling modalities. Balancing client needs with your personal well-being can pose challenges, particularly in the context of time management and financial self-care. Feeling pressured to accept clients may create a conflict between the client's needs and your own. In the current economic climate, financial concerns may impact well-being. If you charge for sessions, you may question whether the amount accurately reflects the service you are providing and the costs that you incur. It is also imperative to consider whether you feel safe in your workplace, as this may have an impact on the hours and clients you feel comfortable working with. If working remotely from home, this may introduce a unique challenge of blending roles, blurring the boundaries between family or personal life and professional responsibilities.

Establishing regular, distinct periods of *time out* – time away from the counselling room to do whatever you enjoy – can be a very effective way of balancing and nourishing important activities in your life. Kottler (2022) suggests that travel can be transformative and helps individuals to face fears and become more resilient, as well as regaining perspective on what is important. Engaging in creative pursuits can also serve as a rejuvenating escape.

Keeping a journal can also be very effective. Liz Cox, a coach, advocates the use of reflective writing to boost personal and professional development (Cox, 2017). Setting aside time to write things down offers an opportunity to consider your thoughts, feelings and reactions to various situations, by reading over your words and observing any patterns or interesting insights.

Exploring your *spirituality*, if this is important to you, may help you gain a deeper sense of purpose. This can play a significant role in self-care and offer sanctuary for counsellors when they are overwhelmed by personal or professional suffering (Sori, Biank and Helmeke, 2012). Consider what brings meaning and enjoyment to your role as a counsellor. Contemplating on your motivations for becoming a counsellor can be a helpful way of tuning in to the meaning and purpose of your role.

3.2 Reflection in action

Reflection in action is a way of practising self-care for moments in the counselling room that might come out of nowhere, and where your thoughts and emotions may feel slightly out of your control. In Chapter 6 you learnt about how to work with some of these unconscious processes. Perhaps a client has disclosed some information or behaved in a way that has left you with a strong emotional response, and you begin to feel signs of physical stress. In the case example with Kayden and Grace in Chapter 5, for instance, you saw how the counsellor and client had different interpretations of what was happening in the therapy room, and the counsellor felt tension rising in her chest. Maybe you suggested something to your client which has made them feel angry and you, in turn, misunderstood. The following strategies have been found to be helpful for counsellor self-care when you are in the room with your client and require some immediate reflexive action in order to work through an issue.

Practicing *mindful self-awareness* during sessions with traumatised clients has been found by a growing body of research to lower rates of vicarious trauma and compassion fatigue in therapists (Thompson, Amatea and Thompson, 2014). In order to work mindfully and stay present in the moment, you could ask yourself: 'How am I feeling now? What's happening in my body right now? How's my breathing?' Regularly check in with your emotions throughout the day. Try to notice any shifts in your emotional state and explore the reasons behind those changes without judgment. You may want to explore whether you are moving out of your 'window of tolerance', or the zone in which you are best able to manage stress, process information and engage in meaningful interactions (Siegel, 1999). Mindful breathing and meditation can help you observe your emotional experiences.

It is important to address *physiological responses to stress*, in part by understanding the connection between physical and emotional health and taking steps to maintain a balance between them, in turn becoming more embodied in your approach. Consider when you are experiencing physical signs of hyperarousal, such as an increased heart rate or muscular tension (e.g. clenching your fists). It is good practice to familiarise yourself with your own autonomic system states and compare what happens within your body when you feel calm, compared to when you are feeling anxious or upset. This way, you will know the signs to look out for. You might also explore whether you are mirroring any of your client's physical states, and think about why this might be.

Cultivate *in-the-moment empathy*. When feeling sudden strong emotions, it can be very helpful to pause and practise empathy by trying to understand your client's viewpoint and emotions. Reflect on how you might feel in a similar situation. As mentioned in Table 7.1, it is possible to over-empathise with clients, which can pose risks to both the therapist and the client (Rothschild, 2023). You might also practise empathy and forgiveness towards yourself by remembering that making missteps in the counselling room is normal and to be expected.

Develop your *internal supervisor*, which is an internalised, mental representation of a supervisor that may help to guide you (this concept is explored in more detail in Chapter 8). An internal supervisor can be useful when you don't have immediate access to external supervision, or when you are faced with on-the-spot decisions during client sessions. You may use this internal 'voice' to identify the situations that trigger specific emotions for you, and notice recurring emotional patterns in your reactions to certain events or people. This can also help you to expand your emotional vocabulary by labelling and describing your feelings. The aim is to use your own knowledge to help yourself in the same way that you help your clients.

Try to *notice boredom*, for example when time appears to have slowed down and you are finding it difficult to stay present with your client. Explore the reasons for this, particularly whether it might be to do with your client or something happening internally with yourself.

Finally, practise *self-compassion in the moment*. Accept that you are not unique in your feelings, and that experiencing a range of positive and negative emotions in therapy is normal and offers an opportunity to grow into a more experienced counsellor.

Conclusion

This chapter has explored how the emotional complexity of counselling impacts the counsellor and how we can recognise the signs of burnout, compassion fatigue, vicarious trauma and secondary traumatic stress. This chapter has also presented a range of self-care techniques – both external to and at the point of counselling – for maintaining the emotional fitness and motivation required to carry out meaningful and rewarding counselling work.

Further reading

- The following article offers a clear summary of the research into self-care:

  Posluns, K. and Gall, T.L. (2020) 'Dear mental health practitioners, take care of yourselves: a literature review on self-care', *International Journal for the Advancement of Counselling*, 42(1), pp. 1–20. Available at: https://doi.org/10.1007/s10447-019-09382-w

- The following book offers exercises on how to help clients while maintaining your own self-care:

  Rothschild, B. (2023) *Help for the helper: preventing compassion fatigue and vicarious trauma in an ever-changing world*. 2nd edn. New York: W.W. Norton & Co.

References

BACP (2018) *Ethical framework for the counselling professions*. Available at: www.bacp.co.uk/events-and-resources/ethics-and-standards/ethical-framework-for-the-counselling-professions (Accessed: 1 March 2024).

BACP (2023) *2022–2023 workforce mapping survey*. Available at: www.bacp.co.uk/about-us/about-bacp/6-march-2022-2023-workforce-mapping-survey (Accessed: 26 September 2024).

Barnett, M. (2007) 'What brings you here? An exploration of the unconscious motivations of those who choose to train and work as psychotherapists and counsellors', *Psychodynamic Practice*, 13(3), pp. 257–274. Available at: https://doi.org/10.1080/14753630701455796

Bennett-Levy, J. (2019) 'Why therapists should walk the talk: the theoretical and empirical case for personal practice in therapist training and professional development', *Journal of Behavior Therapy and Experimental Psychiatry*, 62, pp. 133–145. Available at: https://doi.org/10.1016/j.jbtep.2018.08.004

Bienen, M. (1990) 'The pregnant therapist: countertransference dilemmas and willingness to explore transference material', *Psychotherapy: Theory, Research, Practice, Training*, 27(4), pp. 607–612. Available at: https://doi.org/10.1037/0033-3204.27.4.607

Canady, V.A. (2023) 'More than half of mental health therapists experience burnout', *Mental Health Weekly*, 33(39), pp. 5–6. Available at: https://doi.org/10.1002/mhw.33812

Covey, S.R. (1989) *The 7 Habits of Highly Effective People*. London: Simon and Schuster.

Cox, L. (2017) 'I write, therefore I think', *Therapy Today*, 28(4). Available at: https://www.bacp.co.uk/bacp-journals/therapy-today/2017/may-2017/i-write-therefore-i-think/ (Accessed: 26 August 2024).

Dorociak, K.E., Rupert, P.A. and Zahniser, E. (2017) 'Work life, well-being, and self-care across the professional lifespan of psychologists', *Professional Psychology: Research and Practice*, 48(6), pp. 429–437. Available at: https://doi.org/10.1037/pro0000160

Ellis, A. (2003) 'How to deal with your most difficult client – you', *Journal of Rational-Emotive and Cognitive-Behavior Therapy*, 21(3–4), pp. 203–213. Available at: https://doi.org/10.1023/a:1025885911410

Erikson, E.H. (1968) *Identity: youth and crisis*. New York, NY: Norton

Green, A.E., Albanese, B.J., Shapiro, N.M. and Aarons, G.A. (2014) 'The roles of individual and organizational factors in burnout among community-based mental health service providers', *Psychological Services*, 11(1), p. 41–49. Available at: https://doi.org/10.1037/a0035299

Hernandez, R., Bassett, S.M., Boughton, S.W., Schuette, S.A., Shiu, E.W. and Moskowitz, J.T. (2018) 'Psychological well-being and physical health: associations, mechanisms, and future directions', *Emotion Review*, 10(1), pp. 18–29. Available at: https://doi.org/10.1177/1754073917697824

Jung, C. (1963) *Memories, dreams, reflections*. Glasgow: Random House.

Kottler, J.A. (2022) *On being a therapist*. Oxford: Oxford University Press.

Luther, L., Gearhart, T., Fukui, S., Morse, G., Rollins, A.L. and Salyers, M.P. (2017) 'Working overtime in community mental health: associations with clinician burnout and perceived quality of care', *Psychiatric Rehabilitation Journal*, 40(2), pp. 252–259. Available at: https://doi.org/10.1037/prj0000234

Malinowski, A. (2014) *Self-care for the mental health practitioner: the theory, research and practice of preventing and addressing the occupational hazards of the profession*. London: Jessica Kingsley Publishers.

Maslach, C. and Jackson, S.E. (1981) 'The measurement of experienced burnout', *Journal of Organizational Behavior*, 2(2), pp. 99–113. Available at: https://doi.org/10.1002/job.4030020205

McBeath, A. (2019) 'The motivations of psychotherapists: an in-depth survey', *Counselling and Psychotherapy Research*, 19(4), pp. 377–387. Available at: https://doi.org/10.1002/capr.12225

Moe, F.D. and Thimm, J. (2021) 'Personal therapy and the personal therapist', *Nordic Psychology*, 73(1), pp. 3–28. Available at: https://doi.org/10.1080/19012276.2020.1762713

Norcross, J.C., Bike, D.H., Evans, K.L. and Schatz, D.M. (2008) 'Psychotherapists who abstain from personal therapy: do they practice what they preach?', *Journal of Clinical Psychology*, 64(12), pp. 1368–1376. Available at: https://doi.org/10.1002/jclp.20523

Norcross, J.C. and VandenBos, G.R. (2018) *Leaving it at the office: a guide to psychotherapist self-care*. 2nd edn. New York: Guilford Press.

Posluns, K. and Gall, T.L. (2020) 'Dear mental health practitioners, take care of yourselves: a literature review on self-care', *International Journal for the Advancement of Counselling*, 42(1), pp. 1–20. Available at: https://doi.org/10.1007/s10447-019-09382-w

Rokach, A. and Boulazreg, S. (2022) 'The COVID-19 era: how therapists can diminish burnout symptoms through self-care', *Current Psychology*, 41(8), pp. 5660–5677. Available at: https://doi.org/10.1007/s12144-020-01149-6

Rokach, A. and Sha'ked, A. (2013) *Together and lonely: loneliness in intimate relationships – causes and coping*. New York, NY: Nova Science Publishers.

Rothschild, B. (2023) *Help for the helper: preventing compassion fatigue and vicarious trauma in an ever-changing world*. 2nd edn. New York: W.W. Norton & Co.

Rupert, P.A. and Dorociak, K.E. (2019) 'Self-care, stress, and well-being among practicing psychologists', *Professional Psychology: Research and Practice*, 50(5), pp. 343–350. Available at: http://doi.org/10.1037/pro0000251

Satir, V. (2000) 'The therapist's story', in M. Baldwin (ed.) *The use of self in therapy*. 2nd edn. New York, NY: The Haworth Press, pp. 17–29.

Schön, D. (1983) *The reflective practitioner: how professionals think in action*. New York, NY: Basic Books.

SCoPEd Framework (2022), collaboratively developed by Association of Christian Counsellors (ACC), British Association for Counselling and Psychotherapy (BACP), British Psychoanalytic Council (BPC), Human Givens Institute (HGI), National Counselling and Psychotherapy Society (NCPS) and United Kingdom Council for Psychotherapy (UKCP). Available at: https://www.bacp.co.uk/about-us/advancing-the-profession/scoped/scoped-framework (Accessed: 12 June 2024).

Siegel, D.J. (1999) *The developing mind: toward a neurobiology of interpersonal experience*. New York, NY: Guilford Press.

Sori, C.F., Biank, N. and Helmeke, K.B. (2012) 'Spiritual self-care of the therapist', in K.B. Helmeke and C.F. Sori (eds) *The therapist's notebook for integrating spirituality in counseling: homework, handouts, and activities for use in psychotherapy.* London: Routledge, pp. 3–18.

Thompson, I., Amatea, E. and Thompson, E. (2014) 'Personal and contextual predictors of mental health counselors' compassion fatigue and burnout', *Journal of Mental Health Counseling*, 36(1), pp. 58–77. Available at: https://doi.org/10.17744/mehc.36.1.p61m73373m4617r3

Wampold, B.E. and Imel, Z.E. (2015) *The great psychotherapy debate: the evidence for what makes psychotherapy work.* 2nd edn. New York: Routledge.

Ziede, J.S. and Norcross, J.C. (2024) 'Personal therapy and self-care in the making of psychologists', in A. Rokach (ed.) *Psychologists in making: life lessons and observations from practicing psychologists.* Abingdon: Routledge, pp. 53–86.

Chapter 8

Using reflexivity in supervision

Trudi Macagnino

Contents

Introduction

Comforting Notebook by Kathleen Kettles

Supervision is considered essential for ensuring good practice throughout your professional life. It allows you to reflect, and it also supports you to work safely, ethically and effectively while maintaining the resilience you need as a therapist. The British Association for Counselling and Psychotherapy (BACP) defines supervision as:

> a specialised form of professional mentoring provided for practitioners responsible for undertaking challenging work with people. Supervision is provided to ensure standards, enhance quality, stimulate creativity and support the sustainability and resilience of the work being undertaken.
>
> *(BACP, 2020)*

Supervision has been described as having three functions (Proctor, 1988):

- *normative*, which deals with professional, ethical and legal issues
- *formative*, which helps to develop knowledge and skills
- *restorative*, which deals with the emotional impact of the work.

Early definitions tended to see the process as one where an expert supervisor imparted knowledge to a less knowledgeable supervisee. More relational models have challenged this conception and instead frame supervision as collaborative, with supervisor and supervisee each bringing their own understanding and reflections, with the aim of facilitating clients' therapy (McNamee, 2021).

As emphasised in previous chapters, supervision is an essential part of reflexive practice, particularly in relation to the themes of self-care, improving your practice and working with unconscious material. This chapter is about using supervision effectively and adapting it as your needs evolve and change. You will be encouraged to take a reflexive and active role in your own supervision by asking questions about yourself, your practice, your clients and the relational aspects of your supervision.

This chapter contributes towards achieving the **SCoPEd competency 5.6.B**:

Ability to review and evaluate supervision arrangements and take responsibility for adapting supervision to the evolving and changing requirements of ongoing practice.

(SCoPEd Framework, 2022, p. 31)

This chapter aims to:

- help you identify how you are developing as a counsellor and relate it to your supervision needs

- consider how to prepare effectively for supervision

- outline how to evaluate supervision time to assess how well it meets your needs

- explore the advantages and disadvantages of peer supervision

- guide you to develop your own 'internal supervisor'.

1 Supervision and your developmental journey

Pause for thought 8.1

Complete this sentence with as many possible answers as are relevant to you:

'I experience supervision as ...'

You may notice that your experience of supervision has changed over time. When thinking about what you need from supervision, it may be helpful to consider your developmental stage as a therapist within the various contexts you are working. If you are a trainee, you will need different things compared to someone with several years of counselling, training and supervision experience. Your relationship with your supervisor may vary as a result.

One well-known and empirically supported model which links therapists' supervision needs with their level of development was developed by Stoltenberg and McNeill (2010). They describe four levels of progressive therapist development: Level 1, 2, 3 and 3i ('i' stands for integrated).

Each level is based on how a practitioner functions across the following seven domains of practice:

- *Therapeutic intervention*, which is dependent on theoretical modality (e.g. mirroring, interpretation, reframing, etc.).
- *Assessment*, which may incorporate use of assessment tools (covered in Part 3 of this book).
- *Diagnosis and/or formulation*, which could include use of DSM/ICD if appropriate (these systems are covered further in Chapter 9).
- *Diversity matters* (covered in Part 1 of this book).
- *Theoretical understanding* across modalities.
- *Treatment plans and goals*, which are dependent on modality and context.
- *Professional ethics* and how they are incorporated into practice.

Table 8.1 describes the key features of Stoltenberg and McNeill's (2010) development levels and how these relate to supervision needs.

Table 8.1 Developmental stages and supervision needs

Level	Key features	Supervision needs
1	Anxious about competence and performance	Validation and encouragement to build confidence
	Supervisor seen as role model/expert	Direct guidance and advice on how to work with client
	Focused on technique and theory rather than process	Help linking theory and practice
	Difficulty developing treatment plans and goals	
	Diversity issues may be overlooked	
2	Comfortable with a range of interventions and approaches	Broadening understanding of different conceptualisations and approaches
	More independent	
	More focused on client's process and experience	Help in understanding when progress is not being made with client
	Deeper empathy and understanding	Making sense of emotional experiences in sessions
	Possible overwhelm, overidentification with client and/or countertransference reactions	Exploration of individual differences
	Awareness of socio-cultural factors	Help with ethical dilemmas
	Treatment plans may still be vague	
	May find ethical and boundary issues difficult	
3	Autonomous and confident	Collegiate relationship (consultation or mentoring)
	Understands own strengths/weaknesses	Exploration of alternative perspectives
	Skills flow naturally and automatically	Identification of specific areas requiring further development
	Can handle unexpected situations in sessions	Exploration of career and professional progression
	Moves between intense presence with client and reflection	
	Integrates empathic attunement with understanding of socio-cultural factors	
	Implements ethical guidelines	

3i	As for Level 3, plus:	As for Level 3, plus:
	Moves across different areas of practice smoothly and easily	Personal and professional goals dictate areas of focus
	Monitors impact of personal life on performance	

(Based on Stoltenberg and McNeill, 2010)

You may be functioning at different levels of development in each of the domains and when working in different contexts. For instance, you may be functioning at Level 3 in most domains when working with individual clients but at Level 1 when working with couples. Or you may be very practised at doing assessments, therefore functioning at Level 3 in that domain, but need to develop in the area of establishing treatment plans. If you are a trainee, you are likely to be at Level 1 across nearly all domains. Also, stressful life events can lead to temporary regression to a lower level.

Of course, the boundaries between levels are not always clear-cut and there can be overlap. Someone functioning at the upper end of Level 1 may be very similar in practice to someone functioning at the lower end of Level 2.

Although taking a developmental perspective can be helpful in identifying specific supervision needs, a good **supervisory alliance** that includes warmth, acceptance, respect, understanding and trust is important whatever your level of development. The supervisory relationship is discussed later in the chapter.

supervisory alliance
Similar to the therapeutic alliance between therapist and client, this is composed of a bond between supervisor and supervisee, who collaboratively agree the goals and tasks of supervision.

2 Getting the most out of your supervision

Your supervision time is precious, so it is important to get the most out of it. You will need to take responsibility for getting the supervision you want and need. Who you have supervision with, the practical arrangements, what you talk about, preparation and reflection are all key considerations for effective supervision.

2.1 Choosing a supervisor

The relationship with your supervisor is an important one and it often becomes a long-term commitment, so it is worth taking time to carefully choose your supervisor if you are in a position to do so. As already discussed, your supervision needs are likely to change as you develop your practice, so it is worth revisiting your arrangements periodically. There are several factors you could consider when making this choice:

- What modality/philosophy would you like your supervisor to work within? Would you prefer this to be the same as your own, or different to it?
- Do you need a supervisor with a specific specialism, such as addiction, sexual abuse or working with children?
- How much experience would you like them to have?
- Are any identity considerations important? For example, do you want to work with a supervisor with a particular ethnicity? Do you have accessibility needs? Is their gender or sexual orientation important to you?
- Are there practical considerations? If you are in private practice, how much can you afford? How far can you travel? Do you prefer online supervision?

Once you have arranged your supervision, the next step is to think about what you will discuss in your sessions.

2.2 What to talk about in supervision

Navigating supervision sessions can sometimes feel confusing

A wide range of topics can be discussed in supervision. These can include:

- managing professional and ethical dilemmas, and safeguarding
- setting up and maintaining a practice (premises, marketing, note taking and records, financial planning, etc.)
- managing caseloads (e.g. getting more clients, reducing clients, handling a mix of client issues)
- managing your time
- examining the therapeutic relationship with particular clients
- seeking an alternative viewpoint, or looking for your biases/filters
- developing skills (e.g. learning new techniques and interventions)
- building theoretical knowledge
- integrating theory and practice
- examining the supervisory relationship (style, level of satisfaction, cultural differences, etc.)
- exploring organisational issues, tensions and conflicts
- building confidence through validation and affirmation
- considering the impact of personal life on client work
- gaining support for overwhelm, stress or burnout
- considering training needs, interests and overall career development.

Pause for thought 8.2

Which topics do you regularly take to supervision? Are there particular topics or clients that do not get discussed? If there are, why is that? Are there things that you would never tell your supervisor? What do you imagine would happen if you did?

You may be unsure about what is important, relevant or appropriate to discuss in supervision. However, there may be other barriers to using supervision to its fullest extent. Research by Ladany *et al.* (1996) has shown that nondisclosure in supervision is very common, especially among trainees, and particularly if their supervisor formally assesses them. Non-disclosure can lead supervisees to feeling frustrated, disappointed, embarrassed, guilty and less confident, and it can have a negative impact on client work.

The results of the Ladany *et al.* (1996) study offer several examples of information commonly not shared in supervision, including:

- perceived clinical 'mistakes', such as getting names wrong, forgetting a session or mistiming an intervention
- challenges in managing boundaries, for example over-running sessions and issues with getting clients to complete payments
- sexual attraction towards a client
- positive or negative reactions to a client, including hateful or discriminatory thoughts, or wanting to 'rescue' them
- positive or negative reactions to supervisor, including feeling angry, unsupported or envious, or idealising (exaggerating positive qualities) them
- personal issues, for example bereavement, divorce, physical and mental health, and finances.

The choice to hold back certain information or experiences may be intentional or unintentional, possibly even unconscious. These omissions will be related to your relationship with your client(s) and to your supervisor, or specific to you personally. Recognising your blocks is an important step towards getting the most out of supervision for you and your clients.

You may have had a negative experience of supervision in the past which has led you to be wary. Conversely, you may have had a very positive experience with a previous supervisor and believe no one else will be as good. As discussed in Chapter 6, you may fear being judged by your supervisor. You may feel embarrassed or ashamed about something. You may want to appear competent or want to avoid confrontation. You may have concerns about qualifying or career progression. You may even perceive your supervisor to be inadequate or unable to help. These concerns are very common, and they can lead us to become defensive in supervision.

The following case illustration is loosely based on a real-life example of difficulty in discussing an issue in supervision; the issue in this case is sexual attraction (erotic transference) between the client and the therapist (note that names have been changed for anonymity).

Case example: Chris and the frothy coffee

Chris has been a therapist for two years when he starts working with Diane, who has been having relationship difficulties. Diane has no problem attracting boyfriends, but after about 12 months into each relationship she starts losing interest in them sexually. She admits to then engaging in promiscuous sexual behaviour. During their sessions, Chris explores her early attachment relationships and how these might be relevant, and this seems productive. After a few weeks, Diane begins to arrive for her sessions with a takeaway coffee for them both. Although Chris feels uncomfortable, he accepts the coffee each time, thanking Diane, and they drink their coffees together.

Although they speak about Diane regularly, Chris does not share this with his supervisor. He feels embarrassed, like he is doing something 'wrong' by accepting the coffee. He imagines his supervisor would judge him even though they have a good working alliance. As time goes on, Chris feels increasingly uncomfortable withholding this from his supervisor and eventually tells her. His supervisor helps him safely explore the situation in a supportive and gentle way, referring to Diane as Miss Frothy Coffee. This dispels much of Chris' embarrassment, and they are able to discuss more seriously the erotic transference occurring in the therapeutic relationship. Chris is then able to bring this into the work, and help Diane understand that her seduction is an attempt to achieve emotional closeness.

A significant disclosure in supervision can often lead to a turning point or deepening of the supervisory relationship, particularly when the supervisor meets the disclosure with validation and careful exploration of the supervisee's feelings. The supervisor should create a safe space for you to share personal or difficult information in the interest of supporting your client work. You will return to the supervisory relationship in Section 3.

2.3 Preparing for your session

> The key to getting the most out of supervision is reflection before, during and after a session.
>
> *(van Ooijen, 2021, p. 53)*

How you prepare for supervision will depend to some extent on your modality, the context you work in and your supervision arrangement (individual, group or peer-to-peer). You may be required to bring tangible evidence of your work, such as audio/visual extracts, session notes, self-ratings of sessions, and so on. Taking time to look over your client notes is a good place to start. Table 8.2 contains some suggestions of reflective questions for you to consider.

Table 8.2 Reflective questions for supervision

Reflective stage	Self-directed questions
Before supervision	What's on my mind?
	What/who do I need to talk about?
	What am I anxious about bringing? Why?
	What are my intentions for this session?
	What outcome am I looking for?
During supervision	Does my supervisor know why I am bringing this issue?
	How long do I want to spend on it?
	Am I getting what I need?
	Am I avoiding sharing something?
After supervision	What did I gain from the session?
	What did I learn about myself/my client(s)?
	How will I use what I have learnt?
	What actions do I need to take?
	Is there anything I want to revisit next time?

Irrespective of your theoretical modality, preparation and reflection are important; they ensure that you get the most out of your supervision. Another important factor to attend to in supervision is something called parallel process.

2.4 Parallel process in supervision

Parallel process has traditionally been understood as an unconscious reenactment – in supervision, by the supervisee – of a dynamic that is occurring in client work; often, this dynamic is one which has been making the work difficult. More recently, the process is understood as a two-way activity that involves both the supervisee's and the supervisor's unconscious enactments (Sarnat, 2019). The contexts of therapy and supervision are very similar: both involve a helping aspect; both work with powerful emotional content; and both involve the use of self. It is, therefore, not surprising that interpersonal patterns of relating can be readily transmitted from one context to the other.

It is the supervisor who is likely to notice and suggest that a parallel process may be happening. Exploring this in supervision can be extremely useful for providing insight into unconscious dynamics in the therapeutic relationship that may otherwise go unnoticed. It also provides the opportunity for learning therapeutic techniques, as the supervisor works with the dynamic in the present and in the context of the supervisory relationship. The supervisee can then take this experiential learning into their work with the client.

In the following case example, I recount a personal experience of parallel process with one of my supervisees, 'Andy' (a pseudonym and further detail changes have been applied).

parallel process

Refers to the way in which dynamics operating in one relationship (e.g. between therapist and client) are mirrored in another relationship (e.g. between therapist and supervisor).

Case example: parallel process between Andy and myself

Andy presented a client to me in supervision that he found difficult to work with. He reported that the client talked a lot in their sessions, but Andy was unclear what the client really wanted from therapy. Andy gave me lots of detail about his client's history and current life. Initially, I listened carefully to all of the details but eventually found myself losing interest and drifting off. Was this a parallel process? Rather than continuing to listen, I decided to share my experience with Andy:

'Let's pause for a minute. I hear there is a lot of story here, but I don't feel connected to you or your client. Take a breath. What are you feeling in relation to this client?'

Andy then told me that he felt there was a barrier between them. We explored the way in which the client's continual talking was part of the barrier and that it resulted in Andy retreating and becoming passive, listening while not really being present. My pausing enabled us both to be present again for the client in the supervision session. Andy was then able to similarly pause the client in their sessions to explore what feelings the client may have been avoiding.

3 Evaluating supervision

Research into the effectiveness and impact of supervision has historically been problematic due to methodological difficulties such as small sample sizes, reliance on self-report measures and lack of control for confounding variables (factors that are not the main point of interest in a study but can affect the outcome) (Watkins, Vîşcu and Cadariu, 2021). In particular, it has been very difficult to definitively prove that supervision positively impacts client outcomes (Watkins, 2020) and empirical studies report a range of values for effect on client outcome, from less than 1% to 16.4% (Teichman *et al.*, 2023). (You will read more about the challenges associated with therapy research in Part 4 of this book.)

However, studies do show that effective supervision contributes to skill development and competence, increased confidence and self-efficacy, and job satisfaction (Khoshfetrat, Moore and Kiernan, 2022a). Supervision support can also help to reduce work-related stress (Aggarwal and Bhatia, 2020).

Good supervision should enhance your professional practice. For example, you should feel you that are learning and developing. You should also feel supported, and that supervision is contributing to a positive outcome for your clients. In contrast, problematic supervision will lead to frustration, confusion and/or disappointment. You may feel hurt if your supervisor has not provided enough positive feedback or has even been harshly critical. You may feel uncomfortable disclosing certain issues or that you lack a voice in your supervision sessions (Khoshfetrat, Moore and Kiernan, 2022b). There may be some conflict related to differences in theoretical orientation between you and your supervisor. The supervision contract may be unclear or there may be problems related to the triadic relationship between you, your supervisor and your organisation.

Box 8.1 offers real examples of problematic supervision experienced by some of the authors of this textbook.

Box 8.1 Problematic supervision

Example 1

My supervisor's interventions/questions/suggestions were often not connected to what I had been talking about. It made me feel uncomfortable. I finally realised that this happened because he couldn't hear me properly. He was the Director of my training placement so I never felt able to say anything to him about it.

Example 2

I discussed a client who had been racially abusive towards me. His abuse seemed to fluctuate with his anxiety levels. Although the supervisor acknowledged the inappropriateness of the client's comments, when I tried to talk about the impact on me my supervisor said, 'Aah – you let them get into you!'

He didn't ask me how I was, or about the impact on me as a Black therapist. He didn't advise me to take it to personal therapy or discuss how to manage similar situations. I was left feeling I'd done something wrong by allowing the content of the session to get to me. I felt unheard.

From then on, I avoided sharing personal parts of myself. I took race-related issues to other forums where consideration of race, difference and identity was encouraged.

Example 3

My supervisor has a wonderful, easy manner and is insightful and person-centred, but he challenges me so gently, so sometimes I feel I might be missing something because I'm relying so much on my own perceptions. I sometimes wonder whether he doesn't always say what he is thinking. It's very hard to know at times!

Example 4

I had a supervisor who consistently misgendered a client – I felt confused, frustrated, embarrassed, angry … I began to question my supervisor's beliefs and practice. Initially, I avoided bringing clients with trans or non-binary genders, but in the end I spoke to the supervisor about it and we resolved it.

Example 5

I had a placement supervisor who didn't agree with using drawing as an intervention with adult clients. I felt completely undermined by them and changed supervisors.

Activity 8.1 Reviewing problematic supervision

Allow about 15 minutes

Carroll and Gilbert (2011) outline four unhelpful approaches to supervision:

- *constrictive*, where the focus is on technique and rules
- *amorphous*, where there is too little input or guidance
- *unsupportive*, where the supervisor is unapproachable
- *therapeutic*, where the supervisor takes on the role of therapist and turns the supervisee into a 'client'.

Reread the examples of problematic supervision in Box 8.1, then answer the following questions:

1   What do you think was going wrong in each example?
2   Do any of the examples fit Carroll and Gilbert's categories?
3   What impact do you think this had on:

    ○   the supervisee?

    ○   the supervisory relationship?

    ○   the work with the client?

4   What would you have done in that situation?

Discussion

You may have noticed issues such as unequal power between supervisor and supervisee, a lack of attention given to issues of diversity, misalignment between the supervisor's approach and supervisee's stage of development, or differences in theoretical orientation.

It is important recognise that some ruptures can be due to your own defences. Unconscious processes related to your own history can occur, and old beliefs and drivers can be triggered. For example, do you try to be perfect or please others? Are you someone who tries hard at life or feels they must be strong? The following questions could be helpful to consider if you think unconscious processes may be involved.

> In the presence of my supervisor:
>
> - Do I feel small and vulnerable?
> - Do I experience similar feelings to those I have experienced with other authority figures in my life?
> - Do I feel in awe of my supervisor?
> - Am I prone to feeling shame in supervision?
> - Am I scared to ask for what I need?
> - Do I feel as though I have a crush on them?
> - Do I silence myself?
>
> *(Adapted from Carroll and Gilbert, 2011, p. 65)*

When supervision becomes problematic, it is best, if possible, to openly discuss with your supervisor how you are feeling – many issues can be resolved in this way. Most supervisors will be open to discussing what you would like more or less of in supervision. However, there may be occasions when problems cannot be resolved, and, if possible, you may need to find an alternative supervisor with whom you can work well.

One of the most important predictors of effective supervision is the relationship between the supervisee and the supervisor; you will explore this next.

3.1 The supervisory relationship

The supervisory relationship is complex, multilayered and encompasses several aspects. One of the most important is the provision of a 'safe base' that supports development and learning. This safe base has been termed the 'supervisory bond' and 'represents a relationship which is positive, supporting, empathic, respectful and warm, facilitative and collaborative, flexible, affirming and encouraging, interested and engaged' (Teichman *et al.*, 2023, p. 518). A strong supervisory bond leads to an increase in supervisee self-confidence and autonomy (Teichman *et al.*, 2023).

Another component of the supervisory relationship is the educative element, which is important for supporting theoretical thinking, understanding the therapeutic relationship with clients and defining therapy goals. The combination of the supervisory bond and the educative element leads to respectful and supportive feedback and critique.

Several measures have been developed to assess the quality of the supervisory relationship. The Supervisory Working Alliance Inventory (SWAI) (Efstation, Patton and Kardash, 1990) is a seven-point Likert scale questionnaire that measures how much the supervisor helps the supervisee's understanding of their clients (client focus) and the level of support and encouragement the supervisee receives (rapport). Examples of items on the questionnaire are 'I feel comfortable working with my supervisor' and 'My supervisor helps me work within a specific treatment plan with my clients' (Efstation, Patton and Kardash, 1990, p. 327).

However, the SWAI is based on the therapeutic relationship between the therapist and their client. To address this limitation, a specific Supervisory Relationship Questionnaire (SRQ) has been developed (Palomo, Beinart and Cooper, 2010). The SRQ also uses a seven-point Likert scale and consists of 67 questions divided into the following subscales:

- safe base (e.g. 'my supervisor was non-judgemental in supervision')
- structure (e.g. 'supervision sessions were focused')
- commitment (e.g. 'my supervisor appeared interested in supervising me')
- reflective educative (e.g. 'my supervisor encouraged me to reflect on my practice')
- role model (e.g. 'I respect my supervisor as a professional')
- formative feedback (e.g. 'my supervisor's feedback on my performance was constructive').

(Adapted from Palomo, Beinart and Cooper, 2010, pp. 147–149)

real relationship

Understood as person-to-person interactions as opposed to technical, educational or interventive interactions. It includes the feelings, thoughts and behaviours of supervisor and supervisee that are separate from the supervisory alliance.

Another aspect of the supervisory relationship, termed the **real relationship** (Watkins, 2011), is much harder to describe and measure. It refers to a sense of realness and genuineness that exists between two human beings and includes qualities such as mutual warmth, openness and acceptance. In such a relationship, the supervisor is likely to praise, encourage and advise the supervisee; they will show empathy for the supervisee's vulnerability; and they are able to share their own experiences, mistakes and doubts. The real relationship is often experienced at moments of greeting and parting, through friendly chat, mutual interest and the sharing of feelings regarding life events. Overall, there is a sense of 'clicking' with each other.

As you have learnt in this section, there are various elements that contribute to the overall usefulness of your supervision. A general and simple Supervisory Satisfaction Questionnaire (SSQ) developed by Ladany *et al.* (1996, p. 12) consists of eight questions, such as 'How would you rate the quality of the supervision you have received?' and 'In an overall, general sense, how satisfied are you with the supervision you have received?' The higher the score on the questionnaire, the higher the level of satisfaction. This questionnaire can be used to help you measure your supervision experience.

There is a high correlation between measures of the supervisory relationship, supervisee-rated satisfaction and levels of supervisee disclosure (Schweitzer and Witham, 2018). In other words, the better the quality of your supervisory relationship, the more likely it is that you will disclose things to your supervisor, and therefore feel more satisfied with your supervision.

4 Other forms of supervision

As well as one-to-one supervision, there are a number of other formats in which supervision can take place, each with its own strengths and limitations. For example, in group supervision a supervisor will work with a group of supervisees rather than individuals, and these supervisees could be part of the same team. This section will focus on two forms in particular: peer supervision, and the use of your own internal supervisor.

4.1 Peer supervision

Peer supervision involves two or more practitioners working together in a mutually collaborative way to supervise each other's practice. Each member of the group takes equal responsibility for sessions and takes the role of supervisor and supervisee in turn. Although this is a valid form of supervision that can contribute to part of your supervision arrangements, it is generally not advised as an alternative to individual supervision with a qualified supervisor for newly qualified counsellors (BACP, 2022). In addition, your professional organisation or place of work may stipulate certain parameters regarding peer supervision.

There are many advantages of this practice. Peer supervision doesn't cost anything, allows you to work with a colleague in a particular specialism, fosters team building in organisations, counters feelings of isolation in private practice, allows collaboration, promotes reassurance (e.g. when others have similar experiences), offers mutual support and exposes you to different perspectives. However, peer supervision can have some drawbacks. Peers may lack the breadth of experience needed, issues of power and responsibility can develop, the group may be intimidating for some and group dynamics may lead to problematic patterns (such as one person dominating discussions or conflict between members).

It is important to remember that peer supervision is not the same as peer support; it involves looking closely at each other's practice. The following guidelines for peer supervision can help you avoid the most common pitfalls:

- Try to form a group with shared values but with a range of approaches. It is helpful to view client work from different perspectives.
- Think about the number and mix of members, the criteria for membership and how to allow enough time to meet the needs of everyone in the group.
- Establish a clear contract (e.g. frequency and duration of sessions, confidentiality and record keeping, communications regarding arrangements, how to deal with difficulties, joining and leaving processes and ground rules for how sessions will be run).
- Check your professional body's guidance regarding peer supervision.

- Be clear about roles and expectations regarding the sessions.
- Allow time at the end of sessions for feedback on the process.
- Review arrangements regularly.

(Adapted from Hawkins and Shohet, 2006, p. 167–168)

4.2 Developing an internal supervisor

internal supervisor

A concept that describes the way in which aspects of the supervisory relationship are internalised by the therapist and used for self-support.

You were introduced to the concept and processes of internalisation in Chapter 6; the concept of an **internal supervisor**, which was first developed by psychoanalyst Patrick Casement (1985), expands on this learning. Indeed, there are times when you will need to reflect on your work without the presence of your supervisor; for instance, when in sessions with your clients, between supervision sessions and if your supervisor is unavailable for any length of time.

The internal supervisor can be understood as a valuable, friendly companion that can help monitor your work and guide you in your thinking (Rickard, 2011). It is an essential component of reflexive practice, although it should not be considered a replacement for formal supervision. Engaging with a compassionate internal supervisor has been shown to reduce shame, self-criticism, anxiety and worry when reflecting on difficulties (Bell, Dixon and Kolts, 2017).

Development of an internal supervisor is an ongoing process that begins when you yourself are going through therapy as a client, learning to observe and think about what you are experiencing. Casement (1985, p. 31) refers to this process as going to 'an island of intellectual contemplation', which is a metaphor for the therapist distancing themselves in order to reflect on what is happening, and what they are thinking and feeling. As a therapist, you initially rely a great deal on your real-world supervisor. You are likely to take on board their thoughts and guidance when difficult situations arise in a session, perhaps trying to think how your supervisor might think. At this stage, your internal supervisor will most likely resemble the borrowed 'voice' of your external supervisor. With time, though, you will develop your own internal monologue as you develop your autonomy. Your formal supervision can then become a dialogue between your internal and external supervisor. If you go on to become a supervisor yourself, your internal supervisor will enter another period of growth: as a result of reflecting on your supervisees' practice, you will reflect further on your own practice.

Your internal supervisor can be used for reflection in action or reflection on action (Rickard, 2011). You came across these terms in Chapters 5 and 7, in relation to reflexive practice. Reflection in action refers to the use of the internal supervisor within a therapy session. Utilising Casement's 'island of intellectual contemplation', reflective questions your internal supervisor could ask are:

- What does it feel like to put myself in the position of this client?
- How might the client receive what I am thinking of saying?
- How might the client have interpreted what I have just said?
- How can I understand the client's response to me?
- Rather than focusing on the detail of the story, what themes are evident? How do these themes connect?
- What alternative responses could I give? What would serve the client and the therapeutic process best?
- Are any ethical issues emerging?

Reflection in action requires practice. It can be difficult to stay 'present' with the client while standing on your island of intellectual contemplation with your internal supervisor. However, you can get better at this with time, experience, and the encouragement and support of your external supervisor.

Reflection on action refers to the time after the session that is used to think about and reflect on what has happened. Your internal supervisor might ask the following questions:

- What seemed to work?
- What did not work well?
- Did I notice any possible unconscious dynamics? What did they tell me?
- What might have been left unsaid?
- Are there any ethical issues to consider?
- What do I need to take to supervision?

Making regular time and space to think deeply about your work will lead to a stronger and more confident internal supervisor, and this will be reflected in your practice.

Conclusion

In this chapter you have learnt how your needs will change and evolve as you develop and work in different contexts. You have considered how to prepare for supervision, reflected on what topics you choose to discuss and the issue of non-disclosure. You have also been introduced to the ways in which you can evaluate your supervision and the particular importance of the supervisory relationship for its effectiveness. Finally, the advantages and drawbacks of peer supervision have been discussed, alongside the value of developing your own internal supervisor.

Supervision is an essential part of your reflective practice and, in a reciprocal dynamic, reflective practice should be part of your supervision as well. Supervision contributes to your continuing professional development, self-care and client work. The responsibility for ensuring you receive the supervision you need is yours.

Further reading

The following books are excellent sources to help you take responsibility for your own supervision and learning:

- Carroll, M. and Gilbert, M.C. (2011) *On being a supervisee: creating learning partnerships*. 2nd edn. Victoria, Australia: PsychOz Publications.
- Creaner, M. (2013) *Getting the best out of supervision in counselling and psychotherapy: a guide for the supervisee*. London: SAGE Publications.

References

Aggarwal, P. and Bhatia, P. (2020) 'Clinical supervision in forensic psychiatry in India', *Journal of Psychotherapy Integration'*, 30(1), pp. 9–15. Available at: https://doi.org/10.1037/int0000177

BACP (2020) *Good practice in action 054 commonly asked questions: introduction to supervision in the counselling professions (member version).* Available at: https://www.bacp.co.uk/events-and-resources/ethics-and-standards/good-practice-in-action/publications/gpia054-introduction-to-supervision-for-members-caq/ (Accessed: 4 October 2024).

BACP (2022) *Good practice in action 121 fact sheet: peer supervision within the counselling professions.* Available at: https://www.bacp.co.uk/events-and-resources/ethics-and-standards/good-practice-in-action/publications/gpia121-peer-supervision-within-the-counselling-professions-fs/ (Accessed: 14 June 2024).

Bell, T., Dixon, A. and Kolts, R. (2017) 'Developing a compassionate internal supervisor: compassion-focused therapy for trainee therapists', *Clinical Psychology and Psychotherapy*, 24(3), pp. 632–648. Available at: https://doi.org/10.1002/cpp.2031

Carroll, M. and Gilbert, M. (2011) *On being a supervisee: creating learning partnerships.* 2nd edn. Victoria, Australia: PsychOz Publications.

Casement, P. (1985) *On learning from the patient.* London: Routledge.

Efstation, J.F., Patton, M.J. and Kardash, C.M. (1990) 'Measuring the working alliance in counselor supervision', *Journal of Counseling Psychology*, 37(3), pp. 322–329. Available at: https://doi.org/10.1037/0022-0167.37.3.322

Hawkins, P. and Shohet, R. (2006) *Supervision in the helping professions.* 3rd edn. Maidenhead: Open University Press.

Khoshfetrat, A., Moore, G. and Kiernan, G. (2022a) 'What do psychoanalytic supervisees say about good supervision?', *Counselling Psychology Quarterly*, 35(2), pp. 421–443. Available at: https://doi.org/10.1080/09515070.2020.1857701

Khoshfetrat, A., Moore, G. and Kiernan, G. (2022b) 'Problematic psychoanalytic supervision: an interpretative phenomenological analysis study', *Counselling and Psychotherapy Research*, 22(1), pp. 225–237. Available at: https://doi.org/10.1002/capr.12415

Ladany, N., Hill, C.E., Corbett, M.M. and Nutt, E.A. (1996) 'Nature, extent, and importance of what psychotherapy trainees do not disclose to their supervisors', *Journal of Counseling Psychology*, 43(1), pp. 10–24. Available at: https://doi.org/10.1037/0022-0167.43.1.10

McNamee, S. (2021) 'Theoretical foundations of relational processes in supervision', in O. Ness, S. McNamee and Ø. Kvello (eds) *Relational processes in counselling and psychotherapy supervision.* Cham, Switzerland: Palgrave Macmillan, pp. 9–24.

Palomo, M., Beinart, H. and Cooper, M.J. (2010) 'Development and validation of the Supervisory Relationship Questionnaire (SRQ) in UK trainee clinical psychologists', *British Journal of Clinical Psychology*, 49(2), pp. 131–149. Available at: https://doi.org/10.1348/014466509x441033

Proctor, B. (1988) 'Supervision: a co-operative exercise in accountability', in M. Marken and M. Payne (eds) *Enabling and ensuring: supervision in practice.* 2nd edn. Leicester: National Youth Bureau and Council for Education and Training in Youth and Community Work, pp. 21–34.

Rickard, A. (2011) 'The internal supervisor', *Therapy Today*, 22(1), pp. 26–29.

Sarnat, J.E. (2019) 'What's new in parallel process? The evolution of supervision's signature phenomenon', *American Journal of Psychoanalysis*, 79(3), pp. 304–328. Available at: https://doi.org/10.1057/s11231-019-09202-5

Schweitzer, R.D. and Witham, M. (2018) 'The supervisory alliance: comparison of measures and implications for a supervision toolkit', *Counselling and Psychotherapy Research*, 18(1), pp. 71–78. Available at: https://doi.org/10.1002/capr.12143

SCoPEd Framework (2022), collaboratively developed by Association of Christian Counsellors (ACC), British Association for Counselling and Psychotherapy (BACP), British Psychoanalytic Council (BPC), Human Givens Institute (HGI), National Counselling and Psychotherapy Society (NCPS) and United Kingdom Council for Psychotherapy (UKCP). Available at: https://www.bacp.co.uk/about-us/advancing-the-profession/scoped/scoped-framework (Accessed: 12 June 2024).

Stoltenberg, C.D. and McNeill. B.W. (2010) *IDM supervision: an integrative developmental model for supervising counselors and therapists*. Hove: Routledge.

Teichman, Y., Berant, E., Shenkman, G. and Ramot, G. (2023) 'Supervisees' perspectives on the contribution of supervision to psychotherapy outcomes', *Counselling and Psychotherapy Research*, 23(2), pp. 516–529. Available at: https://doi.org/10.1002/capr.12540

van Ooijen, E. (2021) 'How do I prepare for supervision and get the most out of it?', *Therapy Today*, 32(1), p. 53.

Watkins, C.E. Jr (2011) 'The real relationship in psychotherapy supervision', *American Journal of Psychotherapy*, 65(2), pp. 99–116. Available at: https://doi.org/10.1176/appi.psychotherapy.2011.65.2.99

Watkins, C.E. Jr (2020) 'What do clinical supervision research reviews tell us? Surveying the last 25 years', *Counselling and Psychotherapy Research*, 20(2), pp. 190–208. Available at: https://doi.org/10.1002/capr.12287

Watkins, C.E. Jr, Vîşcu, L-I. and Cadariu, I-E. (2021) 'Psychotherapy supervision research: on roadblocks, remedies, and recommendations', *European Journal of Psychotherapy & Counselling*, 23(1), pp. 8–25. Available at: https://doi.org/10.1080/13642537.2021.1881139

Part 3

Assessment

Chapter 9

Foundations of psychological assessment

Gina Di Malta

Contents

Introduction

Silhouette in a Box by Gina Di Malta. Much like the structure in this image frames the person and their perspective, a consistent theoretical approach can frame psychological assessment and ongoing therapy.

Imagine you are working with a new client for the first time. How would you go about determining what they want from therapy, and how would you monitor progress throughout your sessions together? In psychological therapies, the initial client assessment, followed by ongoing assessment, plays a pivotal role in guiding the therapeutic journey (Youngstrom and Prinstein, 2020). Psychological assessment generally consists of data gathering and sometimes encompasses the interpretation of the data using a formulation. It departs from a psychiatric assessment, which gathers data in order to establish a diagnosis and prescribe medication. In counselling and psychotherapy, effective psychological assessment guides the therapeutic process and ensures that the service provided is suited to the client's needs. The initial assessment sets the tone for future ongoing assessment and reformulation when moving forward in therapy. In cases where the assessor is also the therapist, the initial assessment lays the groundwork for the commencement of the new therapeutic relationship. Furthermore, assessments are also an opportunity to embed a culturally sensitive lens from the beginning of therapy. As emphasised in Part 1 of this book, cultural norms, values and diverse backgrounds profoundly impact an individual's psychological experience (Sue *et al.*, 2022) and, as such, the process of an initial assessment.

Importantly, initial and ongoing assessments can be considered an integral part of the therapeutic process, one that contributes positively to the therapeutic relationship and outcome (Durosini and Aschieri, 2021). Sadly, research still shows how assessment processes can lead to a person experiencing stigma and discrimination (Reynolds, Altmann and Allen, 2021). A core principle across this book is that the assessment of mental health problems should be client-centred, specifically in terms of being respectful of the autonomy of the client and collaborative in approach. Such processes of assessment starts from the client's own understandings of themselves, and are then co-created between the client and the counsellor.

The aim of this chapter is to guide you to a nuanced understanding of the foundational processes of assessment. You will reflect on the case of Sahar, a 28-year-old Omani woman who has recently moved to the UK and is experiencing depressive symptoms and culture shock. This chapter contributes towards achieving the **SCoPEd competency 2.1.B**:

> Ability to use an initial and ongoing clinical assessment strategy that is informed by a consistent, coherent and in-depth theoretical approach.
>
> *(SCoPEd Framework, 2022, p. 18)*

This chapter aims to:

- define the psychological assessment process
- outline an initial and ongoing clinical assessment strategy that is informed by a consistent, coherent and in-depth theoretical approach
- explore how to engage with assessment within theoretical frameworks
- examine how to undertake assessment within a culturally sensitive framework.

1 The difference between assessment, formulation and diagnosis

Before delving into the theoretical foundations of psychological assessment, it is important to differentiate between the following processes:

- assessment, which gathers data
- formulation, which offers a comprehensive understanding of presenting problems
- diagnosis, which categorises these according to an established system.

These are all fundamental processes in the field of mental health, and each serves a distinct yet interrelated purpose (Summers, 2022).

Psychological assessment involves the systematic collection and evaluation of information about an individual's psychological well-being, encompassing their thoughts, emotions, behaviours and interpersonal relationships. It aims to provide a comprehensive understanding of the client, and often serves to gauge or establish clients' suitability for the service, to match them with a therapist, and to determine which types of therapy could be offered and sometimes the length of it.

A psychological formulation often follows the assessment process. It is a broader, more holistic process that aims to synthesise and make sense of the information gathered in an assessment. It constitutes the assessor's working understanding (based in the model in which they work) and hypotheses about why the client is manifesting the difficulties that they are (Johnstone, 2018). With a formulation, the assessor creates a coherent narrative or conceptualisation of the client's psychological functioning, taking into account their unique life experiences, strengths and challenges. By delving into the contributing factors and underlying causes of the client's issues, a formulation offers a deeper understanding of their problems (Summers, 2022).

Diagnosis, on the other hand, represents the categorisation or labelling of a client's presenting problem based on established criteria and classification systems, such as the *International Classification of Diseases* (World Health Organization, 2022), now in its eleventh revision (**ICD-11**), or the *Diagnostic and Statistical Manual of Mental Disorders* (American Psychiatric Association, 2022), now in its fifth revision (**DSM-5-TR**). These are the most used systems, although there are others. The Health of the Nations Outcome Scales (HoNOS) clustering, used in the NHS in England, is an assessment and classification system for all mental health patients, which is also used to record outcomes of therapy (James *et al.*, 2018). While diagnosis provides a standardised framework for communication among professionals and can guide treatment planning, it has been criticised for oversimplifying complex human experiences and potentially stigmatising individuals (Summers, 2022). Despite this, in many countries, the provision and funding of physical and psychological treatment relies on a person receiving a diagnosis. Providing a

ICD-11

A standardised system for categorising and coding diseases, health conditions and related factors which is published by the World Health Organization and widely used in healthcare for accurate and consistent medical record-keeping and billing.

DSM-5-TR

A comprehensive classification system published by the American Psychiatric Association, used by mental health professionals to diagnose and classify mental health conditions. It provides standardised criteria for the identification and classification of psychiatric disorders.

diagnosis requires additional training and it is often done by an appropriately trained medical professional, such as a general practitioner (GP), prior to a referral for therapy.

The assessment, formulation and diagnosis processes are interconnected: assessment provides the raw material for formulation, and then this formulation contributes to the diagnostic process. However, each aspect differs in scope, depth and the implications that they hold for understanding and addressing psychological issues. In this chapter, the main focus is on the assessment process.

Pause for thought 9.1

Consider one of your clients. How do the assessment, formulation and diagnosis processes interact with each other and apply to your work with that client?

2 Background and context of psychological assessment

The history and evolution of conducting psychological assessment within the context of psychotherapy reflects shifts in our understanding of human behaviour (note that psychological assessments can occur in other contexts, e.g. to determine entitlement to state benefits for a disability or for additional educational support). Assessments evolved with the increasing recognition of the importance of a comprehensive understanding of clients' psychological states and needs (Wright, 2020).

Early psychotherapy approaches, like psychoanalysis, primarily relied on open-ended conversations and clinical observations (e.g. Freud, 1905). The mid twentieth century marked a significant turning point in the field, with the emergence of structured interviews and psychological testing (Benjamin, 2018). The Rorschach inkblot test, developed by Hermann Rorschach in the early twentieth century, offered a **projective approach** to uncover hidden aspects of an individual's personality, emotions and thought processes. By presenting ambiguous inkblot patterns and asking participants to describe what they see, the Rorschach test aimed to tap into the depths of the unconscious mind. The use of psychological assessments was later significantly influenced by people such as David Wechsler, who introduced the Wechsler Adult Intelligence Scale (WAIS) to measure cognitive abilities (Wechsler, 2008). This contributed to a shift towards more standardised and objective assessments in psychotherapy (Benjamin, 2018). The later decades of the twentieth century saw a diversification of existing assessment tools to encompass new cognitive, emotional and behavioural domains, and even domains tailored to specific populations (Benjamin, 2018). These innovations allowed for a broader understanding of the therapeutic process and its impact on patients' well-being.

projective approach

A psychoanalytic approach used to uncover aspects of the unconscious. It involves presenting ambiguous stimuli, such as inkblots or pictures, to elicit unconscious thoughts and emotions, allowing analysts to explore deeper aspects of a person's psyche.

Today, practitioners can draw from a wide range of assessment tools – including standardised tests, clinical interviews and self-report questionnaires – to tailor their assessment and treatment plans, and also to monitor therapeutic progress and outcomes (Benjamin, 2018). The twenty-first century has witnessed an integration of technology into the therapeutic process, with online assessments, telehealth and artificial intelligence playing a significant role in some settings (Andersson *et al.*, 2019). Ideally, the approach to assessment for counselling and psychotherapy today should be holistic and culturally sensitive, and it should acknowledge the interplay of socio-cultural factors on an individual's mental health and well-being (Graves and Aston, 2016; Sue *et al.*, 2022). This recognition underscores the importance of considering cultural diversity, gender, socio-economic factors and other dimensions in the assessment process.

3 Grounding assessment in a theoretical approach

Effective assessment serves as a compass that guides therapists in understanding their clients' unique needs and enables them to tailor their interventions. To conduct effective assessments that empower clients, therapists should select an assessment method and process informed by their chosen theoretical approach to therapy (Wright, 2020). A theoretical approach provides a structured lens through which assessments are conducted. There are several key reasons why using a theoretical approach may support the assessment process:

congruence

Agreement between one's thoughts, feelings and behaviours, creating a state of authenticity and consistency in self-expression.

- It ensures that assessments are consistent with the therapist's core approach and principles. This consistency can help to build trust and rapport with clients, as they sense a **congruence** between what the therapist says and does.
- It ensures that all components, from initial intake to ongoing evaluations, are aligned with the chosen theoretical model. This cohesive approach can foster a deeper understanding of the client's concerns.
- It can support therapists to delve deeper into clients' issues because it enables them to identify the root causes of emotional distress (as conceptualised by the therapist's chosen modality) and to create a more comprehensive treatment plan.

Taken together, these points illustrate that a theoretical approach can not only inform the counsellor's understanding of human behaviour and emotional processes, but can also guide the development of relevant assessment tools and techniques. Before reading the next sections of this chapter – which focus on humanistic approaches, along with some coverage of cognitive behavioural therapy (CBT) and psychoanalytic therapy to illustrate different assessment practices – consider the fictional case of Sahar.

Case example: Sahar seeks therapy

Sahar is a 28-year-old woman from Oman who has recently migrated to the UK for work. She's seeking therapy due to the increased levels of anxiety and mild depressive symptoms she has experienced since her arrival. She has a successful career but is struggling with feelings of isolation and homesickness, as well as the challenges of adapting to a new culture. Sahar's primary language is Arabic, and while she speaks English, she often finds it challenging to express her thoughts and emotions accurately in her non-native language.

Pause for thought 9.2

If you were working with Sahar, how do you think your own theoretical approach might inform the assessment you conduct with her? What sort of information would you want to find out, and what methods might you use?

3.1 Humanistic approach to assessment

A humanistic theoretical foundation for conducting psychological assessment in psychotherapy is rooted in the fundamental tenets of humanistic psychology, which is a school of thought that places a strong emphasis on the uniqueness, autonomy and intrinsic worth of each individual (Rogers, 1961). This approach seeks to understand and address clients' concerns from a holistic and humanistic standpoint. Unique to this approach to assessment is the rejection of the assessor's goal of being the 'objective observer' (e.g. Tonsager, 2020).

There is not an agreed set structure to conduct a humanistic assessment. Instead, the process is unstructured and tends to unfold over several sessions. Therapists may employ a clinical interview with open-ended questions and use **active listening** to encourage clients to explore their experiences in depth (Rogers, 1961). The most important characteristic of such assessment is probably the emphasis on the creation of a safe and empathetic therapeutic environment. Therapists aim to build a genuine and compassionate relationship with their clients, and they seek to foster a climate of trust and acceptance (Hanson *et al.*, 2022; Mearns and Thorne, 1999). This atmosphere allows clients to freely express their thoughts, emotions and concerns without fear of judgment or criticism. Traditionally, such assessment rarely relies on standardised questionnaires or diagnostic labels, and focuses instead on the client's subjective experience and meanings (Bugental, 1965). It seeks to understand the client's life goals, values and the barriers they face in achieving personal growth and fulfilment.

active listening

A communication technique that involves fully focusing on, understanding and responding to a speaker with genuine interest. It can involve providing feedback, paraphrasing and fostering effective and empathetic communication.

A humanistic clinical interview typically involves open-ended questions that encourage clients to share their thoughts, feelings and experiences. Table 9.1 includes questions that a therapist might use in a humanistic clinical interview.

Table 9.1 Example questions in a humanistic clinical interview

Focus of the question	Example questions
Introduction and building rapport	Can you tell me a bit about yourself and what brings you to therapy?
	How are you feeling today as we start our journey?
Current concerns	What has been happening in your life recently that prompted you to seek therapy?
	Can you share more about the challenges or concerns you're currently facing?
Personal narrative and life story	Can you walk me through your life story, including significant events or transitions?
	How would you describe the major themes or chapters in your life so far?
Self-perception and identity	How do you see yourself in this moment? What words come to mind when you think about who you are?
	Can you share your thoughts on your strengths and areas for growth?
Exploration of feelings	How are you feeling right now, and how have your emotions been lately?
	Can you describe any specific emotions that have been particularly prominent for you?
Values and beliefs	What values are important to you in your life?
	How do your values influence the decisions you make and the way you live your life?
Goals and aspirations	What do you hope to achieve through our time together in therapy?
	Are there specific goals or changes that you would like to work towards?
Relationships and connection	How would you describe your relationships with others currently?
	What do connection and meaningful relationships mean to you?
Coping strategies	How do you typically cope with stress or challenges in your life?
	Are there coping mechanisms that have been more or less effective for you?
Cultural considerations	Are there aspects of your cultural background or identity that you would like me to be aware of as we work together?
	How has your cultural background influenced your experiences and perspectives?

| Reflection on changes and growth | Can you recall a time in your life when you felt a sense of personal growth or positive change? |
| | What would positive change look like for you in the context of therapy? |

These questions aim to create a therapeutic space that fosters self-reflection, self-expression and collaboration between the therapist and the client. The specific questions asked may vary based on the clinician's empathic listening to the client's responses and the therapeutic context. For example, in the case of Sahar, the clinician may decide to emphasise cultural considerations over other aspects of the clinical interview. Below is an example of how a clinical interview with Sahar might go.

Case example: Conducting a clinical interview to inform Sahar's assessment

Therapist: Sahar, it's good to meet you. To start, can you share with me what led you to seek therapy?

Sahar: Good to meet you. It's just been really hard since I moved to the UK. I have a good job, but everything feels different. I miss home a lot and I find it challenging to connect with people here. I feel lonely and my anxiety has been getting worse.

Therapist: Thank you for sharing that, Sahar. It sounds like you have had a significant life change and it has brought about a range of emotions. Can you tell me more about what you miss most about home and the challenges you've faced in connecting with others?

Sahar: I miss the familiarity, the way people understand me without many words. Here, I struggle with the language, even though I can communicate in English. It's not the same. I miss my family and the sense of community we had.

Therapist: I hear that the language barrier has been a significant challenge for you. Your feelings of homesickness and the struggle to express yourself in a new language are making this change difficult. How do you typically cope with low moods and the anxious feelings you have?

Sahar: I try to keep myself busy with work, but it's not enough. I've thought about going back home, but I also want to succeed in my career here. I just don't know how to balance it all.

Therapist: Balancing your work and personal well-being sounds like a delicate challenge, especially in a new country. It's commendable that you're seeking balance. We can explore ways to address these feelings of isolation and help you find that balance. Can you share more about what you would like to achieve in your career and personal life?

Sahar: Success for me is not just about work; it's about feeling happy and connected. I want to build a life here, but it feels like I'm on my own.

Therapist: It sounds like you value feeling happy and connected as much as your career success. We can work together to explore strategies that align with your values and help you build connections in this new environment. We can also discuss ways to manage anxiety and homesickness. How does that sound to you?

Sahar: That sounds good. I just want things to get better.

Therapist: I'm here to support you, Sahar. Together, we'll try to navigate these challenges and work towards the changes you're seeking. If there are specific cultural aspects you'd like me to consider in our sessions, please do share them with me. I am sure there is much that I don't know, so if you feel that I'm getting things wrong, I hope you will tell me.

This example illustrates the humanistic approach by acknowledging Sahar's unique experiences, emphasising empathy and collaboratively exploring her goals for therapy. It also recognises the importance of cultural sensitivity, which you learned about in Part 1 of this book.

Pause for thought 9.3

Considering Sahar's Omani background and her challenges in adapting to a new cultural and linguistic context, which questions from Table 9.1 would you want to ask her in your assessment? Are there some you would not want to ask her, and if so, why?

3.2 Psychodynamic approach to assessment

A psychodynamic theoretical approach originates with the groundbreaking work of Sigmund Freud in the late nineteenth and early twentieth centuries (Freud, 1913). Classical psychoanalysis put an emphasis on the unconscious mind, early childhood experiences and the dynamics of the different parts of the mind (ego, id and superego) (Freud, 1920). Important developments have included object relations theory, which focuses on the impact of early interpersonal relationships on psychological development. This strand delves into the internalised unconscious representations of significant others (objects) and their influence on an individual's self and relationships (e.g. Winnicott, 1960). Another contemporary development emphasises the therapeutic relationship as a central focus, and the use of transference – and countertransference – dynamics as tools to foster healthier connections (Mitchell, 1988; Benjamin, 1990).

Like the humanistic assessment, the psychodynamic assessment is also typically unstructured and strives to create a safe and confidential space where clients feel comfortable sharing their thoughts and feelings (e.g. Gabbard, 2014). The process can also involve unstructured, in-depth clinical interviews. However, the psychodynamic approach puts the focus of the assessment on an exploration of early relationships and experiences, as well as current patterns of relating within and outside the therapeutic space. A historical exploration helps reveal patterns of relating and coping that may underlie current issues, as well as possible traumatic or developmentally adverse experiences. In addition, the aim of the assessment is less about the exploration of values and what may block a person's growth (as emphasised in the humanistic approach), and more about forming hypotheses for how early experiences may impact present issues.

A psychodynamic assessment may sometimes include structured interviews such as: the Adult Attachment Interview (AAI), to assess the client's attachment patterns and determine their attachment style; or an Object Relation Interview (ORI), to explore internalised representations of early relationships (referred to as 'objects'). Depending on the context the psychodynamic practitioner is working within, some will use standardised assessment tools (especially within the NHS and NHS-funded third sector organisations).

Alessandra Lemma (2016) offers a comprehensive guide for how to conduct a psychoanalytic assessment. The assessment consists of conversation to assess whether the client would benefit from the modality and involves direct questions. It takes place over a period of between three and six sessions and informs a formulation and treatment plan.

Pause for thought 9.4

Based on what Sahar describes, what do you think might be important to explore in a psychodynamic assessment? For instance, you might want to ask about Sahar's early relationships.

3.3 Cognitive-behavioural approach to assessment

A cognitive-behavioural approach to assessment places a strong emphasis on a structured and goal-oriented way of understanding and addressing clients' concerns (e.g. Hofmann *et al.*, 2012). This approach relies on the identification of specific cognitive and behavioural patterns, the establishment of measurable treatment goals and ongoing monitoring of client progress using outcome measures (Beck, 1979; Doran, 1981).

The CBT assessment process is structured. It consists of a range of questions which provide an overview of a person's situation and history. Clinicians use a structured clinical interview to explore present issues, psychiatric history, use of medication, precipitating events, family history, alcohol and drug consumption, sleep patterns, safeguarding concerns, risk and more. CBT assessment places a strong focus on understanding the client's automatic thoughts, beliefs and interpretations of their experiences, with the view to identify cognitive biases and maladaptive thinking patterns that contribute to emotional distress or behavioural issues (Beck *et al.*, 1979). A CBT-based assessment also prioritises the establishment of measurable and attainable treatment goals. The therapist collaborates with the client to create specific targets for therapy, employing the SMART criteria (Specific, Measurable, Achievable, Relevant, and Time-bound) (Doran, 1981).

One aspect of the CBT-based assessment process is to acquire baseline data against which clients' improvements can be measured as part of ongoing assessment. The outcome data from these assessments informs the therapeutic process by helping therapists to make necessary adjustments to treatment strategies. For example, the Generalised Anxiety Disorder 7-item scale (GAD-7) is widely utilised in CBT assessments (Spitzer *et al.*, 2006).

3.4 Pluralistic approach to assessment

A pluralistic approach is built upon the idea that there is no one-size-fits-all way of helping clients. Instead, it draws on a range of therapeutic modalities and methods, and the assessment process is tailored to the unique needs and preferences of the client (Cooper and McLeod, 2011). Decisions for treatment rely on empirical research, clinical expertise, and clients' strengths and preferences (Cooper *et al.*, 2023). The pluralistic approach also places a strong emphasis on client feedback. A central emphasis in pluralistic assessment is the recognition that clients have diverse backgrounds, concerns and goals, as well as their own agency in the therapeutic process.

In a pluralistic framework, the assessment process is structured and begins with a comprehensive exploration of the client's background, life experiences and presenting concerns. This phase often involves the use of structured clinical interviews to gather relevant information. However, the specific assessment tools employed can vary widely, depending on the client's preferences and the therapist's approach (Cooper and McLeod, 2011).

The pluralistic toolbox is characterised by its eclecticism. Its tools encompass psychometric assessments, interviews, observations and self-report measures. The choice of assessment tools is determined by the client's unique needs and preferences, allowing for a customised assessment experience (Cooper and McLeod, 2011; Di Malta *et al.*, 2023). Assessors ensure that assessment tools are culturally relevant and respectful (this is covered in Section 4).

In the pluralistic approach, the assessment process is directed towards empowering the client to actively participate in shaping their treatment (Cooper and McLeod, 2011). Collaborative decision making is encouraged, ensuring that the assessment goals and methods align with the client's needs and objectives. For this, assessors actively engage in dialogue with clients, practise active listening and invite feedback. This collaborative relationship empowers clients and aims to ensure that they feel heard and respected throughout the assessment process (Di Malta, Oddli and Cooper, 2019).

Therapists adopting the pluralistic approach also continually assess the client's progress and the effectiveness of the chosen therapeutic methods. If certain approaches are not yielding the expected results, therapists are open to making adjustments and trying alternative strategies (Cooper and McLeod, 2011; Di Malta *et al.*, 2023).

4 Cultural sensitivity in psychological assessments

The principles of equality, diversity and inclusion (EDI) should be integral in the realm of psychological assessments, independent of the theoretical approach used. The fundamental aim of EDI considerations during the assessment process is to guarantee equitable, unbiased and culturally proficient evaluations for all clients (Reynolds, Altmann and Allen, 2021). These considerations stand as the cornerstone for fostering an ethical, client-centric and effective assessment procedure in psychotherapy.

As discussed in Part 1 of this book, cultural awareness involves a therapist having a high degree of sensitivity towards the potential influences of their clients' diverse backgrounds on their mental health (Reynolds, Altmann, and Allen, 2021). This entails the recognition of the profound impact that culture can wield over therapists' and clients' world-views, life experiences, and modes of expressing and understanding emotional distress. It also entails the understanding that culture and context can contribute to mental health issues (e.g. experiences of discrimination). Cultural awareness necessitates an attitude of cultural humility and for the therapist to continually educate oneself about a wide array of cultural norms and values (Bhui *et al.*, 2007). In psychological assessments, it may be important to ask clients about the aspects of their identity that are salient to them, and to acknowledge if they have identities that are discriminated against as well as their experience of minority stress.

Linguistic proficiency may be a consideration for an assessing therapist (Bhui *et al.*, 2007). The presence of language barriers can significantly impede the assessment process, so it may be important to offer assessments (and counselling itself) in multiple languages if required. Additionally, therapists are encouraged to remain highly attuned to non-verbal communication, as cultural nuances may render this pivotal in understanding clients' modes of expressing emotional distress and their individual coping mechanisms.

Assessment could also encompass any aspects of identity (e.g. religious identity or sexual orientation) that have been identified by a client as important for discussion in counselling. Such assessments should account for the unique experiences and challenges faced by individuals whose identities may be socially stigmatised (Suzuki *et al.*, 2019).

Considerations also encompass the critical realm of physical and sensory accessibility. To ensure that assessments remain inclusive, evaluation tools, materials and methods of communication need to be selected with careful consideration for clients with neurodivergence or disabilities, with the intention of equitable access for all individuals (Dunn and Andrews, 2015).

Lastly, the concept of intersectionality is pivotal within psychological assessments. Intersectionality addresses the reality that clients may belong to multiple marginalised groups and, as a result, their experiences and identities may intersect in intricate ways. To conduct a comprehensive assessment, it is essential to consider and inquire about the collective influences of these intersecting identities on the mental well-being of the client (Cole, 2009).

Pause for thought 9.5

With the above considerations, reflect on how you would integrate cultural discussions within your theoretical approach in your assessments with clients.

4.1 Cultural considerations in an initial assessment with Sahar

An initial assessment meeting would typically begin with explaining the assessment process to ensure that Sahar understands the purpose of the meeting, how long it is likely to take and what to expect. As part of the assessment, the use of active and empathic listening would support the establishing of rapport and the creation of a safe and non-judgmental space in which Sahar can share her concerns. In addition, it would be useful to consider and discuss the following cultural aspects:

- *Assessment validity*: First and foremost, the assessor should be cautious about the validity of the assessment tools used and consider potential cultural biases in the assessment questions. In the case of Sahar, the assessor would also need to ensure that the selected questionnaires are culturally appropriate (Chapter 12 expands on this). They may consider personalised measures to better fit Sahar's cultural context.

- *Language and communication*: Language proficiency may impact the accuracy and depth of Sahar's self-expression. To address this, the assessor may explore with Sahar whether she would prefer to receive therapy in Arabic through a translator, and what the possibilities and potential pros and cons for this might be. This respects Sahar's potential need to communicate in her primary language.

- *Respecting cultural and religious norms*: If the cultural norms and values of Sahar's Omani background are different to the assessor's, it may be especially important to be sensitive to potential cultural differences in various topics, such as family dynamics, gender roles and religious beliefs. The assessor needs to avoid making assumptions and should instead seek to understand how these cultural aspects influence Sahar's experiences and expectations by asking questions about her culture. As was covered in Chapter 6, some of these might be unconscious and may require approaches that account for this.

Understanding that many Middle Eastern cultures may emphasise community more than British cultures do, the assessor may want to consider the impact of social support systems, such as family and social or religious community, on Sahar's well-being. The assessor may want to explore how these factors affect Sahar's experience of isolation and homesickness.

- *Cultural humility*: Having cultural humility would involve the assessor acknowledging the limitations of their knowledge of Middle Eastern cultures and making a commitment to ongoing learning. It would involve having an open dialogue with Sahar and allowing her to educate them about her cultural background, but it may also involve the assessor doing further independent reading while, importantly, reflecting on their own conscious and unconscious biases.

- *Empowering decision making*: Informing Sahar about the assessment process and explaining the treatment options can empower Sahar by involving her in the decision making around her treatment. In addition, the assessor may want to foster a collaborative approach to setting goals and planning treatment to further empower Sahar to take an active role in her treatment.

By applying these considerations throughout the assessment process, the assessor aims to create a culturally sensitive and inclusive therapeutic environment that respects Sahar's unique needs and experiences.

Conclusion

The aim of this chapter was to support you in using an initial and ongoing clinical assessment strategy that is informed by a consistent, coherent and in-depth theoretical approach. The four main approaches contrasted in this chapter each bring a different emphasis to assessment, from the humanistic and psychodynamic approaches, which are more exploratory, to the cognitive behavioural and pluralistic approaches, which are more structured. Grounding assessments in a theoretical approach can help therapists reach a deeper understanding of their clients and can help them to identify the root cause of problems. It can also help to provide a consistent narrative in therapy, which may help build trust with clients. Across all theoretical approaches, assessments should be guided by ethical, compassionate and culturally sensitive methods. In the next chapter you will learn about another essential aspect of assessment: assessing suicidality and risk to ensure the client's safety.

Further reading

- The following text provides further information about the humanistic assessment approach:

  Hanson, W.E., Zhou, H., Armstrong, D.L. and Liwski, N.T. (2022) 'A humanistic approach to mental health assessment, evaluation, and measurement-based care', in J.J.W. Andrews, S.R. Shaw, J.F. Domene and C. McMorris (eds) *Mental health assessment, prevention, and intervention: promoting child and youth well-being.* Cham: Springer International Publishing, pp. 361–390.

- This text provides information about the psychodynamic assessment approach:

  Lemma, A. (2016) *Introduction to the practice of psychoanalytic psychotherapy.* 2nd edn. Chichester: Wiley-Blackwell.

References

American Psychiatric Association (2022) *Diagnostic and statistical manual of mental disorders: DSM-5-TR*. 5th edn, text rev. Washington, DC: American Psychiatric Publishing.

Andersson, G., Carlbring, P., Titov, N. and Lindefors, N. (2019) 'Internet interventions for adults with anxiety and mood disorders: a narrative umbrella review of recent meta-analyses', *The Canadian Journal of Psychiatry*, 64(7), pp. 465–472. Available at: https://doi.org/10.1177/0706743719839381

Beck, A.T. (ed.) (1979) *Cognitive therapy of depression*. New York: Guilford Press.

Benjamin, L.T., Jr (2018) *A brief history of modern psychology*. Hoboken, NJ: John Wiley & Sons.

Benjamin, J. (1990) 'An outline of intersubjectivity: the development of recognition', *Psychoanalytic Psychology*, 7(Supp.), pp. 33–46. Available at: https://doi.org/10.1037/h0085258

Bhui, K., Warfa, N., Edonya, P., McKenzie, K. and Bhugra, D. (2007) 'Cultural competence in mental health care: a review of model evaluations', *BMC Health Services Research*, 7(1), article number 15. Available at: https://doi.org/10.1186/1472-6963-7-15

Bugental, J.F. (1965) 'The existential crisis in intensive psychotherapy', *Psychotherapy*, 2(1), pp. 16–20. Available at: https://doi.org/10.1037/h0088602

Cole, E.R. (2009) 'Intersectionality and research in psychology', *American Psychologist*, 64(3), pp. 170–180. Available at: https://doi.org/10.1037/a0014564

Cooper, M., Di Malta, G., Knox, S., Oddli, H.W. and Swift, J.K. (2023) 'Patient perspectives on working with preferences in psychotherapy: a consensual qualitative research study', *Psychotherapy Research*, 33(8), pp. 1117–1131. Available at: https://doi.org/10.1080/10503307.2022.2161967

Cooper, M. and McLeod, J. (2011) *Pluralistic counselling and psychotherapy*. London: SAGE.

Di Malta, G., Cooper, M., Bond, J., Raymond-Barker, B., Oza, M. and Pauli, R. (2023) 'The Patient-Perceived Helpfulness of Measures Scale: development and validation of a scale to assess the helpfulness of using measures in psychological treatment', *Assessment*, article number 10731911231195837. Available at: https://doi.org/10.1177/10731911231195837

Di Malta, G., Oddli, H.W. and Cooper, M. (2019) 'From intention to action: a mixed methods study of clients' experiences of goal-oriented practices', *Journal of Clinical Psychology*, 75(10), pp. 1770–1789. Available at: https://doi.org/10.1002/jclp.22821

Doran, G.T. (1981) 'There's a S.M.A.R.T. way to write management's goals and objectives', *Management Review*, 70(11), pp. 35–36.

Dunn, D.S. and Andrews, E.E. (2015) 'Person-first and identity-first language: developing psychologists' cultural competence using disability language', *American Psychologist*, 70(3), pp. 255–264. Available at: https://doi.org/10.1037/a0038636

Durosini, I. and Aschieri, F. (2021) 'Therapeutic assessment efficacy: a meta-analysis', *Psychological Assessment*, 33(10), pp. 962–972. Available at: https://doi.org/10.1037/pas0001038

Freud, S. (1905) 'On psychotherapy', in *The standard edition of the complete psychological works of Sigmund Freud*, volume 7(267), pp. 64–145.

Freud, S. (1913) *The interpretation of dreams.* Translated from the German by A.A. Brill. New York: The Macmillan Company.

Freud, S. (1920) 'Transference', in *A general introduction to psychoanalysis.* Horace Liveright, pp. 372–387.

Gabbard, G.O. (2014) *Psychodynamic psychiatry in clinical practice.* 5th edn. London: American Psychiatric Publishing.

Graves S.L., Jr and Aston, C. (2016) 'History of psychological assessment and intervention with minority populations', in S.L. Graves and J.J. Blake (eds) *Psychoeducational assessment and intervention for ethnic minority children: evidence-based approaches.* Washington, DC: American Psychological Association, pp. 9–21.

Hanson, W.E., Zhou, H., Armstrong, D.L. and Liwski, N.T. (2022) 'A humanistic approach to mental health assessment, evaluation, and measurement-based care', in J. J.W. Andrews, S.R. Shaw, J.F. Domene and C. McMorris (eds) *Mental health assessment, prevention, and intervention: promoting child and youth well-being.* Cham: Springer International Publishing, pp. 361–390.

Hofmann, S.G., Asnaani, A., Vonk, I.J.J., Sawyer, A.T. and Fang, A. (2012) 'The efficacy of cognitive behavioral therapy: a review of meta-analyses', *Cognitive Therapy and Research*, 36(5), pp. 427–440. Available at: https://doi.org/10.1007/s10608-012-9476-1

James, M., Painter, J., Buckingham, B. and Stewart, M.W. (2018) 'A review and update of the Health of the Nation Outcome Scales (HoNOS)', *BJPsych Bulletin*, 42 (2), pp. 63–68. Available at: https://doi.org/10.1192/bjb.2017.17

Johnstone, L. (2018) 'Psychological formulation as an alternative to psychiatric diagnosis', *Journal of Humanistic Psychology*, 58(1), pp. 30–46. Available at: https://doi.org/10.1177/0022167817722230

Lemma, A. (2016) *Introduction to the practice of psychoanalytic psychotherapy.* 2nd edn. Chichester: Wiley-Blackwell.

Mearns, D. and Thorne, B. (1999) *Person-centred counselling in action.* 2nd edn. London: SAGE.

Mitchell, S.A. (1988) *Relational concepts in psychoanalysis: an integration.* Cambridge: Harvard University Press.

Reynolds, C.R., Altmann, R.A. and Allen, D.N. (2021) 'The problem of bias in psychological assessment', in C.R. Reynolds, R.A. Altmann and D.N. Allen (eds) *Mastering modern psychological testing: theory and methods.* 2nd edn. Cham: Springer International Publishing, pp. 573–613.

Rogers, C.R. (1961) *On becoming a person.* Boston, MA: Houghton Mifflin.

SCoPEd Framework (2022), collaboratively developed by Association of Christian Counsellors (ACC), British Association for Counselling and Psychotherapy (BACP), British Psychoanalytic Council (BPC), Human Givens Institute (HGI), National Counselling and Psychotherapy Society (NCPS) and United Kingdom Council for Psychotherapy (UKCP). Available at: https://www.bacp.co.uk/about-us/advancing-the-profession/scoped/scoped-framework (Accessed: 12 June 2024).

Spitzer, R.L., Kroenke, K., Williams, J.B.W. and Löwe, B. (2006) 'A brief measure for assessing generalized anxiety disorder: The GAD-7', *Archives of Internal Medicine*, 166(10), pp. 1092–1097. Available at: https://doi.org/10.1001/archinte.166.10.1092

Sue, D.W., Sue, D., Neville, H.A. and Smith, L. (2022) *Counseling the culturally diverse: theory and practice.* 9th edn. Hoboken, NJ: John Wiley & Sons.

Summers, A. (2022) 'Formulation and diagnosis', in C. Maloney, J. Nelki and A. Summers (eds) *Seeking asylum and mental health: a practical guide for professionals*. Cambridge: Cambridge University Press, pp. 132–149.

Suzuki, L.A., O'Shaughnessy, T.A., Roysircar, G., Ponterotto, J.G. and Carter, R.T. (2019) 'Counseling psychology and the amelioration of oppression: translating our knowledge into action', *The Counseling Psychologist*, 47(6), pp. 826–872. Available at: https://doi.org/10.1177/0011000015602595

Tonsager, M.E. (2020) 'How therapeutic assessment became humanistic', in S.E. Finn (ed.) *In our clients' shoes. Theory and techniques of therapeutic assessment*. New York: Routledge, pp. 33–41.

Wechsler, D. (2008) *Wechsler Adult Intelligence Scale–fourth edition (WAIS–IV)*. San Antonio, TX: The Psychological Corporation.

Winnicott, D.W. (1960) 'The theory of the parent-infant relationship', *International Journal of Psychoanalysis*, 41(6), pp. 585–595.

World Health Organization (2022) *International classification of diseases: eleventh revision (ICD-11)*. Available at: https://icd.who.int/en (Accessed: 12 January 2024).

Wright, A.J. (2020) *Conducting psychological assessment: a guide for practitioners*. 2nd edn. Hoboken, NJ: John Wiley & Sons.

Youngstrom, E.A. and Prinstein, M.J. (2020) 'Introduction to evidence-based assessment', in E.A. Youngstrom, M.J. Prinstein, E.J. Mash and R.A. Barkley (eds) *Assessment of disorders in childhood and adolescence*. 5th edn. New York: The Guilford Press, pp. 3–29.

Chapter 10

Working with risk

Andrew Reeves

Contents

Introduction

moonsquarepluto2019

Miserere by Martina Morrow. The darkness in this image, devoid of clear meanings and colours, could represent a person's emotional and psychological state when they are contemplating suicide.

Working with clients at risk can challenge all of us, from those just starting out on their training journey through to those who have been in practice for years. There are many features of working with risk in the therapy room that can raise anxieties, but the overarching challenge is the uncertainty that we experience: in truth, no matter what we ask and how we might explore risk, we will never definitively know whether a client is going to act on their thoughts. There have been attempts over the years to try to introduce objective measurement for considering risk but, as you will explore in this chapter, best practice guidance now specifically directs practitioners away from using risk assessment tools.

The intention of this chapter is to unpack some of the key elements of working with risk. It will also explore what we mean by risk, and how we – and our clients – can approach it to create opportunities for positive change. Essentially, the theme of this chapter is about collaboration: it's about counsellors and clients working together in a shared endeavour.

The chapter brings this theme to life by drawing on the fictional case of Abeba, who undergoes bereavement counselling. The case explores how Abeba's therapist, Ashe, may work with her to assess her risk and create a safety plan.

This chapter contributes towards achieving the **SCoPEd competency 2.8.B**:

Ability to devise and use a comprehensive risk assessment strategy.

(SCoPEd Framework, 2022, p. 19)

This chapter aims to:

- consider what the term 'risk' means in the therapy context
- explore ways in which the counsellor's personal perspectives might shape how they approach risk
- describe how the professional context of practice informs how counsellors respond to clients at risk
- explain how to ask clients about risk, and the options to consider having asked these questions
- describe how safety plans can be used to support clients at risk.

1 What do we mean by 'risk'?

Before thinking about what risk means, it is useful to reflect on what risk can feel like: fear, danger, excitement and ambivalence are just a few examples. For some, risk is something to embrace in life, whereas for others it feels best avoided. Such responses are contextual as well: our attitude to risk might inform how we travel, where we go on holiday, the sports we engage with or how we manage our money. Risk as an emotional concept is fluid and profoundly shaped by context, including our own history and life journey.

Risk is further defined through a cultural lens; much of our understanding of risk is shaped by a Western definition of action and behaviour. This is no truer than for therapeutic environments: one service might be very risk-embracing, while another is risk-averse. This might also be true for individual counsellors in their work. It is helpful to remember that different clients will present with risk in different ways, and the task is to engage with the meaning and definition of risk that is pertinent for their context.

In terms of context, it could be argued that counselling has become increasingly shaped by a diagnostic framing of risk over the last few decades, where risk assessment – which draws on scientific research through a process of an identification of risk factors – has dominated thinking and practice (Reeves, 2017; Johnstone, 2022). Risk has often been reduced to a binary concept: people are either 'at risk', or they are not. The task of the counsellor is to identify if they are and, if so, to act accordingly through a process of mitigation and probably referral to a general practitioner (GP) or mental health team. The reality is, however, that risk is far from binary and presents in different ways, nuanced by context, culture, perspective and individuality; this is true for all of us, including our clients (Reeves, 2015).

A typical dictionary definition of risk will note a kind of exposure to the possibility of an adverse event (e.g. loss or injury), or will describe taking a risk as something bold or daring. Here we see both a negative and positive association with risk.

Pause for thought 10.1

What feelings come up for you when thinking about working around risk with your own clients? How might these feelings shape your work? Do you think your response might depend on the context of practice (e.g. a public organisation compared to private practice)?

1.1 Risk in counselling

In my own research, I have previously offered five areas of risk in counselling: situational, relational, contextual, professional, and personal (Reeves, 2015). These are further defined in Table 10.1.

Table 10.1 Definitions of risk

Type of risk	Definition	Example scenario
Situational	Relates to a specific event or situation, or the potential for that event or situation. Risks include suicide, self-injury, child protection and safeguarding (e.g. against a terrorism threat).	Janin is 12 and is attending school counselling. He attends one session and talks of his 'angry family', and shows bruising on his arm.
Relational	Relates to the relational dynamics in the therapeutic process. They might include sexual attraction or financial mismanagement.	Dana is 19 and has been attending a young person's counselling service. She finds her counsellor, Sasha, very attractive and plucks up the courage to ask her out on a date.
Contextual	Relates to the context in which counselling is delivered. This might include an inequitable delivery of a service, processes that hinder equal access, or poor working practices.	A community centre offers free counselling to people living locally in a diverse community. The service only accepts self-referral by completion of an online form, which is only available in English.
Professional	Relates to acts that have the potential to undermine the integrity of counselling or the wider profession. This might include criticising other professionals or inappropriate posts on social media.	Ahmed is a counsellor working in a busy service. He has a difficult afternoon and posts on his social media account how frustrating he has found some of his clients that day. He thinks this is okay because his account can only be accessed by friends and family.
Personal	Relates to the personal cost of working as a counsellor in the event of poor self-care. This might include vicarious trauma, burnout or difficulties in personal relationships.	Mike has a busy caseload of clients, many of whom have suicidal thoughts. He notices how he is becoming irritable both in his therapeutic practice and in his personal relationships.

> **Pause for thought 10.2**
>
> Having considered Table 10.1, do certain types of risk worry you more than others? If so, why might that be the case?

1.2 Responding to risk as people and practitioners

There is very little certainty in assessing risk (in terms of an externally definable truth) and much that is subjective (interpreted through one's individual social, cultural and relational lens). The most important starting point for working with risk, therefore, is us, the counsellors. It is critically important that we not only reflect on those factors that shape our individual perspectives, but that we question them too. This is not to say there is one single way of thinking, but that we need to ensure that how we think about risk doesn't inadvertently shape what we do, consciously or unconsciously. As Khan (2023) suggests, working with diversity demands that counsellors do not simply see difference as sitting within their client (the 'normative' position), but rather that both counsellor and client work together with the individual differences they both bring to the relationship. In doing so, counsellors can gently begin to push the limitations of how we see risk, and move to adopt a more inclusive, less risk-averse position (Part 1 of this book discussed diversity issues). By constructing risk collaboratively, client autonomy and judgement is respected, and there is less chance that the client's behaviour (e.g. particular kinds of sexual behaviour) is inappropriately labelled as creating risk.

Reflecting on your personal responses to risk in the context of your social, cultural and relational experience is critical for working effectively with clients. Take suicide risk as an example: depending on one's cultural, religious or political experiences, responses can range from accepting it is everyone's right to make that choice, through to considering it to be a mortal sin (e.g. Kawashima *et al.*, 2020).

It is critical too that we engage with our emotional responses to risk and how that shapes our responses. Risk can relate to actions that may evoke significant anxiety in counsellors – such as suicide, self-injury and acts of violence – but can equally relate to events that are harder to spot (and thus do not evoke emotion) like online bullying, emotional harm and neglect. Counsellors may focus on the risks that can be clearly identified and evoke a strong emotional reaction, while unintentionally overlooking those that are less apparent but just as damaging, as outlined in Table 10.1.

2 Factors informing current practice

risk assessment tools

Tools used for generating a measurable risk in counselling. Common tools include self-report questionnaires that touch on self-harm or suicide, and questionnaires completed by mental health professionals which systematically screen for risk.

Some scholars have argued that counselling has become increasingly dominated by a medical discourse of risk factors; this medical discourse arose from the extensive research on risk factors in the context of mental health and the subsequent creation of **risk assessment tools** (Kinderman, 2019; Watson, 2019). In relation to risk, an increased use of – and perhaps dependency on – risk assessment tools may, in part, be a response to individual and organisational anxiety about 'getting it wrong' (Reeves, 2010; 2017). This has permeated counselling too: it is not uncommon for counsellors to use risk assessment tools as part of assessing risk (Rossouw, Smythe and Greener, 2011). However, many have argued for some considerable time that risk assessment tools have limited efficacy in determining risk, and that these have instead moved practitioners away from meaningful discussions about risk with their clients to superficially completing the task simply because it is expected (making it a 'box-ticking exercise') (Large *et al.*, 2016).

In the UK, there has been a significant shift in what is considered good practice around managing suicide and self-harm risk, specifically in response to ongoing concerns about the efficacy of such tools: the Royal College of Psychiatrists (2020) has now advised against the use of risk assessment tools. Additionally, in their guidance on working with suicide and self-harm that was published in late 2022, the National Institute for Health and Care Excellence (NICE) specifically directed against using risk assessment tools to: predict suicide and self-harm risks; differentiate levels of risk; and determine who should be allocated to services and when they should be discharged (NICE, 2022). While such guidance is often focused on health and social care, the strength of the NICE guidance is likely to permeate through all working contexts.

> ## Pause for thought 10.3
>
> What do you consider to be the challenges and opportunities of talking with clients about risk, rather than relying on risk assessment tools?

The NICE guidance talks of the need to undertake a 'risk formulation', or a clear assessment of the client, at the outset of therapy or during the assessment in order to identify risk (NICE, 2022). It also recommends that practitioners review this assessment in an ongoing way (the general principles of formulation were introduced in Chapter 9). Additionally, they advise the use of safety plans, which will be discussed in Section 3. Considering what we know about risk generally, it could be fair to say that all risks are better explored through the core business of what we do, fostering the therapeutic relationship and using our counselling skills to ask questions, reflect, paraphrase and explore meaning. By doing so, we become less reliant on broad-brush risk factors and instead help ourselves – and, importantly, the client – to identify the specific factors that might either lead that individual into danger or be worked with as a mechanism for change.

2.1 Dialogue as a liberating approach

The move away from relying on risk assessment tools brings us back to the consideration of how risk is talked about in counselling and how this dialogue can also begin to attend to unconscious processes. The call for dialogue is not new; a good example of this challenge can be seen as far back as the late 1990s:

> Our best route to understanding suicide is not through the study of the structure of the brain, nor the study of social statistics, nor the study of mental diseases, but directly through the study of human emotions described … in the words of the suicidal person. The most important question to a potentially suicidal person is not an inquiry about family history or laboratory tests of blood or spinal fluid, but 'Where do you hurt?' and 'How can I help you?'
>
> *(Shneidman, 1998, p. 24)*

With this approach, Edwin S. Shneidman, one of the most respected and accomplished researchers on suicide, challenged the predominant use of risk factors for determining and managing suicide risk – for example, brain studies, social statistics and diagnostic frameworks – in favour of dialogue. However, while the presumption here is that the use of dialogue 'liberates' counsellors to reconnect with our core therapy values, it does not come without some challenges. Michaud *et al.* (2021, p. 416) state that 'countertransference towards suicidal patients may blur healthcare professionals' clinical judgment and lead to suboptimal decision-making'. In my own research (Reeves *et al.*, 2004), it was found that counsellors often actively avoided dialogue about suicide risk with their clients, regardless of their working modality, due to unacknowledged countertransference feelings (for more on this, see Leenaars, 2004).

The fear of talking about risk is often based on a belief that finding out about risk would be the worst outcome. The reality, of course, is that *not* asking about risk, but instead speculating and ruminating on it as a possibility, may lead to higher anxiety. As is often the case in life, we can deal with what we know; it is what we fear that can cause us the most emotional turmoil.

You will now consider the case illustration of Abeba, who is introduced in the next example.

> ## Case example: Abeba starts bereavement counselling
>
> Abeba is 19 years old and has been seeing a bereavement counsellor for four months, following the unexpected death of her mother. Much of her extended family lives in Ghana, but Abeba's parents and her older brother moved to the UK before she was born. She is devastated at her mother's death and, while close to her father and brother, feels that she has lost her primary female familial connection. Her counsellor, Ashe, is very much aware of the importance of a trauma-informed approach to understanding Abeba's loss, and an early assessment identified some self-injury and suicidal thoughts, though with no intent. Abeba continues to present as highly distressed. Risk has not been revisited since the initial meeting.

From a comprehensive 'risk assessment' perspective (as required by SCoPEd competency 2.8.B), there are several risk factors here for Ashe to consider:

- traumatic bereavement
- age
- loss of key support figure
- distance from support of extended family
- self-injury
- thoughts of suicide
- high level of distress.

Perhaps the biggest risk, however, is that the specific discussion about risk took place four months prior, and does not appear to be embedded as part of the ongoing counselling. Discussing risk early on is important for informing the following actions:

- *Determining the appropriateness and scope of counselling.* Talking about risk helps to establish some of the contractual parameters of the work, and provides a space for both the counsellor and the client to think about whether counselling is right at a particular time. It is critical that Ashe ensures Abeba can make an *informed* decision about beginning counselling, because if she can't, then alternative support might be more appropriate.
- *Bringing risk into the therapeutic space.* A lot of stigma still sits around risk. Research suggests that many clients will be wary of talking about those aspects of themselves, for fear of how the counsellor might respond (Reeves, 2010). Ashe asking about risk early on served to both determine Abeba's safety and to offer 'permission' for Abeba to talk about it.

- *Setting a benchmark.* Risk factors are generally too broad to be helpful when applied at an individual level (Large *et al.*, 2016). Moreover, by talking about risk, a shared understanding of Abeba's specific risk can be achieved – but this is only useful if it is then carried forward in an ongoing dialogue, where Ashe can reflect with Abeba on what, if anything, is changing for her.

Dialogue has the potential to liberate both client and counsellor so that risk becomes *part* of the therapy, rather than something that sits separately from it, simply to be managed.

2.2 What to do after asking the question

Here lies the conundrum: while the primary focus of working with risk tends to be on the importance of asking and then continuing to talk about risk, less attention is given to what to do after the question has been asked. For example, if areas of risk are explored early in the process and no risk is identified, the temptation for many counsellors can be to see it as a 'job done'. Perhaps because of a genuine belief that there is no risk present, or because of anxiety about revisiting it, or because of the countertransferential dynamics highlighted earlier, risk can too easily slip out of the dialogue, as you saw in Abeba's case illustration.

When asked about risk, there is usually one answer out of a possible three:

1 risks are present, which can then be further explored
2 no risks are present
3 there may be risks, but these are not identified because the client is not yet ready to talk about them.

This third scenario emphasises the need for Ashe to maintain the possibility of risk in the therapeutic dialogue and to create space for Abeba to revisit her thinking about it.

Pause for thought 10.4

If you were Ashe, how would you feel about revisiting a discussion with Abeba about the risks identified earlier on? How might you go about bringing that into the dialogue so that the discussion remains therapeutically driven, rather than driven by anxiety or a 'box-ticking' exercise?

Case example: Making sense of Abeba's risk

Ashe asks Abeba about how she thinks things are progressing, and whether she continues to have thoughts of suicide or is still self-injuring. Abeba says that her thoughts of suicide are daily, but that she doesn't think she has plans to act on them. She says she actually finds them comforting: her faith gives her the belief that she will eventually be reunited with her mother, and that death, ultimately, is simply the moving on from one state to another. She feels distraught by the loss of her mother, but comforted by her sense that through her own eventual death she will be reunited − albeit right now she does not actively want to join her mother in death. Likewise, Abeba explains that cutting oneself is not uncommon in her culture, and that it is understood as a mechanism through which one can connect the spiritual, cultural, emotional and physical together in one act.

The risk factors that remain are: Abeba's suicidal thoughts, self-injury, traumatic loss and relative isolation. However, the dialogue has enabled Ashe to develop a more nuanced and relevant understanding of what these factors mean to Abeba.

2.3 Relational ethics

How we work with risk is essentially about navigating different ethical possibilities. As practitioners and members of a professional association, we have usually given a commitment to work to a code or framework of ethics. We could refer to such codes and frameworks as 'top-level' ethics (Gabriel and Reeves, 2024), in that they provide overarching principles that relate to all client work and all contexts. In part, this is often why practitioners can also be frustrated by them: they turn to such frameworks at times of difficulty for specific answers, but find that the specifics are not there. To bring this back to Abeba's case, such top-level ethics will not tell Ashe how she should respond to Abeba.

relational ethics

Ethical considerations that arise from the therapeutic relationship between therapist and client. They emphasise the importance of mutual respect, empathy and collaborative attentiveness to ethical issues as they arise, ensuring that both parties' needs are honoured.

It is impossible to provide definitive answers about what you should actually do once you have asked the question about risk. Outcomes can vary from: counselling no longer being a desired approach for either the client (e.g. when different services are needed) or the counsellor (e.g. if they reach a limit of confidence or competence); continuing with counselling; referring to another agency with consent; referring to another agency without consent; or instigating an emergency response in the event where risk is considered *immediate*. However, the principles of **relational ethics** provide a helpful structure that supports an ongoing dialogue with the client and, where possible, involves the client in any decision-making processes following the emergence of any risks.

3 Keeping the client safe

'Keeping it safe' in therapy

Approaches to risk have tended to focus on the binary approach, as already discussed. As such, if someone is identified as being 'at risk', then the next steps can often be centred around referral to another service – though this must always be managed with care, so that the client's needs are not overlooked in this process. However, retaining risk as a part of the ongoing therapeutic dialogue means that the client and counsellor can take a more nuanced approach, which better supports the therapy. It remains important, of course, that the safety of the client and others is a key consideration, and where there are concerns that need a response (e.g. immediate risk of suicide or child protection), these should be acted on. If working in an organisational context, it is crucial that the counsellor and their supervisor are clear about policy or procedural expectations around risk and work consistently with these. Likewise, if the counsellor is working in a multidisciplinary setting, they need to be able to find appropriate ways to collaborate with their colleagues; it is always important to remember that, regardless of context, counselling is rarely the only thing that will benefit a client at risk, and other services and support will often bring meaningful benefits as well.

The first step in 'keeping it safe' is ensuring that risk continues to be part of the dialogue. This does not mean simply asking questions about risk, but using risk as a gateway for therapeutic exploration. Ashe perhaps could talk with Abeba about her suicidal thoughts and how that relates to her connection with her mother, or her self-injury and its meaning for her in expressing what she finds hard to put into words. These discussions are therapeutically central, but attention also needs to be given to how the client can be safe in that process. Counsellors, like other mental health professionals, have increasingly used 'keep safe plans' (a type of safety plan) as a way of structuring such discussions (Knapp, 2023).

3.1   The importance of action

There are instances in the UK context where counsellors are required to act due to legal requirements even without client consent: in matters of child protection or terrorism threat, for example. Beyond legal requirements, it might be necessary for a counsellor to break confidentiality, if consent cannot be obtained, in order to seek help (e.g. if threats of violence are made to another person or the counsellor). If the risk of suicide is considered imminent (i.e. suicide is likely in the short term), a referral to a mental health crisis service may be required. Likewise, if a client leaves the counselling room saying it is their intention to end their life and cannot be persuaded to give consent, a call to emergency services might be required to prevent harm to themselves or others. Where possible, a discussion with your supervisor or another manager should take place, but if this would cause a delay, the counsellor should act immediately. The client's capacity here is an important consideration. The scope of this chapter does not allow for a full discussion, but the NHS (2024) provides useful guidance around the relevant UK legislation, which is titled the Mental Capacity Act.

Case example: Developing a safety plan with Abeba

Ashe suggests to Abeba that it might be helpful to think more specifically about her thoughts, feelings and struggles now, as a way of offering additional support. Abeba agrees, and they develop a safety plan together. The plan helps Abeba to really understand what makes her feel worse (too much time alone) and what makes her feel better (spending time with her aunt). This plan is reviewed regularly to remove any aspects that turn out not to be helpful, and to incorporate others that are working better for Abeba in practice.

3.2 Planning for safety

Developing a safety plan in collaboration with a client essentially involves exploring with them those factors that make things feel more safe or unsafe – supplemented with key helpline numbers as well as contact information for their GP and other services – and drawing up a menu of resources or strategies that they can refer to at points of higher crisis. Sometimes this process begins with scaling, where the client is asked to score how they feel now, when it feels the worst and when it feels the best on a scale from 10 (high risk) to 1 (no risk). Scaling is subjective and is not about assessing degrees of risk, but is simply a mechanism through which the client can reflect on their experiences with some structure. Some additional considerations about approaches to managing risk are detailed in Box 10.1.

Box 10.1 'Keep safe' or 'no harm'?

A keep safe plan is a mechanism whereby, through collaborative dialogue with the client, exploration focuses on what helps the client to keep safe, and builds that into a tailored plan that the client can take away. Adapted versions of these can be used in both in-person and online counselling, and with adults, children and young people. A 'no-harm contract' is a mechanism through which the client makes a commitment, to themselves and their therapist, not to act on any thoughts related to self-harm or harm towards others in between sessions. The former approach can be hugely effective, while the latter has been subject to much debate and criticism (Rozek *et al.*, 2022). The use of safety plans as opposed to no-harm contracts has generally emerged as a consensus, and is the approach recommended by NICE in their guidance (NICE, 2022).

There are several key advantages in this approach to keeping the client safe. Safety plans:

- are *collaborative and empowering*. They are typically developed collaboratively, which empowers the client by involving them in creating strategies that are specific to their needs and preferences.
- offer an *individualised approach*. They are tailored to the individual needs and circumstances of the client, by considering the client's unique triggers, warning signs and coping mechanisms.
- are *preventative and proactive*. Safety plans focus on identifying and managing potential risks before they escalate.
- help to *structure the response* to crisis. Safety plans offer specific steps and coping strategies that the client can use during difficult moments. Having a plan in place can help the client to feel more prepared and in control when faced with challenging situations.

- promote *communication and trust*. The process of developing a safety plan involves open communication through discussing potential risks, coping strategies and support networks, which can strengthen the therapeutic relationship. Clients may feel more comfortable sharing their concerns and experiences, in turn fostering a sense of trust and understanding.

It's important to note that safety plans are just one component of a comprehensive therapeutic approach. While they can be valuable in managing immediate risks, other factors are crucial for long-term well-being, including ongoing therapy, exploration of underlying issues, fostering emotional regulation capacity and addressing the root causes of distress. Additionally, the effectiveness of a safety plan depends on the willingness of the client to engage in the process and the ongoing collaboration between the client and the counsellor.

Case example: Making sense of Abeba's case in supervision

Ashe discusses with her supervisor her concerns about Abeba. They talk about Abeba's thoughts of suicide and Ashe's supervisor expresses some concern. However, having talked it through in some depth with Abeba, Ashe feels more reassured that any risk is not imminent. While she agrees with her supervisor that a dialogue with the GP (with Abeba's consent) would be of potential value, she does not want to break Abeba's confidence at this point. There is a sense of friction between Ashe and her supervisor about this.

In this chapter you have already explored the importance of understanding the social, cultural and relational lenses that shape the experience of working with risk in the therapeutic space. This is equally true for supervision, where the relational dynamics are likely to be paralleled in the supervisory relationship. What is critically important is that counsellors talk with their supervisors *before* such issues arise to ensure a shared understanding and that agreed expectations are in place. Instead, what often happens is that such issues are brought into supervision at the point of concern. The challenge, therefore, is for the supervisor and counsellor to find a way of navigating both the ethical issues emerging from the therapy process as well as the relational challenges in supervision at the same time. It is not unheard of for supervisory ruptures to be encountered at the point where a counsellor realises that their perspective on working with risk is quite different from their supervisor's. This can, and should, be avoided through an early dialogue that explores not only each person's attitude towards risk in therapy, but also an exploration of how risk might be effectively engaged with in therapy, in the specific context in which the counsellor works.

> ### Pause for thought 10.5
>
> Have you talked to your supervisor about what you expect of each other when working with risk? How do you feel about having this discussion?

Good supervision doesn't just happen; it needs to be continually worked on (as discussed in Chapter 8). Given the challenges that arise during practice while working with risk, it is an ethical imperative that early discussion about risk takes place in the supervisory space to ensure that the supervision can be an important place of support and not a potential cause of stress.

3.3 An action plan for client safety

All of what you have explored so far points to a set of actions that you can incorporate into your own practice when working with risk:

1 *Engage* in an initial, and ongoing, dialogue around risk, ensuring that clients are given space and time to talk about those aspects of themselves that cause hurt, danger and uncertainty.

2 *Collaboratively explore* those factors with the client, such as their perceived severity of the problems encountered and how able they feel to identify, and access, a system of support.

3 *Develop a safety plan* with your client through a collaborative dialogic process, including coping strategies, emergency contacts and steps to take during moments of crisis.

4 *Double-check* with the client to ensure that the safety plan is something they are engaged with and consent to; make sure the plan isn't ultimately there to support you with your anxiety, but rather that it supports the needs of the client.

5 *Clearly communicate* the limits of confidentiality to the client, explaining in clear terms what that means; for example, if you were to refer them on to other services, when that would be with the client's consent and when it might be without it.

6 *Obtain informed consent* for any necessary disclosures or interventions.

7 *Consult with colleagues and/or supervisors* so that you are already prepared for discussions around risk.

8 *Work collaboratively with other professionals* as needed.

9 *Share relevant information* with appropriate professionals to ensure a comprehensive and coordinated approach to client care.

10 *Regularly engage in supervision* to discuss challenging cases, ethical considerations and personal reactions to client issues.

11 *Stay informed* about the latest research, guidelines and best practices related to working with clients at risk.

12 *Engage in continued professional development* to enhance your skills in working with risk and ethical decision making.

Both the client and the counsellor may feel empowered by these steps as they work together to identify and manage risk. This chapter finishes by illustrating how this might be experienced in Abeba's case.

Case example: Abeba's final sessions

Over time, Abeba moves from crisis to having some sense of security, feeling more grounded in her experience of loss. She acknowledges that her mother's death has created a profound and irrefutable emotional scar that she will always carry.

In her final sessions with Ashe, she is quite reflective, saying: 'I really felt listened to here, honoured … it's hard to put it into words. You were prepared to really go there, you know, to be alongside me in my most frightening places without panic or hurrying me along. That was the thing that really changed things for me; that you were prepared to not only listen to me, but to try and see things from where I was standing. You can't even begin to imagine how important that was.'

Pause for thought 10.6

Where are you now in terms of your understanding of the issues raised in this chapter? What might you want to do to further develop your ability to work with risk?

Conclusion

The aim of this chapter was to explore the concept of risk in the context of therapy, and how counsellors can respond to it. The principles outlined throughout this chapter have hopefully offered a scaffold through which you can consider your practice and work to embed relational ways of working with risk.

These principles will help you engage in good practice and bring confidence to your work, therefore mitigating the dangers that we might encounter and supporting you to connect with clients to ensure a collaborative approach. Ultimately, collaboration is key; if a client is unable to agree, disagree or engage with a discussion about risk, this might suggest that counselling is either an unsafe option for them at that point, or that other services should be brought under consideration.

Further reading

- The following online resource (with videos) demonstrates how to work relationally with risk:

  BACP (2024) *Exploring suicidal risk with clients (GPiA EL002).* Available at:

  https://www.bacp.co.uk/cpd/exploring-suicidal-risk-with-clients-gpiael2

- The following book provides resources on how to work effectively and ethically with risk:

  Reeves, A. (2015) *Working with risk in counselling and psychotherapy.* London: SAGE

- The following book provides resources on working with risk in the context of domestic violence:

  Roddy, J. (ed.) (2023) *Working with client experiences of domestic abuse: a handbook for counsellors, psychotherapists, and other mental health professionals.* London: Routledge.

References

Gabriel, L. and Reeves, A. (2024) *Navigating relational ethics in day-to-day practice: ethics in the counselling professions*. London: Routledge.

Johnstone, L. (2022) *A straight talking introduction to psychiatric diagnosis*. 2nd edn. Ross-on-Wye: PCCS Books.

Kawashima, D., Kawamoto, S., Shiraga, K. and Kawano, K. (2020) 'Is suicide beautiful? Suicide acceptance and related factors in Japan', *Crisis:*, 41(2), pp. 114–120. Available at: https://doi.org/10.1027/0227-5910/a000612

Khan, M. (2023) *Working within diversity: a reflective guide to anti-oppressive practice in counselling and therapy*. London: Jessica Kingsley.

Kinderman, P. (2019) *A manifesto for mental health: why we need a revolution in mental health care*. London: Palgrave MacMillan.

Knapp, S. (2023) 'The essentials of creating effective safety planning-type interventions for suicidal patients', *Practice Innovations*, 8(2), pp. 131–140. Available at: https://doi.org/10.1037/pri0000205

Large, M., Kaneson, M., Myles, N., Myles, H., Gunaratne, P. and Ryan, C. (2016) 'Meta-analysis of longitudinal cohort studies of suicide risk assessment among psychiatric patients: heterogeneity in results and lack of improvement over time', *PLoS One*, 11(6), article number e0156322. Available at: https://doi.org/10.1371/journal.pone.0156322

Leenaars, A.A. (2004) *Psychotherapy with suicidal people: a person-centred approach*. London: Wiley.

Michaud, L., Greenway, K.T., Corbeil, S., Bourquin, C. and Richard-Devantoy, S. (2021) 'Countertransference towards suicidal patients: a systematic review', *Current Psychology*, 42, pp. 416–430. Available at: https://doi.org/10.1007/s12144-021-01424-0

NHS (2024) *Mental Capacity Act*. Available at: https://www.nhs.uk/conditions/social-care-and-support-guide/making-decisions-for-someone-else/mental-capacity-act (Accessed: 3 June 2024).

NICE (2022) *Self-harm: assessment, management and preventing recurrence*. NICE guideline NG225. Available at: https://www.nice.org.uk/guidance/ng225 (Accessed: 3 June 2024).

Reeves, A. (2010) *Counselling suicidal clients*. London: SAGE.

Reeves, A. (2015) *Working with risk in counselling and psychotherapy*. London: SAGE

Reeves, A. (2017) 'In a search for meaning: challenging the accepted know-how of working with suicide risk', *British Journal of Guidance & Counselling*, 45(5), pp. 606–609. Available at: https://doi.org/10.1080/03069885.2017.1377338

Reeves, A., Bowl, R., Wheeler, S. and Guthrie, E. (2004) 'The hardest words: exploring the dialogue of suicide in the counselling process — A discourse analysis', *Counselling and Psychotherapy Research*, 4(1), pp. 62–71. Available at: https://doi.org/10.1080/14733140412331384068

Rossouw, G., Smythe, E. and Greener, P. (2011) 'Therapists' experience of working with suicidal clients', *Indo-Pacific Journal of Phenomenology*, 11(1), pp. 1–12. Available at: https://doi.org/10.2989/ipjp.2011.11.1.4.1103

Royal College of Psychiatrists (2020) *Self-harm and suicide in adults: final report of the Patient Safety Group*. CR229. Available at: https://www.rcpsych.ac.uk/improving-care/campaigning-for-better-mental-health-policy/college-reports/2020-college-reports/cr229 (Accessed: 3 June 2024).

Rozek, D.C., Tyler, H., Fina, B.A., Baker, S.N., Moring, J.C., Smith, N.B., Baker, J.C., Bryan, A.O., Bryan, C.J. and Dondanville, K.A. (2022) 'Suicide intervention practices: what is being used by mental health clinicians and mental health allies?', *Archives of Suicide Research*, 27(3), pp. 1034–1046. Available at: https://doi.org/10.1080/13811118.2022.2106923

SCoPEd Framework (2022), collaboratively developed by Association of Christian Counsellors (ACC), British Association for Counselling and Psychotherapy (BACP), British Psychoanalytic Council (BPC), Human Givens Institute (HGI), National Counselling and Psychotherapy Society (NCPS) and United Kingdom Council for Psychotherapy (UKCP). Available at: https://www.bacp.co.uk/about-us/advancing-the-profession/scoped/scoped-framework (Accessed: 12 June 2024).

Shneidman, E.S. (1998) *The suicidal mind*. Oxford: Oxford University Press

Watson, J. (ed.) (2019) *Drop the disorder! Challenging the culture of psychiatric diagnosis*. Ross-on-Wye: PCCS Books.

Chapter 11

Conceptualising and assessing mental health difficulties

Naomi Moller

Contents

Introduction

Alone by Carys Treadwell

As defined in Chapter 9, assessment in the context of counselling involves working collaboratively with the client to more deeply understand the issues that have brought them into counselling. Assessment is important not only at the beginning, but across therapy, as it helps the work to be focused where it needs to be. From a service perspective, assessment is also about identifying whether a client is appropriate for a particular service and/or counsellor. While assessment in counselling is very different from psychiatric assessment, which aims to arrive at a psychiatric diagnosis of the patient, there is an overlap, as in both cases the central concern is understanding a client's mental health difficulties. This chapter consequently considers how 'mental health difficulties' can be conceptualised, and how different understandings shape both treatment and what is assessed. The aim of the chapter is to stimulate your thinking about what can or should be included in a counselling assessment while reminding you that how you conduct an assessment is as important as what you assess. This chapter argues for a respectful, client-centred and holistic approach.

Across this chapter you will follow the story of a (fictional) client, Eli, providing a case against which you can consider and apply elements of assessment. Like Chapter 1, this chapter contributes towards achieving the **SCoPEd competency 2.5.B**:

Ability to conceptualise, evaluate and take account of a range of mental health problems, symptoms of psychological distress, functioning and coping styles (with due understanding of cultural norms), during assessment and throughout therapy.

(SCoPEd Framework, 2022, p. 19)

Chapter 1 argued for a central consideration of the role of culture in conceptualising mental health and for the importance of taking a culturally sensitive approach to working therapeutically with psychological distress.

This chapter aims to:

- consider theories of mental health difficulties, including the debates around different understandings of causation

- explore systems of classification for mental health difficulties and the implications of these

- examine non-symptom-based ways of assessing mental health difficulties, including functioning and coping styles

- consider what can be included in holistic assessments of mental health difficulties

- reflect on how to assess client suitability for a particular service/ counsellor.

1 Theorising causation

Theories that seek to explain why people develop mental health difficulties are important because they often logically suggest what the treatment approach should be. For example, if you understand the problem to lie in brain dysfunction, then cutting into the brain (cutting out the problem?) might seem like a logical response. Indeed, performing lobotomies – a procedure which involved 'inserting surgical instruments resembling ice picks into the frontal lobes of patients and blindly destroying neural tissue' (Acharya, 2004, p. 2) – was popular in the 1940s for the treatment of mental illness. Lobotomies were performed on thousands of people worldwide, leading to its pioneer, António Egas Moniz, receiving a Nobel Prize in 1949 (Terrier, Lévêque and Amelot, 2019).

Lobotomies, however, also resulted in unwanted side effects in terms of cognitive decline and personality changes (Hoffman, 1949). These side effects, plus the advent of new classes of psychotropic drugs, in particular antipsychotics (Cunningham Owens and Johnstone, 2018), as well as advances in understandings of the brain (including the importance of the frontal lobes), led to lobotomies losing their appeal as a treatment. Nonetheless, the idea of a biological or genetic basis to mental health difficulties is still prevalent (as discussed in the following section). However, there are other ways to think about causation.

1.1 What causes mental health difficulties?

The Mental Health Foundation (a charity working to promote better mental health in the UK) identifies three main categories of factors that impact mental health: biological, psychological and social (Mental Health Foundation, 2023). While the biopsychosocial model of mental health is well known, the factors that are included in each category, and how much each category is emphasised or valued, has varied across time, and likely also across professional discipline.

Biomedical

The biomedical model maintains that mental health difficulties have biological and genetic origins. The term 'biomedical' is used here, rather than 'biological', to highlight the association with the medical/psychiatric approach to mental health, which has been hugely influential, both historically and globally, in how mental health difficulties are understood and treated.

The biomedical approach has also been strongly criticised. In 2023, the World Health Organization declared that it was formally moving away from endorsing a biomedical paradigm for mental health on the basis that, by failing to acknowledge the social and environmental factors that are causative for mental health difficulties, this approach allows these factors to be ignored by healthcare systems and governments (World Health Organization, 2023).

While it is important to acknowledge criticisms of an exclusionary biomedical model, it is also important to acknowledge that biological or genetic factors can play a part in mental health difficulties. Brain disease (including brain tumours and Lewy body dementia) and hormonal imbalances (particularly hypo- and hyperthyroidism) significantly impact mental health. Emerging research implicates even common conditions such as iron deficiency (Lee *et al.*, 2020) or vitamin D deficiency (Parker, Brotchie and Graham, 2017) as potentially causing depressive symptoms. There is also lots of research that suggests a genetic component to mental health difficulties; for example, substantial research suggests a significant genetic component (and hence heritability) for schizophrenia (Henriksen, Nordgaard and Jansson, 2017).

Psychological

Psychological factors in mental health are those that are individual but not biological or genetic. These might include a person's general beliefs and perceptions but also their personality traits, their understanding of their experiences/history and their behaviours, and how these might be interrelated. Relevant factors include the following:

- *Negative beliefs about the self*: Research suggests that low self-esteem makes a person more vulnerable to depression (Sowislo and Orth, 2013; see also Orth and Robins, 2022).

- *Optimism*: Being more optimistic may act as a protective factor against mental health difficulties (Weitzer *et al.*, 2022).

- *Neuroticism*: This is a personality characteristic associated with the propensity to feel negative emotions (including anxiety, fear, sadness, anger and guilt). Unsurprisingly, neuroticism is associated with mental health difficulties, with an analysis of multiple prior studies finding that it *prospectively* predicts the development of future depression and anxiety (Jeronimus *et al.*, 2016).

- *Exercise*: There is accumulating evidence that being physically active reduces an individual's vulnerability to depression (Biddle, 2016; Weinstein, Koehmstedt and Kop, 2017). The relationship might reflect the biological impacts of exercise, but exercising first requires a person to *decide* to do it. Thus, how a person approaches exercise (and many other behaviours, such as how a person eats, sleeps, engages with alcohol or social media) can be considered an individual psychological factor that influences mental health.

Social

A person's social environment can affect their mental health. The World Health Organization (2023, p. xvii) states: 'Mental health and well-being are strongly associated with social, economic, and physical environments, as well as poverty, violence, and discrimination.' Through its central focus on diversity, the current textbook acknowledges the profound negative impact of discrimination and prejudice on mental health (as well as in counselling). Increasing research also evidences – unsurprisingly – how poverty increases risk of mental health difficulties. For instance, poverty is associated with anxiety about, for example, being able to pay for basic living costs; it is also associated with living in inadequate housing, increased exposure to environmental stressors such as pollution and temperature extremes, as well as violence and crime, and poorer physical health, including effects due to diet (Ridley *et al.*, 2020).

Trauma can also be understood as a social/contextual factor. There is a lot of research that evidences that trauma and neglect, particularly in childhood, increase the risk of developing mental health difficulties (e.g. Hughes *et al.*, 2017). Growing recognition of this has contributed to a global rise in **trauma-informed care** in mental health services, including in the NHS (Emsley *et al.*, 2022).

trauma-informed care
An approach that acknowledges that trauma is common in the population, and that clients/patients might be responding in particular ways because of a history of trauma.

Pause for thought 11.1

Consider your own personal theories about where mental health difficulties come from – what explanations do you favour? Do you think that some theories of causation are more prevalent than others in your own professional context?

The case study below introduces Eli, who is experiencing mental distress. Read through the description, keeping in mind the biomedical, psychological and social explanations of mental health covered in this section.

Pause for thought 11.2

What might you want to know about how Eli understands the causes of what they are currently experiencing? For example, does Eli make sense of their own distress in terms of the discrimination experienced by the trans (including non-binary) community in the UK? If so, what might this mean for how you work with them?

Also consider the service perspective. Based on this limited information, what is your current assessment of whether Eli is appropriate for counselling in the third-sector organisation they have approached?

---

2 Symptoms and taxonomies

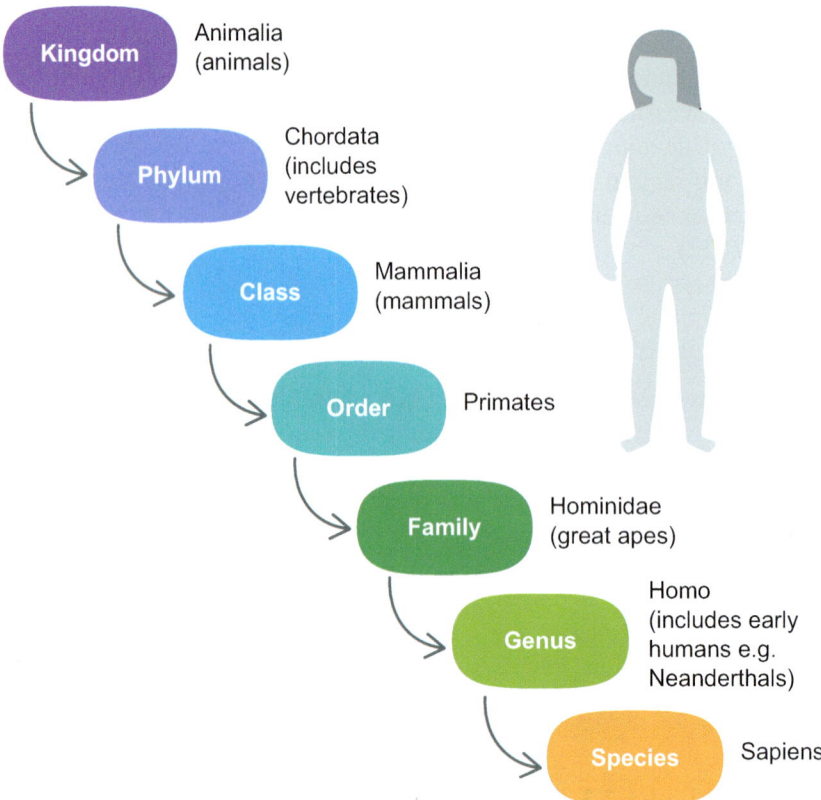

Figure 11.1 A taxonomy of modern humans that shows how they are biologically classified

In order to fully understand a concept or system, conceptual maps can be a useful tool. Taxonomies are conceptual maps which classify phenomena using categories and subcategories. You are likely familiar with zoological classification systems, an example of which is shown in Figure 11.1. Zoological taxonomies are based on evolutionary and genetic similarity. In other words, the categorisation process is based on underlying theories and empirical evidence about how living things relate to each other. As outlined in Chapter 9, within the field of mental health there are two major classification systems:

- The International Classification of Diseases, currently in its eleventh revision (ICD-11), is published by the World Health Organization (2022) and covers both physical and mental health.
- The Diagnostic and Statistical Manual of Mental Disorders, currently in its fifth revision (DSM-5-TR), is published by the American Psychiatric Association (2022).

The ICD-11 is used more in the UK, but the DSM system is also very influential. Both classification systems, developed by medical and psychiatric organisations, can be understood as broadly 'biomedical' and are modelled on approaches to the diagnosis of physical health conditions. This means that psychiatric diagnoses are based on diagnostically trained mental health professionals identifying, in conversation with patients, whether their patients meet the diagnostic threshold in terms of a list of symptoms. For example, in DSM-5-TR, the first criteria for the diagnosis of a 'major depressive episode' is that the patient experiences 'depressed mood most of the day, nearly every day, as indicated by either subjective report (e.g. feels sad, empty, hopeless) or observation made by others (e.g. appears tearful)' (American Psychiatric Association, 2022, p. 6).

While diagnostic processes follow on from theories of the cause of a disease in medicine (e.g. if hypothyroidism is suspected, a doctor will order a blood test to establish blood levels of thyroid hormones), there has been a further move away from formally making assumptions about such causes with each iteration of the DSM and the ICD. There is no blood or saliva test for depression or schizophrenia, for instance, and as discussed above, the idea that all mental health difficulties are caused by something that begins in the body has been hugely contested. Because psychiatric diagnoses are not based on explicit causal theories, one criticism of these systems is that the diagnoses themselves may not be valid.

2.1 Arguments for and against psychiatric diagnosis

Psychiatric diagnosis evolved for important – and positive – reasons: to name, map and differentiate the range of mental health difficulties; to give practitioners a common language; and to support research on causation and treatment. Psychiatric diagnosis also has important real-world influence. Having a psychiatric diagnosis is typically necessary for a person to receive mental health treatment within the NHS, but it is also required in other contexts, including when:

- deciding whether a person should be involuntarily detained in a psychiatric institution
- determining criminal responsibility
- defining eligibility for unemployment and disability benefits (Szmukler, 2013).

Because of their social significance (evident from the list above), diagnoses can be influenced by individual and group campaigns. For example, post-traumatic stress disorder entered the DSM in 1980 in part as a result of campaigns from Vietnam war veterans because this diagnosis created a pathway to military service-related disability benefits (Hermes, Hoff and Rosenheck, 2014). The social influence of diagnosis means that even mental health professionals and clients who reject psychiatric diagnosis may still be impacted by diagnosis in material ways. This creates an argument for counsellors, a professional group that typically receives little education in psychiatric diagnosis, to develop some level of understanding of this domain.

Despite its influence, psychiatric diagnosis has been widely critiqued (e.g. Pilgrim, 2007), not least by those who have been subject to it (Perkins *et al.*, 2018). The empirical and theoretical literature questioning psychiatric diagnosis is extensive and has spanned decades, but as a brief summary, some key criticisms are that psychiatric diagnosis:

- *lacks validity and reliability.* The validity of diagnostic categories themselves are questioned, as well as the process of diagnosis. There is evidence that different clinicians reach different decisions about diagnosis based on the same information (Jablensky, 2016; Cohen, 2017).

- *increasingly pathologises 'normal' human distress.* Each DSM edition, for instance, includes more diagnoses. For the first time it now includes criteria for 'prolonged grief disorder', which enables psychiatric diagnosis of a level of grief response deemed 'disabling'.

- *is stigmatising.* To exemplify the research on this, two large-scale studies found that young people (predominantly from Europe, the United States and Canada) and adults (from six countries in Asia) experienced discrimination and stigma as a result of their psychiatric diagnoses (O'Connor *et al.*, 2018; Zhang *et al.*, 2020).

- *is racist, sexist and heteronormative.* A substantial body of research evidences that the practice of diagnosis is shaped by contemporary discrimination towards marginalised groups. For example: the DSM historically categorised 'homosexuality' as a psychiatric disorder; racialised minorities are disproportionately likely to be diagnosed with psychosis and schizophrenia; and gender stereotypes play out in how men and women are diagnosed with different personality disorders (Garb, 2021).

3 Holistic mental health assessment

Arguments for and against psychiatric diagnosis, as well as its enduring influence, were outlined in the previous section. This section will now move on to explore alternative ways to think about assessing mental health difficulties. The core aim of holistic assessment is to deeply understand the difficulties being experienced by the client; however, as already discussed, before counselling starts it is also critical that a client's suitability for the service and/or counsellor is carefully assessed. For example, is the service appropriate for the client's level and type of distress? In counselling, 'appropriate' typically means working with clients in the mild, moderate and 'low severe' spectrum in terms of level of distress, and additionally with clients who are not showing any signs of psychosis. This is parallel with the typical remit of primary care mental health services in the NHS. However, for people doing counselling assessments, it is not always so easy to judge a client's suitability for the service. For this reason, assessment may be done by more senior or experienced clinicians, and also discussed in team meetings.

Case example: Continuing Eli's assessment

The service clinic manager and the counsellor who assessed Eli are discussing how to think about Eli's self-described 'paranoid' thoughts. In particular, they are trying to decide if the paranoia means that Eli is not suitable for the service that they offer. In the conversation, the assessor says that although Eli described a pattern over about a month of having 'paranoid thoughts', when questioned, Eli also said that even at the time they knew that these thoughts, despite being disturbing, were not real.

During the month that Eli was having these thoughts, they were also experimenting with cannabis 'edibles' to see if these improved their mood. Since this time, Eli has learned that if they are beginning to feel 'paranoid' they can distract themselves by listening to music or reaching out to a friend.

Pause for thought 11.3

Now that you have a bit more information on the case study, have your thoughts changed about whether Eli is suitable for treatment with a third-sector counselling organisation that offers a part-time service and is largely staffed by volunteers? Consider Eli's self-described 'paranoia' and the organisation's likely level of in-house expertise about such complex mental health presentations.

There are, of course, other considerations in assessment. As a counsellor, you will have your own approach to assessment that will be influenced by your training, modality and service setting, as well as any practice specialisms that you might have. While recognising that there is not a single, set approach to assessment in counselling, it may be useful to consider:

- risk (see Chapter 10)
- client suitability for the service/counsellor (discussed further in Section 4)
- client suitability for the modality
- core domains, such as mental health symptoms (and any psychiatric diagnoses that have been given), general functioning, coping, relationships, strengths and resources (discussed in Section 3.1)
- any additional domains that are collaboratively identified by you or your client as important.

3.1 Core assessment domains

Holistic assessment of a person's functioning includes, but is not exclusively focused on, their mental health difficulties. Depending on a client's presenting concerns and a counsellor's theoretical approach, many domains could be assessed, such as: sleep patterns; trauma history; ability to work; transference; attachment style; and eating, drinking or spending behaviour. The following domains appear relevant for all clients.

Functioning

In counselling, it can be useful to get a broad sense of how a person thinks they are doing in terms of managing everyday tasks, including around work and relationships. A counsellor can directly ask this question of a client (e.g. 'How are you?' or 'On a scale of 1 to 10, how are you today?'). For tracking functioning across time, specially developed questionnaires can also be helpful (which will be discussed further in Chapter 12). Two examples are the CORE-10 (Barkham *et al.*, 2013), which is widely used in counselling settings in the UK and assesses 'psychological distress', and ReQoL, a measure developed with significant input from mental health service users that assesses current quality of life (Keetharuth *et al.*, 2018).

In working with a client like Eli, tracking functioning over time can help to uncover patterns – perhaps, for example, that Eli's well-being dips after they spend too much time checking social media to see what their ex-girlfriend is posting about them. Additionally, when Eli is feeling down, it can act as a useful reminder to them that they do not always feel this way.

Coping

The dictionary definition of 'coping' is to successfully manage a difficult situation. In the psychological literature, the concept is used more broadly to determine how a person *attempts* to manage something difficult.

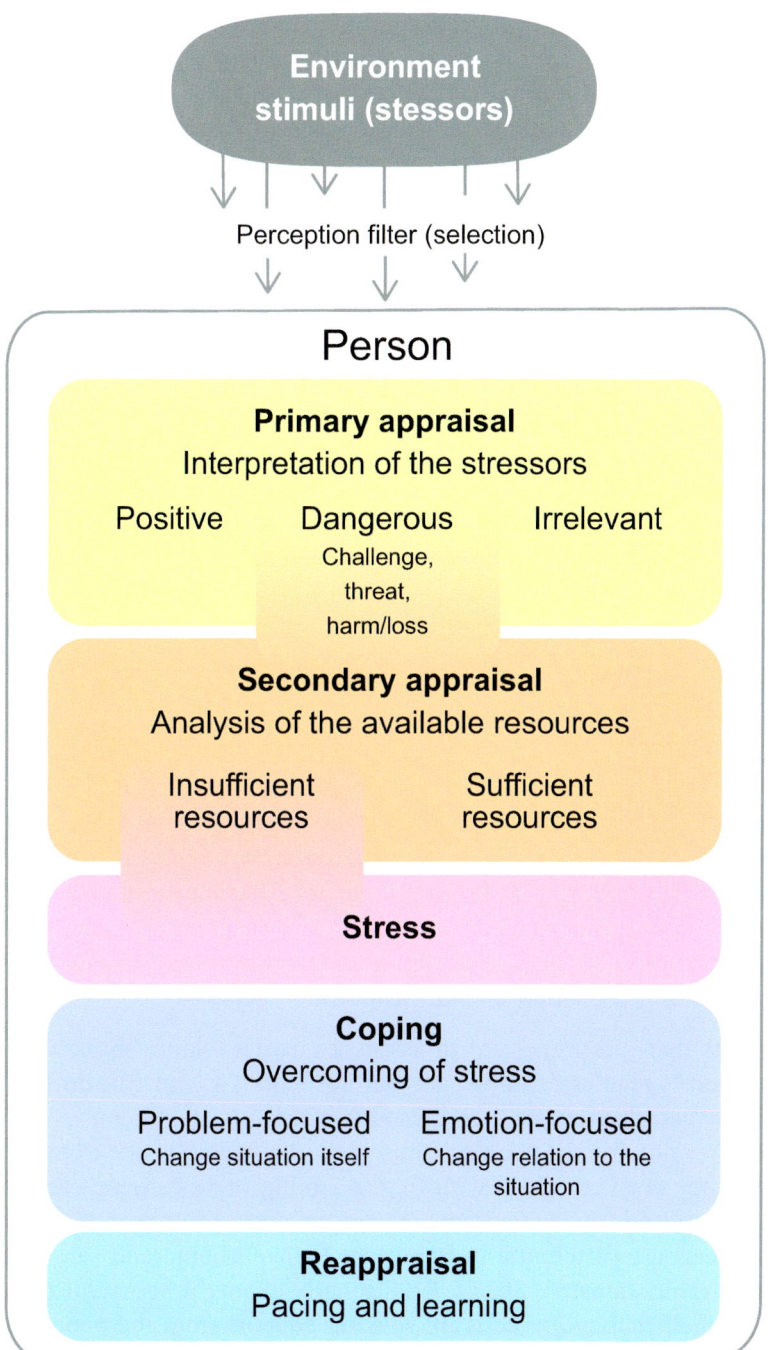

Figure 11.2 Transactional model of stress and coping (Source: Lazarus and Folkman, 1984, p. 16)

The most influential coping theory – the transactional model of stress and coping (Lazarus and Folkman, 1984) – is depicted in Figure 11.2. The figure shows that how a person makes sense of something influences how likely they are to be stressed and, moreover, that there are two key appraisals: of the thing itself (how bad is it?) and of one's own ability to manage that thing. The other key aspect of the model is that it distinguishes between attempts to cope that are focused on the stressor itself (problem-focused coping) and on managing one's own response to the stressor (emotion-focused coping). Historically, problem-focused coping has been seen as 'better', but for some stressors (e.g. having a family member with a terminal illness) there is little a person can do to change a feared outcome. It is therefore increasingly recognised that in such contexts, emotion-focused coping (including repression or avoidance) can be useful, for example to help a person provide support to their family (Biggs, Brough and Drummond, 2017).

In counselling, it can be useful to get a sense of how a person typically copes, or attempts to cope, and to work with the person to establish whether what they are doing is genuinely helpful. For example, is our case study client Eli someone who responds to stressors mostly by trying to avoid them (trying not to think about them, or using alcohol or drugs to block out feelings)? If so, it might be useful to discuss with them possible alternative responses – perhaps reaching out to people in the local trans (including non-binary) community, rather than using edibles.

Relationships

There is a great deal of research that evidences the positive impact of 'good' relationships on the physical and mental health of individuals, as well as the negative impact of 'poor' relationships and lack of relationships (loneliness). To give just one example, a **meta-analysis** of research conducted over a 50-year period, which looked at the associations between physical health and quality of marital relationships in over 72,000 individuals, found that while the impact is statistically small, it is as big as the relationship between physical health and eating fruit and vegetables or doing regular exercise (Robles *et al.*, 2014). In other words, having a good relationship may be as important for your health as eating enough fruit and vegetables!

meta-analysis

A statistical method of combining the results of multiple individual studies, which investigated the same research question, to provide findings that are more compelling because they are based on larger samples.

All of this suggests that it is important to assess a client's relationships: their quantity, quality and type. For example, for our case study client Eli, do they have support from their family and a community of friends and peers, including from other non-binary people if this feels relevant? Do they have both people who they are very close with (e.g. a sibling or best friend) and a broader social network of friends, colleagues, neighbours and acquaintances? All such relationships are differentially important for well-being and to prevent loneliness (Holt-Lunstad, 2021). Additionally, it might be useful to talk to Eli about whether they are actively seeking support from the people around them rather than, for example, just trying to manage alone.

Strengths and resources

One criticism of psychiatric diagnosis is that it is focused only on what is wrong with a person. Increasingly, however, it is recognised that it is also important to assess what positive personal qualities and resources a person might have – such as a good sense of humour, or being determined or clever. There is research evidence for a strengths-based approach in mental health settings (e.g. Tse *et al.*, 2016), one that is celebratory rather than pathologising and, by definition, in the spirit of holistic assessment.

A focus on strengths is further justified by the fact that 'mental illness' and 'well-being' are mostly (statistically) independent of each other, which means that 'treating' mental health difficulties does not necessarily result in improvements in a person's reported well-being. This is problematic given that persistent low well-being still matters in relation to mental health; the former is associated with vulnerability to the re-emergence of mental health difficulties (Chakhssi *et al.*, 2018).

There is emerging research from the field of positive psychology on the value of supporting people to focus on relevant positive aspects, including their own positive qualities. For example, one study found that focusing on the positives increases well-being, and decreases depression and anxiety (Chakhssi *et al.*, 2018). Another meta-analytic study has also shown that asking people to identify their biggest character strengths and then asking them to actively try to use one of these every day for a week results in increases in well-being (Schutte and Malouff, 2019). There are resources for incorporating positive psychology into psychotherapy (e.g. Rashid and Seligman, 2018) but it is also possible to integrate a focus on strengths into assessment in counselling, for example by engaging in 'strength spotting' – that is, noticing and drawing attention to a client's strengths. Eli's counsellor, for example, might note how funny they are or that it seems like their friends really care for them.

Pause for thought 11.4

To what extent do you consciously work with clients to identify their strengths?

What do you think your *own* strengths are as a counsellor?

---

4 Assessing client suitability for service

In the previous section, the focus was on thinking about what domains a holistic assessment might incorporate. In this section, the focus is on how to determine whether a client is suitable for counselling in a particular setting.

Bearing in mind the point at the beginning of Section 3 – that counselling is typically expected to work with mild, moderate and 'low severe' presentations – two key questions can be useful:

1   Is the client's level of problem severity and risk appropriate for the service and/or proposed counsellor?
2   Are there any other indicators which might suggest that the client is not suitable to work with in this setting and/or with this counsellor?

The answer to each of these questions will of course depend on both the client(s) and the service setting, but a core issue is whether the proposed counsellor and their supervisor and/or clinical manager have the competence (training and experience) to work with the client's presenting problems and level of risk (see Chapter 10). For example, taking on a client who has an established or current dependence on drugs or alcohol would make sense in a service that works with addiction, but might not work in a service without such a specialism. Cognitive capacity (including the ability to consent to a service) is typically required for counselling, but there are counsellors and services that specialise in working with people with learning disabilities or people who are in the early stages of dementia. A service might be open to working with a client experiencing anger issues and currently under investigation for assault, but potentially not if the client can only attend a satellite site where the counsellor would be the only person in the building.

Section 3 mentioned that, in general, counselling services or NHS primary care are not deemed appropriate for people with psychosis because staff don't have the right training or expertise to work effectively or safely with this population (National Collaborating Centre for Mental Health, 2024). The case study of Eli, however, illustrates that it is not always easy to assess whether a client is or is not presenting with symptoms that might indicate a first episode of psychosis. Psychosis is characterised by the person being out of touch with reality in some way. A person might see, hear or feel something that is not there (hallucinations); they might strongly believe something that other people do not (such as Eli believing that malevolent others have installed cameras in their bedroom) (delusions); they might be talking and thinking very fast and incoherently (disordered thinking and speaking). For the counselling service, the task is to decide whether Eli might be on the brink of their first psychotic episode, in which case a volunteer-run service would not be right for Eli, who instead would require psychiatric referral.

In NHS secondary care mental health services, a tool developed by the Royal College of Psychiatrists – the Health of the Nation Outcome Scales (HoNOS) – is used in making this judgement (Wing *et al.*, 1998). HoNOS is a 12-question measure that is scored by the clinician and is used to assess the mental and social functioning of people with severe mental health difficulties (James *et al.*, 2018). There is one specific HoNOS item that assesses for problems with hallucinations and/or delusions, and the clinician's job is to rate these on a scale from 0 to 4, as below:

> 0 No evidence of hallucinations or delusions during the period rated.
>
> 1 Somewhat unusual or eccentric beliefs not in keeping with cultural norms.
>
> 2 Hallucinations or delusions are present, but there is little distress to patient or manifestation in bizarre behaviours, i.e. clinically present but mild.
>
> 3 Marked preoccupation with hallucinations or delusions, causing much distress and/or manifested in obviously bizarre behaviour, i.e. moderately severe clinical problem.
>
> 4 Mental state and behaviour is seriously and adversely affected by hallucinations or delusions, with severe impact on patient.
>
> *(Adapted from NHS England, 2021, p. 14)*

However, in addition to scoring a minimum of a 1 on this item, the protocol expects people who merit the 'first episode psychosis' label to also have a current and prior history of self-harm, current depression, problems with drug and alcohol use, as well as a history of vulnerability and agitated behaviour or manic mood. Considering the information you have so far about Eli, perhaps it does not seem like they would meet the criteria for first episode psychosis and thus that they could be deemed suitable for the service (assuming also that there is someone in the service who has experience/knowledge in working with non-binary clients). However, the counsellor might want to monitor Eli's 'paranoia' going forward or consider a psychiatric referral, just in case.

Conclusion

The aim of this chapter has been to support you in developing your ability to do holistic assessments of your clients, not just at intake, but across counselling, as a way of deepening your understanding of your clients and improving their counselling outcomes. The chapter has therefore considered what holistic assessment of mental health difficulties could include. The chapter has also considered how assessment can be used to determine whether a client is appropriate for a particular service or counsellor. Chapter 12 will focus on another important aspect of assessment: the use of routine outcome measures, which can be really helpful for assessing whether or not counselling is actually working for a particular client.

Further reading

- The following paper reviews research on the initial assessment session in counselling and makes suggestions for evidence-based, 'better' ways of doing assessment:

  Hilsenroth, M.J. and Cromer, T.D. (2007) 'Clinician interventions related to alliance during the initial interview and psychological assessment', *Psychotherapy: Theory, Research, Practice, Training*, 44(2), pp. 205–218. Available at: https://doi.org/10.1037/0033-3204.44.2.205

- This paper from Australia also argues for holistic assessments:

  Lynch, J.M., Askew, D.A., Mitchell, G.K. and Hegarty, K.L. (2012) 'Beyond symptoms: defining primary care mental health clinical assessment priorities, content and process', *Social Science & Medicine*, 74 (2), pp. 143–149. Available at: https://doi.org/10.1016/j. socscimed.2011.08.043

- The following book chapter provides a template for doing pluralistic assessments:

  McLeod, J. and McLeod, J. (2016) 'Assessment and formulation in pluralistic counselling and psychotherapy', in M. Cooper and W. Dryden (eds) *The handbook of pluralistic counselling and psychotherapy*. SAGE Publications Ltd, pp. 15–27.

References

Acharya, H.J. (2004) 'The rise and fall of the frontal lobotomy', *Proceedings of the 13th annual history of medicine days*, Calgary, 19–20 March. Calgary: University of Calgary, pp. 32–41.

American Psychiatric Association (2022) *Diagnostic and statistical manual of mental disorders: DSM-5-TR*. 5th edn, text rev. Washington, DC: American Psychiatric Publishing.

Barkham, M., Bewick, B., Mullin, T., Gilbody, S., Connell, J., Cahill, J., Mellor-Clarke, J., Richards, D., Unsworth, G. and Evans, C. (2013) 'The CORE-10: a short measure of psychological distress for routine use in the psychological therapies', *Counselling and Psychotherapy Research*, 13(1), pp. 3–13. Available at: https://doi.org/10.1080/14733145.2012.729069

Biddle, S. (2016) 'Physical activity and mental health: evidence is growing', *World Psychiatry*, 15(2), pp. 176–177. Available at: https://doi.org/10.1002/wps.20331

Biggs, A., Brough, P. and Drummond, S. (2017) 'Lazarus and Folkman's psychological stress and coping theory', in C.L. Cooper and J.C. Quick (eds) *The handbook of stress and health: a guide to research and practice*. Hoboken, NJ: John Wiley & Sons Ltd, pp. 349–364.

Chakhssi, F., Kraiss, J.T., Sommers-Spijkerman, M. and Bohlmeijer, E.T. (2018) 'The effect of positive psychology interventions on well-being and distress in clinical samples with psychiatric or somatic disorders: a systematic review and meta-analysis', *BMC Psychiatry*, 18, article number 211. Available at: https://doi.org/10.1186/s12888-018-1739-2

Cohen, B.M.Z. (2017) *Routledge international handbook of critical mental health*. Abingdon: Routledge.

Cunningham Owens, D. and Johnstone, E.C. (2018) 'The development of antipsychotic drugs', *Brain and Neuroscience Advances*, 2, pp. 1–6. Available at: https://doi.org/10.1177/2398212818817498

Emsley, E., Smith, J., Martin, D. and Lewis, N.V. (2022) 'Trauma-informed care in the UK: where are we? A qualitative study of health policies and professional perspectives', *BMC Health Services Research*, 22(1), article number 1164. Available at: https://doi.org/10.1186/s12913-022-08461-w

Garb, H.N. (2021) 'Race bias and gender bias in the diagnosis of psychological disorders', *Clinical Psychology Review*, 90, article number 102087. Available at: https://doi.org/10.1016/j.cpr.2021.102087

Henriksen, M.G., Nordgaard, J. and Jansson, L.B. (2017) 'Genetics of schizophrenia: overview of methods, findings and limitations', *Frontiers in Human Neuroscience*, 11, article number 322. Available at: https://doi.org/10.3389/fnhum.2017.00322

Hermes, E.D.A., Hoff, R. and Rosenheck, R.A. (2014) 'Sources of the increasing number of Vietnam era veterans with a diagnosis of PTSD using VHA services', *Psychiatric Services*, 65(6), pp. 830–832. Available at: https://doi.org/10.1176/appi.ps.201300232

Hoffman, J.L. (1949) 'Clinical observations concerning schizophrenic patients treated by prefrontal leukotomy', *The New England Journal of Medicine*, 241(6), pp. 233–236. Available at: https://doi.org/10.1056/nejm194908112410604

Holt-Lunstad, J. (2021) 'The major health implications of social connection', *Current Directions in Psychological Science*, 30(3), pp. 251–259. Available at: https://doi.org/10.1177/0963721421999630

Hughes, K., Bellis, M.A., Hardcastle, K.A., Sethi, D., Butchart, A., Mikton, C., Jones, L. and Dunne, M.P. (2017) 'The effect of multiple adverse childhood experiences on health: a systematic review and meta-analysis', *The Lancet Public Health*, 2(8), pp. e356–e366. Available at: https://doi.org/10.1016/S2468-2667(17)30118-4

Jablensky, A. (2016) 'Psychiatric classifications: validity and utility', *World Psychiatry*, 15(1), pp. 26–31. Available at: https://doi.org/10.1002/wps.20284

James, M., Painter, J., Buckingham, B. and Stewart, M.W. (2018) 'A review and update of the Health of the Nation Outcome Scales (HoNOS)', *BJPsych Bulletin*, 42(2), pp. 63–68. Available at: https://doi.org/10.1192/bjb.2017.17

Jeronimus, B.F., Kotov, R., Riese, H. and Ormel, J. (2016) 'Neuroticism's prospective association with mental disorders halves after adjustment for baseline symptoms and psychiatric history, but the adjusted association hardly decays with time: a meta-analysis on 59 longitudinal/prospective studies with 443 313 participants', *Psychological Medicine*, 46(14), pp. 2883–2906. Available at: https://doi.org/10.1017/S0033291716001653

Keetharuth, A.D., Brazier, J., Connell, J., Bjorner, J.B., Carlton, J., Taylor Buck, E., Ricketts, T., McKendrick, K., Browne, J., Croudace, T. and Barkham, M. (2018) 'Recovering Quality of Life (ReQoL): a new generic self-reported outcome measure for use with people experiencing mental health difficulties', *The British Journal of Psychiatry*, 212(1), pp. 42–49. Available at: https://doi.org/10.1192/bjp.2017.10

Lazarus, R.S. and Folkman, S. (1984) *Stress, appraisal, and coping*. New York: Springer Publishing Company.

Lee, H.S., Chao, H.H., Huang, W.T., Chen, S.C.C. and Yang, H.Y. (2020) 'Psychiatric disorders risk in patients with iron deficiency anemia and association with iron supplementation medications: a nationwide database analysis', *BMC Psychiatry*, 20, article number 216. Available at: https://doi.org/10.1186/s12888-020-02621-0

Mental Health Foundation (2023) *Factors that affect mental health*. Available at: https://www.mentalhealth.org.uk/explore-mental-health/factors-affect-mental-health/ (Accessed: 3 January 2024).

National Collaborating Centre for Mental Health (2024) *NHS Talking Therapies for anxiety and depression manual*. Available at: https://www.england.nhs.uk/publication/the-improving-access-to-psychological-therapies-manual/ (Accessed: 23 May 2024).

NHS England (2021) *Annex DtD: technical guidance for mental health clusters*. Available at: https://www.england.nhs.uk/wp-content/uploads/2021/03/21-22NT_Annex-DtD-Technical-guidance-for-mental-health-clusters.pdf (Accessed: 23 May 2024).

O'Connor, C., Kadianaki, I., Maunder, K. and McNicholas, F. (2018) 'How does psychiatric diagnosis affect young people's self-concept and social identity? A systematic review and synthesis of the qualitative literature', *Social Science & Medicine*, 212, pp. 94–119. Available at: https://doi.org/10.1016/j.socscimed.2018.07.011

Orth, U. and Robins, R.W. (2022) 'Is high self-esteem beneficial? Revisiting a classic question', *American Psychologist*, 77(1), pp. 5–17. Available at: https://doi.org/10.1037/amp0000922

Parker, G.B., Brotchie, H. and Graham, R.K. (2017) 'Vitamin D and depression', *Journal of Affective Disorders*, 208, pp. 56–61. Available at: https://doi.org/10.1016/j.jad.2016.08.082

Perkins, A., Ridler, J., Browes, D., Peryer, G., Notley, C. and Hackmann, C. (2018) 'Experiencing mental health diagnosis: a systematic review of service user, clinician, and carer perspectives across clinical settings', *The Lancet Psychiatry*, 5(9), pp. 747–764. Available at: https://doi.org/10.1016/s2215-0366(18)30095-6

Pilgrim, D. (2007) 'The survival of psychiatric diagnosis', *Social Science & Medicine*, 65(3), pp. 536–547. Available at: https://doi.org/10.1016/j.socscimed.2007.03.054

Rashid, T. and Seligman, M.P. (2018) *Positive psychotherapy: clinician manual.* Oxford: Oxford University Press.

Ridley, M., Rao, G., Schilbach, F. and Patel, V. (2020) 'Poverty, depression, and anxiety: causal evidence and mechanisms', *Science*, 370(6522), article number 214. Available at: https://doi.org/10.1126/science.aay0214

Robles, T.F., Slatcher, R.B., Trombello, J.M. and McGinn, M.M. (2014) 'Marital quality and health: a meta-analytic review', *Psychological Bulletin*, 140(1), pp. 140–187. Available at: https://doi.org/10.1037/a0031859

Schutte, N.S. and Malouff, J.M. (2019) 'The impact of signature character strengths interventions: a meta-analysis', *Journal of Happiness Studies*, 20, pp. 1179–1196. Available at: https://doi.org/10.1007/s10902-018-9990-2

SCoPEd Framework (2022), collaboratively developed by Association of Christian Counsellors (ACC), British Association for Counselling and Psychotherapy (BACP), British Psychoanalytic Council (BPC), Human Givens Institute (HGI), National Counselling and Psychotherapy Society (NCPS) and United Kingdom Council for Psychotherapy (UKCP). Available at: https://www.bacp.co.uk/about-us/advancing-the-profession/scoped/scoped-framework (Accessed: 12 June 2024).

Sowislo, J.F. and Orth, U. (2013) 'Does low self-esteem predict depression and anxiety? A meta-analysis of longitudinal studies', *Psychological Bulletin*, 139(1), pp. 213–240. Available at: https://doi.org/10.1037/a0028931

Szmukler, G. (2013) 'When psychiatric diagnosis becomes an overworked tool', *Journal of Medical Ethics*, 40, pp. 517–520. Available at: https://doi.org/10.1136/medethics-2013-101761

Terrier, L.M., Lévêque, M. and Amelot, A. (2019) 'Brain lobotomy: a historical and moral dilemma with no alternative?', *World Neurosurgery*, 132, pp. 211–218. Available at: https://doi.org/10.1016/j.wneu.2019.08.254

Tse, S., Tsoi, E.W.S., Hamilton, B., O'Hagan, M., Shepherd, G., Slade, M., Whitley, R. and Petrakis, M. (2016) 'Uses of strength-based interventions for people with serious mental illness: a critical review', *International Journal of Social Psychiatry*, 62(3), pp. 281–291. Available at: https://doi.org/10.1177/0020764015623970

Weinstein, A.A., Koehmstedt, C. and Kop, W.J. (2017) 'Mental health consequences of exercise withdrawal: a systematic review', *General Hospital Psychiatry*, 49, pp. 11–18. Available at: https://doi.org/10.1016/j.genhosppsych.2017.06.001

Weitzer, J., Trudel-Fitzgerald, C., Okereke, O.I., Kawachi, I. and Schernhammer, E. (2022) 'Dispositional optimism and depression risk in older women in the Nurses' Health Study: a prospective cohort study', *European Journal of Epidemiology*, 37(3), pp. 283–294. Available at: https://doi.org/10.1007/s10654-021-00837-2

Wing, J.K., Beevor, A.S., Curtis, R.H., Park, S.G.B., Hadden, S. and Burns, A. (1998) 'Health of the Nation Outcomes Scale (HoNOS): research and development', *British Journal of Psychiatry*, 172(1), pp. 11–18. Available at: https://doi.org/10.1192/bjp.172.1.11

World Health Organization (2022) *International classification of diseases: eleventh revision (ICD-11)*. Available at: https://icd.who.int/ (Accessed: 12 January 2024).

World Health Organization (2023) *Mental health, human rights and legislation: guidance and practice*. Available at: https://www.who.int/publications/i/item/9789240080737 (Accessed: 5 January 2023).

Zhang, Z., Sun, K., Jatchavala, C., Koh, J., Chia, Y., Bose, J., Li, Z., Tan, W., Wang, S., Chu, W., Wang, J., Tran, B. and Ho, R. (2020) 'Overview of stigma against psychiatric illnesses and advancements of anti-stigma activities in six Asian societies', *International Journal of Environmental Research and Public Health*, 17(1), article number 280. Available at: https://doi.org/10.3390/ijerph17010280

Chapter 12

Using outcome measures to inform psychological assessment

Gina Di Malta, Jo-anne Carlyle and Chris Evans

Contents

Introduction

Pier Pointing to the Ocean by Gina Di Malta. The pier symbolises the aim of an outcome measure, which is to assess a uniform construct believed to represent a specific human experience.

Underpinned by a desire for more 'evidence-based' and transparent practice, the use of outcome measures in counselling and psychotherapy has developed rapidly over the last few decades. This stark increase in the use of measures has brought new – and sometimes confusing – terminology. Outcome measures are standardised tools or assessments used to systematically evaluate the effectiveness of therapy practice and services by tracking the progress of clients within and across therapy.

Outcome measures are designed to provide data on various aspects of a client's experience – such as well-being, symptoms, general functioning and overall quality of life – and they aim to make that data fairly comparable across clients. They can be used at the start and end of treatment to determine outcomes of treatment, or at regular intervals (e.g. on a session-by-session basis). Terminology varies, but this chapter uses 'routine outcome monitoring' (ROM) to refer to the routine use of such measures in counselling services. In some contexts, the term 'ROM' has been used interchangeably with 'embedded change management' (ECM), to refer to scores on outcome measures that are monitored during treatment and used to change the direction of work. ECM is usually, but not always, done by sharing and discussing scores with the client to support treatment decisions.

Greater funding challenges for mental health services have contributed to the increase in the use of outcome measures. More people are now seeking help due to their experiences of increasing social dislocation and deprivation, emotional impacts from global events and socio-cultural disturbance. In this context, ROM has been implemented to support and potentially advance psychotherapeutic services by giving valuable data on the effectiveness of particular interventions with specific client groups. The ECM model enables practitioners to adapt their interventions in therapy, with some evidence that, where it is appropriate to the therapy model, it may shorten the duration of therapies that are progressing well and perhaps reduce the rate of early drop out (Barkham *et al.*, 2023).

The overall aim of this chapter is to support your ability to use outcome measures as a tool to monitor and maintain standards of practice with due understanding of cultural norms. The chapter contributes towards achieving the **SCoPEd competency 4.15.B**:

Ability to utilise audit and evaluation tools to monitor and maintain standards within practice settings.

(SCoPEd Framework, 2022, p. 29)

This chapter aims to:

- outline the background and context behind the use of outcome measures
- explain how ROM can be used to improve counselling practice and support counsellors' professional development
- review commonly used outcome measures, and their function and application in counselling practice
- detail some challenges in using ROM in practice and consider how these can be addressed
- consider innovations and future directions for outcome monitoring.

1 Historical and theoretical context of outcome measures

Therapy has always involved feedback: in counselling, we continually monitor both what the client says as well as many non-verbal cues. The use of formal outcome measures within psychological assessment grew in the mid twentieth century, spurred by a commitment to empirical accountability and evidence-based practice (Margison *et al.*, 2000). This time was marked by a paradigm shift in the evaluation of therapeutic outcomes, away from solely subjective (and potentially inaccurate) clinical judgement to standardised and objective metrics (e.g. Barkham *et al.*, 1998). In tandem with the broader movement towards continuous improvement in mental health care, outcome measures emerged as valuable tools that can support the systematic appraisal of psychological interventions. In the United Kingdom, the growing influence of the National Institute for Health and Care Excellence (NICE) guidelines meant that psychotherapy modalities which lacked a quantitative evidence base were less likely to receive funding both for treatment and for further research. In parallel, third-sector organisations increasingly mandated the use of outcome measures to secure funding. Practitioners in these sectors began to engage with outcome measures even where the therapy modality might have theoretical reservations surrounding their use (e.g. Remfrey Foote, 2023).

Although the overarching aim of ROM is to evaluate treatment, different theoretical frameworks tend to rely on different underlying rationales for using outcome measures. For instance, cognitive behavioural therapy (CBT) focuses on measuring cognitive and behavioural changes as key indicators of treatment effectiveness. This more structured model commonly uses **nomothetic measurement**, where scores are thought to be fairly comparable across the majority of clients. Person-centred approaches, on the other hand, emphasise the significance of capturing subjective well-being and personal growth, which is reflective of the individual's experiential journey within the therapeutic process. Associated humanistic theoretical approaches tend to embrace **idiographic measurement**, which is more personalised. In the pluralistic model, for instance, the integration of outcome measures aligns with the approach's ethos of evidence-based practice, alongside a theoretically informed commitment to customising interventions according to individual needs (e.g. Boswell *et al.*, 2015). In such approaches, idiographic measurement can be used to focus on understanding the unique characteristics and experiences of individuals by providing in-depth, context-specific insights into their psychological processes (Sales *et al.*, 2023).

nomothetic measurement

Uses general measures and principles thought to apply equally or comparably across clients.

idiographic measurement

Used to describe phenomena unique to an individual. Most qualitative assessments are idiographic, emphasising detailed and context-specific information.

Pause for thought 12.1

In your own practice, has the use of outcome measures been aligned with your therapeutic approach? Have you encountered any challenges?

2 Measurement as a path to improvement

> We need to be open to where our therapies may not be effective or may even cause harm. If we hold this brave openness, we can explore the complexities that may be operating, and be better fitted to adapt and change.
>
> *(Evans and Carlyle, 2021, p. 23)*

Measurement is important for assessing client and service improvement, and can also support counsellor improvements. This section looks at these in turn.

2.1 Improving client outcomes

embedded change management

Also termed 'feedback-informed treatment', 'measurement-based care' and 'progress monitoring', this reflects an 'embedded' use of scores to inform treatment.

The use of outcome measures can improve client outcomes at national, service and individual levels (Brattland *et al.*, 2018). That is, where measures align with service monitoring needs, therapeutic modality and the clients' wishes, outcome measures can enhance transparency and accountability by establishing a common language for communication about change. At the national level, for example, securing political investment in the UK's Improving Access to Psychological Therapies (IAPT) programme (now termed NHS Talking Therapies) was based on a commitment to monitoring and improving outcomes. At the individual level, services have used **embedded change management** (ECM) to identify some therapies as 'off track', in order to either reduce the rate of negative outcomes or to reduce the number of sessions for clients reporting good outcomes (Lambert, 2013). At the service level, ROM can be useful not only for evaluation, but also for audit.

2.2 Service audit and evaluation

audit

A cyclical process of measuring service performance against a target and reviewing progress or deterioration at regular intervals (typically quarterly, six-monthly or annually) and making adjustments to practice in light of the data.

Audit and **evaluation** are broad methods which support quality improvement in psychology services. Auditing usually involves measuring service performance against a predefined standard or target at regular intervals. Lots of aspects of counselling can be audited – for example, whether paperwork is complete or up to date, whether the service is reaching the intended population, or whether the service's best practice guidelines are being followed. A charity, for instance, might audit their completed cases to establish that their average 'recovery rate' meets the standard required by funders. Auditing assesses existing practice and data; it's not the same as research, which involves investigating a new question, so it does not require additional data collection, or burden users or the service.

evaluation

The process of routinely reviewing service performance. It includes audit, service improvement, needs assessment and formal evaluative research.

Evaluation is used to explore how well a service is able to meet its stated aims. It looks at existing service delivery and is not about trialling new approaches. Evaluation may look at costs, user experience, strengths and weaknesses of a service. The charity doing the audit in the example just given might also evaluate its strengths and weaknesses by investigating whether there are different rates of recovery for different types of clients. Evaluation methods can include qualitative questions, pre–post measurement and experimental designs to assess service quality as well as the use of outcome measures for evaluating the effectiveness of a service.

Pause for thought 12.2

Does the service setting in which you work/have worked use audit and service evaluation for quality improvement? Have you 'audited' your own practice?

2.3 Counsellor professional development

Within counsellor professional development, exploring the meaning of change scores can contribute to a learning and improvement cycle. Measures can provide insights into the effectiveness of interventions and the progress of clients (Boswell *et al.*, 2015), and it becomes possible to compare scores across different clients or with colleagues. The data can offer insights into both strengths and areas for further development, potentially affirming successful strategies and interventions. It can also support professional reflection on the impact of interventions, complementing traditional qualitative, narrative supervision and case discussion. Engaging with feedback can help a counsellor cultivate a reflective and responsive mindset, enhancing their ability to meet the evolving needs of clients. This iterative process of self-reflection and improvement therefore becomes a cornerstone of their professional development.

As with all therapy skills, familiarity and expertise when using outcome measures can be enhanced with supervision and by continuing professional development. The integration of both ROM and ECM data into supervision is a developing area in therapeutic practice. Increasingly, trainees and recently qualified practitioners may be more familiar with the use of measures than some supervisors. Specific training programmes centred on the use of ROM and ECM are now well-established in the United States and Germany (Lutz *et al.*, 2021) and are emerging in other countries (e.g. Valdiviezo-Oña *et al.*, 2023).

Supervision that provides a structured and supportive space to discuss and reflect on the use of outcome measures, neither overvaluing nor dismissing scores, ensures that the feedback obtained can be integrated into counselling practice. This requires both supervisee and supervisor to be comfortable with the measures, to have sufficient time to digest the findings and to have access to those findings in tables and graphs (Aafjes-van Doorn and de Jong, 2022).

In addition, approaches to working with the data available may be informed by the level of experience of the practitioner. For example, where ECM is new to the practitioner, supervision should be frequent and possibly focused on specific, individual clients. It may also be helpful to use role play to practise how to introduce outcome measures. By contrast, where supervision is less frequent, or where both the supervisor and supervisee are familiar with ECM and with each other's ways of working, it may be better to review trajectories across clients. This would involve a balanced review of work that produced good outcomes alongside work that went less well. The integration of outcome measures feedback into supervision therefore becomes a dynamic and proactive approach, one that ensures that therapeutic practices remain evidence-based, responsive and aligned with the evolving needs of clients (Aafjes-van Doorn and de Jong, 2022).

Pause for thought 12.3

Think of your work with a specific client. What might you find useful when exploring the outcome data from this work with your supervisor?

---

3 Outcome measures and their application

As mentioned in Section 1, outcome measures can be categorised as either idiographic, where the client's particular circumstances and context define the problem to be measured, or nomothetic, where scores are intended to be comparable between clients. It can be good practice to use both a short nomothetic and a short idiographic measure. This section presents an overview of a few commonly used idiographic and nomothetic instruments, most of which have also been validated for use in research. For more detailed information on a wider range of clinical outcome measures, you can refer to Evans and Carlyle (2021).

Examples of idiographic measures

The Psychological Outcome Profiles (PSYCHLOPS) is a measure that is used in some clinics in the UK as well as internationally (Ashworth *et al.*, 2004). It is a brief self-report tool designed to assess the subjective experiences and concerns of individuals undergoing therapy. It allows clients to identify and rate up to five areas of personal significance that they wish to address in therapy. PSYCHLOPS has four items (questions) which cover three domains.

- *Problems*: Two free-text, patient-generated items regarding the problems that trouble them most.
- *Function*: One free-text, patient-generated item corresponding to what has become hardest to do because of their problem.
- *Well-being*: A pre-set, standardised item about how the client felt in themselves in the previous week.

Items are scored on a six-point rating scale (from 'not at all affected' to 'severely affected') and for duration (from 'under one month' to 'over five years') (e.g. Ashworth *et al.*, 2017). The PSYCHLOPS total scoring is obtained by summing the scores of the four scales.

The Goals Form (Cooper, 2015) is used in some clinics in the UK and internationally to collaboratively establish and articulate up to seven goals for therapy between clients and therapists. The Goals Form encourages open dialogue between clients and therapists, and supports a shared understanding of the desired outcomes of therapy. The goals are scored on a seven-point Likert scale from 'not at all achieved' to 'completely achieved'. Goals can be revised when they are no longer relevant. By explicitly outlining and then regularly revisiting these goals, this form helps the therapist track progress and adapt interventions to better meet the evolving needs of their client.

Examples of nomothetic measures

The Outcome Rating Scale (ORS) is widely used in the US and in some clinics internationally (Miller *et al.*, 2003). It is a brief, four-item scale designed to assess change in clients following psychological intervention. It assesses three areas of functioning – individual, relational and social – using a visual analogue (sliding scale) format, which ranges from low to high. Its instructions invite the client to look back over the last week (or since their last appointment). The client is asked to indicate, by marking the scale, how they have been feeling by rating how well they have been doing in the three areas. The scale takes approximately one minute to complete.

The Patient Health Questionnaire (PHQ-9) (Kroenke, Spitzer and Williams, 2001) is used internationally, and primarily in IAPT/NHS Talking Therapies settings alongside the Generalised Anxiety Disorder Scale (GAD-7), Work and Social Adjustment Scale (WSAS) and IAPT Phobia Scales. The PHQ-9 is a nine-item questionnaire that assesses diagnostic symptoms of depression. Items cover experiences of pleasure, feeling down, sleep disruption, energy levels, appetite, feeling a failure, trouble concentrating, speaking slowly (or the opposite, being fidgety), and having thoughts around suicide or self-harm over the previous two weeks. At the initial assessment, the PHQ-9 can assist a counsellor to identify depression. At the follow-up visits, the PHQ-9 is used to assess treatment outcomes and can help identify specific symptoms that are not responding to treatment. Higher scores indicate more severe depression.

The Clinical Outcomes in Routine Evaluation Outcome Measure (CORE-OM), and shorter versions of it, are used in both IAPT/NHS Talking Therapies settings and in clinics internationally (Evans, 2012). The CORE-OM is a 34-item self-report instrument of mental health distress which asks the client to reflect on the extent to which they have felt certain ways over the last week. The items cover four domains: subjective well-being, problems/symptoms, life functioning and risk to self and to others. Items are rated on a five-point scale ranging from 'not at all' to 'most or all the time'. Higher scores indicate more psychological distress.

Case example: Applying ROM in Tom's treatment for depression

Tom, 42, self-refers for open-ended therapy partly based on advice from a friend who recommended Bobby's private counselling practice. Tom is recognising that he has long-standing difficulties and that they impinge on his work, relationships and parenting. His GP has diagnosed depression and Tom has been taking antidepressants for seven years, which he says have helped, but now he feels he wants therapy.

Partly because of the depression diagnosis, Bobby suggests using the depression measure PHQ-9. Bobby suggests to Tom that they also monitor things with a more general measure, and suggests the CORE-

OM with its measures of well-being, relevant problems, functioning and risk. Tom and Bobby agree to use both measures fortnightly. They also agree that questionnaire scores are useful but not the only monitor of change for Tom's therapy.

The work proceeds and after three months Tom is finding the sessions hard. Bobby and Tom find that his PHQ-9 scores have deteriorated slightly but his CORE-OM scores, particularly his risk and functioning scores, have improved. Bobby reviews the scores and writes some notes to himself about the work. As with all ROM data, he takes this to his quarterly peer supervision session to look at the information with his colleagues.

After one year, Bobby and Tom agree to terminate the work and schedule a three-month follow-up. Scores on both measures at the end of therapy and at the follow-up are markedly improved. Tom takes the plots of the scores away, laughing, and says, 'They seem a bit like my exam results, which weren't the whole story of my school career!'

Pause for thought 12.4

Does the process outlined in Tom's case seem familiar, or does it differ from your work? Are you doing, or might you do, something similar in terms of using ROM?

For some modalities of therapy – perhaps including yours – the best approach can be to assess outcome measures outside the therapy rather than embedding this within the work (using ECM). This can be particularly appropriate for psychodynamic and arts therapies, which focus on unconscious processes. It can also be easier in group and some couple and family interventions to complete outcome measures outside the therapy. This is because responses will inevitably be individualistic rather than systemically driven, thus potentially changing the discourse of the therapy. Clearly, much will depend on the working practice of the therapist, which again highlights the importance of a reflective approach towards the use of measures.

4 Ethical considerations

Umbrellas representing diversity and individuality (photo by Ana Santos)

As you have seen, outcome measures and ROM systems can be valuable tools for counselling and psychotherapy practice. As with other aspects of practice, however, counsellors must adhere to professional ethical guidelines, such as those of the American Psychological Association (2017) and the BACP (2023). This ensures that the integration of ROM into the work with clients always prioritises the clients' needs.

One important initial step when using measures includes obtaining informed consent from clients to ensure that they understand the purpose and potential implications of measurement, and that the process serves to underline and respect their right to decline participation. As part of informed consent, practitioners should be transparent about the limitations and potential risks associated with the use of outcome measures (Börjesson and Boström, 2020). This also means checking that the measure used is appropriate to the setting and client, particularly whether the measure is accessible to the client in terms of literacy, cognitive functioning, language fluency, and so on.

Confidentiality also constitutes a key issue when using measures. Although scores themselves do not reveal a client's identity, in a small dataset other variables, particularly demographic ones, could do so. It is the counsellor's responsibility to ensure that confidentiality is maintained. The increasing use of computerised systems means that adhering to General Data Protection Regulation (GDPR) guidelines is crucial; practitioners must implement secure data storage and transmission methods that uphold privacy standards (Muir *et al.*, 2019).

In the process of selecting outcome measures or implementing ROM systems within counselling practice, it is important to consider whether the measures are suitable for the specific client population and whether they are culturally relevant and sensitive to diverse backgrounds. As noted, measures have generally been developed within a particular socio-cultural context. While there are advantages to using the same measures across a range of settings and client groups, there are dangers to this for subgroups of clients. A range of important considerations may be relevant here, including (but not limited to) the following:

- The expression of symptoms varies across different cultural groups (Birtel and Mitchell, 2023).

- Stigma associated with emotional distress or mental health differs across different groups (Birtel and Mitchell, 2023).

- The experience of individualistic or collectivistic cultures and of egalitarian or embedded social frameworks impacts people's expressions of distress (Heim, Wegmann and Maercker, 2017).

- Most measures require respondents to identify their gender as either female or male, making them inappropriate for people who reject this binary.

- The experience of distress may arise from social circumstances (e.g. social deprivation, experiences of discrimination and prejudice, experiences of mobility and migration, etc.). This can mean that scores may not change much for clients even when the work is strengthening resilience (Marmot, 2020).

- Although some measures may be translated into other languages, their referential data (validity and reliability checks) will not be transferable across languages. New data would need to be collected for each language to conduct these checks.

Case example: Cultural sensitivity between Hasan and Masha

Hasan, a humanistic counsellor, is working with Masha, a client from a North African background who sought therapy to address feelings of anxiety and adjustment difficulties related to her sexual orientation. Hasan recognises the importance of cultural sensitivity in his approach. While Hasan typically incorporates ROM in his practice to ensure a comprehensive understanding of his clients' progress, he is unsure whether appropriate instruments exist that will properly reflect the challenges that Masha faces.

In the initial sessions, Hasan collaborates with Masha to establish culturally attuned outcome goals, focusing on reducing anxiety linked to the exploration of her sexuality, and fostering a sense of acceptance within her cultural context. To ensure a tailored assessment, Hasan suggests a personalised idiographic measure: the Goals Form. Masha and Hasan collaboratively formulate three therapy goals: to reduce her anxiety, to better understand her sexual feelings and to improve her relationships with family and friends. The Goals Form was then brought back into every session to monitor Masha's progress towards her goals and to review the wording and priorities, if necessary. Hasan felt that this approach would best accommodate cultural nuances, wording preferences and the unique challenges that Masha was encountering.

The data gathered became an integral part of their discussions, allowing Hasan to adjust his humanistic approach based on Masha's evolving needs and the insights gleaned from the outcome measure. By incorporating ROM, Hasan not only gained a nuanced perspective on Masha's progress, but it also ensured that his humanistic interventions were culturally informed and responsive to Masha's unique journey.

This case illustrates the integration of outcome measures within a humanistic framework, highlighting how ROM can provide a tailored approach to counselling individuals from diverse cultural backgrounds.

Pause for thought 12.5

What proportion of the clients you have seen would find using a client-generated idiographic measure preferable to a nomothetic measure? What might be lost if counsellors only used client-generated measures?

5 Challenges in using outcome measures

The use of outcome measures in practice is not without its challenges, which itself reflects the multilayered nature of the therapeutic process. Addressing these challenges requires a thoughtful integration of outcome measures into the therapeutic process in a way that's appropriate to the modality in use.

Generally, clients are not averse to the use of outcome measures, particularly if they are concise and pertinent to them (Barkham *et al.*, 2023). One key concern is the additional (cognitive and time) burdens that outcome measures typically put on clients, which could impact on their engagement. Selecting efficient and client-friendly assessment tools can promote sustained engagement and facilitate accurate data collection (de Jong, Delgadillo and Barkham, 2023).

As with the case of Hasan and Masha, another concern is the inappropriateness of using certain measures with certain clients. This may be particularly important where there are cultural differences in the expression of emotional states, or if a client has a learning difference or disability that makes the use of measures difficult. The use of outcome measures may also be limited when a client presents with certain characteristics or symptoms (e.g. disabilities or psychotic symptoms). Counsellors should be guided by individual and cultural factors when selecting measures and ensure that they are contextually relevant and appropriately tailored to best reflect individual progress.

Solstad, Castonguay and Moltu (2019) identified some areas of concern around the use of ROM among clients:

- *Transparency around adopting ROM*: Clients may be concerned about what the results are going to be used for. As part of informing the client and obtaining their consent, being open and transparent about how the measures will be used in the service can help build trust and engagement.

- *Emphasis on symptom tracking*: Clients may doubt the applicability of a measure to their personal problems and goals (e.g. Aafjes-van Doorn and Meisel, 2023). This may be exacerbated when identity factors are not fully integrated within a measure. It is important to be realistic and transparent about the limitations of such scales, which are not intended to reflect the rich and nuanced story of the therapy journey. Instead, they provide a particular snapshot of symptoms and experiences that are thought to be common to many people, in a way that allows progress to be charted.

- *Integration and collaboration*: ROM data should enrich therapeutic discussions. Maintaining ongoing dialogue with clients can best ensure a comprehensive and accurate representation of therapeutic progress (e.g. Cooper *et al.*, 2023). Key skills here can include supplementing nomothetic outcome measures with qualitative data and incorporating open-ended questions and narrative feedback during sessions. Counsellors can collaborate with clients to identify personalised goals and benchmarks (Di Malta, Oddli and Cooper, 2019). The completion of outcome measures is not imposed on clients, especially where it would be perceived as meaningless, difficult or shaming.

It is worth noting these points so that you can consider how you would introduce or use ROM with your clients in a way that can reassure them.

Case example: Applying ROM flexibly in Andrew's treatment

Andrew, aged 25, has a mild to moderate intellectual disability and limited education. He is referred to the local NHS Talking Therapy service following several incidents of self-harm. He is allocated to Jan, a practitioner with some previous experience working as a care assistant in intellectual disability services.

Jan recognises that the routine measures used in the service don't really address the frustrations and, at times, rage that Andrew experiences. After discussion with her supervisor and her manager, Jan decides that she will use the Learning Difficulties/Disabilities – Clinical Outcomes in Routine Evaluation (LD-CORE), a measure of mental distress co-designed by and intended for adults with learning difficulties or disabilities. The self-report items have been worded very simply and supported with images. Jan believes the LD-CORE will be accessible for Andrew and will avoid triggering negative feelings such as shame.

Keen to avoid placing Andrew under time pressure, Jan opts to use the 14-item version of the LD-CORE over the longer, 30-item version. Jan takes some time to explain to Andrew what it is about, how it works and what it is used for. She asks Andrew if he would be willing to try it in their therapy.

Andrew is offered 26 sessions with the service – the maximum available – within which they will use the LD-CORE once a month. Jan shares a simple hand-drawn graph with Andrew each time he completes the measure. They also discuss the items where the scores are changing, particularly, 'Have you felt frustrated or upset with your learning disability?' and 'Have you bottled up angry feelings?', for which Andrew particularly likes the alternative phrasing of, 'Have you felt ready to blow inside?'

Pause for thought 12.6

This case study exemplifies the need to be careful when using measures. Thinking about your own practice, have there been cases where the use of outcome measures was clearly not appropriate? What might you do if your practice nonetheless required their use?

6 Future horizons: innovation and developments in outcome measurement

The use of outcome measurement in counselling practice is an evolving process, not least in addressing the challenges described in the previous section. There is also vast potential to enhance the effectiveness and client-centred nature of therapeutic interventions. Areas of potential growth for ROM and ECM exist at both the professional level and also across service development in different national or global contexts.

One prominent limitation of outcome measures is that most have been developed in a Global North or Western context with embedded assumptions about well-being, identities and relationships, the meaning of symptoms and a specific set of diagnostic frameworks. All of these elements reflect a particular cultural view. As noted, for substantial subsets of clients, ECM and ROM are limited by language and cultural markers, and they are also limited in their use for clients experiencing psychotic states or whose problems are highly specific. The field is therefore ripe for a careful and reflective critique of the assumptions inherent in research and practice in the Global North. This may lead to some fundamental changes in approaches to both the outcomes that are measured and the way that they are measured (e.g. the items used in scales). Over time, this may be achieved if practitioners are continuously reflective about the measures used and the impact on their clients.

An important development, therefore, is designing measurement tools and approaches to capture the complexity of human experiences more accurately, moving beyond traditional self-report questionnaires, and combining these with qualitative and client-generated measures (Evans, Carlyle and Paz, 2023). In particular, the development and validation of outcome measures in a range of contexts and cultural groups would support a more inclusive future for outcome measurement.

Another developing area relates to patient choice and how this can be integrated in the selection of outcome measures and systems. One novel tool developed to support and contribute to patient choice in the selection of measures is the Patient-Perceived Helpfulness of Measures Scale (ppHMS) (Di Malta et al., 2023). The ppHMS is a brief scale that provides a structured way for clients to express their perspectives on the usefulness and relevance of outcome measures for their own therapeutic journey. The tool can guide the selection of optimal outcome measures for individuals or groups of clients, enhancing client engagement and outcomes by selecting measures that align with the specific issues faced by each client. It can also support dialogue between clients and psychotherapists, encouraging collaboration and shared decision making.

Technology already plays an increasing role in the future of outcome measurement in counselling, and sophisticated software systems that support data collection, analysis and feedback continue to emerge. Mobile applications and online platforms can offer clients more accessible and convenient ways to engage with assessments, which promotes regular and timely feedback (Gual-Montolio *et al.*, 2020). The use of artificial intelligence and machine learning has the potential to enhance the predictive power of outcome measures, contributing to more personalised and efficient treatment plans (Chekroud *et al.*, 2021). Finally, it also seems likely that the exploration of therapy outcomes and processes will better align and link with physiological measurements to provide more complete and integrated data on patients' outcomes (e.g. Avdi and Evans, 2020).

Conclusion

The aim of this chapter was to provide a foundation for understanding the use of outcome measures as they are applied to evaluating practice and therapy services. The chapter provided the context in which the use of ROM evolved, reviewed common outcome measures and their use, and showed how ROM can contribute to service and counsellor development. There are several challenges associated with the use of outcome measures, in particular in terms of client engagement and also in the relevance of outcome measures when clients have diverse cultural and individual needs. One possible future for outcome measurement in counselling would be marked by a commitment to facing and tackling these challenges, particularly the integration of collaborative and individualised care. These advancements would not only reflect a holistic understanding of mental health, but would also empower clients and counsellors in their collaborative efforts towards achieving positive therapeutic outcomes.

Further reading

To learn about a range of outcome measures and their applications, you can refer to the following texts:

- Evans, C. and Carlyle, J. (2021) *Outcome measures and evaluation in counselling and psychotherapy*. London: SAGE.
- de Jong, K., Delgadillo, J. and Barkham, M. (2023) *Routine outcome monitoring and feedback in psychological therapies*. Maidenhead: Open University Press.

References

Aafjes-van Doorn, K. and de Jong, K. (2022) 'How to make the most of routine outcome monitoring (ROM): a multitude of clinical decisions and nuances to consider', *Journal of Clinical Psychology*, 78(10), pp. 2054–2065. Available at: https://doi.org/10.1002/jclp.23438

Aafjes-van Doorn, K. and Meisel, J. (2022) 'Implementing routine outcome monitoring in a psychodynamic training clinic: it's complicated', *Counselling Psychology Quarterly*, 36(3), pp. 446–465. Available at: https://doi.org/10.1080/09515070.2022.2110451

American Psychological Association (2017) *Ethical principles of psychologists and code of conduct*. Available at: https://apa.org/ethics/code (Accessed: 18 April 2024).

Ashworth, M., Shepherd, M., Christey, J., Matthews, V., Wright, K., Parmentier, H., Robinson, S. and Godfrey, E. (2004) 'A client-generated psychometric instrument: the development of "PSYCHLOPS"', *Counselling and Psychotherapy Research*, 4(2), pp. 27–31. Available at:https://doi.org/10.1080/14733140412331383913

Ashworth, M., Schofield, P., Ayis, S., Godfrey, E., Salisbury, T. and Lund, C. (2017) *Psychological Outcome Profiles questionnaire (PSYCHLOPS), Pre-Therapy, Version 5*. Available at: http://www.psychlops.org.uk/versions (Accessed: 18 June 2024).

Avdi, E. and Evans, C. (2020) 'Exploring conversational and physiological aspects of psychotherapy talk', *Frontiers in Psychology*, 11, article number 591124. Available at: https://doi.org/10.3389/fpsyg.2020.591124

Barkham, M., de Jong, K., Delgadillo, J. and Lutz, W. (2023) 'Routine outcome monitoring (ROM) and feedback: research review and recommendations', *Psychotherapy Research*, 33(7), pp. 841–855. Available at: https://doi.org/10.1080/10503307.2023.2181114

Barkham, M., Evans, C., Margison, F., McGrath, G., Mellor-Clark, J., Milne, D. and Connell, J. (1998) 'The rationale for developing and implementing core outcome batteries for routine use in service settings and psychotherapy outcome research', *Journal of Mental Health*, 7(1), pp. 35–47. Available at: https://doi.org/10.1080/09638239818328

Birtel, M.D. and Mitchell, B.L. (2023) 'Cross-cultural differences in depression between White British and South Asians: causal attributions, stigma by association, discriminatory potential', *Psychology and Psychotherapy: Theory, Research and Practice*, 96(1), pp. 101–116. Available at: https://doi.org/10.1111/papt.12428

Börjesson, S. and Boström, P.K. (2020) '"I want to know what it is used for": clients' perspectives on completing a routine outcome measure (ROM) while undergoing psychotherapy', *Psychotherapy Research*, 30(3), pp. 337–347. Available at: https://doi.org/10.1080/10503307.2019.1630780

Boswell, J.F., Kraus, D.R., Castonguay, L.G. and Youn, S.J. (2015) 'Treatment outcome package: measuring and facilitating multidimensional change', *Psychotherapy*, 52(4), pp. 422–431. Available at: https://doi.org/10.1037/pst0000028

Brattland, H., Koksvik, J.M., Burkeland, O., Gråwe, R.W., Klöckner, C., Linaker, O. M., Ryum, T., Wampold, B., Lara-Cabrera, M.L. and Iversen, V.C. (2018) 'The effects of routine outcome monitoring (ROM) on therapy outcomes in the course of an implementation process: a randomized clinical trial', *Journal of Counseling Psychology*, 65(5), pp. 641–652. Available at: https://doi.org/10.1037/cou0000286

British Association for Counselling and Psychotherapy (BACP) (2023) *Ethical framework for the counselling professions*. Available at:

https://www.bacp.co.uk/events-and-resources/ethics-and-standards/ethical-framework-for-the-counselling-professions/ (Accessed: 12 June 2024).

Chekroud, A.M., Bondar, J., Delgadillo, J., Doherty, G., Wasil, A., Fokkema, M., Cohen, Z., Belgrave, D., DeRubeis, R., Iniesta, R., Dwyer, D. and Choi, K. (2021) 'The promise of machine learning in predicting treatment outcomes in psychiatry', *World Psychiatry*, 20(2), pp. 154–170. Available at: https://doi.org/10.1002/wps.20882

Cooper, M. (2015) *Goals Form: guidance on use*. Available at: www.researchgate.net/publication/286928866_Goals_Form (Accessed 12 June 2024).

Cooper, M., Di Malta, G., Knox, S., Oddli, H.W. and Swift, J.K. (2023) 'Patient perspectives on working with preferences in psychotherapy: a consensual qualitative research study', *Psychotherapy Research*, 33(8), pp. 1117–1131. Available at: https://doi.org/10.1080/10503307.2022.2161967

de Jong, K., Delgadillo, J. and Barkham, M. (2023) *Routine outcome monitoring and feedback in psychological therapies*. Maidenhead: Open University Press.

Di Malta, G., Cooper, M., Bond, J., Raymond-Barker, B., Oza, M. and Pauli, R. (2023) 'The Patient-Perceived Helpfulness of Measures Scale: development and validation of a scale to assess the helpfulness of using measures in psychological treatment', *Assessment*, 31(5), pp. 997–1010. Available at: https://doi.org/10.1177/10731911231195837

Di Malta, G., Oddli, H.W. and Cooper, M. (2019) 'From intention to action: a mixed methods study of clients' experiences of goal-oriented practices', *Journal of Clinical Psychology*, 75(10), pp. 1770–1789. Available at: https://doi.org/10.1002/jclp.22821

Evans, C. (2012) 'The CORE-OM (Clinical Outcomes in Routine Evaluation) and its derivatives', *Integrating Science and Practice*, 2(2), pp. 12–15.

Evans, C. and Carlyle, J. (2021) *Outcome measures and evaluation in counselling and psychotherapy*. London: SAGE.

Evans, C., Carlyle, J. and Paz, C. (2023) 'Rigorous idiography: exploring subjective and idiographic data with rigorous methods – the method of derangements', *Frontiers in Psychology*, 13, article number 1007685. Available at: https://doi.org/10.3389/fpsyg.2022.1007685

Gual-Montolio, P., Martínez-Borba, V., Bretón-López, J.M., Osma, J. and Suso-Ribera, C. (2020) 'How are information and communication technologies supporting routine outcome monitoring and measurement-based care in psychotherapy? A systematic review', *International Journal of Environmental Research and Public Health*, 17(9), article number 3170. Available at: https://doi.org/10.3390/ijerph17093170

Heim, E., Wegmann, I. and Maercker, A. (2017) 'Cultural values and the prevalence of mental disorders in 25 countries: a secondary data analysis', *Social Science & Medicine*, 189, pp. 96–104. Available at: https://doi.org/10.1016/j.socscimed.2017.07.024

Kroenke, K., Spitzer, R.L. and Williams, J.B. (2001) 'The PHQ-9: validity of a brief depression severity measure', *Journal of General Internal Medicine*, 16(9), pp. 606–613. Available at: https://doi.org/10.1046/j.1525-1497.2001.016009606.x

Lambert, M.J. (ed.) (2013) *Bergin and Garfield's handbook of psychotherapy and behavior change*. 6th edn. Hoboken, NJ: John Wiley & Sons, Inc.

Lutz, W., de Jong, K., Rubel, J.A. and Delgadillo, J. (2021) 'Measuring, predicting, and tracking change in psychotherapy', in M. Barkham, W. Lutz and L.G. Castonguay (eds) *Bergin and Garfield's handbook of psychotherapy and behavior change*. 7th edn. Hoboken, NJ: John Wiley & Sons, Inc., pp. 89–133.

Margison, F.R., Barkham, M., Evans, C., McGrath, G., Mellor-Clark, J., Audin, K. and Connell, J. (2000) 'Measurement and psychotherapy: evidence-based practice and practice-based evidence', *The British Journal of Psychiatry*, 177(2), pp. 123–130. Available at: https://doi.org/10.1192/bjp.177.2.123

Marmot, M. (2020) 'Society and the slow burn of inequality', *The Lancet*, 395 (10234), pp. 1413–1414. Available at: https://doi.org/10.1016/S0140-6736(20)30940-5

Miller, S.D., Duncan, B.L., Brown, J., Sparks, J.A. and Claud, D.A. (2003) 'The outcome rating scale: a preliminary study of the reliability, validity, and feasibility of a brief visual analog measure', *Journal of Brief Therapy*, 2(2), pp. 91–100.

Muir, H.J., Coyne, A.E., Morrison, N.R., Boswell, J.F. and Constantino, M.J. (2019) 'Ethical implications of routine outcomes monitoring for patients, psychotherapists, and mental health care systems', *Psychotherapy*, 56(4), pp. 459–469. Available at: https://doi.org/10.1037/pst0000246

Remfrey Foote, C. (2023) 'Outcome measures in transactional analysis clinical practice', *International Journal of Transactional Analysis Research & Practice*, 14 (2), pp. 3–16. Available at: https://doi.org/10.29044/v14i2p3

Sales, C.M.D., Ashworth, M., Ayis, S., Barkham, M., Edbrooke-Childs, J., Faísca, L., Jacob, J., Xu, D. and Cooper, M. (2023) 'Idiographic patient reported outcome measures (I-PROMs) for routine outcome monitoring in psychological therapies: position paper', *Journal of Clinical Psychology*, 79(3), pp. 596–621. Available at: https://doi.org/10.1002/jclp.23319

SCoPEd Framework (2022), collaboratively developed by Association of Christian Counsellors (ACC), British Association for Counselling and Psychotherapy (BACP), British Psychoanalytic Council (BPC), Human Givens Institute (HGI), National Counselling and Psychotherapy Society (NCPS) and United Kingdom Council for Psychotherapy (UKCP). Available at: https://www.bacp.co.uk/about-us/advancing-the-profession/scoped/scoped-framework (Accessed: 12 June 2024).

Solstad, S.M., Castonguay, L.G. and Moltu, C. (2019) 'Patients' experiences with routine outcome monitoring and clinical feedback systems: a systematic review and synthesis of qualitative empirical literature', *Psychotherapy Research*, 29(2), pp. 157–170. Available at: https://doi.org/10.1080/10503307.2017.1326645

Valdiviezo-Oña, J., Montesano, A., Evans, C. and Paz, C. (2023) 'Fostering practice-based evidence through routine outcome monitoring in a university psychotherapy service for common mental health problems: a protocol for a naturalistic, observational study', *BMJ Open*, 13, article number e071875. Available at: https://doi.org/10.1136/bmjopen-2023-071875

Part 4

Research

Chapter 13

Why research matters for counsellors

Femke Truijens and Rebeka Pázmányová

Contents

Introduction

Scattered by Jamie Roscoe-Jones. Much like one's understanding of research, the perception of this image (colour, shape, meaning) depends on the viewer's perspective

Research evidence is increasingly used to make decisions about which psychotherapies get recommended and which services get funded. This chapter highlights the intricate relationship between: scientific research evidence; therapeutic experience, skills and sensitivity; and local, contextual and client-based circumstances. As a counsellor, you have a central role in balancing this triad. This chapter therefore takes you through the kind of choices that are made by researchers, how these might affect the evidence base for practice, how these may shape your implicit or explicit assumptions about therapeutic work and, above all, how crucial it is to be aware of and actively reflect on these choices to facilitate clients' well-being. The chapter aims to provide a context for what it means to be an 'evidence-based practitioner', by focusing on the role of evidence in 'evidence-based practice' (EBP).

What is evidence-based practice? What counts as evidence? Why does research matter to counsellors? These are core questions that are important for all counsellors. As counsellors, we do not simply adopt evidence-based practice; we actively *shape* it. This chapter therefore positions EBP as a practice in which *you*, the reader, play a vital role. To play that role well, it is crucial to be aware of what it entails.

The chapter provides an overview of different research paradigms, methodologies and methods, and encourages a reflexive approach to evidence – one that is open to navigating the complexities of a rich, varied evidence base in order to improve clinical practice. The chapter will first look at the function of evidence in EBP. Next, it discusses several concepts and debates that are important for understanding how counselling research evidence comes about. It then goes on to explore the role of the researcher-practitioner in evidence-based clinical practice.

Throughout the chapter you will review a 'trainer–trainee' dialogue, between the authors, on the impact of research evidence on clinical understanding. Through this dialogue, along with several reflection points and examples based on our own clinical experience, we, the authors, invite you to consider what evidence-based practice means for you as a clinical professional.

This chapter contributes towards achieving the **SCoPEd competency 4.16.B**:

> Ability to draw upon and evaluate published research on counselling and psychotherapy and integrate relevant research findings to enhance practice.
>
> *(SCoPEd Framework, 2022, p. 29)*

This chapter aims to:

- introduce evidence-based practice and describe how it differs from evidence-based treatment
- facilitate reflection on how methodological choices and assumptions – such as realism and constructivism – in different types of clinical research impact scientific evidence
- outline and promote a reflexive and pluralist approach towards evidence-based practice to actively evaluate the merit of sources of evidence in counselling.

1 What is evidence-based practice?

The American Psychological Association (APA) defines EBP as 'the integration of the best available research with clinical expertise in the context of patient characteristics, culture, and preferences' (APA, 2006, p. 273). Importantly, evidence-based practice (EBP) is not the same as evidence-based treatment (EBT). EBTs are treatments found to be 'effective' in scientific research, of which 'ingredients' (ranging from core principles or basic modules to session-by-session planning) are therefore concretely described in a manual. Thus, EBTs are also known as empirically supported treatments. Whereas EBT forms the evidence that supports clinical practice, EBP is much broader, bringing together:

- scientific evidence
- practice-based knowledge (i.e. clinical experience or judgement)
- the local circumstances and contexts of the particular person seeking treatment (think of individual characteristics, but also local socio-economic circumstances, culture and values, and healthcare organisation and accessibility).

In the middle of this EBP triad we find the counsellor, who is actively bringing together and balancing these three elements to provide healthcare that is fit for the actual person sitting across from them in their consultation room. Figure 13.1 displays this dynamic.

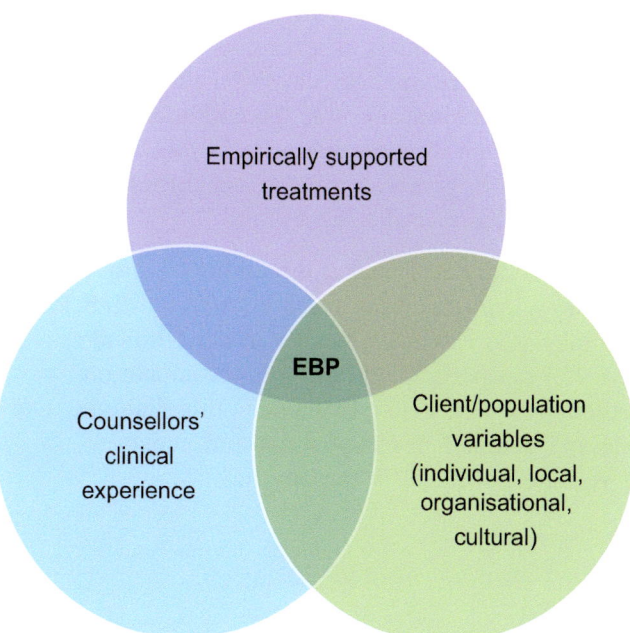

Figure 13.1 Evidence-based practice is a triad between research evidence, clinical knowledge and client context, balanced by the evidence-based practitioner

Pause for thought 13.1

Can you think of a case where you had to adjust your treatment plan due to particular characteristics of a client or local circumstances? What steps did you take to justify these adjustments (to yourself, your client or your institution/employer)?

In considering the question above, you may have remembered some atypical cases. For example, you might have had a client who avoided using the word 'depression' throughout their treatment, for fear of mirroring a parent who had experienced depression. Or perhaps a client opted for self-care training through local social services over a full therapeutic trajectory. Maybe you even found that there are more exceptions than rules when it comes to following standard procedures. This highlights an important feature of EBP: it is a multiperspectival understanding (Cooper and McLeod, 2007). Consequently, there is no 'gold standard' or protocol for how to adjust a treatment plan to a particular person's needs. Therefore, EBP always requires the counsellor to balance research evidence with clinical knowledge and contextual information.

To do that, practitioners need to know how to read, understand and evaluate research evidence. They also need to learn how to balance that evidence with clinical observation, contextual characteristics and professional experience. Thus, it is vital that you become aware of your own perspectives, beliefs and values with respect to EBP. Such awareness is an ever-evolving and personal process. Although such evolution is necessary for development and growth, at times it can feel unsteady and even a bit scary. We, the authors of this chapter, know this well because we go through this process too. We will share some of our own experiences to give you a bit of insight (and hopefully reassurance) as to what one might learn in the process.

Throughout the chapter, we – Femke and Rebeka, the authors – provide excerpts of our dialogue on how learning about research affected Rebeka's perspective on practice. (Femke was Rebeka's teacher in her Clinical Psychology Masters, where Rebeka participated in Femke's course on qualitative and mixed methods research.) Box 13.1 opens this dialogue. Our aim is to invite you to imagine yourself in our position and, most importantly, to show that you are not alone in this journey.

1.1 The place of 'evidence' in evidence-based practice

The principle of EBP is derived from the scientist-practitioner model for the education of clinical psychologists in the latter half of the twentieth century. As the field was scattered over several different 'therapy schools', the idea arose that for fair and adequate treatment of people with mental health issues, decision making on diagnoses and treatments should be grounded in impartial science rather than allegiance to a particular theory. This was substantiated by studies that, for example, showed how outcome studies found large effects for the therapy types that the authors preferred (e.g. Wampold and Imel, 2015). In turn, this showed that it is important to control for **researcher bias**, or researcher allegiance. This, among other things, led to an increasing emphasis on research procedures and methodologies that control for preferences and biases.

researcher bias

Bias formed by the belief of superiority in the intervention that the researcher prefers, which leads to better outcomes for that intervention than the comparison (placebo, waiting list or alternative condition).

The procedures were adopted from medical science, where the efficacy of medical and pharmaceutical interventions are systematically tested in controlled experiments. As such, the intervention of interest (e.g. a pill, surgical procedure or treatment) is compared to a non-active control (e.g. doing nothing, being on the waiting list, receiving a placebo). In this experimental set-up, it is thus possible to check whether:

1   people are better off after the intervention than before (i.e. check for a pre–post difference)

2   that effect is actually due to the intervention rather than some other factor (e.g. simply the passing of time, a normal course of change, or common factors such as attention and relief).

Another way to ensure that the found effect is due to the intervention is to allocate participants randomly to the experimental conditions. This design, in which interventions are tested pre–post against a control and with random allocation, is known as the randomised controlled trial (RCT). In psychology, the RCT has been set as the 'gold standard' methodology for therapeutic outcome research (Wampold and Imel, 2015). In fact, for a treatment to be viewed as evidence-based or empirically supported, it must have been found to be effective in a minimum number of RCT studies.

Setting RCTs as the gold standard for therapeutic research has had a huge impact on the organisation of mental health care – not just in respect to methodology and research, but also on the way we think about treatment more generally. What 'works' in treatment, for example, is increasingly defined in terms of symptom reduction. Why? Because RCTs test the efficacy of treatments by comparing symptoms pre- and post-treatment. In addition, treatment success is defined on a group level, because the design presupposes the comparison of randomly allocated groups rather than individuals. Importantly, these groups are comprised of people who share particular characteristics. For example, they might all have a certain level of depression, but no signs of anxiety, personality disorders or substance abuse disorders. The more similar the people in the experimental groups, the more confident the researcher can be that a found therapeutic effect is due to the intervention and not to other so-called confounding factors or variables (this quality is known as internal validity; see Chapter 14). In formal terms, strict inclusion and exclusion criteria enable homogeneous samples, which are necessary to conclude that found pre–post differences are *caused* by the treatment of interest. Adopting this approach to therapeutic research has, therefore, affected how clinical concepts such as treatment effect and success are defined.

1.2 The research–practice gap

The emphasis on evidence-based principles led to over six decades of scientifically rigorous research, resulting in over 350 EBTs (Kazdin, 2008) and a global wave of reform in local mental health organisations. A downside of this increased emphasis on RCTs is the fact that such systematic, highly specified and uniform research does not resemble the messiness of the real world. As clinicians, of course, we want to know which treatments work *in general*, but we also want to know what to do for or offer an individual client.

Generally, clinicians (and even researchers) do not have the capacity to review the full body of relevant evidence, and often turn to guidelines for practice. The National Institute for Health and Care Excellence (NICE) develops and updates treatment guidelines across England and Wales for specific health issues, such as depression and trauma, by reviewing the available scientific evidence as it is published, and reflecting changes in scientific or clinical knowledge. However, imagine you have a client who presents with symptoms of both depression *and* trauma resulting from childhood abuse. While the NICE guidelines will provide you with a recommendation of an EBT for either issue, it will not provide you with the answer you probably need in this case. Most of us would look for guidance on how to adapt or combine available treatments in such a case of comorbidity (i.e. when different psychopathological experiences occur at the same time or are interrelated).

This example shows that *group-level systematic controlled research evidence* is not always sufficient. It might be more helpful to read case reports of specific individuals who share particular features with your client. The difference between the highly systematised world of research evidence on the one hand, and the messy, individual and contextual particularities and needs of clinical practice on the other, is known as the research–practice gap (McLeod, 2001).

So why does research matter for counsellors? It matters because evidence *shapes* practice. Therefore, it is important to be aware of the kind of evidence that is formed in research and whether, or how, your practice reflects that evidence every day. The way in which you are expected to work with individuals within an organisation is for a large part defined by that evidence but, as discussed, that does not cover the whole story of practice. As your role as a counsellor is to balance the research evidence, individual client factors and your clinical experience, it is vital that you are well aware of the role and scope of evidence in your work.

1.3 The importance of reflecting on evidence

Pause for thought 13.3

What kind of evidence have you found helpful as a counsellor in tailoring treatment plans to your clients? What are the obstacles in formulating or administering such an adjusted or personalised treatment plan?

The questions above put you in the centre of the EBP triad. As a clinical practitioner balancing this triad, you might answer these questions differently for each case you think of. When a client tells you that she is expected to suffer to prove that she is worthy of God's love, you have to be sensitive to the cultural and religious aspects of her experience of symptoms, as well as to the appropriateness of interventions. It might be that you yourself hold different beliefs, but in clinical practice what you believe cannot drive your actions, which might be at odds with the belief system of your client. This asks you to combine your self-awareness and cultural sensitivity (as was covered in Part 1 of this book) with an awareness of what the evidence tells you about treatment options.

This professional (and personal) self-awareness is central to reflexive clinical practice. As explained in Chapter 7, reflexivity is seen as imperative to becoming aware of one's own assumptions, values, and personal and cultural beliefs, which is of course a prerequisite to being able to notice that the beliefs and values of the person sitting across from you can differ from your own. Such self-reflection is a well-known and often taught virtue of clinical professional behaviour, but as argued in this chapter, it does not stop at *self*-awareness. Rather, for EBP, reflexivity also means reflecting on the *production*, *use* and *justification* of evidence in our daily practices (Willig, 2019). When you apply evidence in your practice, you give it more value. Vice versa, when applying evidence does not work or is not sufficient in your practice, it is important to feed this back to the producers of evidence (i.e. researchers). This way, EBP becomes a self-learning practice too, which is necessary for development and growth both for the individual clinician and for the counselling field in general, as discussed in Box 13.2.

Box 13.2 Trainer–trainee dialogue: EBP and reflexivity

Rebeka: While experimental research sees researcher influence as detrimental, in qualitative research and clinical practice it is often seen as a strength. I was lucky enough to be involved in teams that put emphasis on reflexivity: the supervisors always taught me this practice of knowing how my own frame of reference influences my work.

Femke: Is that what reflexivity means to you, knowing yourself and your blind spots?

Rebeka: Yes. In reflexive research, I would have to think of how I influence the research or the client, but I also need to reflect on how my work makes me feel. It's a circle: how my own frame of reference influences the client, how the client influences me and how all of that, in turn, influences my frame of reference.

Femke: What you're describing is how a hermeneutic circle works: how you listen to a person from your own understanding, while also being adaptive to their story. By doing so, you influence how you're listening, and then that affects your way of speaking with the person, which affects the way the person feels heard. That becomes a circle.

---

2 Principles and approaches for evidence formation

When designing studies, researchers make several choices that have an impact on how evidence is produced, and the applicability and relevance of that evidence for practice. This section focuses on conceptual and methodological concepts that are important to grasp in order to understand how researchers develop the evidence that serves as a basis for evidence-based practice.

2.1 Nomothetic versus idiographic approaches

When we experience the world through our senses, we automatically make assumptions about what is 'real' and 'true'. That the sun rises every morning is a truth regardless of what we believe; this is considered a law of nature. Understanding the world as being made up of such law-like processes and patterns reflects a nomothetic approach to understanding (this is related to 'nomothetic measurement', which was defined in Chapter 12, Section 1). This approach is also at the heart of medical science, where we understand and study diseases as real, universal processes that work according to natural laws. In psychology, the nomothetic approach is central to the understanding of psychological suffering in terms of mental diseases. In the disease model, it is assumed that major depressive disorder (MDD), for example, has a natural cause (e.g. a neurological deficit), and a cure means that this cause should be eliminated. Accordingly, since this model understands diseases as being governed by objective laws of nature, it treats patients with that disorder in the same way by, for example, using the same treatment protocol that targets similar symptoms in different people.

On the other hand, idiographic approaches (see also 'idiographic measurement', defined in Chapter 12, Section 1) do not assume that mental illnesses present in such a law-like fashion. Rather, it is assumed that people develop and understand their symptoms in unique ways. For example, while two clients can both be diagnosed with MDD, one could develop it gradually within an ongoing abusive relationship, while the other is surprised by a sudden depressive episode. This would make a huge difference in how they experience depression and construct their self-narrative, and how they might benefit from treatment. So, rather than assuming regularities over people, the idiographic approach starts from the unique and personal perspectives of the individual.

2.2 Ontology and epistemology

ontology

Theory of being (i.e. understandings of what is real and true in the world).

The paradigms discussed in Section 2.1 both make assumptions about how the world works, and what constitutes truth and reality. These questions together form a 'theory of being', or the **ontology** of the paradigm. From a nomothetic perspective, MDD is understood as a real, biological disease, whereas from an idiographic perspective, the focus is on how people experience, understand and explain depressive complaints, and how that affects what they consider to be real or true. The next question is therefore: how can we learn something about truth? This question is central to the 'theory of knowledge', or epistemology (defined in Chapter 4, Section 2, as the nature of learning and generating knowledge about the world).

Researchers adhering to a nomothetic approach tend to look for patterns or regularities in (large) groups of people, which can be generalised to other people or circumstances, and can be used to make predictions. The style of writing in nomothetic enquiry is usually impersonal and emphasises objectivity. This fits with the epistemic goal of *Erklären* (explanation): when one holds the ontological position that there is a real, universal and law-like outside world, the epistemological consequence is that the universal world can be *explained* by deducting universal patterns of phenomena. In this, the patterns or laws underlying the phenomena are understood as the *cause* of those phenomena, such as when neurological disease (disordered neurotransmitters) is considered a cause of symptoms of depression.

Idiographic approaches assume that to know anything about people's sense of truth, you must start by asking how people themselves understand those truths. The idiographic approach often explores complex constructs or narratives, where the context and interpretation of an individual play a central role. The writing is often descriptive, detailed and highlights subjectivity. This fits with the epistemic goal of *Verstehen* (understanding): when one's ontological position is that people make sense of phenomena in their personal contexts and from their own framework of meaning, the epistemic implication is that researchers can *understand* this meaning-making by observing it and taking personal contexts into account. Hence, the goal would be to understand how people make meaning of phenomena. It is vital to remember that, in this approach, the researcher also tries to make sense of these phenomena from their own framework of meaning, so they must closely reflect on the relation between how researchers understand participants and how they understand their own meaning-making, worldviews and preferences (which calls for reflexivity, as outlined in Section 1.3). For example, a clinician who follows the idiographic approach would try to understand how different factors (e.g. the client's unique stressors and coping strategies, and how they make sense of their distress) contribute to their anxiety, rather than solely adhering to the diagnostic criteria of generalized anxiety disorder.

To sum up, researchers typically adhere to a particular paradigm, which is characterised by certain ontological assumptions about how the world works and by epistemological assumptions about how a human researcher can gain knowledge about that world. The ontological and epistemic assumptions can be directed to a more nomothetic approach or a more idiographic approach, which are related to the understanding of reality and truth, causation, generalisability and objectivity.

2.3 Realism and constructivism

Realism and constructivism are two well-known, related paradigms that are adhered to in the field of mental health care and research. It is important to understand these widely used terms, since the assumptions that follow from them impact how evidence is understood and produced.

In the realist paradigm, reality is considered to be singular and independent of our understanding of it. For example, the sun is real, and whether we find the sun beautiful or annoying does not affect its 'realness'. By systematically observing a phenomenon, we can gain knowledge. Systematic observation can indeed be done by impartial observation (meaning that the observation should not depend on who is watching). This can be done by using the same tool across observations and observers (e.g. a diagnostic interview or observation), or by systematically intervening and observing the outcome (e.g. comparing symptoms after a treatment, in an experimentally controlled setting). Importantly, systematic observation presupposes many observations, so that one can, in fact, speak of a 'pattern' or 'regularity' over time or different situations. Therefore, when adopting a realist, nomothetic approach, researchers tend to focus on patterns that happen at the population level, and they aggregate a large amount of observation data to represent patterns of the population.

In the constructivist paradigm, the central assumption is that reality is constructed by the individual. Therefore, in principle, there can be as many 'realities' as there are people. People construct their sense of reality *in context*: how they understand the world – *their* world – is shaped by what they have learned (e.g. from parents, school, society) and experienced individually, but also as part of social and cultural groups. To take a very simple example, a person from a cold climate may experience a day that is 20 degrees Celsius very differently to someone from a hot climate. As people are always part of social systems (based on society, socio-economic status, culture and religion), people's constructions of reality can be highly similar. Nonetheless, as people also grow up and develop in their own smaller systems (such as their own family or peer groups), people colour their realities in their own unique ways.

Social-constructivist research is thus in principle idiographic research, in which the starting point is the individual experience. However, this does not mean that constructivist research is individual or case-based research. Given the paramount role of social factors in how people make sense of their world, aggregation of experiences allows us to understand how such shared realities come about and are experienced. This aggregation is often bottom-up, meaning that it starts from the singular and builds up to the general, in which context and meaning remain vital to understanding. Creating a sense of reality and making sense of everything that happens in one's life is also known as hermeneutics. The constructivist approach acknowledges that researchers are also human and therefore they too make sense of the lifeworlds of the people they study. This process is known as double hermeneutics: researchers make sense of how people make sense of the phenomenon of interest (as was shown in the trainer–trainee dialogue in Box 13.2).

Pause for thought 13.4

Have you ever encountered an argument or interpretation that you really disagreed with? Maybe you met a person (e.g. teacher, colleague, client) who had a fundamentally different understanding of human behaviour and experiences than you do. Were you able to remain engaged, or did you dismiss the information? Can you think of how your paradigmatic assumptions might have affected how you understood or accepted the information?

The paradigms (realism and constructivism) and epistemic goals (*Erklären* and *Verstehen*) discussed so far are connected to methodologies. Your ideas and assumptions about the world (ontology) and the best way to gain knowledge on that world (epistemology) form the foundation of your methodology or methodological stance. Methodology, in turn, is your theoretical understanding that explains or drives the choice of a type of method, or the concrete procedures or tools that you can use to address a particular research problem and generate evidence. Many factors will be driven by your methodological approach:

- how you understand data, informed by your theoretical/research paradigm
- what or who constitutes the object or subject of the study
- how you collect your data
- how you assure the quality of the study
- what type of analysis you perform
- how you interpret your findings
- how you disseminate your overall research.

Table 13.1 summarises the inherent relation between paradigmatic philosophical assumptions, methodological principles and the concrete form or design of clinical research. The next chapters discuss in detail how quantitative (statistics-based) research methods (Chapter 14), qualitative (narrative-based) research methods (Chapter 15) and mixed methods (Chapter 16) can be utilised by researchers, and how these types of methods can be read and understood by evidence-based practitioners.

Table 13.1 Paradigmatic assumptions and imperatives for research in realist and constructivist approaches

	Realism	**Constructivism**
Paradigmatic (philosophical) assumptions	Ontology: generalisable laws or rules (nomothetic) Epistemology: systematic observation or controlled intervention for objective knowledge generation Focus on causality and explanation (discourse of *Erklären*)	Ontology: subjective experiences of individuals/groups (idiographic) Epistemology: focus on experiences and (social) construction of reality Focus on understanding how people make sense of their lifeworld (discourse of *Verstehen*)
Methodological principles	Top-down aggregation of data, group-level analyses Often statistical and experimental design yielding quantitative data Impartial researcher (aims for objectivity and limits personal involvement)	Bottom-up understanding and aggregation of idiosyncratic meaning-making Often in-depth qualitative or quantitative analysis of individual data Involved researcher (double hermeneutics)
Research design	Identifying the efficacy of interventions Studying treatment outcomes in controlled settings Looking for a causal explanation (e.g. by specific treatment factors)	Studying processes, experiences and dynamics Studying people in natural circumstances Adapting interventions to the needs of specific individuals/groups

3 Reflexivity and pluralism as guiding principles for evidence-based practice

As covered earlier in the chapter, EBP is considered to follow from 'gold standard' research (i.e. RCT studies). Consequently, in counselling and psychotherapy research, some methodologies are valued more than others. Ironically, however, such methodological preferentialism is at odds with the definition of EBP: evidence-based practice is in principle an integration of several perspectives to serve the needs of real people in the messy context of clinical practice. This integration can be *based* on evidence, but not *dictated* by evidence or methodology.

Section 1 gave an example of a client who avoided saying the word 'depression' throughout their treatment for the condition, because they had a parent who experienced depression. Knowing this, some counsellors would be inclined to enquire about the parent, while adapting their language to suit the client. Others might directly adopt the term to generate an exposure effect that decreases anxiety, which could be a primary step to recovery. Both approaches might be evidence-based, and both might work for the client. But which one would work best for them remains an open question: hitherto, there is very little evidence that answers the question, which is so often asked in clinics, of what works for whom.

As Cooper and McLeod state, 'psychological difficulties may have multiple causes and … there is unlikely to be one, "right" therapeutic method that will be appropriate in all situations – different people are helped by different processes at different times' (2007, p. 135). Moreover, it is important to remember that in clinical practice, there are many more exceptions than in clinical research. While an EBT protocol is a great vehicle to get treatment started, it is up to the counsellor to administer it in such a way that it fits with the specific needs of the client. That process is seldom the same – even though, by experience, the counsellor will become aware of the similarities/patterns within one's target population. This emphasises the importance of the counsellor who remembers that the research evidence is but a tool within the multidimensional toolkit of the counsellor.

Based on this insight, Cooper and McLeod argue for a 'pluralist' perspective on clinical practice: 'In relation to counselling and psychotherapy, a pluralistic standpoint maintains that a multiplicity of different models of psychological distress and change may be "true" and that there is no need to try and reduce these into one, unified model' (Cooper and McLeod, 2007, p. 136–137). Thus, pluralism implies the use of a plurality of methods and approaches to cover the wide array of issues that come together in clinical practice. A major benefit of pluralism is that all stakeholders involved in EBP must argue for *why* their preferred or used means are actually fit to target their particular problem. This is discussed further in Box 13.3.

Box 13.3 Trainer–trainee dialogue: adopting a pluralist approach

Femke: I think it is necessary that researchers who adhere to different paradigms coexist, because if we only did research from, let's say, the qualitative point of view, we would miss out on population level information; and likewise, while RCTs provide that general information, we cannot stop there but have to come up with a roadmap of how to get from this general or average knowledge to this person in my consultation room.

Rebeka: Indeed, because what do we do with the client who doesn't fit the average? What if people who come in show different types of comorbidities? To work in clinical practice, we need knowledge from different types of research, providing information both on the general and the individual. And with this mix of evidence and research paradigms, we can improve our work.

Femke: Absolutely. Rather than prioritising one method over another, we'd better work on the whole spectrum of methods, with the different paradigms alongside each other.

It may have become clear that a pluralist scientific approach inherently requires reflexivity (see Willig, 2019) because when you go by one type of method out of a plurality of options, you have to be able to argue for and justify your choice for that method rather than another. This question of justification is not only relevant to researchers who are tasked with generating evidence, but also to clinical counsellors who intend to *use* this knowledge as part of their evidence-based practice. This makes EBP an ethical imperative: the counsellor has the ethical responsibility to validate interpretations in the context of the individual person and their circumstances. The overarching ethical imperative of EBP is to balance, navigate and weigh the stakes in each situation again.

This comes back to the inherent relationship between reflexivity and pluralism, which are guiding principles for EBP. Pluralism does not just regard the reflexive flexibility of counsellors in practice to adjust treatments to the needs of clients, but also addresses the researchers who produce evidence for EBP. In fact, while evidence-based principles might sometimes come across as top-down, where researchers tell practitioners what to do, this chapter has argued that EBP should be an *iterative* process which moves back and forth between research and practice. This implies that researchers should listen to practitioners about research priorities, practitioners should use and refine research evidence in practice, and both should work towards improving our understanding of individual people and contexts. In this way, EBP becomes a co-creation among people and perspectives.

Conclusion

This chapter has overtly addressed you as a professional who works in evidence-based clinical practice. It has sketched out evidence-based practice as a triad between research evidence, contextual and patient characteristics, and clinical experience and knowledge. In this triad, *you* make the difference, given that counsellors play a central role in balancing the stakes and making sure the treatment fits with the needs of the individual. Given this important role, the aim of this chapter was to engage you in thinking about what EBP means to you, rather than tell you how to do it. You are not just the 'receiver' or the 'disseminator' of evidence that was developed in a lab. Instead, you play a vital role in evaluating and adapting scientific evidence to the day-to-day realm of clinical practice. Thus, it is crucial to be aware of your own beliefs and values, and those of your clients, but also of researchers who draw from their own methodological and philosophical perspectives and use a plethora of methods to form the evidence base for practice. This chapter therefore established reflexivity and pluralism as guiding principles for EBP, in which a multitude of perspectives can facilitate a person-centered *and* research-informed clinical practice.

Further reading

- The ideas in this chapter align with the perspectives on the intricate relation between science and practice. You can read more about this in the following sources:

  McLeod, J. (2016) *Using research in counselling and psychotherapy.* London: SAGE.

  Wampold, B.E. and Imel, Z.E. (2015) *The great psychotherapy debate.* 2nd edn. Oxfordshire: Routledge.

- A great discussion on outcome research appears in the anniversary issue of the journal *Psychotherapy*. All papers in this special issue give a great reflection on the merits of decades of outcome research:

  Hilsenroth, M.J. (2013) 'Introduction to the 50th anniversary special issue on psychotherapy outcome: a return to the beginning', *Psychotherapy*, 50(1), pp. 1–2. Available at: https://doi.org/10.1037/a0031718

References

American Psychological Association, Presidential Task Force on Evidence-Based Practice (2006) 'Evidence-based practice in psychology', *American Psychologist*, 61 (4), pp. 271–285. Available at: https://doi.org/10.1037/0003-066X.61.4.271

Cooper, M. and McLeod, J. (2007) 'A pluralistic framework for counselling and psychotherapy: implications for research', *Counselling and Psychotherapy Research*, 7(3), pp. 135–143. Available at: https://doi.org/10.1080/14733140701566282

Kazdin, A.E. (2008) 'Evidence-based treatment and practice: new opportunities to bridge clinical research and practice, enhance the knowledge base, and improve patient care', *American Psychologist*, 63(3), pp. 146–159. Available at: https://doi.org/10.1037/0003-066X.63.3.146

McLeod, J. (2001) 'Developing a research tradition consistent with the practices and values of counselling and psychotherapy: why *Counselling and Psychotherapy Research* is necessary', *Counselling and Psychotherapy Research*, 1(1), pp. 3–11. Available at: https://doi.org/10.1080/14733140112331385188

SCoPEd Framework (2022), collaboratively developed by Association of Christian Counsellors (ACC), British Association for Counselling and Psychotherapy (BACP), British Psychoanalytic Council (BPC), Human Givens Institute (HGI), National Counselling and Psychotherapy Society (NCPS) and United Kingdom Council for Psychotherapy (UKCP). Available at: https://www.bacp.co.uk/about-us/advancing-the-profession/scoped/scoped-framework (Accessed: 12 June 2024).

Wampold, B.E. and Imel, Z.E. (2015) *The great psychotherapy debate*. 2nd edn. Oxfordshire: Routledge.

Willig, C. (2019) 'Ontological and epistemological reflexivity: a core skill for therapists', *Counselling and Psychotherapy Research*, 19(3), pp. 186–194. Available at: https://doi.org/10.1002/capr.12204

Chapter 14

Understanding and using quantitative research evidence

Felicitas Rost

Contents

Introduction

Anxiety by Carys Treadwell

Quantitative research reflects a nomothetic understanding of phenomena. It assumes the existence of an objective, knowable truth that can be quantified, tested and scientifically proven. As such, it deals with objective phenomena and the discovery of general laws. This chapter will focus on the aims, key principles and outcomes of quantitative research applied to the field of counselling and psychotherapy. The aim is to provide you with a 'map' to orient yourself when reading quantitative studies and to help you evaluate whether findings are useful for your clinical practice.

The image that opens this chapter reflects the worry that some people feel about approaching quantitative methods and data, not only through its title (*Anxiety*) but also through its abstract quality: quantitative methods require us to think in abstract terms. While these methods do rely on statistics, to borrow a phrase by healthcare researcher and academic Trisha Greenhalgh, 'you do not need to be able to build a car in order to drive one' (2019, p. 62). In other words, you do not need to be, or become, an expert in statistics in order to understand and engage with quantitative research. However, having a basic understanding of the key principles and concepts will help you to both make sense of and critically engage with quantitative findings.

How do you feel about approaching this chapter? Do you feel comfortable, apprehensive or maybe somewhat anxious? Whatever emotion you notice, hopefully reading this chapter will increase your curiosity about the quantitative approach that has served the counselling discipline exceptionally well. Perhaps it might even spark an interest in reading more about it, so that you can critique research and practice from an informed position. I strongly believe that, as healthcare professionals, we have a responsibility to offer therapeutic help that is beneficial and does not cause harm. To this end, systematic quantitative research investigations provide us with helpful tools and insights that can improve our ways of working. Relying entirely on our own clinical experience or theoretical beliefs can become problematic; we can get used to working in a particular way, which might benefit some clients but not others. Therefore, quantitative findings – in addition to supervision and consultations with colleagues – help us to challenge ourselves and guide our own thinking and reflexivity.

This chapter contributes towards achieving the **SCoPEd competency 4.16.B**:

Ability to draw upon and evaluate published research on counselling and psychotherapy and integrate relevant research findings to enhance practice.

(SCoPEd Framework, 2022, p. 29)

This chapter aims to:

- introduce key principles of quantitative research

- cover basic theoretical and statistical frameworks used within the quantitative paradigm

- suggest criteria for the evaluation of quantitative research and its usefulness to clinical practice.

1 The importance of quantitative research evidence

Quantitative research aims to answer questions such as 'what is the effect of?', 'how much?', 'how often?', 'what relates to this?' or 'what is causing that?'. To answer these questions, it collects and relies on numerical data that is analysed using mathematically based methods, particularly statistics (Aliaga and Gunderson, 1999). This contrasts with qualitative research, which involves collecting and analysing in-depth narrative data (which is the focus of Chapter 15).

Quantitative research findings cover a wide range of topics relevant to the field of counselling. Broadly, research in counselling falls within two areas: outcome and process research. Outcome studies investigate which psychotherapies are most effective for particular situations or conditions. Process studies provide insight into how and why interventions are beneficial or not. If you looked at the progress of studies over the past 50 years or so, you'd probably be amazed at the advances that have been made in being able to study the intricacies and complexities involved in psychotherapy.

Outcome studies, for example, have helped to build a solid evidence base for many psychotherapeutic approaches, which allows for wider access and availability of these treatments. Studies on the therapeutic process have begun to explore important questions around mechanisms of change as well as factors that help and hinder interventions. For example, the investigation of relational processes – such as the role of the therapeutic relationship, or how ruptures and their repair shape both the process and outcome of therapy – has led to many important findings. Similarly informative for counsellors are the studies that explore client and therapist characteristics and attitudes towards change, and how these can either facilitate or hinder the process of therapy. Quantitative research has also highlighted the usefulness of specific therapeutic techniques – such as transference interpretations, mirroring and homework – for specific populations or conditions.

Admittedly, approaching the wealth of literature on this kind of research can be daunting. You could start by reading summaries or reviews of available studies. *Bergin and Garfield's Handbook of Psychotherapy and Behavior Change* (Barkham, Lutz and Castonguay, 2021), for example, provides a comprehensive summary and review of past and current research findings within the psychotherapy field.

McLeod (2011) made an important point when he argued that all counsellors are intuitive scientists. Think about it: in your sessions with clients, are you not indirectly engaged in collecting evidence, coming up with hypotheses, and then 'testing' them against what is happening in subsequent sessions or with what comes out of a discussion with your supervisor or with other clients?

Pause for thought 14.1

Take a minute to notice how you feel about research in general, and about quantitative research in particular. Have the findings from a quantitative study ever made you question or rethink a particular intervention with a client?

To effectively apply quantitative research to your practice, it is first important to familiarise yourself with the key principles of quantitative methods; this will be the topic of the following sections. Examples from the Tavistock Adult Depression Study (TADS) will be used throughout to make the concepts more understandable and meaningful. I, the author of this chapter, have been involved in the TADS for many years and I owe the development of my identity as a practitioner-researcher to it. Some information on the study is provided in Box 14.1.

Box 14.1 The Tavistock Adult Depression Study

The TADS was developed to investigate the effectiveness of psychoanalytic therapy on treatment-resistant depression. The details of this study are given below.

Research context

Worldwide, 175 million people are said to suffer from major depressive disorder (Institute for Health Metrics and Evaluation, 2021). Most vulnerable are those who experience chronic and severe forms of this depression, and who have tried multiple courses of medication or short-term therapies without benefit. The diagnostic term for this form of depression is 'treatment-resistant depression'. Unfortunately, there is still a lack of research to appropriately guide clinical management, which leaves these individuals at a severe disadvantage.

Study aims and design

The TADS was designed to respond to the lack of research. The aim was to investigate whether long-term psychoanalytic psychotherapy was more effective than standard GP care (treatment-as-usual) at treating this depression. The study was a randomised controlled trial, in which 129 participants were randomly allocated to either the therapy group or the control group. Participants met with the research team at regular intervals during the 18-month duration of therapy and over the two-year follow-up. During these meetings, participants were interviewed and completed questionnaires about their depression, measuring its severity and remission rates, as well as other outcomes including functioning and well-being.

Participant example: Lydia

A participant example is given here for the purposes of clinical context.

Lydia (a pseudonym used for anonymity) was a 40-year-old woman whose parents emigrated to the UK from Ireland. She reported having been severely depressed since university and struggled to function on many levels. She had been unable to work for over ten years and lived a very isolated life, with only her youngest daughter visiting her sporadically. She struggled with sleep. Memories of repeated physical and sexual abuse during childhood and as a young adult had become increasingly intrusive. In addition to having anxiety, she also experienced a range of physical ailments, including fatigue and severe muscular pain. She had tried several types of antidepressants and two courses of cognitive behavioural therapy, neither of which helped. She felt hopeless and experienced frequent thoughts about ending her life.

One day, while waiting for a GP appointment, she noticed a poster calling for participants to take part in a research study. She spoke to her GP about it, who made a referral. The research team ascertained that she met the inclusion criteria and made sure that she understood the aims and process of the study, and gave informed consent to take part. Lydia was subsequently randomised to the therapy group in the study.

Published details

The full description of the study was published by Taylor *et al.* (2012), and the main findings were published by Fonagy *et al.* (2015). Rost *et al.* (2024) published a detailed description of the participant group, highlighting the severity and complexity of the condition, and offering a discussion on the diagnostic term 'treatment-resistant depression'.

2 The breadth and key principles of quantitative research

variable

In quantitative research, a variable is any factor or characteristic that can produce a measurable change (e.g. demographic information, test scores or treatment interventions).

The overarching goal of quantitative research is to be able to draw general conclusions from the data: statistical prediction is used to do this. A data item that is collected can also be referred to as a **variable**, a term which is used because the data is expected to *vary* between individuals and conditions. The aim is thus to look at both the averages and spread around this variation. This is a hallmark of the quantitative paradigm: the approach provides information for the average person in a study, and the results revolve around the average of whatever variable is being measured. However, it does not provide information about person-specific measures and unique experiences. Thus, going back to Lydia, the participant in the TADS who was introduced in Box 14.1, her depression severity scores contributed to the overall average score of depression severity of those randomised into the therapy group, which was then compared to the average score of those in the treatment-as-usual group.

Broadly, quantitative research can be categorised into three domains:

- *Descriptive research* aims to summarise the data (e.g. 'how much?', 'how many?', 'what's the average of?').
- *Correlational research* aims to investigate relationships (associations) between variables.
- *Experimental research* aims to investigate cause-and-effect relationships between variables.

Quantitative research is further distinguished between *cross-sectional* research and *longitudinal* research. The former describes studies that collect data from participants at a single point in time, often to explore trends or associations; the latter describes studies that collect data over a longer period – participants provide information repeatedly, for example, to explore the trajectory of change.

hypothesis

An assumption or proposed explanation that is put to the test in order to see if it is true.

Quantitative research is question specific; it is centred around at least one hypothesis that is put to the test, which subsequently allows researchers to draw general conclusions from the results. Researchers therefore need to carefully design and plan their study. From reformulating the research question into a testable **hypothesis**, to choosing a valid **representative sample** and adequate measurements, to choosing the appropriate statistical test(s), each step requires careful consideration and decisions to be made before the study begins. What researchers need to evaluate is whether their overall study design allows for certainty or confidence in the findings.

representative sample

A subgroup of the whole population of interest, one that reflects the characteristics of the larger group as accurately as possible.

There are five quality standards that should be met when conducting a quantitative study:

- *Objectivity*: the findings should not be influenced by researcher bias or preference.
- *Reliability*: the findings should be replicable.
- *Internal validity*: the findings should be due to the phenomena of interest and not to methodological choices or errors.
- *External validity*: the findings should be generalisable to other relevant situations and people.
- *Ecological validity*: the findings should be applicable to real-world situations (i.e. clinical practice).

As you will learn, it is not always possible to meet the criteria for both internal and external validity in psychotherapy studies. Thus, not only do these criteria provide guidance to those devising and conducting the research, they are also helpful benchmarks for those who – perhaps like yourself – read the published studies to establish their quality and trustworthiness, and to determine whether the findings are relevant to clinical practice. You can often identify good studies by how transparent the authors are in reporting their methodological choices as well as how far they report and discuss their findings in relation to these, and the potential resulting limitations.

Sections 3 and 4 will introduce the key principles of quantitative research in relation to each of these factors and highlight what needs to be done to adhere to them.

3 The importance of the research framework

Like all forms of research, quantitative research begins with posing a question. The next step entails choosing the right research design to answer this question. Let's look at each step in turn.

3.1 The research question

According to Timulak (2015), quantitative research questions relevant to the counselling field are one of the following: descriptive, difference-assessing or relationship-assessing. As you can see, these fall broadly within the areas of quantitative research described above (descriptive, correlational and experimental).

Considering again the theme of depression, interesting descriptive questions you might explore could be:

- 'What is the frequency of treatment-resistant depression among women?'
- 'What percentage of people have a diagnosis of major chronic depressive disorder with comorbid physical health conditions?'

Difference-assessing questions could include:

- 'Are there gender differences in the prevalence of chronic forms of depression?'
- 'Is intervention x better than intervention y in treating treatment-resistant depression?'

Finally, to explore research questions that assess relationships, you could consider questions such as:

- 'Is the number of counselling sessions associated with treatment success?'
- 'Does having particular personality features predict better or worse treatment outcomes in intervention x?'

In practical terms, research questions are reformulated as hypotheses, which are proposed explanations based on existing theory or research findings. For example, the main hypothesis in the TADS was: 'Long-term psychoanalytic psychotherapy is more effective than treatment-as-usual in reducing depression severity' (Fonagy *et al.*, 2015). Note that this hypothesis makes a prediction about the direction of the difference or relationship to be tested.

3.2 The research design

The research design refers to the method used to investigate the hypothesis. There are several design possibilities, and it is important that the research questions and ethical considerations guide the choice of the most appropriate one. Table 14.1 describes the most frequent designs in mental health research.

Table 14.1 Types of research design

Research design	Description	Preferred study aim and example
Randomised controlled trial (RCT)	Experimental comparison study where participants are randomly allocated to two or more groups (i.e. intervention or control group).	Used to study efficacy of interventions, i.e. to test whether intervention x is better than intervention y under condition z.
Cohort study	Observational longitudinal study where specific groups of people (or data) are followed over a period of time (can be retrospective or prospective).	Used to study predictive risk factors or determine prognosis of an illness (e.g. following children of a parent with post-natal depression and comparing to a control group) or psychotherapy outcomes in the natural setting.
Case-control study	Observational study where individuals with a certain outcome or condition are compared ('matched') with an appropriate control group to identify the possible cause. Often retrospective.	Used to observe effects in existing groups; it is the only valid design to study rare occurrences. For example, studying the likelihood of developing treatment-resistant depression following developmental trauma. Does not require large sample sizes. Useful for preliminary research.
Cross-sectional study	Observational study where data is collected and analysed at a single time point.	Best for quantifying prevalence or prognosis. Also good for assessing validity and reliability of tests/questionnaires. For example, assessing prevalence of suicidality in chronic depression or developing a new measure of psychological well-being.
Case study	Study of a specific subject, e.g. a person, event or phenomenon. Allows a systematic in-depth investigation in a real-world setting.	Best vehicle for making sense of complex clinical situations. For example, exploring the treatment process of one (or several) participant(s) in a study who have not benefited from the therapy.

Chapter 13 introduced you to the claim that RCTs are the gold standard in producing research evidence. To identify and develop empirically supported psychotherapies, the evidence-based practice movement adopted the hierarchy of evidence used in medical science. This hierarchy classifies research designs by its epistemological strength or 'rigour', and thereby identifies RCTs as the most 'powerful' design in yielding the 'strongest' evidence. Sadly, this classification system led to a restrictive approach in which other designs are seen as less valuable, with the consequence that many important findings are being ignored by developers of treatment guidelines because they have not been produced using RCTs.

However, let's take a look at why RCTs are regarded as the gold standard. In terms of the common quality criteria, they attempt to address all of these in the most robust and rigorous way. The RCT is the only design able to establish causality by ruling out alternative explanations. Figure 14.1 shows the basic design of a randomised controlled study.

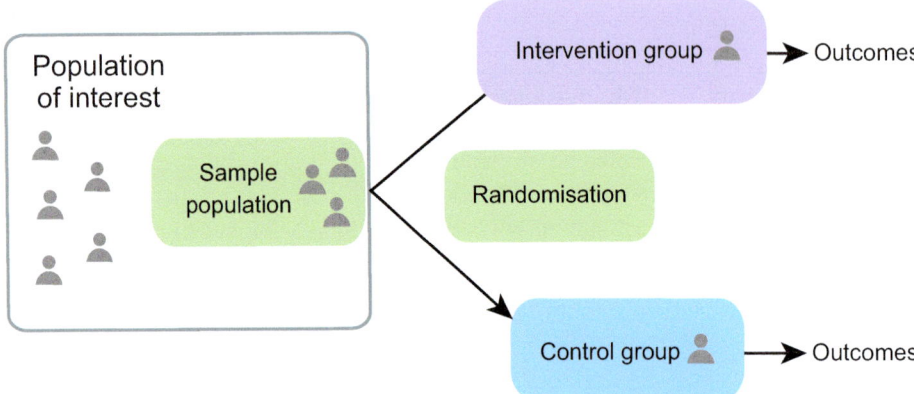

Figure 14.1 Basic design of a randomised controlled study

The TADS used this design. The population of interest was adults experiencing treatment-resistant depression. We included a sample population of 129 participants from GP practices in London. Participants were randomly allocated, by a process akin to the flip of a coin, to receive either 18 months of psychoanalytic psychotherapy or continued care from their usual GP (treatment-as-usual). The primary outcome measured was depression severity. If you compare this against Figure 14.1, you can see that the TADS was set up as an experiment, where the effect of one variable (receiving treatment or not) was observed and measured on another variable (level of depression severity). The technical terms often used to refer to these variables are **independent variable** and **dependent variable** respectively.

independent variable

The experimental variable that remains independent from, or is not influenced or changed by, other variables.

dependent variable

The experimental variable that is dependent on other factors and could therefore change as a result of the independent variable.

To maximise confidence that a study can identify a cause-and-effect relationship, other elements of the study also need to be controlled. In addition to randomly allocating participants and having a control or comparison group, well-designed RCTs need the following elements:

- Participants should be carefully selected according to well-defined inclusion and exclusion criteria.

- Participants should not differ too much from each other, especially in terms of characteristics and initial levels of the independent variable (e.g. depression severity) between the test conditions.

- Those who conduct the measurements should not know to which group the participants are allocated (this process is called 'blinding' or 'masking').

- Ideally, the test intervention should be standardised and manualised – that is, carefully described so that it can be consistently applied and replicated.

- In addition, both the participants and those providing the intervention (i.e. therapists) should not know which is the test intervention and which is the control group (a process known as 'double-blind').

As you can imagine, some of these criteria might be easier to implement than others in psychotherapy studies. The criteria were originally devised to test medical interventions, where testing against a placebo (designed to have no therapeutic value, e.g. a sugar pill) is possible, as is a double-blind trial. However, a counsellor cannot be unaware of the approach they are practising. Furthermore, while some approaches, like cognitive behavioural therapy, are better suited to meet the criteria of standardisation or manualisation, other counselling approaches cannot be prescribed in that way; some counsellors would even regard it as anomalous to the whole endeavour of psychotherapy.

Pause for thought 14.2

What might be the implications of the fact that some therapy modalities lend themselves to this type of quantitative research more than others?

Another important question when evaluating a research study is its relevance to the real world. Does the experimental setting create an artifact or 'ideal' circumstance that does not exist in the real world? This refers to external validity, or the extent to which the findings can be generalised to other settings and people. And, most importantly, does it have ecological validity? What use is a perfectly designed RCT when the findings cannot be generalised to real clinical settings?

Thus, in practice, outcome research in psychotherapy requires a trade-off between choosing elements that maximise internal validity and those that maximise external validity. One way to approach this is to adjust an RCT design to increase its external validity. These studies are referred to as pragmatic trials. The TADS is such a trial: it attempts to increase external validity by keeping the client group and the therapy as close as possible to how they are in real-world practice. Other studies utilise a cohort design or case-control design (described in Table 14.1) to observe counselling as it happens in ordinary clinical settings. These are referred to as effectiveness studies, in contrast to efficacy studies where the interventions are investigated under experimental conditions.

Another approach that is gaining in popularity is practice-based research. As McLeod (2022) points out, there are two types:

- large-scale data collection of therapy services within large healthcare systems
- smaller-scale data collection for specific groups of people or types of problems (e.g. adults with addictions or therapeutic communities for young people), or regional/local networks of practitioners.

Practice-based research studies don't have a formal control group, although different groups could be compared. The most well-known large-scale dataset in the UK is the NHS Talking Therapies (formerly IAPT) dataset, which includes session-by-session data collected from thousands of people seen within NHS psychotherapy services. By choosing an instrument to record a patient's progress and to audit one's practice, it is also a good way for individual practitioners, like yourself, to make research part of your professional life.

Pause for thought 14.3

Thinking about your practice or service, what opportunities exist for you to collect data or get involved in some research? What barriers might you encounter?

---

4 Understanding quantitative data, analysis and the effect of sample size

What is quantitative data?

This section focuses on the remaining decisions that a quantitative researcher will have to make before conducting a study. Any findings will be dependent on these choices, and critically evaluating these will give insight into their trustworthiness. Let's start by reviewing what's important when considering the sampling strategy.

4.1 Sampling and bias

To draw valid conclusions, researchers must carefully decide how they will select individuals that are representative of the entire group that they want to draw conclusions about. This entire group is referred to as the 'population', and the specific group of individuals that participate in the research is referred to as the 'sample'.

Overall, there are two types of sampling methods: probability and non-probability. Probability sampling involves randomly selecting from a large pool of people by following either minimum criteria or preselected inclusion and exclusion criteria. By design, each member of the population has an equal chance to be selected. Non-probability sampling involves selecting participants based on the researcher's knowledge or interest. While commonly used, it is important to bear in mind that non-probability sampling can lead to sampling bias (where some people are systematically more likely to be selected than others), which in turn can lead to systematic errors, biased findings, and weaker inferences and conclusions.

A second important consideration is the sample size. A quantitative study needs a 'large enough' sample for statistical tests to be able to detect a difference. This is also referred to as 'power', or the likelihood of a statistical test being able to detect a difference, if one exists (in other words, it is more likely to reject false positives). What constitutes a large enough sample, however, depends on many aspects, including the number of variables in the study, how many people are expected to drop out, and so on. Luckily, the minimum number of participants needed can easily be calculated, which researchers should do and report in their write-up. When reading studies and critically evaluating their findings, pay attention to how many participants dropped out, and check whether the researchers conducted separate analyses and compared the findings for completers and non-completers. This is important, because by excluding the data of those who dropped out, the overall findings might be biased and, for example, erroneously show a positive outcome. Those who stopped participating might have done so because they felt worse, for instance. By comparing findings from non-completers to those of completers, this important bias can be assessed and controlled.

4.2 What is quantitative data?

Quantitative data is collected or converted into numerical form. The most frequently used methods are questionnaires, since they are quick and efficient in obtaining large amounts of data. Questionnaires use a numerical rating scale and produce a total score, which can easily be compared within and between individuals. Ideally, questionnaires should be established as reliable and valid, and have been used in other studies so that findings can be compared. This is important in order to fulfil the quality criteria of objectivity, reliability and validity. However, they also have limitations in that they rely on recall and provide limited response options. Other forms of data used in psychotherapy research include physical indices, such as heart rate or eye movement. These are, for example, used in studies looking at stress responses. Information from audio- or video-recorded interviews, observations and therapy sessions can also be coded and thus provide an important source of quantitative data that can subsequently be explored and analysed statistically.

The choice of measure is one of the most crucial aspects of a research study. In outcome research, it is customary to predetermine one primary outcome measure that directly relates to the main hypothesis. Other measures can also be included to substantiate or deepen the research question.

Pause for thought 14.4

In your view, how should change be conceptualised in psychotherapy research? What would you use as the main variable to assess outcome?

What the focus of measurement should be has become a topic of great debate. Like her fellow participants in the TADS, Lydia, for example, experienced a great number of severe difficulties, and a sole focus on depression severity ignores these other important observations. There has been a move towards focusing on areas of change, such as functioning and quality of life, in addition to or instead of symptom change.

4.3 Data analysis

As highlighted above, to evaluate published research you don't have to become an expert in statistics; however, it is important to understand the basic principles and how they should be applied. Quantitative research makes use of two types of statistics: descriptive and inferential. Descriptive statistics are used to describe or summarise a data set. They consist of three basic measures:

- a measure of the central tendency of the data (the mean or the average)
- a measure of variability (or spread), describing the dispersion of the data (variance, standard deviation)
- a measure of frequency, describing the occurrence of data within the data set (count).

It is customary to use these to summarise both the participants and the entire data set that was collected in a study. These are usually found in the method section of a published paper, in the form of a table or graph.

Inferential statistics have a different function – they are used to test the study hypothesis. The term 'inferential' refers to the inferences or conclusions that these statistics can allow to be drawn from the study sample about the whole population. The tests ascertain whether an observed difference or an association between two or more variables occurred by chance. A result can be considered credible when the probability that it occurred by chance is less than one in twenty. This is when a finding is said to be *statistically significant*, which is denoted by the expression: $p < 0.05$.

There are many different statistical tests, and there are requirements that determine which ones are most appropriate. Suitability depends on many factors, including the nature of the data. As such, researchers have to complete a number of checks before they can conduct the main analysis.

In psychotherapy research, people often describe whether or not their study has found a **treatment effect**, by which they mean a significant difference. It is important to note here that there are common misinterpretations of *p*-values. When research yields a *p*-value greater than 0.05, is it often concluded that there is no difference or no effect; however, this might not be correct. The study might have had too few participants to reliably detect the difference (which is why a sufficiently large sample size is so important). Or, by chance, the study may have had a sample of participants that did not show a difference (which is why replication is also very important). Additionally, it is important to look beyond statistical significance to ascertain if findings are also clinically meaningful. For example, the results of a study might show a

treatment effect

Refers to the causal effect of an intervention on a chosen outcome variable.

statistically significant difference in depression severity between treatment group and control group, yet when you explore the mean depression severity scores, you might find that it is still very high after the treatment or follow-up phase has ended, indicating no substantial benefits. Therefore, researchers have started to report whether findings are also *clinically* significant through, for example, reporting effect sizes or remission rates, or by calculating whether change is clinically reliable. As such, when you are reading about research findings, pay attention to whether authors report any of these.

Are you curious to find out what the TADS found and whether the results supported the hypothesis? They did indeed! Expressed in statistical terms, we found a significant difference in depression severity between those who received the psychoanalytic treatment and those who did not, with medium effect sizes that emerged over the long-term follow-up. Expressed in clinically meaningful terms, we found that 44% of those who received the psychoanalytic treatment were no longer depressed, compared to 10% of those who were in the control group, at the end of the two-year follow-up (Fonagy *et al.*, 2015, p. 317). In terms of depression severity, Lydia moved from the 'severe depression' category to 'medium depression'. Do you think that is a good outcome for her?

The last section of this chapter focuses on how you could integrate quantitative evidence into your practice.

5 Utilising quantitative findings in clinical practice

As this chapter has highlighted, quantitative research provides a range of opportunities. For example, it can be used to establish the prevalence or predictive risk factors of conditions or problems; it can help us to make objective comparisons between groups of individuals; and it can be used to explore the relationships between variables. Using statistical tests allows us to identify the strengths of patterns or trends, either cross-sectionally or over time, and the experimental design can establish causal effects. The indirect and direct gains for practitioners who engage with quantitative research findings are equally manifold.

Pause for thought 14.5

Let's assume you start to work with a new client who presents with a particular problem or difficulty that you have not worked with before. Given what you have read in this chapter, how could quantitative findings be beneficial to you?

Staying with this scenario, the following examples demonstrate the kind of quantitative findings you might want to look out for.

You might be interested in looking at studies that investigate the prevalence of this condition/problem. To get a better overview, you might also want to consider studies that have investigated associations or predictive patterns between this and other problems/difficulties. It is thanks to these kinds of studies that we know, for example, that women are three times more likely to be affected by depression (Hyde and Mezulis, 2020) and that the prevalence of suicide and developmental adversity is very high in this population (Rost *et al.*, 2024). Exploring some of these risk factors or correlates is likely to influence the way you pay attention to your new client.

You might find it helpful to consult outcome studies, especially meta-analytic studies, which aggregate the findings from several smaller studies, to find out what treatment modality has an established evidence base for this condition.

You might also want to explore findings that report on the mechanism of change. These could include studies on specific therapeutic techniques, or studies that explored therapist or client characteristics which might help you to tailor your interventions with this new client. While the TADS found that individuals benefitted on average from the psychoanalytic treatment, there are many who did not. In my doctorate research, I wanted to empirically explore who these individuals were and whether underlying personality features might explain differential treatment outcomes. What I found was that those with less adaptive personality characteristics and lower functioning did not benefit, while those who functioned better and possessed more adaptive personality characteristics did benefit (Rost *et al.*, 2019). Thus, it is worth searching for studies that delve a little deeper into outcome findings to consider whether these can help you with your clinical decisions.

Overall, the kind of findings that might be most relevant depends on the context you work in, your approach and the clients you work with. In terms of the limitations of quantitative research, one important factor – besides the lack of specific subjective experience – is that context often gets lost. We know that people behave according to historical, social, cultural and identity-based contexts (Adams, 2012), yet these aspects are rarely considered when thinking about meeting the quality criteria of generalisation (external validity). Chapter 16 will expand on this issue a bit more. For now, simply note that it is important to look at the description of the study participants to ascertain whether they include the type of client(s) that you are working with. In the TADS, most of the participants matched the characteristics of Lydia: 66% were women, 81% described themselves as either 'White British' or 'White Other', their average age was 43 years old, and just under half (47%) had a university education (Rost *et al.*, 2024, p. 294). If your client presents with a very different demographic detail, the findings might therefore not be relevant.

Many clinicians equate the quantitative paradigm with RCTs and the traditional top-down approach, where research is conducted in laboratories or academic settings and clinicians are expected to use it unquestioningly. However, hopefully this chapter has shown that there are other designs, as well as a shift in how quantitative research is used in psychotherapy research. Keeping a critical stance when evaluating results is important. A lot of evidence from classical RCTs is not applicable to practice and, while there is a lot of merit in experimental settings, many researchers and clinicians have pointed to the need to focus more on practice-based evidence so that it can be drawn from routine clinical settings to inform clinical practice (e.g. Barkham, Hardy and Mellor-Clark, 2010; Fernández-Álvarez *et al.*, 2020).

Conclusion

This chapter started by asking how you feel about quantitative methodology. Has your initial feeling changed somewhat? The chapter has introduced you to both the key principles of quantitative research as well as the quality criteria by which to judge such studies, which will help you decide if their findings are trustworthy and relevant to your practice. The aim of this chapter was to provide you with a 'map' to help you navigate quantitative research literature more easily. However, it is important to keep in mind that the territory that counsellors inhabit – and thus the many questions they grapple with – often concern the complexity and nuance of human life. Thus, one map may not be sufficient. As Chapter 13 discussed, research paradigms differ in their view of what reality is and how it can be understood and measured. They provide insight from different angles and, when considered together, might allow us to gain a better understanding of human suffering and the ways in which our profession can contribute to alleviating it. In Chapter 15 you will explore another part of the 'territory' of counselling literature: qualitative research.

Further reading

- An excellent introduction to quantitative and qualitative research methods is provided in the following book:

  McLeod, J. (2022) *Doing research in counselling and psychotherapy.* 4th edn. London: SAGE.

- If you want to learn more about quantitative methods and statistics, the following book gives a deeper overview:

  Greenhalgh, T. (2019) *How to read a paper: the basics of evidence-based medicine and healthcare.* 6th edn. Hoboken, NJ: John Wiley & Sons.

References

Adams, G. (2012) 'Context in person, person in context: a cultural psychology approach to social-personality psychology', in K. Deaux and M. Snyder (eds) *The Oxford handbook of personality and social psychology*. Oxford: Oxford University Press, pp. 182–208.

Aliaga, M. and Gunderson, B. (1999) *Interactive statistics*. Upper Saddle River, NJ: Prentice Hall.

Barkham, M., Hardy, G.E. and Mellor-Clark, J. (2010) *Developing and delivering practice-based evidence: a guide for the psychological therapies*. Oxford: John Wiley & Sons.

Barkham, M., Lutz, W. and Castonguay, L.G. (eds) (2021) *Bergin and Garfield's handbook of psychotherapy and behavior change*. 7th edn. Hoboken, NJ: John Wiley & Sons.

Fernández-Álvarez, J., Prado-Abril, J., Sánchez-Reales, S., Molinari, G., Gómez Penedo, J.M. and Youn, S.J. (2020) 'The gap between research and practice: towards the integration of psychotherapy', *Papeles del Psicólogo/Psychologist Papers*, 41(2), pp. 81–90. Available at: https://doi.org/10.23923/pap.psicol2020.2932

Fonagy, P., Rost, F., Carlyle, J., McPherson, S., Thomas, R., Pasco Fearon, R.M., Goldberg, D. and Taylor, D. (2015) 'Pragmatic randomized controlled trial of long-term psychoanalytic psychotherapy for treatment-resistant depression: the Tavistock Adult Depression Study (TADS)', *World Psychiatry*, 14(3), pp. 312–321. Available at: https://doi.org/10.1002/wps.20267

Greenhalgh, T. (2019) *How to read a paper. The basics of evidence-based medicine and healthcare*. 6th edn. Hoboken, NJ: John Wiley & Sons.

Hyde, J.S. and Mezulis, A.H. (2020) 'Gender differences in depression: biological, affective, cognitive, and sociocultural factors', *Harvard Review of Psychiatry*, 28(1), pp. 4–13. Available at: https://doi.org/10.1097/hrp.0000000000000230

Institute for Health Metrics and Evaluation (2021) 'Global Health Data Exchange: Global Burden of Disease (GBD) results tool'. Available at: http://ghdx.healthdata.org/gbd-results-tool (Accessed: 23 April 2024).

McLeod, J. (2011) *Qualitative research: in counselling and psychotherapy*. 2nd edn. London: SAGE.

McLeod, J. (2022) *Doing research in counselling and psychotherapy*. 4th edn. London: SAGE.

Rost, F., Booker, T., Gonsard, A., de Felice, G., Asseburg, L., Malda-Castillo, J., Koutoufa, I., Ridsdale, H., Johnson, R., Taylor, D. and Fonagy, P. (2024) 'The complexity of treatment-resistant depression: a data-driven approach', *Journal of Affective Disorders*, 358, pp. 292–301. Available at: https://doi.org/10.1016/j.jad.2024.04.093

Rost, F., Luyten, P., Fearon, P. and Fonagy, P. (2019) 'Personality and outcome in individuals with treatment-resistant depression—exploring differential treatment effects in the Tavistock Adult Depression Study (TADS)', *Journal of Consulting and Clinical Psychology*, 87(5), pp. 433–445. Available at: https://doi.org/10.1037/ccp0000391

SCoPEd Framework (2022), collaboratively developed by Association of Christian Counsellors (ACC), British Association for Counselling and Psychotherapy (BACP), British Psychoanalytic Council (BPC), Human Givens Institute (HGI), National Counselling and Psychotherapy Society (NCPS) and United Kingdom Council for Psychotherapy (UKCP). Available at: https://www.bacp.co.uk/about-us/advancing-the-profession/scoped/scoped-framework (Accessed: 12 June 2024).

Taylor, D., Carlyle, J., McPherson, S., Rost, F., Thomas, R. and Fonagy, P. (2012) 'Tavistock Adult Depression Study (TADS): a randomised controlled trial of psychoanalytic psychotherapy for treatment-resistant/treatment-refractory forms of depression', *BMC Psychiatry*, 12, article number 60. Available at: https://doi.org/10.1186/1471-244X-12-60

Timulak, L. (2015) 'Introduction to research methodology', in A. Vossler and N. Moller (eds) *The counselling and psychotherapy research handbook*. London: SAGE, pp. 74–87.

Contents

Introduction

Let's Fly a Kite by Louise Newbigging. Qualitative methods allow researchers to capture the complexity of human experience

As Chapters 13 and 14 have shown, research can provide a wide range of evidence to inform counsellors' work with clients. This chapter focuses on qualitative research. It covers the aims, methods and outcomes of qualitative enquiry, showing how the paradigm can provide insights into the experiences, narratives and meanings relevant to your practice. Hopefully this will give you the confidence and motivation to read qualitative studies yourself, if you do not already do so.

The chapter starts by exploring some of the reasons for engaging with qualitative research, before deconstructing key ideas within the qualitative paradigm and outlining some data collection methods. It then introduces three qualitative analytic lenses: experiences, stories and language. The topic of depression is used to illustrate the type of insights that each lens brings. Finally, the chapter lays out how to evaluate qualitative research.

Research may feel alienating or excluding to some people. However, qualitative research can be diverse and creative, pushing the boundaries of what has traditionally been considered valid research evidence. While this chapter will focus on the most common approaches, qualitative research offers an exciting and accessible way to learn more about your client work. Counselling psychologist Carla Willig (2022, p. 3) refers to qualitative research methods as an 'adventure', while psychotherapist Linda Finlay (Finlay and Evans, 2009, p. 1) describes them as a 'voyage of discovery'. It is in this spirit that the chapter outlines qualitative research and provides a grounding so that you can bring these insights into your practice.

This chapter contributes towards achieving the **SCoPEd competency 4.16.B**:

> Ability to draw upon and evaluate published research on counselling and psychotherapy, and integrate relevant research findings to enhance practice.
>
> *(SCoPEd Framework, 2022, p. 29)*

This chapter aims to:

- introduce key principles of qualitative research
- cover theoretical frameworks used within the qualitative paradigm
- outline common data collection and data analysis methods
- suggest criteria for the evaluation of qualitative research.

I The importance of qualitative research evidence

Qualitative research findings can give counsellors insights into a diverse range of relevant topics. For example, there is a substantial body of qualitative evidence about how clients experience counselling (Levitt, Pomerville and Surace, 2016). Qualitative research also explores the counselling process, and researchers have conducted reviews and meta-analyses of this evidence on, for example: building a therapeutic alliance (Lavik *et al.*, 2018); how therapeutic insights occur (Timulak and McElvaney, 2013); helpful and hindering events (Ladmanová, Řiháček and Timulak, 2022); and clients' experiences of routine outcome monitoring (Solstad, Castonguay and Moltu, 2019). Qualitative research can also tell counsellors about presenting issues including mental and physical health conditions; adverse experiences; family dynamics; social contexts; other interventions, services or settings; and many other topics relating to counselling.

Qualitative research provides a good entry point into utilising evidence within your practice. It is:

- *Important*. Qualitative research often engages with minoritised people, including clients and patients whose perspectives have been historically silenced. For this reason, qualitative research offers an important counterpoint to quantitative approaches such as randomised controlled trials.

- *Evocative*. Qualitative research produces rich and nuanced evidence, which resonates with the reader and deepens their understanding. It is usually detailed and specific, focusing on small samples (idiographic research), and providing in-depth and contextualised accounts.

- *Accessible*. Qualitative research findings are generally seen as more accessible to non-experts. While some papers lean heavily on theory that can feel dense, many studies in social and health contexts are written for multidisciplinary audiences.

Becoming familiar with the most common qualitative approaches will provide a scaffolding for making sense of research. This chapter aims to help you do just that.

2 The breadth and key principles of qualitative research

While there are important commonalities, qualitative research encompasses many different approaches. This section outlines some of the different schools of thought that underpin qualitative research and how these theoretical frameworks shape the research process.

As with quantitative research, qualitative research always begins with a research question. This is the question researchers hope to answer by undertaking the research, which is not the same as the questions that researchers may ask participants directly (e.g. in interviews). Qualitative questions tend to ask 'what?' or 'how?' rather than 'why?' Qualitative research does not typically deal in making predictions, examining cause and effect, testing hypotheses or comparing groups like quantitative research does. Instead, researchers are interested in understanding experiences, perceptions, narratives, meanings, attitudes, processes or how people speak about something.

Qualitative counselling research questions could include:

- What are clients' experiences of microaggressions in the therapy room?
- What meanings do counsellors ascribe to therapeutic rupture early in their careers?
- How does erotic transference get discussed within supervision?
- What stories do experienced counsellors tell about how counselling works?
- How do clients make the decision to end counselling?
- What discursive resources (terminology, concepts or phrases) do counsellors utilise on their websites to disclose or hide their sexual and gender identities?

In Chapter 13 you were introduced to the idea that methodological choices are underpinned by how a researcher positions themselves in terms of ontology and epistemology. As outlined in Chapter 13, Table 13.1, a realist ontology aligns with the view that there is a singular, objective truth to pursue; Chapter 14 described how this view tends to underpin quantitative research. The quantitative paradigm has a positivist epistemology, arguing that it is possible to discover truth through scientific, objective and deductive ('top-down') methods. Qualitative researchers typically sit more towards the other end of the spectrum, often believing that multiple truths exist at the same time (relativism), which aligns with epistemologies that think of knowledge as something subjective, contextual and contingent, co-created by those doing research rather than being discovered by them. Qualitative research does not start with a hypothesis, but instead creates knowledge in an **inductive** manner, from exploratory engagement with the data.

inductive

Characterised by drawing conclusions on the basis of what has been observed (i.e. 'bottom-up' reasoning, rather than 'top-down', theory-led reasoning).

2 The breadth and key principles of qualitative research

Within the qualitative paradigm there are a wide range of theoretical perspectives. Table 15.1 outlines some common examples.

Table 15.1 Some common theoretical and methodological approaches within qualitative research

Theoretical framework	Description	Associated methodologies	Type of knowledge produced
Critical realism	Acknowledges context and the co-constructed nature of research, but also suggests there is a 'real', objective world that can be known through research.	Thematic analysis /reflexive thematic analysis (Braun and Clark, 2006; 2019) Note: thematic analysis can be used with any theoretical framework	Sets of themes that describe data by organising it into groups (e.g. around shared meanings).
Constructivism	Suggests that individuals construct their worlds through processes of interpretation and narration.	Constructivist grounded theory (Charmaz, 2014) Narrative enquiry (e.g. Murray, 2003)	A model (or theory) that captures the process of how something comes about. Narratives are identified that reveal insights into the experience, the 'storyteller' and the context.
Social constructionism	Suggests that meaning and knowledge are constructed within society. Associated with the 'turn to language', wherein researchers showed how speech and text reveal the operation of power and knowledge production.	Discourse analysis, e.g. Foucauldian discourse analysis (see Arribas-Ayllon and Walkerdine, 2008) Discursive psychology (Edwards and Potter, 1992) Conversation analysis (see Hepburn and Potter, 2021)	Analytic claims that draw connections between how something is said or written and broader societal power structures, or between the speaker and their audience.

Theoretical framework	Description	Associated methodologies	Type of knowledge produced
Psychoanalysis	Perceives people as 'defended subjects' who may be (unconsciously) motivated to give a particular account of themselves and/or are not fully self-aware, and therefore cannot be relied on to tell the 'truth' about their experiences.	Psychoanalytically informed methodologies (e.g. Hollway and Jefferson, 2013)	Analytic claims that draw inferences about psychic dynamics and a person's internal world from what they say about their lives.
Phenomenology	Considers individual perception to be the only knowledge a person has of the world. Research focuses on understanding lived experience.	Descriptive approaches describe the structure of experience, e.g. descriptive phenomenological method in psychology (Giorgi, 2009) Hermeneutic approaches focus on how experiences are interpreted, e.g. interpretative phenomenological analysis (Smith, Flowers and Larkin, 2021)	Sets of themes or descriptions of the 'structure' of experience, and the meanings people ascribe to them.

Note that while this table makes everything look very coherent, the reality is more messy. You may notice that this chapter uses terms like 'most', 'often' and 'typically'; this is because there are no absolutes in qualitative research. It is perfectly possible for someone to use qualitative methods within a realist and positivist framing, in what Kidder and Fine (1987) call 'small q' qualitative research; indeed, you will find some clinical research that takes this perspective. However, this chapter focuses on 'big Q' qualitative research (also described by Kidder and Fine, 1987) – these approaches share a set of concerns around **subjectivity**, context, nuance, reflexivity and exploration.

So far, this chapter has introduced the idea that qualitative research can have different underpinning theories and address different questions. The following section introduces some common data types, then Section 4 looks in more depth at three approaches to analysis.

subjectivity

Refers to the first-person perspective. The subjective researcher acknowledges their personhood and how that impacts the research, as opposed to the objective, detached stance, held within quantitative research.

3 What is qualitative data?

Once a researcher has decided on a research question and has a clear idea of their theoretical approach, they must then consider what data to collect. There are many possible approaches. The most common are interviews, which are conversations between researchers and participants, usually conducted one-to-one, although dyads, families and groups can also be interviewed. There are a number of different types, including the following:

- *Semi-structured interviews* are probably the most common. These have a written interview guide ('schedule') with questions that can be taken in any order. The researcher may deviate from the schedule.

- *Structured interviews* involve a series of predetermined, fixed questions, with no deviation permitted. Many clinical interviews take this form.

- *Unstructured interviews* have no predetermined questions, although a researcher may cover pre-specified topics. The most common types are biographical or narrative interviews, in which the participant tells their life story or the story of a particular time/event.

- *Free-association narrative interviews* are psychoanalytically informed and enable participants to make their own associations with the topic.

- *Interpersonal process recall interviews* are process-focused interviews that use video playback to aid participants' memories (see Macaskie, Lees and Freshwater, 2015). Often used in counselling research, a session is video recorded then played back during the interview to help participants (i.e. clients and counsellors) explore what they were experiencing at specific moments.

All types of interviews are usually audio recorded (with consent) and then transcribed into a written document. Transcription is typically done verbatim, although more detailed forms can include notation to capture intonation, pauses, and so on. A less detailed transcript will only capture meaning, and will miss out things like repeated words, or 'ums' and 'ahs'.

However, many other data collection approaches also exist beyond interviews (see Table 15.2). Research is built on data, and as most qualitative methods consider the researcher to play an active part in how the findings are established, the choices made here are fundamental.

Table 15.2 Some common qualitative data collection methods

Method	Description	Data produced
Focus group	Participants previously unknown to each other are brought together to discuss a topic. Researchers typically generate a topic schedule to guide the discussion. They may be interested in what the group dynamics reveal about the topic. Some will be interested in what group members say; others will be interested in how they say it, which views get silenced or supported, or how easy it is for a minority view to be voiced. The dynamics can indicate how meanings and dominant views are formed.	Audio data, which is typically transcribed
Open-ended questionnaire	A fixed set of open-ended questions around a particular topic, provided to participants in written form, in person, by post or online. New questionnaires may be created or pre-existing questionnaires may be used, such as the Helpful Aspects of Therapy (Llewelyn, 1988).	Written responses
Naturally occurring talk	Researchers record talk that is happening regardless of the research, including speech or conversation that happens formally (e.g. counselling sessions, doctor–patient consultations) or informally (e.g. held in social spaces).	Audio data, which is usually transcribed to a very high degree of accuracy
Naturally occurring written materials	Researchers find written data about the topic in the form of pre-existing media. Blogs, social media entries, posts within online communities and offline materials such as newspapers and magazines are all potential sources of data. Researchers create parameters for how to select data (e.g. date ranges, specific forums or specific authors).	Written data that is naturally occurring and collated by the researcher
Observation	Researchers observe people or events, usually over an extended period of time, either with or without participating themselves. Participant-observers are typically embedded within the setting of interest (e.g. volunteering at a crisis house). Psychodynamically oriented infant observations are an example where the researcher does not participate in the setting, which is usually a family home.	Observations and reflexive field notes (on what the researcher saw, did, heard and/or felt during data collection)

Pause for thought 15.1

What do you consider to be 'appropriate' ways to collect data for research? How does this relate to your views on what constitutes science or what counts as evidence? Think about what you learnt in Chapters 13 and 14 about different types of research evidence and quantitative approaches.

There are also ethical complexities with every method. For example, interviews need to ensure that the participants are not unduly distressed or offended. With pre-existing online materials, there are questions surrounding ownership and consent. In participant observation – or if using naturally occurring talk, like therapy sessions – there are issues of transparency. As such, there are specific ethical standards and processes for research, which are different to counselling ethics. However, these do overlap; for example, through the requirement to treat everyone with respect and care.

The next section will illustrate how three different qualitative methodologies work in practice by exploring some examples on the topic of depression.

4 Three analytic lenses: experience, stories and language

Creating theoretical coherence between research questions, data collection approaches and the analytic method is important. As illustrated in Table 15.1, there are a wide range of methodologies to choose from, each of which point towards specific analytic methods. These result in different types of findings, which we can think of as *lenses* through which to view the topic. In this section, which uses the topic of depression as an example, you will consider three analytic lenses: experience (**hermeneutic** phenomenological research), stories (narrative enquiry) and language (discursive psychology).

hermeneutics

The theory of interpretation: how language and texts are interpreted and the meanings that can be ascribed to them.

4.1 Experience

Experiential research methodologies, like hermeneutic phenomenology, are interested in understanding how people experience and make sense of their lives. Phenomenological and existential concerns such as embodiment, relationality, agency and meaning are all central to this approach. The aim is to capture the texture of a particular experience to create a resonant account for the reader.

One example of an experiential methodology is interpretative phenomenological analysis (IPA) (Smith, Flowers and Larkin, 2021), which typically uses a small, **homogenous sample** of data – often collected via semi-structured interviews – and analyses it in significant detail, before organising the findings thematically. Themes are significant strands of the data that the researcher has organised into groups; when written up, themes include analytic commentary and key quotations. Analysis pays attention to describing the person's experience (phenomenology) and exploring how the participant and researcher interpret that experience (hermeneutics).

homogenous sample

A set of data or group of participants that share similarities (e.g. in age and gender). This contrasts with a heterogeneous sample, where there are notable differences.

Let's take research done by Smith and Rhodes (2015) as an example. They focused on first episodes of depression, and – like many IPA research studies – explored how participants' metaphors revealed lived experience. The researchers interviewed seven people; an extract from 'Sally' (a pseudonym) is presented below. Sally's depression is precipitated by her son being incarcerated for nine years, which she experiences as a huge loss. In the extract, the authors quote Sally (in italics), then analyse the relevant metaphors and meanings. This extract comes from a theme entitled 'The corporeal domain: being empty' and shows how Sally's separation from her son manifests as an embodied sensation of loss (emptiness).

> *It's emptiness, it's nothing don't matter, it's being locked away, you just don't care about yourself. ... It's like part of you gone, your heart, I don't know. Perhaps half my heart has gone away.*
>
> The metaphors are powerful here. First, being depressed is like being in prison – dishevelled and devoid of freedom. Ironically, it may be that here Sally finds an empathic, imaged connection with the person she has lost, her psychological experience of depression mirroring her son's physical endurance of imprisonment.
>
> The account then becomes even more embodied and the imagery is dense with meaning. The loss of her beloved son leaves her feeling she has lost part of herself. This is realized particularly strongly by describing the loss of her heart. Literally losing her heart would mean losing a vital physical organ, so this depression is like not being alive. At a symbolic level, it points to her having lost an affective base, a joie de vivre because she no longer has the heart for life. But the metaphor also directly speaks to the relational component in her depression; reminding us of a previous heart being given away representing her love for her son. Finally, the anguish of what has happened is captured in the final sentence. It is as though she is left, just alive, but missing her other half, the half that gives her life its meaning, its pulse.
>
> *(Smith and Rhodes, 2015, p. 202, italics added)*

As a counsellor, you may be interested in exploring how an experiential lens can be applied to the topic of depression, because it enables an exploration of multiple dimensions of the experience. The extracts from this IPA study described embodied experience, but experiential research can also illuminate a wide spectrum of experience. This may support you in thinking about your clients' depression in a more nuanced and holistic way. Experiential research also helps to humanise experiences and can provide resonant accounts that bring a topic to life. This can help you attune to potentially salient aspects of a clients' life and experience of the world that you may otherwise overlook.

4.2 Stories

The second analytic lens is narrative enquiry. There is a pervasive human tendency to generate stories about our lives, organising our experiences into narratives with a beginning, middle and end. This structure helps give meaning and stability to our experiences. Narrative theory indicates that there are even shared story templates that we utilise to tell these stories. Significant life events, such as illness or trauma, can disrupt attempts to tell coherent stories about our lives. Looking at illness and adversity through the lens of narrative helps us understand the impacts of these experiences on our identities, the sense of flow and progression in our lives, and how much agency and control we feel we have.

A good example here is research by Kroch *et al.* (2022). In this study, the authors used a narrative interview to ask nine people about their chronic, treatment-resistant depression. They invited participants to tell the story of when their depression first began and followed this up with questions prompted by what they heard. Their analysis followed an approach by Murray (2000) which thinks of stories as co-constructed, with personal, interpersonal and societal meanings. Kroch *et al.* (2022, p. 273) identified a 'narrative of order' and a 'narrative of disorder'. The following lists show how the researchers organised their analysis; these lists include extracts from longer quotes as a means of illustration.

A narrative of order

- Depression has clear causative factors: 'My mother died and we'd just had our first baby' (Darryl).
- Depression is a discernible internal process: 'I'm just much more attuned to stress' (Dean).
- Depression is measurable: 'You're constantly judging ... what level you're at' (Sarah).

(Adapted from Kroch et al., 2022, pp. 278–279)

A narrative of disorder

- Depression is random and unpredictable: 'I don't know why I get depressed' (Chris).
- Depression is not observable or measurable: 'You just think back and think "the past year is just a total stranger"' (Dean).
- Depression is unrelenting: 'It's like it's gonna reoccur and reoccur' (Paul).

(Adapted from Kroch et al., 2022, pp. 280–283)

The authors contextualise each of these narratives with quotes and their own analytic commentary. They then argue that these narratives exist in tension with each other. Here is an extract from that analysis:

> Across the participants' accounts, a tension emerged between narrating depression as understandable and ordered and narrating depression as chaotic and confusing. Rather than drawing on one of these narratives in isolation, each of the participants drew on both. ... The narrative of order made experiences of depression more knowable and predictable. It also allowed participants to remain aligned with medical paradigms or publicly available narratives of depression and position themselves as good patients doing all they could to recover. This is the narrative made available in clinical contexts and there is an expectation by clinicians and patients alike that this will be the narrative adopted. To resist this narrative would be to let go of the alliance with psychiatry and psychology and disrupt the expectations regarding how people conduct themselves within clinical encounters. However, for the participants with [treatment resistant depression],

> this narrative did not completely frame their experiences – they also drew on a narrative of disorder. This narrative allowed them to account for the fact that they continued to experience depressive symptoms long term.
>
> *(Kroch et al., 2022, p. 283)*

Counsellors may be interested in research that takes a narrative lens to depression, as it supports us to recognise the stories that our clients tell about their lives, to become aware of counter-narratives or tensions, and to see the possibilities for narrative development, disruption or repair. Identifying narratives may help us see how our clients are making sense of confusing or contradictory experiences, and how they may be using narrative order to gain a sense of control or predictability. Becoming sensitised to narrative as an aspect of human sense making can be useful for helping clients understand how they have made meaning from significant events and circumstances. Of course, this is a core feature of narrative therapy, but narrative research may also be useful for therapists of all modalities.

4.3 Language

Lead typesetting representing the complexity of language

So far, the chapter has introduced approaches that focus on experiences and narratives. This last approach focuses on language: how it is ordered and arranged, and the impact that has on the audience. As with the other forms of qualitative enquiry, there are also many ways to research language. Some methods, like **discourse** analysis, deal with language at a macro level by exploring how society talks about a particular subject (e.g. researching the

discourse

Written or spoken discussion of ideas that shape actions in the real world (e.g. political discourse, medical discourse).

language of 'recovery' within mental health services). Discourse analysis is often concerned with power and how certain ideas, and the language used to describe them, become dominant within societies. This dominance leads to the marginalisation or exclusion of other ways of thinking, speaking and being. Dominant discourses have tangible effects on how people live their lives, and how they make sense of themselves and their experiences, as you will see in the example that follows. Conversation analysis is another method that focuses on language, this time at the micro level, typically using small snippets of real-life interactions; for example, a GP talking to a client about depression. Here, researchers are interested in how the linguistic interaction constructs a particular outcome. They may pay attention to who speaks first, what gets ignored or responded to, and how turns are taken. Discursive psychology is a middle-ground approach that draws on both macro and micro levels. It explores how language constructs action, 'positions' us within certain identities and interpersonal relationships, and reveals social and political context.

An example that demonstrates the discursive approach comes from LaFrance (2007). The researcher interviewed eight women for the study; the interviews were semi-structured but wide-ranging, lasting several hours. The aim of the analysis was to examine how depression was 'constructed' (through language) as a medical condition. The following extract is taken from the first of the discursive resources that the participants drew on. LaFrance (2007, p. 130) calls this section of her analysis '"It's got a name": depression as diagnosis'.

> The provision of a diagnosis is perhaps the most central way in which experiences are medicalized. An analysis of participants' accounts of being diagnosed revealed remarkable consistency in the structure and effect of their talk. Participants who raised the issue of diagnosis repeatedly constructed it as an experience that brought relief and validation. As illustrated in the following two excerpts, being given a diagnosis is situated as validating participants' assertions that there was a problem.
>
> P: It was a validation that I had never had before and I had a **name** [original emphasis]. It was like, you know, it's a bad attitude, it's not. I'm not ... you know maladjusted, I'm not ill socially or whatever. It's just I'm depressed. And that's cool. Like it was really neat to have a name for that. (Kate)
>
> [...]
>
> Participants' accounts of diagnosis have the effect of validating the reality of their depressive experiences. By giving 'a name' to their distress, in addition to using the pronoun 'it', depression is objectified and constructed as an independent entity. That is, by invoking a medical diagnosis to account for their experiences, their pain becomes 'real-ized'. Further, being constructed as having a reality of its own, depression is isolated from the character of the sufferer. In these accounts, personal flaw and biological flaw are presented as

competing hypotheses, and with the verification of the reality of one (biological flaw verified through medical diagnosis), the other (personal flaw) must be false. Thus, a medicalized understanding is presented as normalizing depressive experiences. According to Dianne, a diagnosis assured her that it was not all in her mind; indeed, in a perverse way, a diagnosis assured her that she 'wasn't going crazy'. Therefore, as illustrated in these excerpts, diagnosis is drawn on with the dual effect of defending speakers' experiences and identities.

(LaFrance, 2007, p. 130, italics added)

Counsellors may be interested in research that takes a discursive lens to depression in order to think about the broader political and social contexts of their clients' experiences, and how language use has real-world consequences. Becoming more aware of the discourses available to our clients can sensitise us to how these may be limiting or constraining them. Reading discursive research can also help us recognise how our clients may lean on particular discourses, for example a medical discourse, for reassurance, legitimacy or even comfort.

Pause for thought 15.2

Having looked at three different analytic lenses – experiences, stories and language – reflect on how each approach relates to your own understanding of depression. Did any of the examples make you think differently? What did you think were the relative contributions of each approach? Can you imagine approaching your work with a client experiencing depression any differently after reading about the research in these examples?

Each of these analytic approaches offers something different in understanding the topic of depression. Each is based on different theoretical assumptions, has different analytic procedures, and has findings emphasising different things. There is utility in reading a wide range of qualitative studies with differing approaches as this enriches our understanding.

5 How to make sense of qualitative research

Qualitative and quantitative research paradigms operate on the basis of different assumptions about the nature of reality and knowledge. In addition, they have different strategies for every aspect of the research process. It would be unfair to judge one approach on the standards and expectations set for the other (see Finlay and Evans, 2009). You were introduced to the criteria for evaluating quantitative research in Chapter 14: this included things like internal validity, generalisability (external validity) and replicability (reliability). Similarly, this section will introduce you to the criteria used for qualitative research. These will help you decide whether you can trust a piece of research enough to use it as evidence to inform your practice. The criteria below are generic enough that they can help you judge most types of qualitative research, and they are inspired by Finlay's (2006) review. That said, there are ongoing debates about what makes specific types of qualitative research 'good'.

Qualitative research should:

- *Be trustworthy*. You should feel that the claims are credible, that there is a transparent and rigorous methodological approach with theoretical coherence, that there is an acknowledgement of the role of the researcher (reflexivity), and that the research contributes something valuable to the existing literature.

- *Be resonant*. You should be moved by the research: the writing should be vivid, rich and nuanced, and there should be a sense of the researcher as an authentic, feeling person responding to their subject matter.

- *Have ethical integrity*. You should understand how the researcher has respected and cared for those involved in the research, and how they have ensured the integrity of their project at all stages, including how the findings may be used by others.

In addition to asking yourself whether a study meets these criteria, the critical thinking skills you have developed as a counsellor are incredibly helpful in evaluating qualitative research. Your attunement to dilemmas and tensions will be particularly helpful for judging ethical integrity. While there are core expectations for most research studies (e.g. informed consent, anonymity for participants, respect and protection from harm), there are also more nuanced ethical issues at play. Increasingly, qualitative research – especially in the field of mental health – recognises the importance of addressing inequalities and injustice.

With its emphasis on subjectivity, qualitative researchers tend to think carefully about the people who contribute to the research and what the research might mean for them. Originating with feminist approaches, there has long been a concern that research should 'give voice' to people whose experiences have been overlooked or silenced; for example, because of their marginalised identities or relative lack of power within society (on grounds of gender, race, disability, etc.). This requires researchers to seek out alternative perspectives, for example by interviewing service users, rather than relying on the views of clinicians. The idea of 'giving voice' is not unproblematic though, not least because power dynamics are intersectional and because there are particular ethical complexities around sharing first-person mental health stories, especially from minoritised communities (e.g. Carr, 2016). For example, a well-meaning, socially privileged researcher who attempts to give voice to a marginalised or oppressed group may unintentionally reinforce hierarchies of power by assuming the voicelessness of the 'other' and positioning themselves as the one who can provide those 'others' with a platform to speak (e.g. Macmillan, 1995).

There are more opportunities for **epistemic justice** if those people being researched are also the researchers. Indeed, there is a long history of 'insider researchers': academics researching topics closely related to their own experiences. For example, in the 1980s feminist researchers developed their own method – memory groups – to research their experiences of sexual violence and abuse. Autoethnography is another approach where researchers analyse their own experiences. Increasingly, however, you will find research that is co-produced between academics and non-academic stakeholders. For example, experience-based co-design (Bate and Robert, 2023) is a form of participatory action research. It aims to change healthcare settings, such as inpatient psychosis services (Larkin, Boden and Newton, 2015) or adult psychotherapy settings (Cooper, Gilmore and Hogg, 2016), through intensive, research-focused collaboration between stakeholders.

epistemic justice
Fair and equitable access to knowledge sources and means of knowledge production.

The lack of objectivity present when you are personally connected to a topic is not necessarily seen as problematic in qualitative research. Subjectivity is valued, provided that all of the choices and interpretations in the research are interrogated through a process of reflexivity, and then made transparent within the writing-up process. A reflexive researcher, like a reflexive counsellor, considers all aspects of their involvement with the project, including power dynamics and social positioning, their own thoughts and feelings, personal history and motivation with the topic, and so on. Reflexivity is therefore a key strength of qualitative research when used as a resource to develop the researcher's analysis.

Conclusion

This chapter has provided you with a brief overview of the qualitative methods that counsellors may encounter, but it has also offered only a tiny glimpse into a vast and emergent field. The aim was to give you the basic building blocks you need to confidently seek out qualitative research papers which might support your counselling practice. These could be as varied as descriptions of the lived experiences of a particular type of distress, narrative accounts of how counselling helps clients or a discursive study of how counsellors talk to clients about a particular intervention. Each of these are examples of how practice issues can be illuminated through engaging with qualitative research.

Hopefully you have seen that research evidence goes beyond the dominant quantitative paradigm. Qualitative approaches allow us to understand more about how people experience, think about, talk about and shape aspects of their lives. It provides a useful way to demystify the counselling process, for example by evidencing how change happens or how counsellors support clients. Qualitative researchers value subjectivity, context, reflexivity and theoretical engagement. Holding these concerns in mind should provide you with the scaffolding necessary to appreciate the resonance and insight that qualitative research can bring to a topic and your practice.

Further reading

- The following chapter provides further information on qualitative research methods in counselling:

  McLeod, J., Stiles, W.B. and Levitt, H. (2021) 'Qualitative research: contributions to psychotherapy practice, theory, and policy', in M. Barkham, W. Lutz and L.G. Castonguay (eds) *Bergin & Garfield's handbook of psychotherapy and behavior change*. Hoboken, NJ: John Wiley & Sons, pp. 351–384.

- The following sources offer reviews of qualitative counselling research:

  Hissa, J. and Timulak, L. (2020) 'Theoretically informed qualitative psychotherapy research: a primer', *Counselling and Psychotherapy Research*, 20(3), pp. 429–434. Available at: https://doi.org/10.1002/capr.12301

  Ponterotto, J.G., Park-Taylor, J. and Chen, E.C. (2017) 'Qualitative research in counselling and psychotherapy: history, methods, ethics, and impact', *The SAGE handbook of qualitative research in psychology*. London: SAGE, pp. 496–519.

References

Arribas-Ayllon, M. and Walkerdine, V. (2008) 'Foucauldian discourse analysis', in C. Willig and W. Stainton-Rodgers (eds) *The SAGE handbook of qualitative research in psychology*. London: SAGE, pp. 91–108.

Bate, P. and Robert, G. (2023) *Bringing user experience to healthcare improvement: the concepts, methods and practices of experience-based design*. London: CRC Press.

Braun, V. and Clarke, V. (2006) 'Using thematic analysis in psychology', *Qualitative Research in Psychology*, 3(2), pp. 77–101.Available at: https://doi.org/10.1191/1478088706qp063oa

Braun, V. and Clarke, V. (2019) 'Reflecting on reflexive thematic analysis', *Qualitative Research in Sport, Exercise and Health*, 11(4), pp. 589–597. Available at: https://doi.org/10.1080/2159676X.2019.1628806

Carr, S. (2016) 'Narrative research and service user/survivor stories: a new frontier for research ethics?', *Philosophy, Psychiatry & Psychology*, 23(3/4), pp. 233–236. Available at: https://doi.org/10.1353/ppp.2016.0023

Charmaz, K. (2014) *Constructing grounded theory: a practical guide through qualitative analysis*. 2nd edn. London: SAGE.

Cooper, K., Gillmore, C. and Hogg, L. (2016) 'Experience-based co-design in an adult psychological therapies service', *Journal of Mental Health*, 25(1), pp. 36–40. Available at: https://doi.org/10.3109/09638237.2015.1101423

Edwards, D. and Potter, J. (1992) *Discursive psychology*. London: SAGE.

Finlay, L. (2006) '"Rigour", "ethical integrity" or "artistry"? Reflexively reviewing criteria for evaluating qualitative research', *British Journal of Occupational Therapy*, 69(7), pp. 319–326. Available at: https://doi.org/10.1177/030802260606900704

Finlay, L. and Evans, K. (eds) (2009) *Relational-centred research for psychotherapists: exploring meanings and experience*. Chichester: John Wiley & Sons.

Giorgi, A. (2009) *The descriptive phenomenological method in psychology: a modified Husserlian approach*. Pittsburgh, PA: Duquesne University Press.

Hepburn, A. and Potter, J. (2021) *Essentials of conversation analysis*. Washington, DC: American Psychological Association.

Hollway, W. and Jefferson, T. (2013) *Doing qualitative research differently: a psychosocial approach*. 2nd edn. London: SAGE

Kidder, L.H. and Fine, M. (1987) 'Qualitative and quantitative methods: when stories converge', *New Directions for Program Evaluation*, 1987(35), pp. 57–75. Available at: https://doi.org/10.1002/ev.1459

Kroch, E., Breheny, M., van Kessel, K. and Taylor, J. (2022) 'Order and disorder: navigating narrative tensions in the experience of treatment resistant depression', *Qualitative Psychology*, 9(3), pp. 273–288. Available at: https://doi.org/10.1037/qup0000192

Ladmanová, M., Řiháček, T. and Timulak, L. (2022) 'Client-identified impacts of helpful and hindering events in psychotherapy: a qualitative meta-analysis', *Psychotherapy Research*, 32(6), pp. 723–735. Available at: https://doi.org/10.1080/10503307.2021.2003885

LaFrance, M.N. (2007) 'A bitter pill: a discursive analysis of women's medicalized accounts of depression', *Journal of Health Psychology*, 12(1), pp. 127–140. Available at: https://doi.org/10.1177/1359105307071746

Larkin, M., Boden, Z.V.R. and Newton, E. (2015) 'On the brink of genuinely collaborative care: experience-based co-design in mental health', *Qualitative Health Research*, 25(11), pp. 1463–1476. Available at: https://doi.org/10.1177/1049732315576494

Lavik, K.O., Frøysa, H., Brattebø, K.F., McLeod, J. and Moltu, C. (2018) 'The first sessions of psychotherapy: a qualitative meta-analysis of alliance formation processes', *Journal of Psychotherapy Integration*, 28(3), pp. 348–366. Available at: https://doi.org/10.1037/int0000101

Levitt, H.M., Pomerville, A. and Surace, F.I. (2016) 'A qualitative meta-analysis examining clients' experiences of psychotherapy: a new agenda', *Psychological Bulletin*, 142(8), pp. 801–830. Available at: https://doi.org/10.1037/bul0000057

Llewelyn, S. (1988) 'Psychological therapy as viewed by clients and therapists', *British Journal of Clinical Psychology*, 27(3), pp. 223–238. Available at: https://doi.org/10.1111/j.2044-8260.1988.tb00779.x

Macaskie, J., Lees, J. and Freshwater, D. (2015) 'Talking about talking: interpersonal process recall as an intersubjective approach to research', *Psychodynamic Practice*, 21 (3), pp. 226–240. Available at: https://doi.org/10.1080/14753634.2015.1042517

Macmillan, K. (1995) 'Giving voice: the participant takes issue', *Feminism & Psychology*, 5(4), pp. 547–552. Available at: https://doi.org/10.1177/0959353595054017

Murray, M. (2000) 'Levels of narrative analysis in health psychology', *Journal of Health Psychology*, 5(3), pp. 337–347. Available at: https://doi.org/10.1177/135910530000500305

Murray, M. (2003) 'Narrative psychology and narrative analysis', in P.M. Camic, J.E. Rhodes and L. Yardley (eds) *Qualitative research in psychology: expanding perspectives in methodology and design*. Washington, DC: American Psychological Association, pp. 95–112.

SCoPEd Framework (2022), collaboratively developed by Association of Christian Counsellors (ACC), British Association for Counselling and Psychotherapy (BACP), British Psychoanalytic Council (BPC), Human Givens Institute (HGI), National Counselling and Psychotherapy Society (NCPS) and United Kingdom Council for Psychotherapy (UKCP). Available at: https://www.bacp.co.uk/about-us/advancing-the-profession/scoped/scoped-framework (Accessed: 12 June 2024).

Smith, J.A., Flowers, P. and Larkin, M. (eds) (2021) *Interpretative phenomenological analysis: theory, method and research*. 2nd edn. London: SAGE.

Smith, J.A. and Rhodes, J.E. (2015) 'Being depleted and being shaken: an interpretative phenomenological analysis of the experiential features of a first episode of depression', *Psychology and Psychotherapy: Theory, Research and Practice*, 88(2), pp. 197–209. Available at: https://doi.org/10.1111/papt.12034

Solstad, S.M., Castonguay, L.G. and Moltu, C. (2019) 'Patients' experiences with routine outcome monitoring and clinical feedback systems: a systematic review and synthesis of qualitative empirical literature', *Psychotherapy Research*, 29(2), pp. 157–170. Available at: https://doi.org/10.1080/10503307.2017.1326645

Timulak, L. and McElvaney, R. (2013) 'Qualitative meta-analysis of insight events in psychotherapy', *Counselling Psychology Quarterly*, 26(2), pp. 131–150. Available at: https://doi.org/10.1080/09515070.2013.792997

Willig, C. (2022) *Introducing qualitative research in psychology.* 4th edn. London: Open University Press.

Chapter 16

Mixing methods for research–practice integration

Felicitas Rost and Femke Truijens

Contents

Introduction

Life Beyond the Gates by Amy Sears. This image reflects the importance of constantly questioning whether our methods keep valuable viewpoints outside of our frame of reference.

The word 'research' derives from the Middle French word *recherche*, meaning 'to go about seeking'. Chapter 13 provided you with an overview of why research is important for counsellors. Chapters 14 and 15 introduced you to the key principles and methods of quantitative and qualitative approaches respectively, and focused on how counselling researchers engage in knowledge seeking. All three chapters emphasised how important it is to develop a critical capacity when reading research findings, especially when it comes to evaluating whether these are useful for your own clinical practice. This final chapter on research methods offers a further approach to draw on, one that will enable you to critique published research findings, both from a methodological point of view and in terms of content or focus.

We, the authors of this chapter, are both psychotherapy researchers *and* psychotherapists. We share the belief that counselling research always needs to be applied with the clear objective of understanding and improving individual (or communal) suffering. While this aim unites both practitioners and researchers, what is often missing is a common language. The integration of research methods might provide this. Quantitative and qualitative methods are often understood as distinct from each other, given their differences in data collection, understanding and approach towards human behaviour and experience, and the different types of research questions that they can answer. However, notwithstanding their ontological and epistemic differences, quantitative and qualitative methods also share common elements. We would even argue that holding on to a sharp distinction creates a false dichotomy that limits our ability to build an evidence base that is both fundamentally rigorous at the population level *and* useful and relevant in clinical practice.

The need for integration is grounded in the age-old question: is psychotherapy an art or a science? Who should be doing the *seeking*, as it were? Whose voices are being included and heard on that journey, and whose are not? And where does that lead us (both counsellors and clients) regarding an evidence base that serves the broad and colourful array of people in society? These pivotal questions lead to the thesis in this chapter, namely that the field requires a meta-reflection on how we can bring together evidence, experiences and practices. Rather than sticking to dichotomised thinking, which might limit what and whom we 'hear' in research, there is a need for a more integrative, collaborative and socially just approach to counselling research.

This chapter contributes towards achieving the **SCoPEd competency 4.16.B**:

Ability to draw upon and evaluate published research on counselling and psychotherapy, and integrate relevant research findings to enhance practice.

(SCoPEd Framework, 2022, p. 29)

This chapter aims to:

- emphasise the importance of evidence integration for inclusive clinical practice

- highlight the need to involve a range of stakeholders/perspectives in the research process and the appraisal of published research

- explain the core principles of mixing research methods to show how perspectives can be combined.

I Is counselling an art or a science?

In Chapters 12 and 13 you were introduced to the terms 'idiographic' and 'nomothetic', which describe different approaches to gaining knowledge. The former seeks to understand unique, private and subjective 'truths'; the latter is concerned with the discovery of general laws and objective truth. Since their application to psychology in the 1930s, there have been fierce debates that have led to a dichotomy which has framed counselling as *either* an art *or* a science.

Pause for thought 16.1

What do you think: is counselling an art or a science?

The idea that counselling is entirely an art is based on the premise that psychotherapy is a completely unique and creative endeavour where decisions and choices are made spontaneously by the people involved. The idea that counselling is entirely a science assumes that there are general principles determining psychological suffering and how people change, and also that research can discover causal processes and mechanisms responsible for creating change in a specific way.

When you considered the question posed above of whether counselling is an art or science, did you arrive at an either/or position? O'Donohue, Cummings and Cummings (2006) provide compelling arguments for why counselling can't be either an art or a science, and that it instead must be both. Overall, the authors argue that therapeutic practice can't lend itself to pure science as it is based on the uniqueness of all components involved: the uniqueness of the individual undergoing therapy, the relationship with the counsellor or other group members, their problems and the uniqueness of each moment. Therefore, there can't be absolute general laws. On the other hand, the authors point out that it can't be pure art as there exist causal relations that science is best at discovering. Whether or not we, as counsellors, directly speak about it with our clients, we do promise them that we can help them. As O'Donohue, Cummings and Cummings (2006, p. 3) put it, 'art rarely harms, but bad therapy can'. Thus, we need to establish ways to avoid this, and since spontaneity cannot consistently produce benefit, relying on scientific testing is our best option.

However, it is also important to keep in mind that science does not have the answers for everything. It cannot help with value or ethical decisions, including important clinical questions such as how counsellors should address their clients, what they should wear, what the payment policies should be, how to deal with absences and, crucially, whether a stated treatment goal is ethical. It principally falls to the individual clinician to make a judgement call as they balance the triad of research evidence, clinical knowledge and client context (explained in Chapter 13, Figure 13.1). Additionally,

O'Donohue, Cummings and Cummings (2006, p. 2) point out that science cannot 'fully cover the "art" or "craft" of implementing … evidence-based techniques, (i.e. the nuances, the creative maneuvers, the dexterity, the problem-solving strategies when difficulties arise)'. Moreover, science itself is an art and constantly evolving: 'There is no algorithm to spit out the best hypothesis or theory. This is part of the art of science. In addition, there is an art of experimental design. How does one design a simple, elegant, but persuasive study? Scientists differ on this ability' (O'Donohue, Cummings and Cummings, 2006, p. 5). In other words, these researchers stress that there is a very creative element in research.

Thus, best health practices may come from a mixture of science and art. It's not only about following scientific protocol or learning specific counselling skills, it is also about how they are applied. This requires a mixture of theoretical knowledge and a degree of artistic improvisation.

Westen and Weinberger summarise this beautifully in one of their papers:

> Perhaps we would do well to heed the seemingly disparate warnings of Hume, Bacon, Freud, and Meehl. From Hume (and later Kant) we learned that we cannot escape the subjectivity of the observer – that we will never see the world exactly as it is. From Bacon we learned that we must try anyway, and that scientific method is our best guide. From Freud (and later Kahneman and Tversky, Dawes, and others) we learned that our minds can play all kinds of tricks on us, and that systematic self-reflection, self-scrutiny, and knowledge about the biases to which we are prone are as essential for clinicians and scientists as for our patients. And from Meehl we learned that the scientific mind and the clinical mind can coexist, if ambivalently, in a single field – indeed, in a single person – and that the dialectic between the two may be essential for a scientific psychology.
>
> *(Westen and Weinberger, 2004, p. 610)*

2 The stakeholders in evidence-based practice

The chapter began by referring to the origin of the word 'research', with its associated meaning 'to go about seeking'. This section introduces the role and place of the various individuals and organisations that should be involved in this endeavour. The term 'stakeholders' is used to highlight the invested interest in clinically relevant research findings.

Stakeholders should not only include researchers, clinicians, treatment guideline developers, and policymakers, but also – and importantly – those whom the research is about: the participants, along with their families and communities. They all should have a say in what is researched, how research is done and what happens with the findings. Thus, when reading studies, it is worth checking whether and how these stakeholders have been involved.

Pause for thought 16.2

Thinking about yourself as a stakeholder, at what level would you like to be involved in research, or how would you like your voice to be heard?

The next section will look at why full stakeholder involvement is important, and whose voices we need to hear.

2.1 Why stakeholder involvement is important

Stakeholders can be involved at different stages of the research, although not necessarily all at the same time. Stakeholders are crucial in determining what needs to be researched, but also in being involved in the whole research process, starting from devising the research question and method through to its conduct, and finally the dissemination of the results.

As emphasised throughout Part 4 of this book, it is important that interpretations of research findings are representative of the population being studied (i.e. that the research has external validity/transferability) and can be implemented into the real world of clinical practice (i.e. that it has ecological validity). Since the world of health and psychotherapy is complex, we need a range of stakeholder voices to shape and steer this process.

Currently, too few stakeholders are involved, and among those who are, some dominate the discourse and decision-making process. For example, treatment guideline developers, such as the National Institute for Health and Care Excellence (NICE), have been a strong stakeholder. Given their objective to review the available evidence so that policymakers, commissioners and clinical services can make important funding and treatment decisions, it is important that they are. However, although their approaches have changed over the past years – in that they now include more service users and a variety of health professionals at the various stages of the development of a set of guidelines – their overall ethos and way of working is still shaped by medical science and lacks the needed adaptation to the more dynamic and person-centred ethos of the mental health and psychotherapy field. For example, NICE reviews focus primarily on randomised controlled trials (RCTs) to inform treatment recommendations. Additionally, NICE continues to influence what research is seen as important (and is therefore funded), and how it is evaluated (and therefore utilised in treatment guidelines). Thus, it is crucial that other stakeholders are included and that their expertise is taken into account and influences how clinically-relevant research is implemented and utilised.

As was pointed out in Chapter 13, the debate on how to inform evidence-based practice has often focused on a lack of practitioner involvement in research. A lot has been done over the past few years to bridge the practitioner–research gap. There are now, for example, more opportunities for direct dialogue at conferences, where practitioners are invited to engage with researchers to discuss their studies' methods and findings. Practitioners are also much more involved in steering groups (which guide large studies) as well as ethics committees, bridging the gap between the various positions. Furthermore, research methods are increasingly taught in practitioner training programmes, and some offer the choice of doing a clinical doctorate alongside therapy training. Researchers are also asked to attend specific training on clinically relevant ethics. These attempts have been fruitful; there is no doubt that empowering practitioners to become more research-minded – and in turn, allowing researchers to become more mindful of what is important for clinicians – makes research findings more relevant to practice. However, additional work needs to be done to allow for research methods and findings that are clinically relevant.

> ### Pause for thought 16.3
>
> Whose voices do we need to hear? From your perspective as a counsellor, what would you like to know more about, or what would you like to see covered more in research?

2.2 Whose voices do we need to hear?

Who the audience is and who the research is conducted for is an important question that is too often brushed aside. Paquin, Tao and Budge (2019, p. 495) ask 'what type of power are we really interested in?', playing on words by pointing to the principle of statistical power in quantitative research (explained in Chapter 14, Section 4.1) that is often valued more than the potential impact of research on the audience of interest.

However, the vast majority of psychology and psychotherapy research findings are based on studies that predominantly include participants from English-speaking and Western countries. The acronym WEIRD (Western, educated, industrialised, rich and democratic) was coined by Henrich, Heine and Norenzayan (2010), who described this over-reliance as a serious sampling bias. Indeed, it is a problematic position to continue to treat research findings based on WEIRD populations as universal, given that they only represent 11 per cent of the world's population (Thalmayer, Toscanelli and Arnett, 2021).

As discussed in Chapter 14, the way research participants are recruited has an impact on the research. Often, methods such as snowballing (where participants are selected based on who they know) and convenience sampling (where participants are selected based on availability) are relied on. Including a couple of sentences to that effect in the limitation section of research papers, as is often customary, seems to have become a 'get-out clause' rather than a prompt for researchers or clinicians to think about the actual implications of a WEIRD participant group on the findings.

A related bias, and therefore another 'power problem', is that most psychology researchers are also from WEIRD societies, which is not at all representative of the diversity in culture, religion, sexuality, class, socio-economic status and so on, found in the global population. As discussed in Chapters 1 and 2, many of the constructs, theories and measurements utilised in psychotherapy research are based on WEIRD values and cultural influences. This isn't necessarily problematic if the assumption is that the theory or tool applies to those of the same culture. However, it becomes problematic when the assumption is that the theory or tool is superior and/or applies globally across populations and cultures.

Pause for thought 16.4

Can you think of examples in your own life where you were expected to 'fit' a standard that did not feel right for you? Or do you remember a moment, for example when interacting with someone at work, where your assumptions or interpersonal habits did not fit the situation?

To increase the relevance and validity of research practice and findings, we should start with re-evaluating some of these values. However, there is a tendency to undermine or dismiss such efforts. Reviews, for example, often only include literature published in the English language, thereby ignoring valuable research findings from across the world. Moreover, involving and/or funding research carried out in non-Western countries by local teams should be a priority; as Meadon and Spurrett (2010, p. 104) claim, 'a literature in which most data are outliers is flawed'. Importantly, this process should not involve the unconsidered application of research methods and processes developed in Western countries, as this would invariably disrupt or overshadow local ethical considerations, values, customs and knowledge, and thus needs careful re-evaluation as well. Tauri (2018), for example, points to different ethical issues associated with research on Indigenous people. While a common ethical requirement in Western countries is to seek consent from the individual participant (unless they are underage or deemed 'incapacitated', when someone else would consent on their behalf), in other parts of the world there is a need for collective consent that includes people other than the specific participant. Smith (2021) provides an important account of how we can begin **decolonising research** methods to address some of these important aspects.

decolonising research

The process of focusing on concerns and world-views of non-Western individuals, which includes acknowledging that other ways of seeking knowledge and understanding theory and methods might differ.

Finally, there has been growing emphasis on a need to inform both therapeutic practice and research with the social justice agenda. This refers to 'engagement in the active transformation of individual actions, communities, and institutions, to be more equitable for groups marginalized due to their disadvantaged status in society to create a more harmonious system' (Fietzer and Ponterotto, 2015, p. 21). Importantly, this means that in addition to doing more research on topics related to inequality and inclusivity, social justice considerations should be reflected throughout the whole research process. Box 16.1 lists core ideas for involving stakeholders in socially just psychotherapy research.

Box 16.1 Core beliefs and practices for socially just psychotherapy research

- A socially just therapy researcher consistently considers 'the frame,' which means asking, 'what are we not seeing?', 'who is missing from the narrative?', 'who sets up the frame (participants? researchers?)'.

- Researchers should engage stakeholders in the development of research questions and research should seek to serve the needs of the community.

- Building trust is paramount, and requires engaging in real-world relationships with our participants, research team, and co-investigators; it requires consistent movement toward transparency.

- The intentional and unintentional silencing of voices can be considered violations of social justice ethical principles, as well as acts of violence.

- Critically question our default reference groups; for example, when engaging with or writing about our participants, who are we comparing them to? What language are we using? How do we position marginalized individuals in the center?

- All of a researcher's intersecting identities enter into the research frame; research is a whole body and whole self-endeavor (positionality).

- Research should seek to empower research participants, thus reducing the chances of marginalizing and stereotyping study participants. This does not mean pretending everyone has the same expertise, nor does it mean abdicating leadership responsibilities; this means owning one's expertise while honoring and valuing the

---

expertise of others and making informed decisions consonant with one's leadership style and with community values to move a project forward.

- Researchers entering culturally diverse and/or communities historically exploited or ignored by research should demonstrate genuine interest in the lives of participants, treat all persons with respect, and be willing to engage in a process of mutual transformation.

- An underlying question must always be 'how and for whom is this research useful?'

- Research is a political act that encompasses many agendas, including our own. We must ask ourselves what is underlying our questions, design, method, and interpretations. Research can seek to empower participants to effectively navigate complex and often oppressive systems.

- Research should lead to developing, implementing, and/or evaluating therapy interventions in schools, organizations, and agencies that positively contribute not only to individual change, but also to systemic and social change.

- Research should not force participants to respond to predesigned instruments or protocols that were not developed without at least a critical mass of participants from the target group, or entirely with members of the target group. If this is not possible, researchers should assume that is a limitation so significant that it necessitates the development of an alternative research design.

(Paquin, Tao and Budge, 2019, p. 500)

These principles can be reformulated as questions that you can ask yourself to evaluate a paper as you read it:

- Were stakeholders involved in developing the research question?
- Who is being excluded and/or may not benefit from the research question?
- Have the world-views of the researchers guided who they included?
- Has anyone from the relevant community been excluded?
- How and to whom are the research findings useful?
- Are the findings clinically relevant? Do they facilitate social change?

2.3 How to involve stakeholders in research directly

A research design that aims to directly engage and collaborate with those about whom the research is conducted is called 'participatory research' (also sometimes referred to as 'co-production research'). The design is predicated on the motto, 'not about us, without us'. The relevant community or participants are involved at all stages of the research process, guiding it through expertise-by-experience (from asking questions to recruitment, design and interpretation). Indeed, the NHS and social care in the UK now include the criterion to involve service users in all research studies funded by the National Institute for Health and Care Research (NIHR, 2019; 2024).

A further branch is participatory action research (PAR), which goes beyond involving relevant communities; it has a particular social or political agenda with the aim of bringing about direct or indirect change by, for example, informing policy or grassroots collective actions. PAR is surprisingly under-used in counselling research despite its various merits, including its potential to inform better and more just clinical practice (Guiffrida *et al.*, 2011). It's also been very successful in providing opportunities for youth engagement to highlight and address social determinants to health. A systematic review by Anyon *et al.* (2018), for example, identified 63 studies that used PAR and noted that the majority of these achieved systems change, such as implementing effective social-emotional learning programmes or skills development to build civic engagement for youth who are traditionally disempowered.

Pause for thought 16.5

Thinking about your own practice, community and interests, what kind of study would you carry out to attempt to achieve a direct change?

3 Mixing methods for integration in practice

The previous section discussed the importance of involving a range of stakeholders in research to allow for an evidence base that is inclusive and socially just. In this section, you will consider how combining quantitative and qualitative methods can yield more clinically relevant findings.

The terms 'methodological diversity' and 'methodological pluralism' have been used to describe the epistemological position that knowledge needs to be derived from a 'variety of sources in a variety of ways' (Barker and Pistrang, 2005, p. 202). This view stresses that researchers should be guided by the philosophical and/or methodological approach that fits the particular research question (Tashakkori and Teddlie, 2003). It is often associated with mixed methods (the combination of quantitative and qualitative methods) or multiple methods (all of which can be either quantitative or qualitative).

While mixing methods may lead to tension between paradigmatic assumptions and the researcher's interpretation of their findings, a dialogue between these contrasting ideas can provide opportunity for new insights (Creswell and Plano Clark, 2011). Moreover, when such tension appears, researchers must make a conscious decision about *which* assumptions are deemed more important for the given goals, for example the goal of utilising population-level findings in one-on-one mental health settings.

Pause for thought 16.6

Think of your own approach to working with clients. What do you prioritise, and how does this translate into how you might devise a research question?

The principal benefit of mixing methods is that it motivates researchers to start from the question 'what is needed?', which is vital for clinically relevant research. This is just as important for readers of research, like yourself. Often, researchers do not justify their design choice in their publications, nor do they discuss the very questions that they could not answer with their chosen methodology. However, this might give the impression that it is not necessary to think about the impact of the chosen methodology on the obtained findings, or to point to the crucial questions that could not be addressed. When researchers mix methods, however, they are required to explain how they mix them, what they assume and which interpretations they prioritise. This allows for a much more transparent insight into how their interpretations and conclusions came about. This, in turn, allows you to judge more concretely whether the research questions are relevant and whether the findings fit your clinical context.

One way of mixing methods is to utilise existing evidence derived from different methods, for example, in treatment guidelines. Evidence derived from RCTs could be combined with evidence derived from practice-based research, or outcome monitoring (using real-world data), case studies and qualitative studies. A wealth of qualitative studies exist that include hundreds of client voices talking about their experiences, and these could inform treatment recommendations. It is incomprehensible why NICE is not including such important evidence to inform treatment recommendations, while so many have argued that sound policy requires that we draw on a diverse range of evidence, and that a one-size-fits-all approach to mental health is untenable (e.g. Health Foundation, 2017).

3.1 Defining mixed methods research

Another way of mixing methods consists of a more formal research approach, where the study is designed to answer both quantitative and qualitative questions.

A mixed methods approach is used to broaden the understanding of a phenomenon. Epistemological and ontological stances are combined to gain a more holistic insight. Mixing can thereby occur in different ways: sequentially, concurrently, iteratively, or in a sandwich pattern (i.e. a combined approach). Creswell and Plano Clark (2011) identified six different types of mixed methods depending on the following decisions:

- *Weighting*: whether the researcher gives equal priority to qualitative and quantitative methods, or whether one is primary and the other supportive.
- *Timing*: whether the researcher wants to use quantitative and qualitative phases concurrently or sequentially.
- *Mixing*: when and how the mixing happens, whether at several stages or only at the beginning or end, and whether the data is kept separately or integrated and connected.

Table 16.1 summarises Creswell and Plano Clark's designs.

Table 16.1 Types of mixed methods design

Design	Description
Convergent parallel design	The quantitative and qualitative strands of the research are performed independently, and their results are brought together in the overall interpretation (through meta-inference). Quantitative or qualitative research questions can be primary.
Sequential explanatory design	A first phase of quantitative data collection and analysis is followed by the collection of qualitative data, which is used to explain the initial quantitative results. Research questions are interrelated and sometimes evolve during the study.

Sequential exploratory design	A first phase of qualitative data collection and analysis is followed by the collection of quantitative data to test or generalise the initial qualitative results. Research questions are interrelated and sometimes evolve during the study.
Embedded design	In a traditional qualitative or quantitative design, a strand of the other type is added to enhance the overall design.
Transformative design	A transformative theoretical framework, e.g. feminism or critical race theory, shapes the interaction, priority, timing and mixing of the qualitative and quantitative strand.
Multiphase design	More than two phases or both sequential and concurrent strands are combined within a programme of study addressing an overall objective. Mixing occurs across multiple levels of analysis, qualitative and quantitative data are analysed and integrated to answer related aspects of the same research question or related questions.

(Adapted from Schoonenboom and Johnson, 2017, pp. 117–118)

The following sections further explain two of these designs: sequential explanatory design and sequential exploratory design.

3.2 Sequential explanatory design

An often-used design in psychotherapy and counselling research is the sequential explanatory design. Here the data collection and analyses happen sequentially and separately, and the findings are integrated at the very end. The quantitative paradigm is primary, and the qualitative paradigm is secondary. An interesting example of such a study was published by De Smet *et al.* (2020). The authors investigated the research question, 'what does a "good outcome" (of psychotherapy) mean to participants?' The researchers used outcome data from the Ghent Psychotherapy Study, an RCT that investigated the effectiveness of cognitive behavioural therapy versus psychodynamic therapy for adults with major depressive disorder (Meganck *et al.*, 2023).

While it is common to study outcomes based on pre–post therapy symptom difference with measures such as the Beck Depression Inventory, it is seen as good practice to establish whether a statistical significance is also clinically significant. Thus, results are often categorised into 'good outcome' (either fully recovered or improved) and 'poor outcome' (either no response or deterioration). This is especially important in clinical settings, as you would want to know whether a treatment that works well on average might have adverse effects for some individuals.

However, De Smet *et al.* (2020) questioned whether the statistical categorisation of outcome often used is in line with how people experienced change themselves. Therefore, they interviewed the participants of the Ghent Psychotherapy Study asking them about their experience and conceptualisation of what 'good' and 'bad' outcomes mean, and compared these with the quantitative categorisations. Interestingly, the authors found that a 'good therapy outcome' was conceptualised by participants as 'feeling empowered' and 'finding personal balance', but also by 'encountering ongoing struggle', in which they did not consider themselves to be symptom-free (De Smet *et al.*, 2020, p. 25). Thus, the qualitative aspect brought a perspective that clearly differed from the quantitative conceptualisation of a 'good outcome' as being free of any depressive symptomatology. The findings from this mixed method perspective are crucial because they invite both researchers and clinicians to revisit and broaden their understanding of change, or what a good outcome of therapy is.

A similar design was used in the Tavistock Adult Depression Study (TADS) (Taylor *et al.*, 2012), which was introduced in Chapter 14, Box 14.1. At the end of the treatment phase, the authors carried out qualitative interviews with the participants and the therapists, asking:

- how they would describe or make sense of the experienced problems and difficulties
- how they experienced the psychotherapy
- what they found has helped or not helped
- what they thought had changed or not changed.

As with the example by De Smet *et al.* (2020), the inclusion of qualitative data in addition to quantitative data allows for further, deeper investigations about problem and change formulation from various perspectives. However, as you may remember, the authors of the TADS found something rather interesting: the main effect (i.e. the significant difference between those who received the psychoanalytic treatment and those who received usual GP care) emerged during the follow-up, and became larger and more statistically significant with time. This phenomenon is known as 'the sleeper effect'. In counselling research, the sleeper effect refers to a phenomenon where the outcome does not immediately show; it lays dormant and emerges (awakes) over some time. There is a call for more research to fully understand this effect in psychotherapy.

It would therefore be interesting to continue this study by interviewing all participants who showed such an effect based on the quantitative data, asking for their experience of how things had shifted (e.g. asking whether they saw a sleeper effect). This would be another example of a sequential explanatory design, given that the qualitative part would be guided by the outcome of the quantitative analysis. This is not just interesting from a research perspective, it could also help counsellors explain to their clients that while the treatment might work in general, sometimes the benefit might change over time or take a while to appear after treatment. This can help manage expectations or inform aftercare planning, for example.

3.3 Sequential exploratory design

Another commonly used method is the sequential exploratory design. Here, the phases are reversed: qualitative data collection and analysis are primarily used, then findings are followed up with quantitative methods. For example, researchers might want to explore a particular phenomenon first and then test the resulting theoretical assumptions or its distribution or prevalence in a selected population. An example is a study by Zhu *et al.* (2023), who explored the relationship between cultural humility and cultural competence in order to shed light on its conceptual ambiguity and help with existing problems in measuring it. They first carried out interviews with 14 counsellors who were experienced in teaching multicultural and cross-cultural issues. In a second step, they transformed their three themes into quantitative hypotheses: (a) that the two concepts share a strong correlation; (b) that they both have distinguishable underlying features; and (c) that they both predict favourable therapeutic processes, but that cultural humility accounts for unique variance. These were then put to the test in a quantitative study, using a cross-sectional correlational design utilising data collected from 434 adults who received counselling. The authors found that counsellors who were perceived as culturally humble also tended to be perceived as culturally competent. Moreover, both qualities were found to strengthen the therapeutic relationship with clients.

As the examples indicate, mixed methods designs can expand and strengthen the conclusions of a research study. Often, this also enables a more concrete perspective on how to implement findings, what limitations or contraindications to keep in mind for particular groups, or new ideas or hypotheses to explore either clinically, scientifically or both. Despite its various merits, this does not mean that mixed methods should become the norm in counselling research; rather, the sentiments here align with researchers who recognise it as a third research paradigm (e.g. Johnson and Onwuegbuzie, 2004), offering you another tool with which to evaluate research and make judgements about the relevance of the findings to your own clinical practice.

Conclusion

Grounded within the argument that counselling is both an art and a science, this chapter has invited you to look beyond dichotomies towards the need to integrate different research methods and perspectives. The aim of this chapter has been to provide you with another tool that you can draw on when evaluating published research findings. The chapter provided two examples of how to combine different sources of evidence to make them work in clinical practice. Moreover, it has highlighted another key question by which to critically evaluate published research: has the study integrated all relevant stakeholders to allow for more inclusive and socially just findings? Hopefully you have gained insight into how the use and integration of multiple perspectives and methodologies can allow for a comprehensive understanding that is at once rigorous for the researcher and relevant for the practitioner.

Further reading

- For a nuanced and witty account of counselling as both an art and a science you can read the following chapter:

  O'Donohue, W., Cummings, N. and Cummings, J. (2006) 'The art and science of psychotherapy', in W. O'Donohue, N.A. Cummings and J.L. Cummings (eds) *Clinical strategies for becoming a master psychotherapist*. Burlington, MA: Academic Press, pp. 1–10.

- This textbook provides useful information on mixed methodology for counsellors:

  Bager-Charleson, S. and McBeath, A. (eds) (2022) *Supporting research in counselling and psychotherapy: qualitative, quantitative, and mixed methods research*. Cham: Palgrave Macmillan.

- If you are interested in reading more on decolonising research methods, you can read this textbook:

  Smith, L.T. (2021) *Decolonizing methodologies: research and Indigenous peoples*. 3rd edn. London: Bloomsbury Publishing.

References

Anyon, Y., Bender, K., Kennedy, H. and Dechants, J. (2018) 'A systematic review of youth participatory action research (YPAR) in the United States: methodologies, youth outcomes, and future directions', *Health Education & Behavior*, 45(6), pp. 865–878. Available at: https://doi.org/10.1177/1090198118769357

Barker, C. and Pistrang, N. (2005) 'Quality criteria under methodological pluralism: implications for conducting and evaluating research', *American Journal of Community Psychology*, 35(3–4), pp. 201–212. Available at: https://doi.org/10.1007/s10464-005-3398-y

Creswell, J.W. and Plano Clark, V.L. (2011) *Designing and conducting mixed methods research*. 2nd edn. London: SAGE.

De Smet, M.M., Meganck, R., De Geest, R., Norman, U.A., Truijens, F. and Desmet, M. (2020) 'What "good outcome" means to patients: understanding recovery and improvement in psychotherapy for major depression from a mixed-methods perspective', *Journal of Counseling Psychology*, 67(1), pp. 25–39. Available at: https://doi.org/10.1037/cou0000362

Fietzer, A.W. and Ponterotto, J. (2015) 'A psychometric review of instruments for social justice and advocacy attitudes', *Journal for Social Action in Counseling & Psychology*, 7(1), pp. 19–40. Available at: https://doi.org/10.33043/JSACP.7.1.19-40

Guiffrida, D.A., Douthit, K.Z., Lynch, M.F. and Mackie, K.L. (2011) 'Publishing action research in counseling journals', *Journal of Counseling & Development*, 89(3), pp. 282–287. Available at: https://doi.org/10.1002/j.1556-6678.2011.tb00090.x

Health Foundation (2017) *Healthy lives for healthy people: introducing the Health Foundation's healthy lives strategy*. Available at: https://www.health.org.uk/publications/healthy-lives-for-people-in-the-uk (Accessed: 18 April 2024).

Henrich, J., Heine, S.J. and Norenzayan, A. (2010) 'The weirdest people in the world?', *Behavioral and Brain Sciences*, 33(2–3), pp. 61–83. Available at: https://doi.org/10.1017/S0140525X0999152X

Johnson, R.B. and Onwuegbuzie, A.J. (2004) 'Mixed methods research: a research paradigm whose time has come', *Educational Researcher*, 33(7), pp. 14–26. Available at: https://doi.org/10.3102/0013189X033007014

Meadon, M. and Spurrett, D. (2010) 'It's not just the subjects – there are too many WEIRD researchers', *Behavioral and Brain Sciences*, 33(2–3), pp. 104–105. Available at: https://doi.org/10.1017/S0140525X10000208

Meganck, R., Desmet, M., Van Nieuwenhove, K., De Smet, M., Hennissen, V., Truijens, F., De Geest, R., Hermans, G., Bockting, C., Norman, U.A., Loeys, T., Inslegers, R., Van den Abeele, T., Baeken, C. and Vanheule, S. (2023) 'The Ghent Psychotherapy Study: a pragmatic, stratified, randomized parallel trial into the differential efficacy of psychodynamic and cognitive-behavioral interventions in dependent and self-critical depressive patients', *Psychotherapy Psychosomatics*, 92 (4), pp. 267–278. Available at: https://doi.org/10.1159/000531643

National Institute for Health and Care Research (NIHR) (2019) *Resource guide for community engagement and involvement in global health research*. Available at: https://www.nihr.ac.uk/documents/resource-guide-for-community-engagement-and-involvement-in-global-health-research/27077 (Accessed: 1 March 2024).

National Institute for Health and Care Research (NIHR) (2024) *Engage patients to help shape your clinical research*. Available at: https://www.nihr.ac.uk/explore-nihr/industry/pecd.htm (Accessed: 1 March 2024).

O'Donohue, W., Cummings, N. and Cummings, J. (2006) 'The art and science of psychotherapy', in W. O'Donohue, N.A. Cummings and J.L. Cummings (eds) *Clinical strategies for becoming a master psychotherapist*. Burlington, MA: Academic Press, pp. 1–10.

Paquin, J.D., Tao, K.W. and Budge, S.L. (2019) 'Toward a psychotherapy science for all: conducting ethical and socially just research', *Psychotherapy* , 56(4), pp. 491–502. Available at: https://doi.org/10.1037/pst0000271

Schoonenboom, J. and Johnson, R.B. (2017) 'How to construct a mixed methods research design', *Kölner Zeitschrift für Soziologie und Sozialpsychologie*, 69(Supp. 2), pp. 107–131. Available at: https://doi.org/10.1007/s11577-017-0454-1

SCoPEd Framework (2022), collaboratively developed by Association of Christian Counsellors (ACC), British Association for Counselling and Psychotherapy (BACP), British Psychoanalytic Council (BPC), Human Givens Institute (HGI), National Counselling and Psychotherapy Society (NCPS) and United Kingdom Council for Psychotherapy (UKCP). Available at: https://www.bacp.co.uk/about-us/advancing-the-profession/scoped/scoped-framework (Accessed: 12 June 2024).

Smith, L.T. (2021) *Decolonizing methodologies: research and Indigenous peoples*. 3rd edn. London: Bloomsbury Publishing.

Tashakkori, A. and Teddlie, C. (eds) (2003) *Handbook of mixed methods in social and behavioral research*. London: SAGE.

Tauri, J.M. (2018) 'Research ethics, informed consent and the disempowerment of First Nation peoples', *Research Ethics*, 14(3), pp. 1–14. Available at: https://doi.org/10.1177/1747016117739935

Taylor, D., Carlyle, J., McPherson, S., Rost, F., Thomas, R. and Fonagy, P. (2012) 'Tavistock Adult Depression Study (TADS): a randomised controlled trial of psychoanalytic psychotherapy for treatment-resistant/treatment-refractory forms of depression', *BMC Psychiatry*, 12, article number 60. Available at: https://doi.org/10.1186/1471-244X-12-60

Thalmayer, A.G., Toscanelli, C. and Arnett, J.J. (2021) 'The neglected 95% revisited: is American psychology becoming less American?', *American Psychologist*, 76(1), pp. 116–129. Available at: https://doi.org/10.1037/amp0000622

Westen, D. and Weinberger, J. (2004) 'When clinical description becomes statistical prediction', *American Psychologist*, 59(7), pp. 595–613. Available at: https://doi.org/10.1037/0003-066X.59.7.595

Zhu, P., Luke, M.M., Liu, Y. and Wang, Q. (2023) 'Cultural humility and cultural competence in counseling: an exploratory mixed methods investigation', *Journal of Counseling and Development*, 101(3), pp. 264–276. Available at: https://doi.org/10.1002/jcad.12469

Part 5

Developing as a practitioner

Chapter 17

Online counselling

Andreas Vossler

Contents

Introduction

Freedom by Jemma Comerford

Both in the UK and around the world, the Covid-19 pandemic has changed the way in which counselling and mental health services are offered, and it has accelerated the trend towards flexible, hybrid provision. While it has long been recognised as a useful service for certain client groups (e.g. clients in remote geographical areas, young people), remote counselling is now provided routinely across all service types and client populations (Smith *et al.*, 2021). For many practitioners, working therapeutically online – via video platform or phone – has become the 'new normal' and part of their standard service provision.

However, the research evidence for remote therapy as a routine service is lagging behind the increase in provision, and practitioners and researchers are still learning about the specifics of remote therapy and the different ways of working online. The knowledge we have in many areas is still limited, and important practice-related questions are yet to be answered. Additionally, there is a lack of research on how clients experience online delivery, and for which clients and problems this might not be accessible at all (due to digital exclusion; see Heponiemi *et al.*, 2020).

The central argument in this chapter is that clients and therapists behave and relate differently to each other online compared with in-person therapy (Werbart *et al.*, 2024). This difference in behaviour implies that therapeutic practice needs to adapt to these differences to achieve results that are as good as the outcomes of offline services. For example, while clients can experience therapeutic presence in video and phone therapy, this chapter will discuss proactive measures and considerations that might be required to establish this presence online. Similarly, while therapeutic interaction and intimacy does take place in remote therapy, this involves new and different dynamics that practitioners need to be aware of (Essig and Russell, 2017). Following this premise, the chapter aims to support you to adapt and evolve your practice when working therapeutically in an online environment.

This chapter contributes towards achieving the **SCoPEd competency 2.11.B**:

Ability to identify and respond to the impact of the technologically mediated environment on issues of identity and presence, including fantasies and assumptions about the therapist and client or patient.

(SCoPEd Framework, 2022, p. 20)

This chapter aims to:

- identify the impact of the technologically mediated environment on the delivery of remote services via video/phone

- consider psychological concepts that help to explain differences in online counselling, especially regarding therapeutic presence, and also identity and fantasies in a technologically mediated environment

- develop strategies to respond to and address the issues related to the impact of this specific mode of delivery on the therapeutic relationship and process.

1 How is technology transforming counselling?

You will probably have guessed at the multifaceted impact that a technologically mediated environment has on the delivery and experience of counselling. You might wonder whether therapy in remote settings, whether through video- or voice-based methods, can be as effective as when the client and counsellor are sitting in the same room. Research has been conducted on the outcomes of remote therapy both before the Covid-19 pandemic and since, when remote counselling became part of the routine service offer. In Box 17.1 you will find a brief review of what this research has shown.

Box 17.1 Outcome research on remote therapy since Covid-19

Meta-analytic reviews of pre-pandemic research comparing remote therapy (videoconferencing and phone) to in-person therapy reported that video therapy is as effective as in-person (e.g. Batastini *et al.*, 2021). For phone therapy specifically, Irvine *et al.*'s (2020) review of research on the interactional aspects – therapeutic alliance, disclosure, empathy, attentiveness or participation – of phone counselling found little evidence of difference in these areas compared to in-person counselling.

Since the Covid-19 pandemic, there has been a noticeable increase in research activities and publications on phone counselling and, in particular, video-based therapy (Ivey and Denmeade, 2023). These new studies have the advantage that they are based on samples which include many types of clients and also many types of practitioners, who work in all sorts of different ways (as remote delivery became the norm during the pandemic), which means that the study findings can be generalised with more confidence (Smith *et al.*, 2021).

In the UK context, two studies (Nguyen *et al.*, 2022; Capobianco *et al.*, 2023) were recently published that evaluated the effectiveness of remote therapy with large client samples within the NHS Talking Therapies (formerly known as Improving Access to Psychological Therapies, or IAPT).

Capobianco *et al.* (2023) conducted a retrospective, cross-sectional comparison of remote therapy outcomes during the Covid-19 pandemic (5515 patients) with in-person therapy before lockdown (9199 patients – used as a reference point) in the Greater Manchester area. Based on their analyses, the authors concluded that the remote delivery did not have an impact on treatment outcomes – in other words, there was no difference regarding treatment effects – except that recovery seemed to be faster in remote therapy.

Nguyen *et al.* (2022) compared the outcomes of remote therapy delivered during the pandemic with in-person treatment prior to Covid-19 in two London-based IAPT services (5360 clients). The authors reported that remote therapy was associated with a greater decrease in symptoms of anxiety and depression. However, the study also indicated that some client groups – older clients and clients with a diagnosis of social anxiety or health anxiety – did not benefit in the same way from remote delivery. The authors suggested that clients with social anxiety might not have benefitted to the same degree because there was a lack of opportunities for exposure and experimentation during lockdown, which is an essential part of the treatment protocols.

Saunders and Allen (2021) conducted a clinical case study in the NHS/IAPT context during the Covid-19 pandemic to illustrate the benefits and challenges of shifting modalities – from in-person to telephone-based cognitive behavioural therapy (CBT) – during therapy. Despite the switch in modality during the 12 therapy sessions, the patient experienced clinically significant changes in symptoms of anxiety and depression. This suggests that a flexible, hybrid service provision with work in multiple modalities can be effective and lead to positive outcomes for clients.

However, a recent meta-analysis by Aafjes-van Doorn *et al.* (2024), which examined 31 studies and encompassed 4862 total participants, only found a small association between the quality of the therapeutic alliance and video-based therapy (effect size 0.15), which is weaker than usually reported for offline therapy. This suggests that the therapeutic relationship might have a smaller impact on the treatment outcomes in remote therapy.

Most new outcome studies are focused on CBT that is delivered remotely via phone and video. The available post-pandemic publications about psychodynamic therapy through online provision are mainly case studies or anecdotal accounts that paint a rather mixed picture of remote practice (e.g. Rizq, 2020; Scharff, 2020).

Overall, the research so far seems to suggest that, in terms of outcomes, therapy via phone or video can be as beneficial as in-person services. However, from the currently available research, it is not clear what the outcome would be if clients have a free choice between different modalities, or whether the outcomes differ dependent on presenting problems and client groups. In addition, it cannot be inferred from outcome research alone whether practitioners need to work differently online to get the same result as in-person settings.

Pause for thought 17.1

Think about the way you practise online. What have you noticed about your practice? Do you find that there are any differences between this context and working within the therapy room? Have you found yourself noticing any difference in client behaviours?

2 Presence in remote therapy

The value of therapists being in a state of presence with and for their clients is recognised across different therapy traditions, and is seen as one of the core qualities of effective therapeutic relationships (Geller and Greenberg, 2012). This approach is known as 'therapeutic presence'. But what exactly is therapeutic presence, and how can it be established and cultivated in practice?

Geller (2021, p. 688) describes therapeutic presence as a therapeutic stance that 'involves therapists bringing their whole self to the encounter with clients and being fully in the moment on a multitude of levels: physically, emotionally, cognitively, relationally and spiritually'. Therapeutic presence can be seen as a common, trans-theoretical factor that can help clients to feel safe, open up and explore sensitive and painful topics – but only if the client experiences the therapist as being present (Geller and Greenberg, 2012).

> ## Pause for thought 17.2
>
> How can therapeutic presence be developed and maintained remotely via video link or on the phone? What are the specific challenges of cultivating therapeutic presence in remote therapy?

With the mass shift to online therapy during the Covid-19 pandemic, it became apparent to many practitioners that they had to work harder, or differently, to convey a sense of presence to their clients in video and phone therapy (Full *et al.*, 2024).

Establishing and maintaining a therapeutic presence via video link or by phone has a set of specific challenges related to:

- *Reduced ability for practitioners to communicate non-verbally.* The physical distance between therapists and clients can limit the ability of practitioners to express themselves, reducing the range of non-verbal communication with the whole body (e.g. gestures, mutual eye gaze) that can be essential for building trust and a sense of safety with many clients (Geller, 2021). It also limits the opportunities for synchronising physiological rhythms and bodily movements (e.g. by mirroring clients' gestures/expressions) and other non-verbal cues.
- *Reduced non-verbal communication from clients.* Long silences may be difficult for the practitioner to interpret without supporting non-verbal cues.
- *Technological glitches and connectivity issues.* Bad reception, dropouts, and video image and/or audio freezing, which are unique to remote therapy, can impede lucidity and therapeutic presence. Clients might attribute such technical issues to the character of the therapist.

- *Challenges maintaining privacy and confidentiality.* Clients may fear being overheard or interrupted in their own environment.

While therapeutic presence can still be conveyed remotely, it requires specific attention, including the evolvement of remote practice skills (Weinberg, 2020). In video-based therapy, practitioners can take advantage of the psychological experience of 'telepresence', which can be illustrated by how TV presenters 'can pass through the screen and transmit their presence through the ether' (Weinberg, 2020, p. 207). This phenomenon is the illusion of a person being present, as if in the same room with another person, with a concurrent forgetting about being in a virtual space by becoming absorbed in the experience (Rathenau *et al.*, 2022).

The concept of telepresence was initially developed and researched in the areas of virtual and augmented realities, and in the context of videoconferencing. Applied to the realm of online therapy, telepresence can be defined as 'the feeling [or illusion] of being in the same location as the psychotherapist and in a sense, not paying attention that one is attending the session remotely, feeling together' (Bouchard *et al.*, 2023, p. 576). The significance of this concept for online therapy is backed up by research evidence (Rathenau *et al.*, 2022); for example, the feeling of telepresence is associated with the perceived strength of the working alliance between counsellor and clients.

Telepresence is more likely to be felt by a client if the online interaction is emotionally charged and the client is engaged in talking about their personal issues (Bouchard *et al.*, 2023). While more positive attitudes by therapists towards online therapy are related to higher scores of telepresence, it might not surprise you to learn that difficulties and disruptions unrelated to the therapy itself, like interruptions or issues with the technology, seem to have a negative effect on client-rated telepresence. The concepts of telepresence and therapeutic presence can also be complementary, with levels of telepresence potentially directly impacting the perceived therapeutic presence (Rathenau *et al.*, 2022). Although telepresence can't be achieved through voice-only methods of therapy, given it is a visual or physical phenomenon, it is still possible to cultivate a therapeutic alliance by phone based on your engagement and attentiveness as a practitioner (Irvine *et al.*, 2020).

Whether you are working by phone or by video call, the growing amount of theory and research available on this topic suggests that when practising remotely, you need to take active steps to make your *implicit* presence *explicit*. You will learn more about how you might evolve your remote practice in the following section, where you will meet a (fictional) client, Alasdair.

2.1 Developing and maintaining presence

To put theory into practice, this section will look at how the challenge of conveying a sense of therapeutic presence when working with clients online might be addressed. The following case example considers Alasdair, a new online video therapy client.

Case example: Presence in video therapy with Alasdair

At 78 years old, Alasdair isn't a complete stranger to technology. After all, he speaks to his grandchildren using WhatsApp (but by his own admission he now knows not to put his phone up to his ear when the camera is on).

These calls are important to him because he is living on his own in a remote area of Scotland. His wife died suddenly 12 months ago, and they had been married 45 years. He is desperately missing her and is having a hard time navigating his extreme grief.

The distance to travel to the city has prevented him from getting the support he needs, so his grandchildren have given him a tablet to allow him to access online support. But he can't imagine how this can work with a digital device. For starters, his wife always helped him with technology. Also, talking to your grandchild is one thing, but he wonders how he can possibly discuss his feelings with a counsellor on the screen. His wife would call him old-fashioned, but if he could, he'd rather have a real life encounter than meet with a counsellor virtually.

Pause for thought 17.3

Imagine you receive this information about Alasdair, your new online video therapy client, before your first session. What could you do to facilitate telepresence or therapeutic presence in the video therapy sessions with Alasdair?

Alasdair seems to be a client who finds it hard to imagine how therapy can work without seeing the (whole) person and being with them in the same room. It will therefore be important to think carefully about how to set up the sessions and convey a sense of presence right from the start.

First, before the session begins, you should ensure that you have a secure internet connection and that you are using a reliable video platform to minimise the risk of technical disruptions. It might help if you always 'meet' Alasdair in the same room, if possible, as this can provide some consistency that mirrors a therapy room experience (Geller, 2021); so, when selecting the room you intend to use, try to choose a room that you are able and willing to use again.

In your first session, acknowledge the 'weirdness', as Alasdair might experience it, of the environment. You could ask him directly in the first session about things that would help to make the situation feel more natural and right for him. For instance, you could ask Alasdair for feedback on your video image – if the lighting too dark or too bright – and adjust your distance and also that they felt it was easier to bring the countertransference up with their clients.

This research review confirms that the remote and virtual space can shape assumptions and fantasies embedded in the therapeutic process. The next section will focus on strategies that, as a practitioner, you can use to navigate the identity-related impact in remote therapy, specifically the effects of online disinhibition.

3.1 Managing identity-related effects

To demonstrate some of the opportunities and challenges that can emerge from identity-related effects in online practice, let's return to considering Alasdair, our imagined online video client. The following case example assumes that you are Alasdair's counsellor.

Case example: Dealing with Alasdair's grief

It's now Alasdair's fourth video counselling session to help him deal with his grief. He is talking about his wife while looking at a framed photo of her on the desk. All of a sudden, he begins to sob. He's speaking to her directly, as if she's in the room with him. 'Why did you leave me?' he asks. He expresses his anger that she has abandoned him and begs her to come back. After a couple of minutes, he remembers that he is not alone. He is embarrassed that you have witnessed this outpouring of emotions, and also the way he speaks to his deceased wife as if she were there. He admits that he does this when he is alone, but to talk to his wife in the presence of a counsellor is something he never thought he would do. His worry is that, as his counsellor, you will think that he's mad. It's certainly a different side of himself than he has shown before. You have never seen him angry; usually you just talk about how he misses his wife and how great their relationship was, so this is new information to work with.

Pause for thought 17.4

As Alasdair's counsellor, what could you do to deal with this situation? Can you think of a way to harness what you have seen or heard in a therapeutic way?

This case example illustrates how client experiences and behaviour can be impacted by the technologically mediated and remote environment. Triggered by a photograph at his home, Alasdair seems to 'forget' that he is in a therapy session and slips into an imaginary dialogue with his deceased wife. In this process, he reveals emotional aspects of his grieving experience that most likely would have taken longer to surface in an in-person setting, or would have not been disclosed at all. This situation poses both challenges and therapeutic opportunities that you would need to address and deal with in a sensitive way if you were Alasdair's therapist.

While the exchange has potentially provided new insights into Alasdair's grieving process, it has left the client shaken and embarrassed, and worried about how his emotional outpouring might have been perceived by his therapist. You should therefore acknowledge these difficult feelings and offer some reassurances that might help to normalise this expressed anger (e.g. as something that can come up during grieving processes). You could also explain to Alasdair that when working online and on the phone, clients can be inclined to open up more, and more quickly, which can be helpful for the therapy. You might also introduce the concept of the online disinhibition effect at the beginning of the therapy process so that the client is prepared for this possibility, rather than them later feeling regretful for sharing more than they meant to. This can be particularly important when working with traumatic experiences, or when there is a secret or taboo involved.

A high level of sensitivity is also needed for working with emotions that have been freed up in this way. To be able to harness Alasdair's disclosure, you need to be aware of the impact this episode might have on his self-perception and identity. You might slow down your approach and use more grounding to leverage the disclosure, facilitate deeper insight and develop relational depth in the therapeutic work with Alasdair (Full *et al.*, 2024). Depending on your therapeutic approach, you can invite and encourage further exploration and interpretation of the client's internal world, which can have the potential to be clinically meaningful. You can also further explore the underlying feelings and thoughts, as well as the meaning these might have for Alasdair. The episode also offers you an opportunity to focus on the transference and countertransference dynamics, both in this particular therapy session and in a more general way (Matheson and Kegerreis, 2023).

Alasdair's fictitious case highlights the unique opportunities and challenges of video counselling in navigating and working with deeply emotional disclosures. By acknowledging the impact of the remote environment on the therapeutic process, therapists can create a space where clients feel safe to explore these unexpected emotional moments, turning them into valuable opportunities for insight and growth.

Conclusion

How therapists respond to the impact of the technologically mediated environment depends, to a certain degree, on their therapeutic approach/training and the practice specialisms they might have. The aim of this chapter has been to support you to evolve your remote practice, and to develop your ability to identify and respond to the impact of the technologically mediated environment on issues of therapeutic presence and identity.

This chapter has argued that clients and therapists behave and relate differently to each other online compared with in-person therapy, and that practitioners need to adapt to these differences to continue to provide effective and ethically sound therapeutic engagement in an online environment. You have learned about theoretical concepts and research which help to explain the impact that the technologically mediated environment can have on both clients and therapists, and encountered strategies that can address and manage these effects in remote practice. This has been illustrated through the case study of Alasdair, who was initially sceptical about remote therapy and experienced the impact of the technologically mediated environment on emotional aspects of his grieving. The chapter also outlined how clients' experience of online delivery and its suitability for remote therapeutic work is an ongoing area of study, and that more research is needed.

Further reading

- The following paper provides lots of tips for cultivating therapeutic presence online:

  Geller, S. (2021) 'Cultivating online therapeutic presence: strengthening therapeutic relationships in teletherapy sessions', *Counselling Psychology Quarterly*, 34(3–4), pp. 687–703.

References

Aafjes-van Doorn, K., Spina, D.S., Horne, S.J. and Békés, V. (2024) 'The association between quality of therapeutic alliance and treatment outcomes in teletherapy: a systematic review and meta-analysis', *Clinical Psychology Review*, 110, article number 102430. Available at: https://doi.org/10.1016/j.cpr.2024.102430

Batastini, A.B., Paprzycki, P., Jones, A.C.T. and MacLean, N. (2021) 'Are videoconferenced mental and behavioral health services just as good as in-person? A meta-analysis of a fast-growing practice', *Clinical Psychology Review*, 83, article number 101944. Available at: https://doi.org/10.1016/j.cpr.2020.101944

Békés, V., Aafjes-van Doorn, K., Prout, T.A. and Hoffman, L. (2020) 'Stretching the analytic frame: analytic therapists' experiences with remote therapy during Covid-19', *Journal of the American Psychoanalytic Association*, 68(3), pp. 437–446.

Bouchard, S., Berthiaume, M., Robillard, G., Allard, M., Green-Demers, I., Watts, S., Marchand, A., Gosselin, P., Langlois, F., Belleville, G. and Dugas, M.J. (2023) 'The moderating and mediating role of telepresence and cognitive change in cognitive behaviour therapy delivered via videoconference', *Clinical Psychology & Psychotherapy*, 30(3), pp. 575–586. Available at: https://doi.org/10.1002/cpp.2816

Braude, G., Mohi, S., Quinlan, E., Shoullis, A. and Collison, J. (2023) 'A change in frame and countertransference experiences: transitioning from face-to-face to telepsychotherapy', *Counselling and Psychotherapy Research*, 23(4), pp. 1063–1071. Available at: https://doi.org/10.1002/capr.12612

Capobianco, L., Verbist, I., Heal, C., Huey, D. and Wells, A. (2023) 'Improving access to psychological therapies: analysis of effects associated with remote provision during COVID-19', *British Journal of Clinical Psychology*, 62(1), pp. 312–324. Available at: https://doi.org/10.1111/bjc.12410

Drum, K.B. and Littleton, H.L. (2014) 'Therapeutic boundaries in telepsychology: unique issues and best practice recommendations', *Professional Psychology: Research and Practice*, 45(5), pp. 309–315. Available at: https://doi.org/10.1037/a0036127

Essig, T. and Russell, G.I. (2017) 'A note from the guest editors', *Psychoanalytic Perspectives*, 14(2), pp. 31–137. Available at: https://doi.org/10.1080/1551806X.2017.1304111

Full, W., Vossler, A., Moller, N., Pybis, J. and Roddy, J. (2024) 'Therapists' and counsellors' perceptions and experiences of offering online therapy during COVID-19: a qualitative survey', *Counselling and Psychotherapy Research*, 24(2), pp. 703–719. Available at: https://doi.org/10.1002/capr.12707

Geller, S. (2021) 'Cultivating online therapeutic presence: strengthening therapeutic relationships in teletherapy sessions', *Counselling Psychology Quarterly*, 34(3–4), pp. 687–703. Available at: https://doi.org/10.1080/09515070.2020.1787348

Geller, S.M. and Greenberg, L.S. (2012) *Therapeutic presence: a mindful approach to effective therapy*. Washington, DC: American Psychological Association.

Grondin, F., Lomanowska, A.M., Békés, V. and Jackson, P.L. (2021) 'A methodology to improve eye contact in telepsychotherapy via videoconferencing with considerations for psychological distance', *Counselling Psychology Quarterly*, 34(3–4), pp. 586–599. Available at: https://doi.org/10.1080/09515070.2020.1781596

Heponiemi, T., Jormanainen, V., Leemann, L., Manderbacka, K., Aalto, A.-M. and Hyppönen, H. (2020) 'Digital divide in perceived benefits of online health care and social welfare services: national cross-sectional survey study', *Journal of Medical Internet Research*, 22(7), article number e17616. Available at: https://doi.org/10.2196/17616

Irvine, A., Drew, P., Bower, P., Brooks, H., Gellatly, J., Armitage, C.J., Barkham, M., McMillan, D. and Bee, P. (2020) 'Are there interactional differences between telephone and face-to-face psychological therapy? A systematic review of comparative studies', *Journal of Affective Disorders*, 265, pp. 120–131. Available at: https://doi.org/10.1016/j.jad.2020.01.057

Ivey, G. and Denmeade, I. (2023) 'Trainee psychologists' experiences of learning and conducting psychodynamic therapy via telepsychology', *Psychoanalytic Psychotherapy*, 37(2), pp. 155–178. Available at: https://doi.org/10.1080/02668734.2022.2158210

Kelly, K. and Lees-Oakes, R. (2021) *Online and telephone counselling: a practitioner's guide*. Warrington: Counselling Tutor.

Koole, S.L. and Tschacher, W. (2016) 'Synchrony in psychotherapy: a review and an integrative framework for the therapeutic alliance', *Frontiers in Psychology*, 7, article number 862. Available at: https://doi.org/10.3389/fpsyg.2016.00862

Matheson, C. and Kegerreis, S. (2023) '"The genie's out of the bottle": the impact of working online with individual psychodynamic psychotherapy for therapists and clients, and its lessons for psychodynamic training', *British Journal of Psychotherapy*, 39(3), pp. 573–591. Available at: https://doi.org/10.1111/bjp.12853

Mishna, F., Bogo, M. and Sawyer, J.-L. (2015) 'Cyber counseling: illuminating benefits and challenges', *Clinical Social Work Journal*, 43(2), pp. 169–178. Available at: https://doi.org/10.1007/s10615-013-0470-1

Nguyen, J., McNulty, N., Grant, N., Martland, N., Dowling, D., King, S., Neely, L., Ball, J. and Dom, G. (2022) 'The effectiveness of remote therapy in two London IAPT services', *The Cognitive Behaviour Therapist*, 15, article number e23. Available at: https://doi.org/10.1017/S1754470X22000198

Rathenau, S., Sousa, D., Vaz, A. and Geller, S. (2022) 'The effect of attitudes toward online therapy and the difficulties perceived in online therapeutic presence', *Journal of Psychotherapy Integration*, 32(1), pp. 19–33. Available at: https://doi.org/10.1037/int0000266

Rizq, R. (2020) 'What have we lost?', *Psychodynamic Practice*, 26(4), pp. 336–344. Available at: https://doi.org/10.1080/14753634.2020.1845068

Roesler, C. (2017) 'Tele-analysis: the use of media technology in psychotherapy and its impact on the therapeutic relationship', *Journal of Analytical Psychology*, 62(3), pp. 372–394. Available at: https://doi.org/10.1111/1468-5922.12317

Saunders, J. and Allen, C. (2021) 'Transitioning transdiagnostic CBT from face-to-face to telephone delivery during the coronavirus pandemic: a case study', *Clinical Case Studies*, 20(6), pp. 498–514.

Scharff, J. (2020) 'In response to Kristin White "Practising as an analyst in Berlin in times of the coronavirus"', *International Journal of Psychoanalysis*, 101(3), pp. 585–588. Available at: https://doi.org/10.1080/00207578.2020.1775939

SCoPEd Framework (2022), collaboratively developed by Association of Christian Counsellors (ACC), British Association for Counselling and Psychotherapy (BACP), British Psychoanalytic Council (BPC), Human Givens Institute (HGI), National Counselling and Psychotherapy Society (NCPS) and United Kingdom Council for Psychotherapy (UKCP). Available at: https://www.bacp.co.uk/about-us/advancing-the-profession/scoped/scoped-framework (Accessed: 17 November 2024)

Smith, K., Moller, N., Cooper, M., Gabriel, L., Roddy, J. and Sheehy, R. (2021) 'Video counselling and psychotherapy: a critical commentary on the evidence base', *Counselling and Psychotherapy Research*, 22(1), pp. 92–97. Available at: https://doi.org/10.1002/capr.12436

Suler, J. (2004) 'The online disinhibition effect', *CyberPsychology & Behavior*, 7(3), pp. 321–326. Available at: https://doi.org/10.1089/1094931041291295

Walther, J.B. (1996) 'Computer-mediated communication: impersonal, interpersonal, and hyperpersonal interaction', *Communication Research*, 23(1), pp. 3–43. Available at: https://doi.org/10.1177/009365096023001001

Walther, J.B. (2007) 'Selective self-presentation in computer-mediated communication: hyperpersonal dimensions of technology, language, and cognition', *Computers in Human Behaviour*, 23(5), pp. 2538–2577. Available at: https://doi.org/10.1016/j.chb.2006.05.002

Walther, J.B. and Whitty, M.T. (2021) 'Language, psychology, and new new media: the hyperpersonal model of mediated communication at twenty-five years', *Journal of Language and Social Psychology*, 40(1), pp. 120–135. Available at: https://doi.org/10.1177/0261927X20967703

Weinberg, H. (2020) 'Online group psychotherapy: challenges and possibilities during COVID-19. A practice review', *Group Dynamics: Theory, Research, and Practice*, 24 (3), pp. 201–211. Available at: https://doi.org/10.1037/gdn0000140

Werbart, A., Byléhn, L., Jansson, T.M. and Philips, B. (2022) 'Loss of rituals, boundaries, and relationship: patient experiences of transition to telepsychotherapy following the onset of COVID-19 pandemic', *Frontiers in Psychology*, 13, article number 835214. Available at: https://doi.org/10.3389/fpsyg.2022.835214

Werbart, A., Jonsson, M., Jankowski, B. and Forsström, D. (2024) 'New skills for distance regulation: therapists' experiences of remote psychotherapy following the COVID-19 pandemic', *Journal of Psychotherapy Integration*, 34(1), pp. 24–44. Available at: https://doi.org/10.1037/int0000310

Chapter 18

Complex formulation and meaning making

Hayley Ness

Contents

Introduction

The 'relationship dance': couple dynamics can be understood as a kind of dance, signalling levels of harmony or dissonance.

The aim of this chapter is to reflect upon the complex information that clients bring to therapy and to start to unpick the different ways that we, as counsellors, make sense of that information – and how we help our clients to do the same. This task is often referred to as 'formulation'; it is something that you will already be doing in your work as a counsellor, although how formally, explicitly or systematically you do formulation in your practice will likely depend on both your modality and training.

Formulation (first covered in Chapter 9) is sometimes informally referred to as a vehicle for change, or for 'building a meaning bridge' (e.g. Brinegar *et al.*, 2006). The British Psychological Society describes it to clients as:

> a joint effort between you and the psychologist to summarise your difficulties, to explain why they may be happening and to make sense of them. It may include past difficulties and experiences if these are relevant to the present. It acknowledges your strengths and resources. It also helps the psychologist work out what needs to be done in order for you to feel better and recover.
>
> *(British Psychological Society, no date, p. 2)*

While professional bodies such as the Health and Care Professions Council (2023, p. 28) in the UK state that practitioners must be able to 'formulate service users' concerns within the chosen therapeutic models', there is no agreed upon way to formulate (Corrie and Lane, 2010). This is somewhat unsurprising, given the myriad theoretical approaches and frameworks within counselling and psychotherapy. However, several authors do highlight that it is a constructive, collaborative, fluid process. For example, Johnstone (2018) emphasises that it is a process of co-constructing meaning between client and counsellor. Similarly, Cox (2021) states that it is about developing a shared narrative. Nevertheless, as this chapter covers, the extent to which we, as counsellors, formulate collaboratively as well as explicitly – if at all – is very much determined by our theoretical approach.

In its focus on complex formulation, this chapter aims to help you evolve your practice in regard to formulating understandings of your clients. The chapter draws on the fictional case example of a couple, George and Marco, to exemplify key points.

This chapter contributes towards achieving the **SCoPEd competency 4.9.B**:

> Ability to reflect upon the complex and sometimes contradictory information gained from clients or patients and to coherently describe their present difficulties and the potential origins using a clear theoretical model or approach.
>
> *(SCoPEd Framework, 2022, p. 28)*

This chapter aims to:

- exemplify the process of formulating presenting problems within different theoretical frameworks

- consider factors that may not be included in a standard formulation

- introduce relational and systemic approaches to formulation as a way of developing the counsellor's understanding of complex and often contradictory information

- reflect on the positioning of the counsellor when making sense of complex information.

1 How do we make sense of complexity?

Pause for thought 18.1

Consider your current views on formulation. Do you currently use it in your practice? Is it something that (from your perspective) should be a collaborative process? Should it be explicit and formal, or more implicit and fluid? Keep these thoughts in mind as you read through this section.

This section will consider how we, as counsellors, make sense of complex and sometimes contradictory information from clients. To get started, consider the fictional case example of George and Marco, introduced below.

Case example: George and Marco begin counselling

George, 31, and Marco, 28, have been together for three years. Both were brought up in Glasgow, Scotland. George's family were originally from Cork, Ireland, and were what George describes as traditional working class. Marco's family were from Barcelona, Spain, and were a mix of shop owners, GPs and dentists.

George and Marco approach Emma, 58, for counselling. Emma is from Edinburgh, Scotland. While she has 15 years' experience of working with individual adults, she has only recently trained in couples counselling; George and Marco are her third counselling couple. Emma has several degrees and qualifications, and was brought up in a relatively wealthy family.

In their first session, George and Marco explain that they moved in together just under a year ago. They say that their relationship had been very good, but that over the last six months or so, they have argued a lot. Most often these escalate to the point where they don't speak for days, and sometimes sleep in different rooms. They can't understand why this is happening and they don't know how to resolve it. When Emma asks them what they hope to get out of counselling, they say that they want to learn how to communicate better and how to resolve conflict. During the session, George and Marco sit together, hold hands and look at each other frequently, displaying empathy. However, Marco also talks over George at times, and Emma sometimes struggles to give them equal space to speak.

Emma explores the nature of the arguments between them. George says that he is unhappy about several things, most notably that Marco has distanced himself from the relationship and is watching an unhealthy amount of pornography. George feels insecure by the fact that he has gained a lot of weight and feels less attractive, and is worried that

Marco may be having an affair. In response, Marco says that he hasn't heard this before and that it is nonsense – none of it is true. Marco feels that George is obsessive over the house and is more worried about that than about him. He describes a pattern of arguing where Marco becomes upset and George responds by shutting down and cleaning the house. Both agree that their sex life has declined over the last six months, to the point where neither is currently interested in having sex with the other.

Both describe experiencing significant amounts of anxiety throughout their adult lives, and each mention a history of loss and trauma. Marco experienced the death of his mother when he was a young child. George describes a good attachment history with his parents, but a subsequent history of turbulent and abusive romantic relationships. Neither has previously sought counselling.

Pause for thought 18.2

Regardless of whether you have worked with couples before, take a moment to think about how George and Marco come across during their initial meeting with Emma, both as individuals and as a couple. As you reflect on this, notice your process for 'making sense'. What are you curious about and would want to explore further with them? What might inform your initial approach for working with this couple?

1.1 Meaning making in formulation

How did you start to make sense of what was described in the case example? Although it contains limited information, did you find yourself forming questions around what might be happening? Did you focus more on the relational issues or the individual ones? Or, were you focusing more on how Marco and George engaged in the room? Did you base your approach on your theoretical framework(s)?

While many researchers agree that formulation involves developing hypotheses – posing questions that are based on both theoretical understanding and observation (see Challoner and Papayianni, 2018, for a review) – within that overarching process there is no 'right' way to formulate. Is the process of developing a hypothesis based on fact or opinion? Is there a 'right' way to make meaning? Furthermore, the concept of formulation is itself a contentious topic within counselling and psychotherapy, particularly for practitioners from the person-centred school of thought who sometimes disagree with the process of formulation. This is exemplified by Simms' (2011) proposal for formulation – which acknowledges and works with the arguments from the person-centred perspective – and Gillon's (2012) counterargument for gaining more insight into these issues around formulation.

Given that there is no agreed-upon way to formulate, we might consider how the different theoretical frameworks can guide a counsellor's approach to formulation. Consider the approaches outlined in Table 18.1 – which could be applied to a case such as George and Marco's – and use the information to reflect on your own approach to formulation.

Table 18.1 Theoretical frameworks and associated approaches to formulation

Theoretical framework	Formulation	Intervention	Goal
Psychodynamic	Has a relational focus. Considers all behaviour as meaningful. Anxieties might be seen as rooted in unconscious conflicts, maladaptive cycles and unresolved childhood experiences.	The therapist might examine ego strength, emotion regulation, defences and internal states, e.g. emotions and motivations.	To gain insight into how the couple's method of relating achieves a balance between autonomy and intimacy, nurturing and individual needs. To understand how past experiences impact on relationship dynamics.
Cognitive behavioural	Examines triggers, maladaptive thought patterns, behaviours, and strengths and resources. May use a cognitive model such as the five Ps: presenting issues, precipitating factors, perpetuating factors, predisposing factors and protective factors (p. 21).	The counsellor might work with the couple to produce a list of triggers, distorted thought patterns and variations thereof, using concrete examples. They may work on communication, flexible thinking and perspective taking to improve interactions. They might also identify and challenge cognitive distortions related to anxiety.	To help the couple develop more flexible, adaptive ways of thinking and behaving in their relationship, to reduce anxiety and improve relational intimacy and communication.

Theoretical framework	Formulation	Intervention	Goal
Humanistic	May draw on conditions of worth, the couple's values and beliefs, their perceptions of experience, levels of congruence and any psychological difficulties.	The counsellor might provide a supportive and empathic environment where the couple can explore their feelings and experiences without judgment. They would focus on facilitating self-exploration and self-acceptance, staying within the clients' narrative and frame of reference.	To help each person develop a greater sense of self-awareness and self-acceptance, leading to improved communication and a more authentic relationship.
Systemic	Might approach difficulties as though arising from the interactional patterns within the relationship, broader family network and broader cultural, societal and political systems.	The counsellor might explore the dynamics between the couple, their relationships with family, and their cultural and societal backgrounds to understand, identify and externalise the 'problem' and how it impacts the relationship. They might use techniques to map out family relationships.	To identify and change dysfunctional patterns of interaction, promoting healthier communication and relationship dynamics.
Integrative	Might consider the interplay between unconscious conflicts, cognitive patterns, interpersonal dynamics and systemic influences.	The counsellor might tailor interventions based on the unique needs and preferences of the couple, drawing from a range of therapeutic techniques and perspectives.	To help the couple achieve a deeper understanding of themselves and their relationship, leading to increased communication, intimacy and overall well-being.

(Adapted from Johnstone and Dallos, 2013)

As can be seen from the table, the emphasis that each theoretical approach places on understanding distress differs slightly. However, the key aim of all approaches is to work collaboratively with clients such as George and Marco to develop a story, or narrative, of what is going on for them, that aligns with the approach being used. As Simms (2011, p. 27) states, 'all therapists, irrespective of theoretical persuasion are engaging in case formulation', because it is just what we do as humans: we use what we know to make sense of ourselves and the world around us. The only difference with formulation is that, as counsellors, we are making sense in a way that aligns with a core theoretical approach which provides a particular understanding about where distress comes from, and which frames how we help clients to understand their distress.

1.2 An example of a person-centred formulation

Reflect again on your responses to Pause for thought 18.2. What were you curious about in George and Marco's case? What might you like to explore further with them? To help think through how we might frame our curiosity within one theoretical paradigm, let's take George as an example, and consider what types of hypotheses Emma – or you – might form using Simms' person-centred framework for formulation. Simms (2011, p. 31, fig. 1) lays out five stages of formulation: establishing 'conditions of worth laid down in childhood'; understanding 'introjected values and beliefs'; understanding 'denial and distortion of experience'; defining the 'state of incongruence' ('congruence' was defined in Chapter 9, Section 3); and establishing 'psychological difficulties'. These are applied to George's case in the following example.

Case example: Approaching a person-centred formulation for George

This case example considers the evidence we have about George and the questions that we might devise based on Simms' (2011) person-centred framework for formulation (you might have additional ideas).

Conditions of worth laid down in childhood

What might George have been praised for as a child? How did he learn to gain love, acceptance and positive regard? He describes a good relationship with his parents, but then a history of abusive romantic relationships. What might that indicate? Perhaps that he was valued and loved when he put other people's needs before his as a child? Perhaps this was modelled by his parents? Perhaps he was praised for being a 'good boy', for tidying his room, being quiet and for not demanding attention? These are aspects that Emma could explore with George.

Introjected values and beliefs

What external values might George have internalised? There is some evidence that perhaps George puts others before himself and that he doesn't show anger (e.g. he may allow Marco to talk over him), and that he works hard around the house. What might Emma explore from the narrative provided so far? What messages has George internalised? Possible messages to explore could include:

- 'Action speaks louder than words.'
- 'Men shouldn't talk about their feelings.'
- 'Conflict is bad and something to be feared.'

- 'A tidy house makes a happy household.'
- 'Nurturing and caring involves taking care of one's partner.'
- 'You don't need to express how you feel; people that love you just know.'

Denial and distortion of experience

Does George's history of relationships suggest that there may be some denial or distortion of experience from his childhood? He describes a healthy attachment with his parents, but might a history of adult abusive relationships suggest that there may be something to explore here?

Currently, George is fearful that Marco has pulled away from the relationship, but perhaps George has pulled away and is emotionally eating as a result? What hypotheses could be developed?

State of incongruence

Incongruence is when a person's ideal self doesn't match – or is incongruent with – their actual behaviour. Is George behaving in a way that reflects his ideal self? Is he aware of his needs in his relationship with Marco? This could be an area to explore.

Psychological difficulties

These include long-term history of anxiety and his experience of abusive relationships.

Counsellors use their theoretical understanding to help frame questions or hypotheses, which in turn can help clients discover patterns and experiences that may be impacting on their adult relationships, and that they perhaps hadn't been aware of. Done well, the process of formulation can help to build empathy as well as enable insight. Given how unique and complex humans are, framing this process within a theoretical framework is crucial, otherwise the process might become unwieldy and chaotic. As such, Simms' five-stage model may be useful to orient oneself as a counsellor. However, it is important that the process is collaborative and that it enables the client(s) to make sense of themselves and their experiences.

2 What might we miss when formulating?

Formulation requires counsellors and therapists to actively *do* something at various levels. It also necessitates an awareness of how they are situating themselves within their theoretical base. Formulation demands an active engagement in learning, and to then use the processes associated with a particular theoretical framework. It also requires the development of tentative hypotheses, a commitment to continuing to test the validity of those hypotheses (against client understandings and against what is happening in the session), as well as the core counselling skills of listening, exploring and demonstrating empathy (Hill and Norcross, 2023).

This process sounds very precise and almost computerised, but counsellors are human; as much as core training and continuous professional development enhances self-awareness and competencies, it is sometimes good to consider things that we might *not* be doing, or may not be aware of, to maintain best practice. In focusing on what we might miss in our formulations, this chapter picks up on ideas relevant to Part 1 of this book surrounding diversity. It highlights that in the process of trying to understand clients (and helping them to understand themselves), issues related to difference may be ignored or dismissed in ways that are harmful to the clients or are not productive for the counselling work. This section illustrates the point by focusing on two examples of individual difference: social class and sex.

2.1 Social class

Considering a client's wider social and cultural background should (but may not) be standard practice when working with clients of different ethnicities and cultural backgrounds. But what about social class? The way that we understand 'class' in the UK is very different to some other countries because it goes beyond occupational and wealth status; research suggests that class in the UK has economic, social and cultural dimensions (BBC News, 2013; see also Dorling, 2014, for a discussion). Whether or not we question the relevance of social class categorisations, many stereotypes and ways of thinking have become embedded within UK culture. Furthermore, as McEvoy, Clarke and Thomas (2021) highlight, there are very important links for counsellors and therapists to consider between class, oppression, marginalisation and psychological distress. McEvoy, Clarke and Thomas argue that if counsellors aren't taught to be critically aware of wider socio-economic and socio-political issues, then there is a risk of replicating those oppressive experiences in the counselling room. Secondly, it is argued that issues around class are so pervasive that they must be included in counselling and psychotherapy training. Let's consider how class may unconsciously impact on how we work with clients (and how they work with us).

Ballinger and Wright (2007) conducted a 'co-operative inquiry' with nine counsellors, asking the question 'Does class count?'. The reflections and insights from this study demonstrated that class did matter to these counsellors in several ways. For example, one counsellor reported: 'I enjoyed working with a very working class client – something to do with her language. It was like working with my auntie' (p. 160). Counsellors talked about how class impacts identity: 'My mother was ashamed at being the poor one in the family' (p. 160); there was also a 'tendency to pair with people from the same class' (p. 161). The counsellors also made links to politics: 'I can get really cynical about the middle classes unloading their guilt by working for voluntary agencies and failing to see the social context of problems' (p. 161). They also talked about how class impacts access to both counselling services and counselling training: 'As a client it would really matter what came out of my counsellor's mouth – the accent, the words' and 'You need money to train as a counsellor' (p. 160).

Pause for thought 18.3

Before reading on, take a moment to relate this to the case example of George and Marco. How does thinking about class help the process of formulation with this couple?

Emma and Marco have a similar socio-economic and class background (what we might term 'middle' class), whereas George comes from a self-declared traditional working-class background. Marco was talking over George in the room, and Emma was struggling to give each person equal time. Why could that have been? Emma was an experienced counsellor. Was it just that she lacked experience with couples, or did she identify more with Marco than George, and unconsciously allow him more time to talk? What impact might this have on the formulation that Emma develops with George and Marco? What stereotypes and assumptions might each person be holding?

Furthermore, to what extent are class assumptions and stereotypes playing a role in the conflict that George and Marco are experiencing? Are the arguments based on family differences, expectations, assumptions or rituals? Are there feelings of shame, pride, privilege, lack of privilege, resentment, achievement or under-achievement? Class may well be an important aspect to consider when approaching a formulation.

2.2 Sex

The other aspect often not considered is the subject of sex. How many times have you asked a client or a couple about their sex life? How many times have you included that information in a formulation?

Sex is often an important part of a relationship, an important domain for couple exploration and fun (Holmes, 2001), but also frequently associated with marital and relationship difficulties (Trudel and Goldfarb, 2010). While sex of course doesn't have to happen in relationships, if it does, it is impacted by the relationship dynamics, including both individual's attachment. As Holmes states:

> A successful sexual relationship involves a number of features relevant to attachment: mutual emotional attunement, the capacity to contain and not feel overwhelmed by mounting excitement, overcoming fear of transgression while retaining respect for boundaries, the capacity to regress and re-integrate, and the ability to separate and cope with loss, secure in the knowledge that a sexual couple as an internal representation will survive.
>
> *(Holmes, 2001, p. 12)*

So, asking about sex and including it in a formulation can be important. The next section will consider this in more detail within a relational formulation with George and Marco.

3 Relational formulation

relational formulation

The process of identifying and making sense of difficulties within a relational dynamic.

Relational formulation is an approach to formulation where the core goal is to identify and externalise problems and issues within a relationship. When used in couples counselling, it can help the couple to gain insight, awareness and understanding around their issues (Hewison, Clulow and Drake, 2014). Couple dynamics can be understood as a 'dance': when one person moves, the other moves; and when things are going well, both are in harmony. However, sometimes one person may not feel like dancing, or the couple might just be completely out of step. When formulating with a couple, counsellors help them to map their dance by looking at their relational interactions and their dynamics, including any that may have disrupted or interrupted the dance.

3.1 Mapping George and Marco's dance

This section will use George and Marco's experience to work through an example of relational formulation, in order to illustrate how complex and potentially contradictory information from clients can be understood by drawing on attachment theory.

In exploring how George and Marco relate to each other and how they each deal with stress and conflict, it may be useful to help the couple understand their attachment styles so that they can gain an increased understanding of how they behave under stress. This seems relevant because Marco and George have already described past attachment issues. Marco experienced the loss of his mother at a young age, and it is unclear whether there was a consistent attachment figure present while he grew up. George describes a history of difficult and abusive attachments as an adult. George and Marco have also come to counselling with relational (attachment) issues – in their case, difficulties communicating and dealing with stress and conflict.

There is a myriad of research on attachment within psychology, and a growing body of research within the counselling literature. Attachment theory describes the dynamics in people's closest relationships, so it can be a useful theoretical lens to understand distress in adult romantic/sexual relationships.

Box 18.1 Attachment theory and romantic relationships

Bowlby's (1969) attachment theory (introduced in Chapter 4) had, at its heart, two behavioural systems: one based on attachment (for survival of the infant) and one linked to exploration. For the attachment system to function appropriately, Bowlby stated that the primary caregiver needs to be accessible, attentive and responsive to the infant's needs. When this happens, the child perceives love and security, and has the confidence to explore. If the primary caregiver is not consistently available and responsive, then the child would become insecure, anxious or depressed. Bowlby believed that attachment was important across the whole lifespan, and other researchers (e.g. Hazan and Shaver, 1987) have highlighted the importance of attachment styles in adult romantic relationships.

It is thought that there are four main attachment styles: secure, avoidant, ambivalent/anxious and disorganised. Simpson and Rholes (2017) reviewed the research on attachment, stress and relationships, and highlighted the often complex interactions between these factors. For example, people with an avoidant attachment style can be very self-reliant and may withdraw from a partner when under stress. In contrast, those with ambivalent or anxious styles may react negatively to both internal and external stressors, and may become emotionally demanding or 'clingy'. Research has shown that the interaction between experiencing stress and one's attachment style (i.e. one's propensity to react to stress and the form this takes) can negatively impact on a person's relationships. Thus, gaining an understanding of one's propensity may help couples understand and work through their relationship difficulties.

George and Marco described a recent lack of sexual intimacy in their relationship. As described earlier, Holmes (2001) categorises sex in a relationship as a form of exploration and fun. If a partner is anxious, or if the relationship is threatened in any way, then, as Bowlby describes, the 'exploration' part of the attachment system will be 'switched off' and partners will seek reassurance and comfort to reduce stress and anxiety. Therefore, a formulation with George and Marco might need to explore where that anxiety is coming from. To what extent does Marco's use of pornography and George's fear of an affair relate to this anxiety? Research by Moller and Vossler (2015) highlighted that defining infidelity in the internet age can be extremely complex, subjective and often gender-based. Many participants in their study viewed sharing emotional and/or sexual information or images with someone else online as infidelity. As such, a formulation for George and Marco could contain a thorough exploration of what each partner sees as problematic sexual behaviour and their perceptions of what constitutes an affair, together with an understanding of their respective attachment behaviours.

Attachment theory also provides a useful lens to examine a counsellor's positioning when working with clients. Holmes (2001) describes the position that a counsellor adopts as a 'secure base' for a person in distress. When working with two people together, the counsellor still adopts the 'secure base' position, but it may also involve a shifting, dynamic process between each person in the partnership and the counsellor. As a practitioner, an understanding of your own attachment style and how it might impact on your way of working relationally can be very important, particularly when making sense of the changing dynamics in a room. In the case example, this means that Emma needs to think about her own attachment style and how this influences what she is bringing to the dance.

4 Working systemically

Relational formulation is a useful way to think about clients if, typically, you have only conceptualised clients as individuals. This is because even when you see clients on an individual basis, they are almost always going to have relationships, including attachment relationships. In other words, relational formulations may further your sense making about clients by helping you hold in mind the fact that your client lives in a web of relationships which will have effects (positive or negative) on their well-being.

Relational formulation was developed more recently as an approach to making sense of couple dynamics. However, **systemic therapy** is a long-standing approach used to work with couples as well as families. A key principle of this approach is that issues or 'problems' within a couple, family or group of people are situated within the context of those relationships and interactions, rather than within specific individuals. Central to this is the idea of circular causality, which is where problems are maintained by repeated cycles of behaviours and feedback.

systemic therapy

An approach which focuses on the interactions and relational dynamics between groups of people. It also incorporates wider systemic influences from cultural, societal, political and economic structures.

To illustrate these concepts, let's imagine that in his second counselling session, George describes that when he was 14 years old he expressed his anxiety by staying in his room and refusing to go to school. This led his mother to become anxious and demand that he went to school, shouting at him and trying to get him out of bed. His father in turn became overprotective of George. This calmed George but increased his mother's anxiety. This led their 13-year-old daughter Emily (George's sister) to feel ignored and alone. In time, as her sense of isolation increased, she started to experiment with drugs and eventually became addicted.

It is easy to see the repeating patterns of behaviour in this simple example, and how they create a self-sustaining negative loop. George's behaviour back then – not going to school – may have been seen by the family as the problem. However, the 'problem' from a systemic perspective is a *symptom* of stress or distress within the wider family system (Dallos and Stedmon, 2014). Systemically, George's anxiety and school avoidance is understood as indicating that there was a problem with the family dynamic. Working with George and Marco today, a systemic understanding might be useful to help foster curiosity about what was happening back then in George's family.

4.1 Cultural perspectives

Systemic ways of thinking, if not already familiar to you, can be a really helpful aid in making sense of the complex and sometimes contradictory information we get from clients, because they encourage us to think about the impacts of wider social networks (beyond attachment relationships) on individual well-being. During the 1960s and 1970s, this 'new' systemic approach to understanding psychological well-being in Western societies seemed revolutionary (Lindegger and Barry, 1999) because it challenged the predominant individualised understandings of distress. Since then, most research and training in systemic family therapy has been developed and delivered in the West (Asiimwe *et al.*, 2021). However, authors such as Nkosi and Daniels (2007) note that within more collectivised communities and societies, this 'systemic' way of understanding ourselves and others through a relational, societal lens has been evident for many years, particularly in many Indigenous African communities.

Asiimwe *et al.* (2021) argue that in such contexts, distress and healing are traditionally conceptualised collectively, communally, relationally and systemically, conveyed in the saying, 'It takes a village to heal (as well as raise) a child'. As such, mental health professionals in Africa acknowledge the constraints of using Westernised individualised approaches to counselling and instead have been adopting a more systemic lens to understand the issues that individuals, couples and families experience. Asiimwe *et al.* (2021), for example, described the development of innovative systemic family therapy initiatives in both Kenya and Uganda. Thinking about formulation of complex cases, this is an example of why it is important to be responsive to local cultural understandings; for formulation to be useful to both the client and the counsellor, it needs to include the client's frame of reference. If it does not, the formulation will not be collaborative and there is unlikely to be shared agreement about what the purpose of the counselling should be.

Pause for thought 18.4

Having read this chapter, what do you think are the benefits and drawbacks to using the different approaches to formulation that have been outlined? What might be the benefit of combining them?

People bring a complex array of individual, relational and systemic issues to the counselling room, whether they present individually, as a couple or as a family. This complexity has led some theorists and practitioners to argue that formulating using a single theoretical approach may lead counsellors to miss key details and form an incomplete understanding of why particular patterns of behaviour persist, or why someone is unable to 'shift'. Gazzillo, Dimaggio and Curtis (2021, p. 116) suggest that more 'bottom-up', holistic and integrative formulations that incorporate different theoretical understandings are needed in order to be relevant for the individual client. They describe this as a 'what works for whom' (p. 116) approach to formulation.

Conclusion

This chapter started by considering what formulation is in counselling. Through the case example of George and Marco, it examined how counsellors might formulate from the perspectives of the main theoretical approaches. It considered some factors that might not be included in a standard formulation, then considered relational formulation using attachment theory and touched on systemic ways of working. While the chapter drew a distinction between relational and systemic approaches, it is important to note that both can be combined and used with clients. The complex nature of people and the issues they bring to counselling means that a bottom-up, integrative and holistic approach may be needed to develop formulations that are most useful for clients.

Further reading

- The following article offers an extensive review of formulation and its role in counselling psychology:

  Challoner, H. and Papayianni, F. (2018) 'Evaluating the role of formulation in counselling psychology: a systematic literature review', *The European Journal of Counselling Psychology*, 7(1), pp. 47–68. Available at: https://doi.org/10.5964/ejcop.v7i1.146

- The following paper offers some alternative perspectives by providing a person-centred approach to formulation:

  Simms, J. (2011) 'Case formulation within a person-centred framework: an uncomfortable fit?', *Counselling Psychology Review*, 26(2), pp. 24–36.

- The following article highlights many of the issues with Western approaches to formulation in counselling:

  Asiimwe, R., Lesch, E., Karume, M. and Blow, A.J. (2021) 'Expanding our international reach: trends in the development of systemic family therapy training and implementation in Africa', *Journal of Marital and Family Therapy*, 47(4), pp. 813–830. Available at: https://doi.org/10.1111/jmft.12514

References

Asiimwe, R., Lesch, E., Karume, M. and Blow, A.J. (2021) 'Expanding our international reach: trends in the development of systemic family therapy training and implementation in Africa', *Journal of Marital and Family Therapy*, 47(4), pp. 813–830. Available at: https://doi.org/10.1111/jmft.12514

Ballinger, L. and Wright, J. (2007) '"Does class count?" Social class and counselling', *Counselling and Psychotherapy Research*, 7(3), pp. 157–163. Available at: https://doi.org/10.1080/14733140701571316

BBC News (2013) 'Huge survey reveals seven social classes in UK', 3 April. Available at: https://www.bbc.co.uk/news/uk-22007058 (Accessed: 17 December 2024).

Bowlby, J. (1969) *Attachment and Loss. Vol. 1: Attachment*. New York, NY: Basic Books.

Brinegar, M.G., Salvi, L.M., Stiles, W.B. and Greenberg, L.S. (2006) 'Building a meaning bridge: therapeutic progress from problem formulation to understanding', *Journal of Counselling Psychology*, 53(2), pp. 165–180. Available at: https://doi.org/10.1037/0022-0167.53.2.165

British Psychological Society (no date) *Working with a psychologist: understanding formulation* [Leaflet]. Available at: https://cms.bps.org.uk/sites/default/files/2022-07/Forumlation%20WEB%20ID3412.pdf (Accessed: 9 October 2024).

Challoner, H. and Papayianni, F. (2018) 'Evaluating the role of formulation in counselling psychology: a systematic literature review', *The European Journal of Counselling Psychology*, 7(1), pp. 47–68. Available at: https://doi.org/10.5964/ejcop.v7i1.146

Corrie, S. and Lane, D.A. (2010) *Constructing stories, telling tales: a guide to formulation in applied psychology*. London: Routledge. Available at: https://doi.org/10.4324/9780429473173

Cox, L.A. (2021) 'Use of individual formulation in mental health practice', *Mental Health Practice*, 24(1), pp. 33–41. Available at: https://doi.org/10.7748/mhp.2020.e1515

Dallos, R. and Stedmon, J. (2014) 'Systemic formulation: mapping the family dance', in L. Johnstone and R. Dallos (eds) *Formulation in psychology and psychotherapy*. 2nd edn. Hove: Routledge, pp. 67–95.

Dorling, D. (2014) 'Thinking about class', *Sociology*, 48(3), pp. 452–462. Available at: https://doi.org/10.1177/0038038514523171

Gazzillo, F., Dimaggio, G. and Curtis, J.T. (2021) 'Case formulation and treatment planning: how to take care of relationship and symptoms together', *Journal of Psychotherapy Integration*, 31(2), pp. 115–128. Available at: https://doi.org/10.1037/int0000185

Gillon, E. (2012) 'A response to Simms (2011): Case formulation within a person-centred framework: an uncomfortable fit?', *Counselling Psychology Review*, 27(1), pp. 73–76.

Hazan, C. and Shaver, P. (1987) 'Romantic love conceptualized as an attachment process', *Journal of Personality and Social Psychology*, 52(3), pp. 511–524. Available at: https://doi.org/10.1037/0022-3514.52.3.511

Health and Care Professions Council (2023) *Standards of proficiency for practitioner psychologists*. HCPC code 20230901POLPUB PYLSoP. Available at: https://www.hcpc-uk.org/globalassets/resources/standards/standards-of-proficiency—practitioner-psychologists.pdf (Accessed: 17 December 2024).

Hewison, D., Clulow, C. and Drake, H. (2014) *Couple therapy for depression: a clinician's guide to integrative practice*. Oxford: Oxford University Press. Available at: https://doi.org/10.1093/med:psych/9780199674145.001.0001

Hill, C.E. and Norcross, J.C. (eds) (2023) *Psychotherapy skills and methods that work*. Oxford: Oxford University Press. Available at: https://doi.org/10.1093/oso/9780197611012.001.0001

Holmes, J. (2001) *The search for the secure base: attachment theory and psychotherapy*. Hove: Routledge.

Johnstone, L. (2018) 'Psychological formulation as an alternative to psychiatric diagnosis', *Journal of Humanistic Psychology*, 58(1), pp. 30–46. Available at: https://doi.org/10.1177/0022167817722230

Johnstone, L. and Dallos, R. (eds) (2013) *Formulation in psychology and psychotherapy: making sense of people's problems*. 2nd edn. Hove: Taylor & Francis.

Lindegger, G. and Barry, T. (1999) 'Attachment as an integrating concept in couple and family therapy: some considerations with special reference to South Africa', *Contemporary Family Therapy*, 21(2), pp. 267–288. Available at: https://doi.org/10.1023/A:1021655727913

McEvoy, C., Clarke, V. and Thomas, Z. (2021) '"Rarely discussed but always present": exploring therapists' accounts of the relationship between social class, mental health and therapy', *Counselling and Psychotherapy Research*, 21(2), pp. 324–334. Available at: https://doi.org/10.1002/capr.12382

Moller, N. and Vossler, A. (2015) 'Defining infidelity in research and couple counseling: a qualitative study', *Journal of Sex and Marital Therapy*, 41(5), pp. 487–497. Available at: https://doi.org/10.1080/0092623X.2014.931314

Nkosi, B. and Daniels, P. (2007) 'Family strengths: South Africa', *Marriage & Family Review*, 41(1–2), pp. 11–26. Available at: https://doi.org/10.1300/J002v41n01_02

SCoPEd Framework (2022), collaboratively developed by Association of Christian Counsellors (ACC), British Association for Counselling and Psychotherapy (BACP), British Psychoanalytic Council (BPC), Human Givens Institute (HGI), National Counselling and Psychotherapy Society (NCPS) and United Kingdom Council for Psychotherapy (UKCP). Available at: https://www.bacp.co.uk/about-us/advancing-the-profession/scoped/scoped-framework (Accessed: 12 June 2024).

Simms, J. (2011) 'Case formulation within a person-centred framework: an uncomfortable fit?', *Counselling Psychology Review*, 26(2), pp. 24–36.

Simpson, J.A and Rholes, W.S. (2017) 'Adult attachment, stress, and romantic relationships', *Current Opinion in Psychology*, 13, pp. 19–24. Available at: https://doi.org/10.1016/j.copsyc.2016.04.006

Trudel, G. and Goldfarb, M.R. (2010) 'Marital and sexual functioning and dysfunctioning, depression and anxiety', *Sexologies*, 19(3), pp. 137–142. Available at: https://doi.org/10.1016/j.sexol.2009.12.009

Chapter 19

Thinking critically about counselling and psychotherapy

Hayley Ness and Naomi Moller

Contents

Introduction

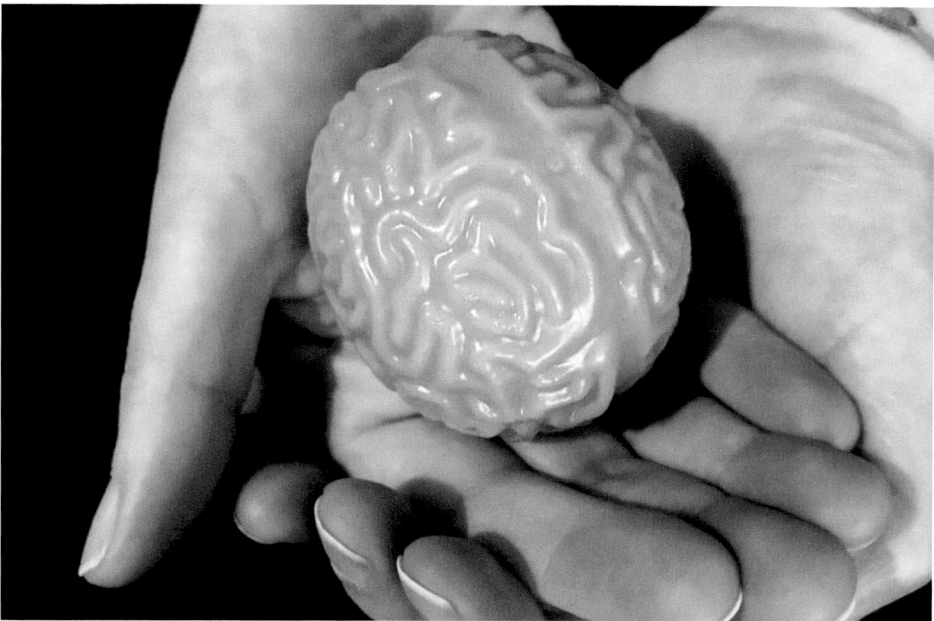

Protection by Karine Mather

This chapter asks you to reflect critically on your practice by introducing you to different concepts, research and perspectives. Of course, this chapter is not the first in this book to do this. What is different in this chapter, however, is the focus on further developing your ability to critically appraise as a counsellor or psychotherapist. In this context, what does it mean to think critically? It involves carefully examining ideas and arguments, systematically considering and evaluating (appraising) different perspectives, and testing the soundness of both the claims being made and the evidence being used to support those claims. It also involves effectively working with ideas, claims and arguments that you may disagree with or have a negative emotional reaction towards, and being open to assimilating new perspectives.

Of course, critical appraisal is harder when you feel emotionally invested in something; as you have chosen to train as a counsellor, it is likely you are emotionally invested in both the profession and your own role as a counsellor. This means that fostering a critical evaluation of what you were taught and your own thinking or beliefs about your own practice may be challenging and uncomfortable at times. However, having the ability to critically appraise how we work as counsellors can improve our ability to practice effectively, ethically and safely.

This chapter contributes towards achieving the **SCoPEd competency 4.2.B**:

Ability to critically appraise a range of theories underpinning the practice of counselling and psychotherapy.

(SCoPEd Framework, 2022, p. 26)

This chapter aims to:

- foster your ability to critically consider your own epistemic stances and how these relate to those of the counselling modalities in which you practice

- evaluate different approaches to evidencing the effectiveness of psychotherapy practice

- develop your appraisal of different theoretical understandings of the therapeutic relationship

- enable you to reflect on critiques of the counselling profession and the implications for practitioners.

I Epistemological foundations

How do individual counsellors and therapists know what they know about counselling and psychotherapy? Chapters 13 and 15 of this book outlined how ontology (the study of the nature of being) and epistemology (the study of ways of knowing) are relevant to the process of reflecting on different assumptions and approaches to research. But how does epistemology relate to counselling theory and your own practice?

Different epistemological stances underlie different counselling theories, as suggested in Table 19.1. Note that this table is just *one* attempt to sort counselling approaches into epistemological categories, as will be explained later in this section.

Table 19.1 Epistemology underlying different counselling theories

Epistemology	Description	Example aligned theory (modality)
Empiricism (also termed positivism or rationalism)	Emphasises the role of observable evidence and experience in acquiring knowledge	Implicit in both cognitive behavioural therapy (CBT) and behavioural therapy. CBT is grounded in empirical research and focuses on observable behaviours and cognitive processes. Behavioural therapy emphasises observable behaviour and learning principles.

Epistemology	Description	Example aligned theory (modality)
Constructivism	Positions knowledge as constructed by individuals based on their experiences, beliefs and interpretations	Narrative therapy explores clients' constructed narratives and meaning-making processes. Solution-focused brief therapy focuses on clients' unique perspectives and strengths, and uses clients' experiences, beliefs and interpretations to identify pathways to making positive changes.
Pragmatism	Emphasises practical utility and problem solving; 'truth' is simply what works in practice	Eclectic approaches draw on multiple theories to address clients' needs effectively. Integrative approaches guide the integration of diverse techniques. Pluralistic counselling is also pragmatic.
Critical realism	Acknowledges that reality exists independently of our perception, but that our understanding is limited and socially constructed	Feminist therapy seeks to challenge the influence of gender-based oppression and discrimination on clients' lives. Psychodynamic psychotherapy acknowledges both a dynamic unconscious and social influences.
Relativism	Holds that knowledge is context-dependent and varies across cultures and perspectives, rejecting the idea of essential 'truths'	Postmodern counselling approaches focus on deconstructing dominant narratives. Family systems therapy considers the multiple viewpoints of family members and how relational context creates different 'truths'.

Researchers and theoreticians differ in how they have categorised epistemic stances (e.g. Royce and Powell, 1983; see also Wilkinson, Shank and Hanna, 2019). As an example, Hauser (2024) makes the argument that person-centred therapy aligns more with a critical realist epistemology than the interpretive-phenomenological epistemology suggested by other theoreticians. However, how the approaches are 'best' sorted is not important here. What is important is the recognition that different therapeutic approaches are embedded in very different epistemologies. Understanding this is a crucial first step in being able to critically appraise counselling theory. It facilitates an understanding of critiques of psychotherapy approaches – such as Dalal's (2018) book-length critique of the empiricist epistemology of CBT, or Renger's (2023) exploration of whether it is appropriate for counsellors who practice non-directive person-centred counselling to ask direct questions of clients.

Moreover, while it is important to recognise that different therapeutic approaches are embedded in very different epistemologies, it is equally as important to understand your own *personal* epistemologies (both how you understand knowledge and the nature of being), which may or may not be in alignment with the epistemology of your counselling approach. Over the past 30 years or so, there has been a growing interest in how a counsellor's philosophy links to their practice. For instance, Lyddon (1989) noted early on that a counsellor's epistemological stance appeared to be linked to their preferences for working with particular approaches. This link has since been investigated by later researchers. Arthur (2000), for example, found not only that individual epistemic stances existed, but also that they appeared to be related to different counselling approaches; cognitive-behavioural counsellors, for instance, appeared to prefer thinking over feeling, relying on reason and logic to reduce emotional input, which relates to an empiricist stance. Lee, Neimeyer and Rice (2013) similarly found a relationship between epistemic stance, the style that a counsellor adopts, the relationship they build with their clients and the types of intervention they use.

The cited research suggests that a counsellor's personal epistemic stance has a strong influence on how they practice. But what happens if this epistemology does not align with the epistemology of their counselling approach? This has the potential make a counsellor less confident in how they work. Alternatively, they may be more likely to bring in other ways of working. While this might not be problematic – eclecticism and integrative approaches are recognised schools of psychotherapy, after all – there is also quite a bit of research that suggests that 'adhering' to one's taught model is associated with better outcomes for clients (Power *et al.*, 2022). This all suggests that it is important to consider the epistemology inherent in your approach to practice *and* your own epistemological understandings, as well as any points of tension between the two.

2 Appraising theories: understanding what works

There is a myriad of different counselling approaches and frameworks in the UK (Allen, 2024). Barth and Moody (2019) found that, in the United States, cognitive behavioural, person-centred, strengths-based and solution-focused approaches to counselling were the most influential. However, results from a survey of UK-trained counsellors could reveal different influences; what is your guess as to which approach is most influential in the UK? Given the plethora of counselling approaches, each with its own theoretical grounding, how can one decide which is the 'best' one to train in and practise? Moreover, how can each practitioner (including yourself) both justify their own approach and evidence why the underlying theoretical approach works with clients? One way is to consider evidence that it 'works'.

The chapters in Part 4 of this textbook discussed the notion of evidence-based practice (EBP), and the various approaches and debates around it. Chapter 14 explored how quantitative research methods can be used to test what therapy works best for which condition, or whether and how some interventions and processes of therapy work in given contexts. As the Part 4 chapters emphasised, there is no absolute consensus on how to investigate the efficacy of different types of therapy due to the many complexities involved (e.g. Norcross and Lambert, 2019a). Nonetheless, solid evidence has come from randomised controlled trials and pragmatic trials – so let's look at what this suggests.

First, there is a great deal of research evidence showing that counselling and psychotherapy is – in general – effective, and second, that the difference in effectiveness between the various schools of therapy are negligible (Barkham and Lambert, 2021). This might suggest that counsellors do not need to be overly concerned with what the research says about their particular counselling approach. Yet, while it seems that 'the facts are friendly' (to quote the title of Mick Cooper's 2008 book on counselling research findings), critical appraisal of counselling theories in general, and of one's own approach in particular, is nonetheless important.

For example, consider the following evidence:

- If you are a non-CBT therapist, you might want to consider that a great deal of research suggests that when there *are* differences between types of therapy in terms of effectiveness, they tend to favour those that are CBT-aligned (Barkham and Lambert, 2021).

- Two rigorously conducted UK studies examined the efficacy of person-centred therapy. The first examined outcomes of CBT and person-centred experiential therapy within NHS primary care; it was found that while the two approaches were equal at six months, outcomes after therapy were better for CBT at one year (Barkham *et al.*, 2021). The second compared humanistic counselling provided within schools to usual pastoral care. This study found that, overall, counselling was not cost-effective; in other words, there was not enough change in psychological distress levels to warrant the cost (Cooper *et al.*, 2021).

- A meta-analysis that examined outcomes for humanistic-experiential (including person-centred) therapies versus CBT therapies also found a clear advantage for CBT (Elliott *et al.*, 2021). However, the authors suggested that their findings might be due to researcher allegiance (i.e. researcher bias, defined in Chapter 13, Section 1.1).

Honing the ability to critically appraise the evidence base for your own therapy approach thus requires fostering the ability to critically appraise the research designs and methods used to demonstrate the effectiveness of different therapeutic approaches. As emphasised throughout Chapter 14, it also requires considering the evidence base not just for a particular counselling approach in general, but also whether the approach works for a particular type of client with a particular problem in a particular context.

2.1 Considering critiques of evidence-based practice

So far, this section has focused on critically evaluating one's own counselling approach by considering and critically appraising the research evidence. However, there are a number of UK practitioners who express considerable reservations about adopting an evidence-based approach to counselling (Lilienfeld *et al.*, 2013; see also Dalal, 2018, as an example of this). When asked what they draw on in order to practise, counsellors and psychotherapists rarely mention research evidence and often mention their clinical intuition (Lucock, Hall and Noble, 2006). Arguments against EBP on the grounds of holding a different epistemological stance still demonstrate critical appraisal of counselling theories; though counsellors sometimes reject EBP in a less thoughtful or valid way.

Lilienfeld *et al.* (2013) suggest a number of reasons counsellors may resist EBP. First, training courses may not have highlighted the importance of research evidence, instead favouring clinical judgement, intuition and experience in the room over the critical evaluation of the research evidence base. Second, practitioners can become used to a specific way of working within a particular approach, and changing that is very challenging. As an example, the authors, citing a 2005 Fisher and Wells paper, state that 'clinicians who have been using psychoanalytic therapy for decades to treat obsessive-compulsive disorder (OCD) may be understandably reluctant to embrace research evidence that exposure and response prevention … is the empirically demonstrated intervention of choice for this condition' (Lilienfeld *et al.*, 2013, pp. 886–887). If both the therapist and client see improvement, then why would they adopt a different approach?

Nonetheless, the focus of this chapter is on the need to critically challenge one's way of working. In this vein, it is important to evaluate the idea that clinical intuition is enough. This is a pretty common argument made by counsellors: that they can best judge whether they are effective (i.e. whether their clients are getting better). And really, so the argument goes, if a client has made meaning, understood their experiences and subjectively feels 'better', does it matter if a 'less evidenced' therapeutic approach has been used?

The issue is that our clinical judgements and decisions can be prone to error. Lilienfeld *et al.* (2014, p. 357) highlight four errors that counsellors tend to make: 'naive realism', 'confirmation bias', 'illusory causation' and 'illusion of control'. Essentially, even though we think that we can view client change and the effectiveness of counselling models objectively, years of psychological research has demonstrated that we tend to assume that how we see things is how they are (naive realism); we favour the information that already fits our way of thinking (confirmation bias); we attribute cause and effect where there isn't any (illusory causation); and we are less aware of these cognitive processes than we think we are (illusion of control). Consider this further by reading Box 19.1.

Box 19.1 Research findings on trusting clinical intuition

Consider the findings related to the following two questions.

Can counsellors judge when clients are 'off-track'?

You might think that you mostly know how your clients are experiencing counselling, and whether they are – broadly – doing better or worse. However, as discussed in Chapter 12 on the use of routine outcome monitoring (ROM) in counselling, research strongly suggests that using ROM improves counselling outcomes, in particular for clients who are getting worse (de Jong *et al.*, 2021).

The reason that ROM helps is because it gives counsellors additional and independent information from clients, and because counsellors may not always have an understanding of their client's current state(s).

The evidence for using ROM is strong. However, in the spirit of critical appraisal, it is important to also note that research that asks clients how they experience ROM suggests that it can be experienced negatively and can sometimes hinder the therapy process (Solstad, Castonguay and Moltu, 2019).

Are counsellors good at judging their overall effectiveness?

There is long-standing research which indicates that therapists tend to overestimate how good they are. One oft-cited study found that 91.6 per cent saw themselves as being in the top 25 per cent of the 129 mental health professionals who participated, while all of the survey respondents saw themselves as in the top 50 per cent of all practitioners (Walfish *et al.*, 2012). While an overinflated view of one's own professional competence is typical in other professions (Dunning, Heath and Suls, 2004), it is just not statistically possible that no therapists are in the worst 25 per cent – or even just average.

More recent research systematically compared the effectiveness of practitioners (as measured by the outcomes of their clients) against their own ratings of their effectiveness in each domain. The authors found that 'therapists were no better than chance at predicting their measurement-based effectiveness classification' (Constantino *et al.*, 2023, p. 474). In general, this study, as well as research by Nissen-Lie *et al.* (2017), suggests that underestimating your own capacity as a counsellor is associated with being a better counsellor, while being overly confident is associated with worse client outcomes.

Pause for thought 19.2

Take a moment to consider how much you trust your own clinical intuition. Do you think the findings outlined in Box 19.1 have helped you to develop appropriate scepticism about your intuition?

This section has considered two sources of 'evidence' that counsellors can draw on to judge whether a counselling approach works: research and clinical intuition. It has also emphasised the importance of fostering critical appraisal skills when considering both. Other ways of evaluating your work with clients can include case discussions in supervision or peer supervision, in addition to reading theoretical and research papers from your own approach as well as others. In all of these contexts, the aim should be to remain open to understandings that potentially challenge one's own thinking and assumptions.

3 Appraising theories of the therapeutic relationship

I appear by Katie Maxsted

Thinking critically about whether our approach 'works' matters, but it is also important to think critically about *how* it works – to review our core beliefs about what good therapeutic work involves. As highlighted throughout this book, counselling theory acknowledges the therapeutic relationship as a critical ingredient in effective counselling (Table 19.2 expands on this). There is extensive empirical research showing that the therapeutic relationship has a 'substantial and consistent' impact on whether clients improve in counselling (Norcross and Lambert, 2019b, p. 631). Moreover, counsellors consider relational skills to be vitally important. This was demonstrated by a survey of US mental health counsellors, which found that the most commonly used counselling skills, regardless of theoretical approach, were: empathy, providing general encouragement, promoting self-care, being genuine and demonstrating unconditional positive regard (Barth and Moody, 2019). These skills can all be thought of as contributing to the formation of a strong therapeutic relationship.

The therapeutic relationship is conceptualised differently by different theoreticians, but it is often understood to include the therapeutic alliance, which itself is conceptualised to include the development of an emotional bond between counsellor and client, as well as an agreement on both the tasks and goals of counselling (Bordin, 1979). The therapeutic alliance is understood as being independent of any counselling approach, but the different schools of therapy understand and enact the therapeutic relationship differently, as summarised in Table 19.2.

Table 19.2 Theorising the therapeutic relationship in different counselling approaches

Counselling approach	Therapeutic relationship
CBT	The therapeutic relationship focuses on building a strong collaborative working relationship between the therapist and client in order to achieve behavioural and cognitive changes. The tasks involve setting shared treatment goals, building shared understandings and fostering agreement on tasks and strategies.
Psychodynamic	The therapeutic relationship is the vehicle for change in psychodynamic psychotherapy. Practitioners work with the transference of the client and pay attention to their own countertransference in order to gain insight into their client's inner world. Traditionally, psychoanalytic psychotherapists are relationally reserved, which creates space for client transference.
Person-centred	For Rogers (1957, p. 95), the 'necessary and sufficient' conditions of the therapeutic relationship are all that is necessary for a client to achieve a good outcome. The conditions include therapist expression of congruence, empathy and unconditional positive regard, which must be genuinely received by the client.

Although this table provides a simplified sketch, it illustrates that counsellors trained in different traditions will typically approach how they should 'do', or enact in practice, the therapeutic relationship quite differently. To help you think about this, compare the idea of a more 'neutral' therapeutic stance with one that provides unconditional positive regard.

Unconditional positive regard (UPR) is, of course, a core concept in person-centred counselling. Rogers (1957, p. 98) wrote that it involves 'warm acceptance of each aspect of the client's experience', no placement of 'conditions of acceptance' on the client, and a 'prizing' of and caring for the client. Theoretically, Rogers saw UPR as an essential ingredient for client growth in counselling, something that allows clients to move past the conditions of worth they internalised in childhood as a result of receiving love that was conditional, towards a radical self-acceptance and self-actualisation.

The neutral therapeutic stance has its roots in Freud's notion of the psychotherapist as a blank screen on to which a client projects their transferences. However, the 'relational turn' in psychodynamic psychotherapy led to an increasing emphasis on the relational dimension of therapy; few practitioners today see themselves as blank screens. Pugh and Polnay (2023) describe the contemporary analytic attitude as encompassing neutrality, anonymity and restraint, involving a non-judgemental open curiosity to all possibilities for a client, and an attempt to be unobtrusive in the therapeutic space in order to leave maximum room for the client. The authors also note that this approach does not mean being cool and aloof or not expressing empathy.

The following case example suggests how these alternative approaches may work in practice.

Case example: Dale's experience of the therapeutic relationship

Dale is a middle-aged man who seeks therapy for low mood. He approaches Sam, a counsellor who uses unconditional positive regard.

The therapeutic relationship with Sam: providing UPR

As Sam believes in UPR, he tries to always show Dale complete support and acceptance, no matter what he is talking about. Sam's UPR helps to create a safe space for Dale. It validates Dale's intrinsic worth and encourages self-acceptance as he talks about his struggles with low mood and his marriage. However, when Dale starts talking in depth about his behaviours as a young man, including criminality and violence, a past that he now feels deeply ashamed by, he finds Sam's expressions of UPR uncomfortable and – ultimately – unbelievable. He abruptly stops counselling with Sam and asks for a new therapist; the service assigns him to Maria, a psychotherapist who uses a neutral stance.

The therapeutic relationship with Maria: taking a neutral stance

For Maria, active expression of UPR is not part of her approach. Maria aims to remain impartial and non-judgmental during sessions. This allows Dale to express himself freely and to talk about his past without the positive feedback that he experienced as jarring from Sam. However, when Dale begins to talk about his experiences of trauma, which pre-dated his criminal and violent behaviour, he finds himself missing Sam's open expression of empathy and UPR, and he experiences Maria's neutrality as cold and frightening. After the session he decides that counselling is just not for him.

The comparison between Maria and Sam expresses extremes; of course, actual counselling relationships are a lot more nuanced. However, hopefully this case has illustrated that the question of the 'right' therapeutic stance is complex and will depend on the specific client and their reason for seeking help. It also depends on the specific counsellor, what is happening in the counselling room at that time, and perhaps the counsellor's ability to catch and respond to a client's ambivalence about the therapeutic relationship.

The discussion up to this point has focused on enacting the therapeutic relationship based on specific psychotherapy approaches. However, as mentioned in Chapter 11, the wider non-counselling literature on relationships is extensive and clearly documents that good relationships are critical to human physical and emotional well-being. This literature broadly supports the idea that the relationship that happens in the counselling room is intrinsically therapeutic (as long as it is 'good'). However, in the view of the authors of this chapter, counselling theory has, with the notable exception of attachment theory and research, largely failed to explore or even acknowledge this broader empirical and theoretical literature on relationships.

While the field of psychotherapy is not alone in being siloed from the rest of psychology, it is important to consider whether this wider literature could suggest anything about, for example, the 'best' stance in a therapeutic relationship. As just one example, a meta-analysis examined whether communication between couples in established relationships predicted later relationship quality and likelihood of relationship breakdown, and found that communication marked by warmth, support, fondness and positive affect was associated with better outcomes for couples (Kanter *et al.*, 2022). Does this kind of research suggest the value of UPR? A core psychotherapy research handbook (now in its third edition), which examines the research evidence related to the therapeutic relationship, concluded that positive acceptance of clients was a definitively 'effective' element of the therapeutic relationship (Norcross and Lambert, 2019a). This conclusion was based on a meta-analysis that examined psychotherapy outcome and positive regard. The authors of the analysis state that 'there is virtually no research-driven reason to withhold positive regard' (Farber, Suzuki and Lynch, 2018, p. 419). The authors also note that a counsellor feeling emotionally warm towards a client is not enough; effort needs to be made so that the client feels this warmth yet is not overwhelmed by it, for example, by receiving 'a stream of compliments' (p. 420).

One last thought on the therapeutic relationship: research on computerised therapeutic self-help programmes and platforms shows that clients develop a therapeutic relationship even in the absence of there being an actual human therapist involved, and also that the quality of this relationship predicts aspects of the intervention outcome (Clarke *et al.*, 2016). Does this finding suggest that, in the future, AI counsellors may be able to replace human counsellors and build robust therapeutic relationships?

Pause for thought 19.3

Having read through this section, reflect on the process of developing a relationship with your clients. What is your epistemic stance on relationship building? Have you uncritically aligned with a particular theoretical approach (practising only UPR or taking a neutral stance, for example) or have you drawn on different theoretical perspectives? Have you drawn on theories and research from outside counselling, such as attachment theory? And does any of this theory or research help you justify more contested aspects of conduct in the therapeutic relationship, such as how and when you self-disclose or whether you will hug a client?

4 Appraising the profession

So far, this chapter has focused on thinking critically about the epistemology of different counselling approaches, how the effectiveness of counselling should be evaluated and the implications of different ways of conceptualising (and working within) the therapeutic relationship. In this section the critical lens is turned on the counselling profession itself.

This book began with four chapters on diversity (Part 1). This is because the editors agreed that a major issue in contemporary counselling practice is a failure to properly consider how social contexts – particularly systemic discrimination and oppression – create psychological distress and shape the lives of clients. In other words, the approach to this book has been heavily influenced by the authors' own critical appraisal of the counselling profession (which you may dispute). In keeping with this, and as a final thought for this chapter, it is worth considering the following idea: that it is important to critically approach the counselling profession itself, not just the theories and research that inform it.

As one example of critical appraisal of the profession, consider this: in some significant ways, the counselling workforce is not representative of the population that it serves. The demographic of BACP counsellors in 2022–2023 was:

- 87 per cent white
- 64 per cent aged between 45 and 65 years old (with 27 per cent aged 45–54, and 37 per cent 55–64) (BACP, 2023).

This compares to 83 per cent white, and 31 per cent in the 45–64 age bracket, in the UK population (BACP compared their data to the results of the 2021 census conducted by the Office of National Statistics; BACP, 2023). Further, 81 per cent of BACP counsellors self-identified as women, compared to 51 per cent in the UK population. BACP counsellors were also less likely than the general population to report that they are disabled and – interestingly – heterosexual. Given how much money, time and emotion one must invest in counselling training, there are important critical questions to be asked about: (a) whether the current workforce is adequate to deliver good outcomes for all clients, in particular marginalised clients; and (b) whether there is a role for activism by counsellors to challenge professional bodies and local, national and NHS counselling funders to do more to actively foster a diverse workforce and to reduce barriers to training.

This criticism of the counselling profession builds on a long history of critiques of mental health systems and of the psychiatry and counselling professions; see, for example, Foucault's *Madness and Civilization* (2003), which was first published in English in 1964, or Kitzinger and Perkins' *Changing Our Minds: Lesbian Feminism and Psychology* (1993). The critiques in this literature are complex and manifold, but a notable argument is that practitioners cause harm through their narrow focus on the individual client. This places undue responsibility on the client for the cause of their distress – even when it is created by the broader social context, such as social tolerance of racism (Prilleltensky, Prilleltensky and Voorhees, 2009). In this view, counselling works to uphold the social status quo by soothing individual distress and thus effectively repressing both social protest and social change and justice.

It can be difficult to consider that one's practice may be part of a system of social control. But this chapter argues for a first step towards preventing this: being open to critical appraisals of the profession.

Pause for thought 19.4

What are your responses to the idea of critiquing the counselling profession in general and to the particular critiques presented in this section? Take a moment to reflect on how *you* might start to critique the profession.

Conclusion

This chapter has emphasised the importance of critically appraising the theories and evidence base you draw on in your practice. It has sought to illustrate how to do this through a focus on epistemology and understanding how to judge whether counselling works, ideas about the 'right' way to enact the therapeutic relationship and critiques of the counselling profession. In doing so, this chapter has built on the invitation implicit in all of the other chapters in this book: to foster your critical thinking.

Further reading

- The following book is an excellent resource to support the development of critical appraisal of counselling theory in terms of race:

  Charura, D. and Lago, C. (eds) (2021) *Black identities + white therapies: race, respect + diversity.* Monmouth: PCCS Books.

- The following book makes an argument against psychotherapy and the theorised mechanisms by which it works:

  Smail, D. (2018) *Taking care: an alternative to therapy.* London: Routledge.

- The following paper argues that although psychotherapy can be critiqued, it is still a valuable practice:

  Brown, L.S. (1992) 'While waiting for the revolution: the case for a lesbian feminist psychotherapy', *Feminism & Psychology*, 2(2), pp. 239–253. Available at: https://doi.org/10.1177/095935359222012

References

Allen, L.R. (2024) *The ultimate list of counseling theories, lens, and treatments.* Available at: https://www.lukeallenphd.com/comprehensive-list-of-counseling-theories (Accessed: 30 April 2024).

Arthur, A.R. (2000) 'The personality and cognitive-epistemological traits of cognitive-behavioural and psychoanalytic psychotherapists', *British Journal of Medical Psychology*, 73(2), pp. 243–257. Available at: https://doi.org/10.1348/000711200160453

BACP (2023) *2022–2023 workforce mapping survey.* Available at: https://www.bacp.co.uk/media/20017/bacp-workforce-mapping-survey-report-2022-to-2023.pdf (Accessed: 18 December 2024).

Barkham, M. and Lambert, M.J. (2021) 'The efficacy and effectiveness of psychological therapies', in M. Barkham, W. Lutz and L.G. Castonguay (eds) *Bergin and Garfield's handbook of psychotherapy and behavior change.* 7th edn. Hoboken, NJ: John Wiley & Sons, pp. 135–189.

Barkham, M., Saxon, D., Hardy, G.E., Bradburn, M., Galloway, D., Wickramasekera, N., Keetharuth, A.D., Bower, P., King, M., Elliott, R., Gabriel, L., Kellett, S., Shaw, S., Wilkinson, T., Connell, J., Harrison, P., Ardern, K., Bishop-Edwards, L., Ashley, K., Ohlsen, S., Pilling, S., Waller, G. and Brazier, J.E. (2021) 'Person-centred experiential therapy versus cognitive behavioural therapy delivered in the English Improving Access to Psychological Therapies service for the treatment of moderate or severe depression (PRaCTICED): a pragmatic, randomised, non-inferiority trial', *The Lancet Psychiatry*, 8(6), pp. 487–499. Available at: https://doi.org/10.1016/S2215-0366(21)00083-3

Barth, A.L. and Moody, S.J. (2019) 'Theory use in counseling practice: current trends', *International Journal for the Advancement of Counselling*, 41(3), pp. 313–328. Available at: https://doi.org/10.1007/s10447-018-9352-0

Bordin, E.S. (1979) 'The generalizability of the psychoanalytic concept of the working alliance', *Psychotherapy: Theory, Research & Practice*, 16(3), pp. 252–260. Available at: https://doi.org/10.1037/h0085885

Clarke, J., Proudfoot, J., Whitton, A., Birch, M.-R., Boyd, M., Parker, G., Manicavasagar, V., Hadzi-Pavlovic, D. and Fogarty, A. (2016) 'Therapeutic alliance with a fully automated mobile phone and web-based intervention: secondary analysis of a randomized controlled trial', *JMIR Mental Health*, 3(1), article number e10. Available at: https://doi.org/10.2196/mental.4656

Constantino, M.J., Boswell, J.F., Coyne, A.E., Muir, H.J., Gaines, A.N. and Kraus, D.R. (2023) 'Therapist perceptions of their own measurement-based, problem-specific effectiveness', *Journal of Consulting and Clinical Psychology*, 91(8), pp. 474–484. Available at: https://doi.org/10.1037/ccp0000813

Cooper, M. (2008) *Essential research findings in counselling and psychotherapy: the facts are friendly.* London: SAGE Publications.

Cooper, M., Stafford, M.R., Saxon, D., Beecham, J., Bonin, E.-M., Barkham, M., Bower, P., Cromarty, K., Duncan, C., Pearce, P., Rameswari, T. and Ryan, G. (2021) 'Humanistic counselling plus pastoral care as usual versus pastoral care as usual for the treatment of psychological distress in adolescents in UK state schools (ETHOS): a randomised controlled trial', *The Lancet Child & Adolescent Health*, 5(3), pp. 178–189. Available at: https://doi.org/10.1016/S2352-4642(20)30363-1

Cushman, P. (1996) *Constructing the self, constructing America: a cultural history of psychotherapy.* Reading, MA: Addison-Wesley.

Dalal, F. (2018) *CBT: the cognitive behavioural tsunami. Managerialism, politics and the corruptions of science.* Abingdon: Routledge.

de Jong, K., Conijn, J.M., Gallagher, R.A.V., Reshetnikova, A.S., Heij, M. and Lutz, M.C. (2021) 'Using progress feedback to improve outcomes and reduce drop-out, treatment duration, and deterioration: a multilevel meta-analysis', *Clinical Psychology Review*, 85, article number 102002. Available at: https://doi.org/10.1016/j.cpr.2021.102002

Dunning, D., Heath, C. and Suls, J.M. (2004) 'Flawed self-assessment: implications for health, education, and the workplace', *Psychological Science in the Public Interest*, 5(3), pp. 69–106. Available at: https://doi.org/10.1111/j.1529-1006.2004.00018.x

Elliott, R., Watson, J., Timulak, L. and Sharbanee, J. (2021) 'Research on humanistic-experiential psychotherapies: updated review', in M. Barkham, W. Lutz and L.G. Castonguay (eds) *Bergin and Garfield's handbook of psychotherapy and behavior change.* 7th edn. Hoboken, NJ: John Wiley & Sons, pp. 421–467.

Farber, B.A., Suzuki, J.Y. and Lynch, D.A. (2018) 'Positive regard and psychotherapy outcome: a meta-analytic review', *Psychotherapy*, 55(4), pp. 411–423. Available at: https://doi.org/10.1037/pst0000171

Foucault, M. (2003) *Madness and civilization: a history of insanity in the age of reason.* London: Routledge.

Hauser, H.J.S. (2024) 'More than my experience: an argument for critical realism in person-centred psychotherapy', *Person-Centered & Experiential Psychotherapies*, 23 (4), pp. 531–548. Available at: https://doi.org/10.1080/14779757.2023.2295528

Kanter, J.B., Lavner, J.A., Lannin, D.G., Hilgard, J. and Monk, J.K. (2022) 'Does couple communication predict later relationship quality and dissolution? A meta-analysis', *Journal of Marriage and Family*, 84(2), pp. 533–551. Available at: https://doi.org/10.1111/jomf.12804

Kitzinger, C. and Perkins, R. (1993) *Changing our minds: lesbian feminism and psychology.* New York, NY: NYU Press.

Lee, J.A., Neimeyer, G.J. and Rice, K.G. (2013) 'The relationship between therapist epistemology, therapy style, working alliance, and interventions use', *American Journal of Psychotherapy*, 67(4), pp. 323–345. Available at: https://doi.org/10.1176/appi.psychotherapy.2013.67.4.323

Lilienfeld, S.O., Ritschel, L.A., Lynn, S.J., Cautin, R.L. and Latzman, R.D. (2013) 'Why many clinical psychologists are resistant to evidence-based practice: root causes and constructive remedies', *Clinical Psychology Review*, 33(7), pp. 883–900. Available at: https://doi.org/10.1016/j.cpr.2012.09.008

Lilienfeld, S.O., Ritschel, L.A., Lynn, S.J., Cautin, R.L. and Latzman, R.D. (2014) 'Why ineffective psychotherapies appear to work: a taxonomy of causes of spurious therapeutic effectiveness', *Perspectives on Psychological Science*, 9(4), pp. 355–387. Available at: https://doi.org/10.1177/1745691614535216

Lucock, M.P., Hall, P. and Noble, R. (2006) 'A survey of influences on the practice of psychotherapists and clinical psychologists in training in the UK', *Clinical Psychology & Psychotherapy*, 13(2), pp. 123–130. Available at: https://doi.org/10.1002/cpp.483

Lyddon, W.J. (1989) 'Personal epistemology and preference for counseling', *Journal of Counseling Psychology*, 36, pp. 423–429. Available at: https://doi.org/10.1037/0022-0167.36.4.423

Nissen-Lie, H.A., Rønnestad, M.H., Høglend, P.A., Havik, O.E., Solbakken, O.A., Stiles, T.C. and Monsen, J.T. (2017) 'Love yourself as a person, doubt yourself as a therapist?', *Clinical Psychology & Psychotherapy*, 24(1), pp. 48–60. Available at: https://doi.org/10.1002/cpp.1977

Norcross, J.C. and Lambert, M.J. (eds) (2019a) *Psychotherapy relationships that work. Volume 1: evidence-based therapist contributions.* 3rd edn. New York, NY: Oxford University Press.

Norcross, J.C. and Lambert, M.J. (2019b) 'What works in the psychotherapy relationship: results, conclusions, and practices', in J.C. Norcross and M.J. Lambert (2019) *Psychotherapy relationships that work. Volume 1: evidence-based therapist contributions.* 3rd edn. New York, NY: Oxford University Press, pp. 631–646.

Power, N., Noble, L.A., Simmonds-Buckley, M., Kellett, S., Stockton, C., Firth, N. and Delgadillo, J. (2022) 'Associations between treatment adherence–competence–integrity (ACI) and adult psychotherapy outcomes: a systematic review and meta-analysis', *Journal of Consulting and Clinical Psychology*, 90(5), pp. 427–445. Available at: https://doi.org/10.1037/ccp0000736

Prilleltensky, I., Prilleltensky, O. and Voorhees, C. (2009) 'Psychopolitical validity in counselling and therapy', in D. Fox, I. Prilleltensky and S. Austin (eds) *Critical psychology: an introduction.* 2nd edn. London: SAGE Publications, pp. 355–372.

Pugh, R. and Polnay, A. (2023) 'Psychodynamic psychotherapy technique', in A. Polnay, R. Pugh, V. Barker, D. Bell, A. Beveridge, A. Burley, A. Lumsden, C.S. Mizen and L. Wilson (eds) *Cambridge guide to psychodynamic psychotherapy.* Cambridge: Cambridge University Press, pp. 98–127. Available at: https://doi.org/10.1017/9781009104425

Renger, S. (2023) 'Therapists' views on the use of questions in person-centred therapy', *British Journal of Guidance & Counselling*, 51(2), pp. 238–250. Available at: https://doi.org/10.1080/03069885.2021.1900536

Rogers, C.R. (1957) 'The necessary and sufficient conditions of therapeutic personality change', *Journal of Consulting Psychology*, 21(2), pp. 95–103. Available at: https://doi.org/10.1037/h0045357

Royce, J.R. and Powell, A. (1983) *Theory of personality and individual differences: factors, systems, and processes.* Englewood Cliffs, NJ: Prentice-Hall.

SCoPEd Framework (2022), collaboratively developed by Association of Christian Counsellors (ACC), British Association for Counselling and Psychotherapy (BACP), British Psychoanalytic Council (BPC), Human Givens Institute (HGI), National Counselling and Psychotherapy Society (NCPS) and United Kingdom Council for Psychotherapy (UKCP). Available at: https://www.bacp.co.uk/about-us/advancing-the-profession/scoped/scoped-framework (Accessed: 12 June 2024).

Solstad, S.M., Castonguay, L.G. and Moltu, C. (2019) 'Patients' experiences with routine outcome monitoring and clinical feedback systems: a systematic review and synthesis of qualitative empirical literature', *Psychotherapy Research*, 29(2), pp. 157–170. Available at: https://doi.org/10.1080/10503307.2017.1326645

Walfish, S., McAlister, B., O'Donnell, P. and Lambert, M.J. (2012) 'An investigation of self-assessment bias in mental health providers', *Psychological Reports*, 110(2), pp. 639–644. Available at: https://doi.org/10.2466/02.07.17.PR0.110.2.639-644

Wilkinson, B.D., Shank, G. and Hanna, F. (2019). 'Epistemological issues in counselor preparation: an examination of constructivist and phenomenological assumptions', *Journal of Counselor Preparation and Supervision*, 12(4), article number 13. Available at: https://digitalcommons.sacredheart.edu/jcps/vol12/iss4/13 (Accessed: 25 January 2025).

Chapter 20

Adapting your way of working for individual clients

Kate Smith

Contents

Introduction

Uncertainty Ahead by Amanda Good

Adapting your practice to fit individual clients is important in counselling and psychotherapy (and mental health care more broadly) because of its potential to improve client experience, outcomes and engagement (Bennett and Shafran, 2023). Conversely, research on the harmful effects of psychotherapy suggests that, as practitioners, we sometimes fail to adapt when clients are not progressing in counselling, and in fact may react to therapeutic impasses by continuing practices or approaches that are not working (Castonguay *et al.*, 2010).

Adaptations – the ways counsellors adapt how they work – occur in different ways in different contexts (Cuijpers *et al.*, 2016). They reflect that both the content of counselling and psychotherapy and the means of delivering it can be changed to enhance the client experience (e.g. Arundell *et al.*, 2021). If a counsellor is failing to adapt the way they work with different clients, this could be due to of a lack of confidence or ability to adapt, a rigid adherence to particular models and ways of working, or simply a lack of recognition of the client experience. However, even if an individual counsellor is limited in terms of what they can offer within their theoretical model, practice training and scope of practice, we can still be open to the many ways that counselling can be undertaken and when adaptation might occur.

Adaptation of counselling in practice must also be seen in the context of the ethical requirement to offer and undertake counselling and psychotherapy which does not systematically exclude any members of society. Unfortunately, the field of counselling and psychotherapy faces significant challenges in regards to the equity of services. Part 1 of this book outlined the importance of being responsive to clients' diverse experiences and encouraged adaptation of ways of working to accommodate cultural differences. The focus in this chapter is broader, looking at adaptation for multiple reasons, as outlined in the chapter aims below.

To exemplify the processes of adaptation in counselling, this chapter draws on the case example of Effia, who comes to counselling for help with a number of different issues.

This chapter contributes towards achieving the **SCoPEd competency 4.7.B**:

Ability to demonstrate the capacity, knowledge and understanding of how to select and adapt interventions and (or) approaches to respond to the needs of the client or patient.

(SCoPEd Framework, 2022, p. 27)

This chapter aims to:

- highlight the need for adaptation in practice
- identify aspects of therapeutic practice which can be adapted to work with individual clients
- provide guidance on when and how adaptation can be undertaken
- encourage you to scope your own practice and identify developments which will help you become more adaptive in your work.

1 Adaptation: what is it and why is it important?

> **Pause for thought 20.1**
>
> Before reading on, consider the times you have adapted or changed what you have done in counselling in response to client context, presentation or identity. Holding these examples in mind, can you identify any possible goals in terms of fostering your ability to adapt your practice to the needs of individual clients?

There are many advantages to adapting practice to fit individual clients, such as being able to *respond to a specific client presentation*. In addition to the considerable theory and research on this topic, your own practice experience will likely indicate that different presentations can benefit from particular therapeutic activities and interventions. This includes understanding the issues that the client is facing – for example, anxiety, depression, stress, disordered eating, the impact of their cultural background and lived experience – and what might be helpful for them given their circumstances (Constantino, Boswell and Coyne, 2021). You have been introduced to some of these potential adaptations throughout the chapters in this book (particularly in Part 1).

Being adaptive also allows the practitioner to more effectively *build and maintain the therapeutic alliance*. Responsiveness and adaptation are desired by clients, and alignment on the purpose of counselling and ways of undertaking it are key factors in maintaining the therapeutic relationship (Norcross and Lambert, 2019). While adherence to a specific theoretical model of counselling is important, most schools emphasise the need to adapt and respond to clients, each of whom will have individual ways of progressing through counselling and undergoing change (Cooper, 2019). So, while we know that there are some aspects of therapy which are reliably helpful, such as the therapeutic relationship, clients will differ in how they prioritise different ways of working, different therapeutic foci and what they find most helpful (Timulak, 2007). This suggests the value in exploring client preferences through feedback and process and outcome monitoring (Swift *et al.*, 2018). Evidence points to this making us, quite simply, better at what we do, because counsellors and psychotherapists who reliably adapt their approach are less likely to feel defensive about the need to be adaptive, and they are perceived by clients to be more engaged and committed to the therapeutic relationship (Goldberg *et al.*, 2016).

Adaptive practice consequently helps to *avoid therapeutic ruptures and drop-out*. When we hold too rigidly to our own model of therapy, theoretical assumptions about client experience, and the boundaries and scope of therapy, we risk losing the client (Constantino, Boswell and Coyne, 2021). Adaptations are central to responding to a lack of client progress, ruptures in the therapeutic relationship, and the risk of client disengagement and drop-out when their needs are not being met (Vybíral *et al.*, 2024). Doing this requires a willingness to receive feedback in order to facilitate adaptation. This is particularly notable given that counsellors appear to be poor at identifying which patients are not progressing well (Hatfield *et al.*, 2010); and, as you read in Chapter 19, counsellors have a tendency to overestimate their own performance (Walfish *et al.*, 2012).

1.1 Types of adaptation in counselling

There are a range of organisational and operational adaptations for therapy delivery, usually decided based on the client population served. The provision of online and phone counselling for people who are geographically isolated (Scogin *et al.*, 2018), as covered in Chapter 17, is one example. For organisations, adaptations to typical counselling practice may be made based on client characteristics and demographics that are determined following intake assessment, such as gender, sexuality, cultural and racial background, or the presence of learning disabilities or health problems. For example, for a client with limited English, a native-speaker counsellor or translator might be required. Organisations (typically through clinical leads) will also often consider the suitability of the match between the (next available) counsellor and the client (e.g. Moore *et al.*, 2021). Research has shown that when matched between client and counsellor, some characteristics – such as self-defined gender (Bhati, 2014) and race and ethnicity (Cabral and Smith, 2011) – result in lower drop-out rates, particularly in the early stages of therapy. However, despite the inherent logic to this approach, the argument for adaptations in the delivery of interventions – for example, offering therapy from different modalities by 'profiling' client features or diagnosis – has mixed results (e.g. Chekroud *et al.*, 2024), with evidence pointing to a more nuanced client-specific dynamic.

meta-competence

An overarching competence that encompasses more specific counselling competencies.

Within the specific therapeutic relationship, aspects of the therapy can be finely tuned, and this **meta-competence** of responsiveness, adaptability and flexibility is well-evidenced as a factor in therapist efficacy (Wu and Levitt, 2020). Ongoing personalisation and 'tailoring' of therapy is of particular importance when considering the uniqueness of each client, as well as the management of power within the relationship (e.g. Timulak and Keogh, 2017). Different types of adaptation are listed in Box 20.1.

Box 20.1 Different types of adaptation

Operational

Description: Adaptations may include the timing, frequency and length of sessions, the duration of the course, the geographic and physical location, and the platform used (e.g. in-person, online, telephone, email or app-based). They may also involve the presence of other people, like translators, family members, and babies or children.

Case example: You agree to see your client with their newborn baby because you/your supervisor judge that continued access to counselling would be in the best interest of the client due to their post-partum depression.

Conceptual and theoretical

Description: Adaptation of the therapeutic intervention may occur either within a single modality or as an aspect of an integrative approach. This may occur during assessment and formulation, but also through the evolution of the therapy, where the counsellor may consider suitable strategies and interventions. For example, a client with substance addiction may be offered counselling based on a model of behavioural change (e.g. the stages of change model; see Prochaska and DiClemente, 1983), while someone with a history of trauma may be offered eye movement desensitisation and reprocessing (EMDR) (Valiente-Gómez *et al.*, 2017) to help them process their experiences (if the counsellor is trained in these modalities). What can be integrated into a single modality will be led by the theory and evidence base, and by the counsellor's training and competence. Competency frameworks based on intervention types can be a useful source of potential adaptations – for example, person-centred counselling for depression (Murphy, 2019).

Case example: You have training in both CBT and person-centred therapy but work in a counselling service for the latter. Your client discloses experiencing frequent panic attacks, for which CBT is the recommended treatment (NICE, 2020). With agreement from your supervisor, you offer your client targeted CBT for panic attacks.

Relational

Description: Counselling and psychotherapy rely on a good therapeutic alliance. But while most counsellors rely heavily on empathy and congruence, adaptations to the relational approach may be useful for some clients. For example, the C-NIP questionnaire (discussed further in Box 20.2) includes questions about the counsellor's degree of directivity, challenge and acceptance of the client.

Case example: Your relational approach is to fully accept the client: to be non-judgemental and non-challenging. However, your client asks you

two-chair work

A technique employed in Gestalt and emotion-focused therapy (among others) which asks the client to speak first from one chair and then the other, voicing different parts of themselves and other important people in their life.

to challenge them if they fail to bring up their problematic alcohol use. You agree to adapt your typical way of relating for this client.

Methodological

Description: This relates to how counsellors deploy different methods and work responsively in therapy. Counsellors can offer the opportunity to undertake different methods relating to the therapeutic task at hand, such as Socratic questioning (a CBT technique), **two-chair work**, use of metaphor and imagery, or emotional focusing.

Case example: Your core training is person-centred, but you have recently completed emotion-focused therapy training and you are beginning to incorporate two-chair work into your sessions. You have agreed this adaptation with your supervisor and you obtain the client's permission each time. You are reviewing (with your supervisor) how this adaptation works in each case.

Pause for thought 20.2

Consider how your capacity to make adaptations came about. Was it through your primary training, continuing professional development, supervision and practice experience, deliberate practice opportunities or something else?

1.2 Making adaptations in practice

You will now be introduced to the case example of Effia, who has come to therapy for help with depression, grief and difficulties with her partner and teenage children.

Case example: Effia – background context

In the first counselling session, Effia, a 54-year-old woman, describes herself as having 'mixed heritage' and explains that she was born in Ghana to an Irish father and Ghanaian mother. Following the breakdown of her parents' relationship when she was 6 years old, she moved to the UK with her father.

On leaving school with few qualifications, Effia became pregnant and got married in order to raise her children 'properly'. Effia has worked a range of part-time jobs in catering and has also worked for a local family as a cleaner. In her adult life, Effia remained close to her father. When he was diagnosed with cancer she became his full-time carer until his death just over a year ago.

Following her father's death, Effia returned to her local further education college to study an access course with the ambition of undertaking teacher training. While at college she received a diagnosis of autism spectrum disorder (ASD) and dyslexia and, ultimately, she did not pass the course. Following this, she says she felt like a 'failure' and lost enthusiasm for studying, feeling that she was not going to be able to 'change her life'. Her mood progressively worsened and this put stress on her relationship with her husband and children. Effia says that she has few friends and that she currently feels very isolated.

She explains that she has recently re-engaged with a local Ghanaian Pentecostal church, which has helped her in establishing a sense of belonging. She cites her new engagement with her faith as one of the reasons she has remained married.

Effia describes her life as pointless beyond her duty to her children (who are 16 and 18). She cannot see a way forward in her marriage but perseveres because she believes it is the right thing to do. She reports that she spends much of her time sleeping or watching television, and she describes her own frustration with herself, wishing she could 'get on' but is finding no pleasure in life. Her children are both at the local college where she had studied, and she is worried that they too may have (as yet 'undiagnosed') neurodiversity that could make study challenging.

Pause for thought 20.3

How do you think you would respond to Effia? Consider the different issues with which she is presenting, as well as your current position as a counsellor.

Perhaps you thought about what is causing Effia's difficulties and what might be helpful for her. Potentially, you drew on different areas of your theoretical knowledge in, for example, minority ethnic experiences, ASD, dyslexia, depression, relationship difficulties, the impact of social isolation and grief. You might have thought about how her presentation fits with your approach/model, but you may also have responded to the case in a personalised way. You will know your own confidence and competence levels, and how this may affect how you work with Effia. You may also have identified knowledge, skills or experience gaps in your ability to respond; some of these might be training-based and some might be contextual, such as the ability to offer suitable counselling adaptations to someone with ASD.

This case helps to demonstrate the types of complex factors that might suggest a need for adapting your way of working with a client. The next section will explore the specifics of adaptation during counselling.

2 Integrating adaptation into the therapeutic process

Pre-planned adaptations informed by counsellor knowledge of the client and client presentation might include inclusivity adaptations for ethnicity, gender and neurodiversity, or client preferences expressed in the assessment (e.g. what has worked and not worked in the past). These allow adaptations to be incorporated into the work from the outset, which can then be monitored for effectiveness.

During case conceptualisation it is important to use an idiographic approach, where you strive to adapt counselling to the client's experience and understanding, and plan the interventions or activities from this basis, rather than strictly applying a theoretical frame or rigidly enacting the interventions. This aids each client in receiving the counselling that works best for them (Silberschatz, 2017). It also ensures that the therapy can be adapted through emergent information in the therapy room, by perhaps changing or reviewing the goals of therapy through paying attention to client insight and meaning making.

Alongside this, counsellors need to adopt an attitude of adaptation in practice which is internal to the counsellor themselves. This attitude is characterised by curiosity and sensitivity towards the client, awareness of their own therapeutic capacity and skills, and an openness to making adjustments. So, while research can inform the overall approaches taken, adaptation at the level of the therapeutic encounter should be navigated to meet the needs of clients. This is illustrated with the case of Effia, which you will read more about in Section 2.2.

2.1 Balancing adaptability with therapeutic fidelity

Adaptability should not come at the cost of coherence: clients are likely to perceive a piecemeal approach to therapy as unhelpful. A practitioner should not, for example, consistently adopt a non-directive, person-centred stance and then, in response to a client presentation of unhelpful thinking styles, automatically introduce a CBT method of structuring the sessions. It is also important to be mindful that from many theoretical perspectives therapy cannot work effectively by relying on client preferences and choice without considering the meaning and impact of these choices. Some argue that blindly following client preferences can lead them to feel comfortable but cause them to remain unchallenged on key aspects of their experience (Dryden, 2012).

Client and counsellor metacommunication and feedback can identify adaptations as well as what is and isn't working about the therapy. But while sensitivity to, and direct feedback from, clients about their experience of counselling is important, their ability to do this may be hampered by deference or politeness norms (e.g. Blanchard and Farber, 2018), as well as a lack of client knowledge about what might be adapted and what adaptation might look like. Active and regular engagement with process monitoring through dialogue and the use of monitoring tools can keep therapy on track and help avoid client drop-out (for more on monitoring tools, see Chapter 12). Examples of monitoring tools which can be integrated into practice include:

- *therapy preference scales*, such as the Therapy Personalisation Form (Bowens and Cooper, 2012) and the C-NIP (described in Box 20.2)

- *process monitoring tools*, which usually consist of client rating reports undertaken at the end of, or between, sessions; for example, session rating scales such as the Helpful Aspects of Therapy questionnaire (Llewelyn *et al.*, 1988) provide personalised indications of what is working from the client perspective

- *routine outcome measures* (covered in Chapter 12), which include both idiographic (client-defined outcomes) and more objective or symptom-based outcomes monitoring, which help in tracking progress and improvement for clients (Sales *et al.*, 2023).

Box 20.2 The Cooper-Norcross Inventory of Preferences

The Cooper-Norcross Inventory of Preferences (C-NIP) is an example of a therapy preference scale (Cooper and Norcross, 2016). It is a questionnaire which can be completed by clients between or within sessions. It serves to highlight aspects of the therapeutic process that the client prefers; this feedback can allow the therapist to adjust to these preferences. The C-NIP (Cooper and Norcross, 2016, p. 87) clusters areas of preference according to:

- 'therapist directiveness' versus 'client directiveness'
- 'emotional intensity' versus 'emotional reserve'
- 'past orientation' versus 'present orientation'
- 'warm support' versus 'focused challenge'.

These areas are further explored in Section 2.2.

The scale also provides other topics which can be used to guide adaptation: the modality/orientation of the work, the language used and the frequency or lengths of sessions, for example.

The C-NIP is designed to encourage open collaboration with clients on what can be undertaken and empowers therapists to make adjustments with the confidence that they are appropriately responding to the client context.

2.2 Adaptations in the context of therapeutic impasse

While it is good practice in general to adapt what we do with clients, it is essential to undertake adaptations when client progress in counselling seems to have stalled. Stalling or impasses (both imply being stuck) need to be first recognised and then responded to by adapting counselling to be more in tune with the client's needs. The timing of this adaptation is important; for example, the counsellor should consider it as soon as they feel the client's progress has stalled.

Let's look at how this might happen in Effia's case.

Case example: Effia's therapeutic impasse

Despite the counsellor Karolina's warm and supportive approach to structuring exploration with Effia, Effia continues to come across as emotionally flat, speaking slowly and quietly, and rarely smiling. In each session, she has described what she has done that week, referring only occasionally to her life history and past events. Her mood score on the CORE-10 (which tracks functioning across time) has remained between 26 and 30, indicating severe psychological distress, and she struggles to identify any aspects of the counselling which she has found helpful.

In their fifth session, Effia states that she would prefer to undertake online counselling as she finds it difficult to get motivated to come to the counselling centre. Her presentation and outcome measures indicate that the therapy is not helping. Karolina begins to wonder if Effia is likely to drop out of therapy due to a lack of progress, and in supervision she shares that she feels 'stuck' on how to help Effia.

In response to Effia's stalled progress, the first consideration might be to open up a conversation to review Effia's hopes and goals for therapy, and then examine what might be undertaken to increase her motivation and engagement, as well as what might be a helpful adaptation. Let's think about Effia's case in terms of the four dimensions of the C-NIP, which were outlined in Box 20.2:

- *Therapist directiveness versus client directiveness*: If the counsellor has held an open space for client exploration and has tracked the client's progress, then client preferences or needs should become clear. For example, it may be that Effia would like more structure, such as keeping the session more focused on a particular issue, walking through structured activities and tasks that she thinks might be helpful, or receiving some feedback from Karolina on what she thinks about Effia's situation and how to improve it. Alternatively, she might be supported to talk to Karolina about her own interpretation of her experience and lead Karolina through this.

- *Emotional intensity versus emotional reserve*: Effia's sessions have been limited in terms of emotional content, and this can be linked to depression which is characterised by anhedonia (the loss of the capacity to feel pleasure) and persistent negative affect (American Psychiatric Association, 2022). Effia may also be overwhelmed by her experiences and be demonstrating a functional avoidance of distress. Adapting the approach to become more open to exploring emotional experiences could start with invitations and prompting of both 'in the room' experience and past events to explore unexpressed emotions.

- *Past orientation versus present orientation*: Effia tends to focus on present day events, but her current ways of being are a result of the past: losing contact with her mother and the death of her father, and perhaps the impact of this – alongside a late diagnosis of learning difficulties – on her sense of identity, for example. Taking her back to these events could potentially help her to structure her understanding and acceptance, and make meaning of her current experiences.

- *Warm support versus focused challenge*: While emotionally warm support (used here in contrast to therapist directiveness) may have enabled the development of the relationship, Effia may benefit from a more challenging stance from Karolina in order to move her towards deeper change processes, through highlighting where alternative actions or beliefs are possible.

Other adaptations may also need to be considered. For example, the costs and benefits of online working, which might fit with Effia's current way of being, could be looked at, but this could also increase her isolation. Adaptations to accommodate aspects of sensory processing experienced by ASD clients may be helpful if Effia is overwhelmed in sensory and relational terms; this may include, for example, asking Effia if she would feel more comfortable with the overhead light or fan turned off. Karolina may also explore Effia's difficulties in her relationship with her husband and how it relates to her sense of social isolation. In addition, Karolina could ask Effia about her spirituality and faith, and undertake a systems map to highlight cultural connections and resources which can be used to improve her mood and experiences. Effia's understanding and interpretation of her experience might also be explored to link to conceptual understandings. For example, if her experience of depression is linked to a spiritual crisis, then counselling might explore this area; if she sees depression as more of a mood or chemical imbalance, psychoeducation and structured CBT-based activities may be preferred.

3 Becoming more adaptive

While the first two sections of this chapter focused on the need for adaptation, this last section will focus on the challenges of being adaptive. One such challenge is that how much any counsellor is able to adapt their practice will depend in part on their career stage (this is explored in Section 3.2).

3.1 The challenges of adaptation

Some factors have an impact on the feasibility of being adaptive in counselling. It is important to consider the following when striving to respond adaptively:

- *Competence, confidence and scope of practice*: You need to understand what adaptations you can make for a client as well as the ways that you might go about this, through self-awareness and knowledge of your expertise and limitations. Reflective practice and supervision will help to identify potential adaptations and support your awareness of whether to undertake them. Active engagement with current research and professional development opportunities is another important process here.

- *Practitioner blind spots and safety zones*: You need to acknowledge what you avoid undertaking and why, especially if it might have been a positive adaptation for the client. Each counsellor should have a sense of why they might avoid some adaptations for practical, conceptual or personal (e.g. confidence) reasons.

- *Presumptive adaptation*: This occurs when you adapt your approach for a particular client based on assumptions about your client's experience but fail to develop a feedback loop with the client to assess whether this has been helpful. Presumptive adaptation involves an imbalance between wanting to be responsive and being effective in your adaptation.

- *The boundary between what therapy is and what it is not*: There may be potential adaptations that a client might value but which are not appropriate. For example, while some counsellors offer 'walk and talk' counselling (Revell and McLeod, 2016), this is not an appropriate adaptation for all clients/settings/counsellors. Understanding what can be incorporated involves understanding personal, organisational and professional boundaries, for example related to developing personal relationships with a client. If activities that could be therapeutic – such as engaging with spiritual activities or mindfulness, or nature-based or arts-based activities – cannot be offered in counselling, consider referring on, outsourcing and working in multidisciplinary contexts.

3.2 Stage of counsellor development

Adaptations in therapy rely on the capacity of the counsellor to: (a) respond to issues and experiences in a range of ways; (b) offer different methodological activities and alternative approaches to counselling; and (c) potentially refer clients on, if appropriate. One thing that will likely impact the counsellor's ability to offer adaptations is their career stage, as illustrated in Table 20.1.

Table 20.1 Adaptation and career stage

Stage	Adaptations
Initial training	Counselling training varies a lot. Some counsellors may not receive training in, or feedback on, adaptation in practice, while others may train in a modality that explicitly incorporates how to adapt ways of working for individual clients. In pluralistic therapy training, for example, there is a focus on identifying 'choice-points', which are points in counselling where an adaptation might be helpful (Smith and de la Prida, 2021). However, by the time they reach the point of qualification, most counsellors will have a sense of what adaptations are possible within their modality, even if they do not always know how they might best go about them.
Post-qualification	Counsellors are required to engage in ongoing continued professional development, which may involve further training and deliberate practice (Rousmaniere *et al.*, 2017). This may support a counsellor's ability to adapt their ways of working for individual clients. However, as counsellors we need to know where our competence boundaries are (a one-day training course may not make us 'competent'). Additionally, there may be limits to what we as individuals can adapt to regardless of what our clients want or need from us, and no matter what we might want from ourselves.
Mastery	Being a practitioner for a long time does not always result in a broader range of response options and increased ability to adapt practice. Nonetheless, there is evidence that those who undertake ongoing and strategic developmental activities and training do improve their overall effectiveness with clients (Chow *et al.*, 2015).

Whatever the counsellor's career stage, they will at some point meet clients whose needs they cannot adequately respond to. It is important to remember that, in general, this does not mean a counsellor is not competent. If a client needs an adaptation you cannot offer, signposting and/or referring to other practitioners or services is the ethically appropriate response.

Conclusion

In this chapter you have explored why it is important for counsellors to be prepared to adapt their way of working to better meet the needs of individual clients. You have considered the various aspects of counselling practice that can be adapted, as well as when and how adaptation can be undertaken. Across the chapter you have been encouraged to consider how you typically work with clients and how confident you are currently about adapting your way of working for individual clients. Hopefully this has allowed you to consider how you might develop your counselling practice to be more adaptive to clients.

Key learning points included the notion that adaptation is especially important when the therapy is failing to work for the client. Additionally, when adaptations are made, it is critical to check whether they are helping by seeking client feedback (formally through routine outcome measures and in general by asking clients) and by reflecting on the adaptation both by yourself and with your supervisor.

Further reading

- Now in its third edition, the following book's second volume focuses specifically on what the evidence base is for different ways of adapting practice for individual clients:

    Norcross, J.C. and Wampold, B.E. (eds) (2019) *Psychotherapy relationships that work. Volume 2: evidence-based therapist responsiveness*. 3rd edn. New York, NY: Oxford University Press.

- The following book examines how client needs and preferences can be assessed and, importantly, uses case examples to explore how a practitioner can go about adapting to these:

    Norcross, J.C. and Cooper, M. (2021) *Personalizing psychotherapy: assessing and accommodating patient preferences*. Washington, DC: American Psychological Association. Available at: https://doi.org/10.1037/0000221-000

- The following article is a nice case study of the application of an adaptive approach in therapy to meet a client's specific needs:

    Ward, T. and Hogan, K. (2015) 'Using client-centered psychotherapy embedded within a pluralistic integrative approach to help a client with executive dysfunction: the case of "Judith"', *Pragmatic Case Studies in Psychotherapy*, 11(1), pp. 1–20. Available at: https://doi.org/10.14713/pcsp.v11i1.1883

References

American Psychiatric Association (2022) *Diagnostic and statistical manual of mental disorders: DSM-5-TR*. 5th edn, text rev. Washington, DC: American Psychiatric Publishing.

Arundell, L.-L., Barnett, P., Buckman J.E.J., Saunders, R. and Pilling, S. (2021) 'The effectiveness of adapted psychological interventions for people from ethnic minority groups: a systematic review and conceptual typology', *Clinical Psychology Review*, 88, article number 102063. Available at: https://doi.org/10.1016/j.cpr.2021.102063

Bennett, S.D. and Shafran, R. (2023) 'Adaptation, personalization and capacity in mental health treatments: a balancing act?', *Current Opinion in Psychiatry*, 36(1), pp. 28–33. Available at: https://doi.org/10.1097/yco.0000000000000834

Bhati, K.S. (2014) 'Effect of client-therapist gender match on the therapeutic relationship: an exploratory analysis', *Psychological Reports*, 115(2), pp. 565–583. Available at: https://doi.org/10.2466/21.02.pr0.115c23z1

Blanchard, M. and Farber, B.A. (2018) 'Lying in psychotherapy: why and what clients don't tell their therapist about therapy and their relationship', in S. Knox and C. Hill (eds) *Disclosure and concealment in psychotherapy*. Abingdon: Routledge, pp. 90–112.

Bowens, M. and Cooper, M. (2012) 'Development of a client feedback tool: a qualitative study of therapists' experiences of using the Therapy Personalisation Forms', *European Journal of Psychotherapy and Counselling*, 14(1), pp. 47–62. Available at: https://doi.org/10.1080/13642537.2012.652392

Cabral, R.R. and Smith, T.B. (2011) 'Racial/ethnic matching of clients and therapists in mental health services: a meta-analytic review of preferences, perceptions, and outcomes', *Journal of Counseling Psychology*, 58(4), pp. 537–554. Available at: https://doi.org/10.1037/a0025266

Castonguay, L.G., Boswell, J.F., Constantino, M.J., Goldfried, M.R. and Hill, C.E. (2010) 'Training implications of harmful effects of psychological treatments', *American Psychologist*, 65(1), pp. 34–49. Available at: https://doi.org/10.1037/a0017330

Chekroud, A.M., Hawrilenko, M., Loho, H., Bondar, J., Gueorguieva, R., Hasan, A., Kambeitz, J., Corlett, P.R., Koutsouleris, N., Krumholz, H.M., Krystal, J.H. and Paulus, M. (2024) 'Illusory generalizability of clinical prediction models', *Science*, 383(6679), pp. 164–167. Available at: https://doi.org/10.1126/science.adg8538

Chow, D.L., Miller, S.D., Seidel, J.A., Kane, R.T., Thornton, J.A. and Andrews, W.P. (2015) 'The role of deliberate practice in the development of highly effective psychotherapists', *Psychotherapy*, 52(3), pp. 337–345. Available at: https://doi.org/10.1037/pst0000015

Constantino, M.J., Boswell, J.F. and Coyne, A.E. (2021) 'Patient, therapist, and relational factors', in M. Barkham, W. Lutz and L.G. Castonguay (eds) *Bergin and Garfield's handbook of psychotherapy and behavior change*. 7th edn. Hoboken, NJ: John Wiley & Sons, pp. 225–262.

Cooper, M. (2019) *Integrating counselling and psychotherapy: directionality, synergy, and social change*. London: SAGE Publications.

Cooper, M. and Norcross J.C. (2016) 'A brief, multidimensional measure of clients' therapy preferences: the Cooper-Norcross Inventory of Preferences (C-NIP)', *International Journal of Clinical and Health Psychology*, 16(1), pp. 87–98. Available at: https://doi.org/10.1016/j.ijchp.2015.08.003

Cuijpers, P., Cristea, I.A., Karyotaki, E., Reijnders, M. and Huibers, M.J.H. (2016) 'How effective are cognitive behavior therapies for major depression and anxiety disorders? A meta-analytic update of the evidence', *World Psychiatry*, 15(3), pp. 245–258. Available at: https://doi.org/10.1002/wps.20346

Dryden, W. (2012) 'Pluralism in counselling and psychotherapy: personal reflections on an important development', *European Journal of Psychotherapy & Counselling*, 14(1), pp. 103–111. Available at: https://doi.org/10.1080/13642537.2012.652399

Goldberg, S.B., Rousmaniere, T., Miller, S.D., Whipple, J., Nielsen, S.L., Hoyt, W.T. and Wampold, B.E. (2016) 'Do psychotherapists improve with time and experience? A longitudinal analysis of outcomes in a clinical setting', *Journal of Counseling Psychology*, 63(1), pp. 1–11. Available at: https://doi.org/10.1037/cou0000131

Hatfield, D., McCullough, L., Frantz, S.H.B. and Krieger, K. (2010) 'Do we know when our clients get worse? An investigation of therapists' ability to detect negative client change', *Clinical Psychology & Psychotherapy*, 17(1), pp. 25–32. Available at: https://doi.org/10.1002/cpp.656

Llewelyn, S.P., Elliott, R., Shapiro, D.A., Hardy, G. and Firth-Cozens, J. (1988) 'Client perceptions of significant events in prescriptive and exploratory periods of individual therapy', *British Journal of Clinical Psychology*, 27(2), pp. 105–114. Available at: https://doi.org/10.1111/j.2044-8260.1988.tb00758.x

Moore, G., Campbell, M., Copeland, L., Craig, P., Movsisyan, A., Hoddinott, P., Littlecott, H., O'Cathain, A., Pfadenhauer, L., Rehfuess, E., Segrott, J., Hawe, P., Kee, F., Couturiaux, D., Hallingberg, B. and Evans, R. (2021) 'Adapting interventions to new contexts – the ADAPT guidance', *The BMJ*, 374, article number n1679. Available at: https://doi.org/10.1136/bmj.n1679

Murphy, D. (2019) *Person-centred experiential counselling for depression*. 2nd edn. London: SAGE Publications.

National Institute for Health and Care Excellence (NICE) (2020) *Generalised anxiety disorder and panic disorder in adults: management*. Clinical guideline 113 (CG113). Available at: https://www.nice.org.uk/guidance/cg113 (Accessed: 10 July 2024).

Norcross, J.C. and Lambert, M.J. (eds) (2019) *Psychotherapy relationships that work. Volume 1: evidence-based therapist contributions*. 3rd edn. New York, NY: Oxford University Press.

Prochaska, J.O. and DiClemente, C.C. (1983) 'Stages and processes of self-change of smoking: toward an integrative model of change', *Journal of Consulting and Clinical Psychology*, 51(3), pp. 390–395. Available at: https://doi.org/10.1037//0022-006x.51.3.390

Revell, S. and McLeod, J. (2016) 'Experiences of therapists who integrate walk and talk into their professional practice', *Counselling and Psychotherapy Research*, 16(1), pp. 35–43. Available at: https://doi.org/10.1002/capr.12042

Rousmaniere, T., Goodyear, R.K., Miller, S.D. and Wampold, B.E. (eds) (2017) *The cycle of excellence: using deliberate practice to improve supervision and training*. Chichester: John Wiley & Sons.

Sales, C.M.D., Ashworth, M., Ayis, S., Barkham, M., Edbrooke-Childs, J., Faísca, L., Jacob, J., Xu, D., and Cooper, M. (2023) 'Idiographic patient reported outcome measures (I-PROMs) for routine outcome monitoring in psychological therapies: position paper', *Journal of Clinical Psychology*, 79(3), pp. 596–621. Available at: https://doi.org/10.1002/jclp.23319

Scogin, F., Lichstein, K., DiNapoli, E.A., Woosley, J., Thomas, S.J., LaRocca, M.A., Byers, H.D., Mieskowski, L., Parker, C.P., Yang, X., Parton, J., McFadden, A. and Geyer, J.D. (2018) 'Effects of integrated telehealth-delivered cognitive-behavioral therapy for depression and insomnia in rural older adults', *Journal of Psychotherapy Integration*, 28(3), pp. 292–309. Available at: https://doi.org/10.1037/int0000121

SCoPEd Framework (2022), collaboratively developed by Association of Christian Counsellors (ACC), British Association for Counselling and Psychotherapy (BACP), British Psychoanalytic Council (BPC), Human Givens Institute (HGI), National Counselling and Psychotherapy Society (NCPS) and United Kingdom Council for Psychotherapy (UKCP). Available at: https://www.bacp.co.uk/about-us/advancing-the-profession/scoped/scoped-framework (Accessed: 12 June 2024).

Silberschatz, G. (2017) 'Improving the yield of psychotherapy research', *Psychotherapy Research*, 27(1), pp. 1–13. Available at: https://doi.org/10.1080/10503307.2015.1076202

Smith, K. and de la Prida, A. (2021) *The pluralistic therapy primer: a concise introduction*. Monmouth: PCCS Books.

Swift, J.K., Callahan, J.L., Cooper, M. and Parkin, S.R. (2018) 'The impact of accommodating client preference in psychotherapy: a meta-analysis', *Journal of Clinical Psychology*, 74(11), pp. 1924–1937. Available at: https://doi.org/10.1002/jclp.22680

Timulak, L. (2007) 'Identifying core categories of client-identified impact of helpful events in psychotherapy: a qualitative meta-analysis', *Psychotherapy Research*, 17(3), pp. 305–314. Available at: https://doi.org/10.1080/10503300600608116

Timulak, L. and Keogh, D. (2017) 'The client's perspective on (experiences of) psychotherapy: a practice friendly review', *Journal of Clinical Psychology*, 73(11), pp. 1556–1567. Available at: https://doi.org/10.1002/jclp.22532

Valiente-Gómez, A., Moreno-Alcázar, A., Treen, D., Cedrón, C., Colom, F., Pérez, V. and Amann, B.L. (2017) 'EMDR beyond PTSD: a systematic literature review', *Frontiers in Psychology*, 8, article number 1668. Available at: https://doi.org/10.3389/fpsyg.2017.01668

Vybíral, Z., Ogles, B.M., Řiháček, T., Urbancová, B. and Gocieková, V. (2024) 'Negative experiences in psychotherapy from clients' perspective: a qualitative meta-analysis', *Psychotherapy Research*, 34(3), pp. 279–292. Available at: https://doi.org/10.1080/10503307.2023.2226813

Walfish, S., McAlister, B., O'Donnell, P. and Lambert, M.J. (2012) 'An investigation of self-assessment bias in mental health providers', *Psychological Reports*, 110(2), pp. 639–644. Available at: https://doi.org/10.2466/02.07.17.pr0.110.2.639-644

Wu, M.B. and Levitt, H.M. (2020) 'A qualitative meta-analytic review of the therapist responsiveness literature: guidelines for practice and training', *Journal of Contemporary Psychotherapy*, 50(3), pp. 161–175. Available at: https://doi.org/10.1007/s10879-020-09450-y

Acknowledgements

Grateful acknowledgement is made to the following sources.

Part 1

Chapter 1: Introduction image: Tanya Frances; Section 3 image: Tanya Frances; **Chapter 2**: Introduction image: Maria Kenyon; Section 3 image: Simon Whitmore; **Chapter 3**: Introduction image: Stuart Timms; Figure 3.1: Sylvia Duckworth; Figure 3.2: Burnham, J. (2019) 'Developments in Social GGRRAAACCEEESS: visible-invisible and voiced-unvoiced', in I.B. Krause (Ed.) *Culture and reflexivity in systemic psychotherapy: mutual perspectives.* London: Routledge, pp. 139-160; **Chapter 4**: Introduction image: Alyssa Sieb/Nappy; Section 2 image: Alyssa Sieb/Nappy.

Part 2

Chapter 5: Introduction image: Jon Tuff; **Chapter 6**: Introduction image: Michael Rost; Section 3 image: Ana Santos; **Chapter 7**: Introduction image: Claudine McFaul; Section 2 image: Kerry Watt; Activity 7.1 text extract: Ellis, A. (2003) 'How to deal with your most difficult client – you', *Journal of Rational-Emotive and Cognitive-Behavior Therapy*, 21(3–4), pp. 203–213. Available at: https://doi.org/10.1023/a:1025885911410; **Chapter 8**: Introduction image: Kathleen Kettles; Section 2.2 image: photo by Emily Morter on Unsplash; Table 8.1 text: Stoltenberg, C.D. and McNeill. B.W. (2010) *IDM supervision: an integrative developmental model for supervising counselors and therapists*. Hove: Routledge.

Part 3

Chapter 9: Introduction image: Gina Di Malta; **Chapter 10**: Introduction image: Martina Morrow; Section 3 image: Brian Norcross. This file is licensed under a Creative Commons Attribution 3.0 Unported License; **Chapter 11**: Introduction image: Carys Treadwell; Figure 11.2: Philipp Guttmann. This file is licensed under the Creative Commons Attribution-Share Alike 4.0 International license. https://creativecommons.org/licenses/by-sa/4.0/; Section 1.1 World Health Organization text quotations: World Health Organization (2023) *Mental health, human rights and legislation: guidance and practice*, The World Health Organization. This file is licensed under the Creative Commons Attribution-Non-commercial-Share Alike Licence https://creativecommons.org/licenses/by-nc-sa/3.0/igo/; Section 4 text extract: NHS England (2021) *Annex DtD: Technical guidance for mental health clusters.* Reproduced under the terms of the OGL, www.nationalarchives.gov.uk/doc/open-government-licence; **Chapter 12**: Introduction image: Gina Di Malta; Section 4 image: Ana Santos.

Part 4

Chapter 13: Introduction image: Jamie Roscoe-Jones; **Chapter 14**: Introduction image: Carys Treadwell; Section 4 image: Unsplash; **Chapter 15**: Introduction image: Louise Newbigging; Section 4.3 image: photo by Etienne Girardet on Unsplash; **Chapter 16**: Introduction image: Amy Sears; Section 1 text extract: Westen, D. and Weinberger, J. (2004) 'When clinical description becomes statistical prediction', *American Psychologist*, 59(7), pp. 595–613. Available at https://doi.org/10.1037/0003-066X.59.7.595; Section 2.2 text extract: Paquin, J.D., Tao, K.W. and Budge, S.L. (2019) 'Toward a psychotherapy science for all: conducting ethical and socially just research', *Psychotherapy* , 56(4), pp. 491–502. United States: Educational Publishing Foundation. Available at: https://doi.org/10.1037/ pst0000271.

Part 5

Chapter 17: Introduction image: Jemma Comerford; **Chapter 18**: Introduction image: Ronaldo Schemidt/AFP via Getty Images; **Chapter 19**: Introduction image: Karine Mather; Section 3 image: Katie Maxsted; **Chapter 20**: Introduction image: Amanda Good.

Cover artwork

Katherine Elizabeth Skelly

Index